Utopia

Stéphanie Roza is a researcher in political philosophy affiliated with CNRS (the French National Centre for Scientific Research) and the École normale supérieure de Lyon. Her expertise lies in the Enlightenment and the French Revolution, and their legacy in socialist and leftist movements during the nineteenth and twentieth centuries. She is currently overseeing the complete works edition of Gracchus Babeuf.

Utopia

From the Novel to Revolution

Stéphanie Roza

Translated by David Broder

London • New York

This English-language edition first published by Verso 2025
First published as *Comment l'utopie est devenue un programme politique: Du roman à la Révolution*
© Classiques Garnier 2015
© Stéphanie Roza 2015, 2025
Translation © David Broder 2025

All rights reserved

This work was published with the help of the French Ministry of Culture – Centre national du livre
Ouvrage publié avec le concours du Ministère français chargé de la culture – Centre national du livre

The Triangle laboratory (ENS Lyon) funded the translation of this book. Our sincere thanks.

The manufacturer's authorized representative in the EU for product safety (GPSR) is LOGOS EUROPE, 9 rue Nicolas Poussin, 17000, La Rochelle, France
Contact@logoseurope.eu

The moral rights of the author have been asserted

1 3 5 7 9 10 8 6 4 2

Verso
UK: 6 Meard Street, London W1F 0EG
US: 207 East 32nd Street, New York, NY 10016
versobooks.com

Verso is the imprint of New Left Books

ISBN-13: 978-1-83976-765-4
ISBN-13: 978-1-83976-767-8 (US EBK)
ISBN-13: 978-1-83976-766-1 (UK EBK)

British Library Cataloguing in Publication Data
A catalogue record for this book is available from the British Library

Library of Congress Cataloging-in-Publication Data
A catalog record for this book is available from the Library of Congress

Typeset in Minion by Hewer Text UK Ltd, Edinburgh
Printed and bound by CPI Group (UK) Ltd, Croydon CR0 4YY

Contents

Abbreviations   vii

Introduction: Enlightenment, Utopia, Socialism?   1

I
MORELLY: THE MANY FAREWELLS TO THE NOVEL   13
1 The Critical Utopia of *La Basiliade*: Introduction to an Atypical Utopia   15
2 The *Code de la Nature* and Its Constructive Utopia   51

II
THE ABBÉ DE MABLY'S UTOPIAN REPUBLIC   95
3 *Des droits et des devoirs du citoyen*: Utopia in Service of the Revolution   97
4 The *Doutes proposés aux philosophes économistes*: Utopia in Service of Polemics   139
5 *De la législation*: Or, Utopia in Service of Reform   163

III
GRACCHUS BABEUF, A UTOPIAN IN REVOLUTION   207

6 Babeuf's 1786 Draft Letter: Utopia in the Villages   209

7 Babeuf in 1789: The *Cadastre perpétuel* and the
   'Preliminary Discourse'; Utopia in the Assembly   265

8 Babeuf During the Revolution: Utopia and the Republic   295

9 The Conspiracy of Equals: Utopia as a Programme   323

Conclusion: An Anti-School of Thought   351

Epilogue: A Post-Revolutionary Avatar of Morellysm   363

Index   369

Abbreviations

CGP – Rousseau, 'Considérations sur le gouvernement de Pologne', in *Œuvres complètes*, edited by Bernard Gagnebin and Marcel Raymond, Paris: Gallimard, 1964–95, vol. III.

CN – Morelly, *Code de la Nature*. Unless indicated otherwise I have cited the edition with my own introduction and notes: Montreuil: La ville brûle, 2011.

DDC – Mably, *Des droits et des devoirs du citoyen*, introduction and notes by Jean-Louis Lecercle, Paris: Librairie Marcel Didier, 1972.

DEP – Rousseau, 'Discours sur l'économie politique', in *Œuvres complètes*, vol. III.

DL – Mably, *De la legislation ou principes des lois*, 1776, vol. IX in *Œuvres*, Paris: Guillaume Arnoux, 1794–5, republished with introduction, bibliography and index of names by Peter Friedemann, Darmstadt: Scientia Verlag Aalen, 1977 (15 vols).

DP – Mably, *Doutes proposés aux philosophes économistes sur l'ordre naturel et essentiel des sociétés politiques*, 1768, in *Œuvres*, vol. XI.

E – Rousseau, *Emile, or Education*, translated by Barbara Foxley, New York: E. P. Dutton, 1921.

EH – Mably, *De l'étude de l'histoire, à Monsieur le Prince de Parme*, 1778, in *Œuvres*, vol. XII.

EdL – Montesquieu, *De l'esprit des lois*, 1748, introduction and notes by Victor Goldschmidt, Paris: Flammarion, 1979 (2 vols).

EP – Mably, *Entretiens de Phocion, sur le rapport de la morale à la politique*, 1763, in *Œuvres*, vol. X.

LB – Morelly, *Naufrage des îles flottantes, ou la Basiliade du célèbre Pilpai*, Messine [Paris]: Société de libraires, 1753 (2 vols).

MEH – Mably, *De la manière d'écrire l'histoire*, 1783, in *Œuvres*, vol. XI.

NH – Rousseau, *Julie, or the New Heloïse*, in *The Collected Writings of Rousseau*, Hannover: Dartmouth College Press, 1997.

OB – Babeuf, *Œuvres*, edited and introduced by Victor Daline, Armando Saitta, and Albert Soboul, Paris: Bibliothèque Nationale, 1977, vol. I: *Babeuf avant la Révolution*.

OG – Mably, *Observations sur l'histoire de la Grèce*, 1766, in *Œuvres*, vol. IV.

OHF – Mably, *Observations sur l'histoire de France*, 1765–72, in *Œuvres*, vols I–III.

PCB – Babeuf, *Pages choisies de Babeuf*, introduction and notes by Maurice Dommanget, Paris: Armand Colin, 1935.

PCC – Rousseau, 'Projet de constitution pour la Corse', in *Œuvres complètes*, vol. III.

THP – Condorcet, *Tableau historique des progrès de l'esprit humain*, edited by Jean-Pierre Schandeler and Pierre Crépel, Paris: INED, 2004.

TP – Babeuf, *Le Tribun du peuple*: up to and including issue 33, included in the same volume as the *Journal de la liberté de la presse* (EDHIS, 1966), labelled as I; beyond that, as II.

Introduction
Enlightenment, Utopia, Socialism?

This book examines a remarkable moment in the second half of the eighteenth century, when utopia evolved into a *political project*. To this end, utopian thinkers developed a specific theory of human nature, their own conception of societies' history, and concrete approaches to action. This book will consider this change essentially by looking at three authors: Étienne-Gabriel Morelly, Gabriel Bonnot de Mably, and François-Noël (or Gracchus) Babeuf. Without doubt, the path from the utopian novel to the utopian programme does not alone encapsulate the entire production and evolution of utopias in the crucial period marked (or better, split) by the French Revolution. But it is surely one of the most striking phenomena of this period, and among the most deserving of attention. This study thus culminates with Babeuf's 'Conspiracy of Equals' in 1795–7, understood as the historical intersection of social utopia, of what is called the Enlightenment's particular optimism, and of the energies of the French Revolution.

Morelly, Mably, and Babeuf have in common the fact that all three proclaimed the superiority of an ideal that was not of their own time. They held up the community of goods as a supreme model of social organisation and traced at least an imaginary outline of what such a form of collective life would look like. We will not venture any new characterisation or definition of utopia in general – an undertaking that would go far beyond the scope of our discussion here.[1] We will, however, point out that the eighteenth century saw profound changes in utopia, which had hitherto been an informal novelistic tradition and, despite its contradictions, a largely identifiable genre of literary, philosophical, and political production. More broadly, utopia as an approach or a way of thinking, or even a state of mind – what we prefer to call 'utopianism' – was also transformed in this period. The first changes came already at the beginning of the century, when Leibniz, in his essays on *Theodicy* (1710), substantiated the term. He used it – and he was first to do so – in a sense that was to flourish, namely as a *representation of a chimerical and only falsely desirable society*:

> It is true that one may imagine possible worlds without sin and without unhappiness, and one could make some like Utopian or Sevarambian romances: but these same worlds again would be very inferior to ours in goodness.[2]

The dominant tone had been set – and it would endure for centuries. On this reading, the idea of a possible world, in essence parallel to, or rather at odds with, the characteristics of the real social world, is massively invalidated by the majority who prefer the world as it is. Yet we may well emphasise, along with Pierre Macherey, that utopians have always used this type of thought experiment as a means of exposing the inadequacies of a given historical reality. It is a contribution to the call to transform this reality, instead of leaving it as is. In this respect, even when utopia is not a programme for action, it could and should be read as a stimulant to transformative thought, as the opposite side of the social

---

1   Among the best and most stimulating general works on utopia are texts by Miguel Abensour (*Utopiques*, Arles: Les éditions de la Nuit, 2010), Ernst Bloch (*The Principle of Hope*, Cambridge, MA: MIT Press, 1995), Pierre Macherey (*De l'utopie!*, Le Havre: De l'incidence éditeur, 2011), Karl Mannheim (*Ideology and Utopia*, London: Routledge, 1991), Pierre-François Moreau (*Le récit utopique*, Paris: PUF, 1982), Jean-Marie Racault (*Nulle part et ses environs*, Paris: Presses de la Sorbonne, 2003), Raymond Ruyer (*L'utopie et les utopies*, Paris: PUF, 1950), Raymond Trousson (*Voyages au pays de nulle part*, Brussels: Presses universitaires de Bruxelles, 1979), Jean Servier (*Histoire de l'utopie*, Paris: Folio, 1991), as well as the special issue of the journal *Europe* devoted to 'Regards sur l'utopie': no. 985, May 2011.

2   Gottfried Wilhelm von Leibniz, *Theodicy: Essays on the Goodness of God the Freedom of Man and the Origin of Evil*, London: Routledge & Kegan Paul, 1951, p. 129.

world which it represents.[3] These two antithetical ways of judging utopia have, in fact, constantly clashed throughout its history.

But, even apart from the political or moral value judgements that could be made, one thing does seem for sure: in the Age of Enlightenment, the term 'utopia' referred to a project for a society in another time, which might or might not take the form of a novel. This is clear in the 1771 edition of Trévoux's Dictionary, the first where the entry 'utopia' appears. The definition reads:

> A region that does not exist anywhere, an imaginary land. From OU TOPOS, *non locus*. In Rabelais, L. II ch. 23, it was the kingdom of Grandgousier or Gargantua . . . The word *Utopia* (the title of a work), is sometimes used figuratively, for the plan for an imaginary government, as in Plato's *Republic*, or Thomas More's *Utopia*.[4]

Remarkably, Plato's *Republic* is considered a utopia in the same manner as More's text, even though it has no novelistic aspect. Yet, this broadening of the definition of utopia in fact corresponds to a diversification of utopian production itself, clearly demonstrated by the specific literature on utopias in the Age of Enlightenment.[5] Bronisław Baczko offered a useful characterisation of this development (indeed, also because he was setting out a research programme more than a strict definition), when he wrote:

> There is no utopia without an overall representation, the idea-image of an alternative society, opposed to the existing social reality, and its

---

3   See Macherey, *De l'utopie!*, especially pp. 75–7.

4   *Dictionnaire universel français et latin, vulgairement appelé Dictionnaire de Trévoux*, Paris: Par la Compagnie des Libraires associés, 1771, vol. VIII, p. 489.

5   We shall mainly refer to the works of Bronisław Baczko, *Utopian Lights*, New York: Paragon House, 1989; Antoine Hatzenberger (ed.), *Utopies des Lumières*, Lyon: ENS éditions, 2010; Mona Ozouf, *L'école de la France, essais sur la Révolution, l'utopie et l'enseignement*, Paris: Gallimard, 1984 and *L'homme régénéré, essais sur la Révolution française*, Paris: Gallimard, 1989; Nicolaas Van Wijngaarden, *Les odyssées philosophiques en France entre 1616 et 1789*, Paris and Geneva: Slatkine Reprints, 1982; Franco Venturi, *Utopia and Reform in the Enlightenment*, Cambridge: Cambridge University Press, 1971, as well as Anne-Rozenn Morel's dissertation *Les fictions utopiques pendant la Révolution française*, doctoral thesis under Isabelle Brouard-Arends, Université Rennes II, 2008.

institutions, rites, dominant symbols, systems of values, norms of interdictions, hierarchies, relationships of dominance and property, its domain reserved to the sacred, and so forth. In other words, *there is no utopia without a synthetic and disruptive representation of social otherness.*[6]

We will hold on to this notion of an 'idea-image', because it recognises the proper role of the imagination in projects that had, moreover, gone beyond the realm of the novel and become attached to a more directly theoretical genre. This is, indeed, the case with the three authors that most interest us. In particular, we will look for the idea-image of the common store – the place where everyone deposits the products of their labour and takes what they need – as the marker par excellence of the utopian community. Working from such a perspective, far from restricting utopia to a literary and philosophical production with well-defined criteria, we can instead ask ourselves where utopia 'exists'. More specifically, we can ask where utopia conformed to the principle of the collective appropriation and distribution of the goods produced – a principle that was not yet called communism – in the era and in the texts of Morelly, Mably, and Babeuf.[7]

It seems that, with a fair degree of probability, if not certainty, we can establish a line of descent between these three utopians in their use of certain concepts and themes. In 1797, during the trial prosecuting the conspiracy of which he was the main leader, Babeuf identified himself with the philosophical and political heritage of Morelly's *Code de la Nature* (which he, like everyone else at that time, attributed to Diderot) and, moreover, claimed the legacy of Mably's writings. He described Morelly, alias Diderot, as 'the most spirited athlete of the system' of

---

6   Baczko, *Utopian Lights*, p. 15, italics in original.
7   According to Jacques Grandjonc, it was Restif de la Bretonne who first used the word 'communism' in its modern sense in one of the last *Monsieur Nicolas* books, written in 1797 (Jacques Grandjonc, *Communisme/Kommunismus/ Communism. Origine et développement international de la terminologie communautaire prémarxiste, des utopistes aux néo-babouvistes, 1785–1842*, Trier: Schriften aus dem Karl-Marx-Haus, 1989, vol. I, p. 75). On what this new use owed to the experience of the French Revolution and to Babouvism, see his second chapter, 'De l'utopie communautaire à la révolution sans-culotte', in J. Grandjonc, *Communisme/ Kommunismus/Communism*, pp. 57–85. Neither Morelly, nor Mably, nor Babeuf ever used this term with such strong historical connotations; this is also why we will avoid it as far as possible.

equality; as for the latter, he spoke of 'the popular, the human, the sensitive Mably';[8] and he referred to himself and his comrades as the 'disciples' of the doctrine of these 'great masters'.[9]

It is true that Babeuf also summoned Rousseau into the courtroom as an 'accomplice' whom his accusers would not dare attack.[10] However, it is notable that the Citizen of Geneva was the subject of only the most lukewarm praise. This is in fact especially remarkable when we place this episode in the context of the French Revolution, which generally idolised the man it considered its main inspirer. Mably was presented, by comparison with Rousseau, as 'a much more pronounced disorganiser', 'a conspirator of a very different fibre'; the praise went up a notch further for Diderot-Morelly, who was said to be 'the most determined', 'the most fearless'. In general terms, it is surely necessary to consider the strategic element at work, here. This was, after all, a plea made before judges, and clearly sought to play down both the originality and subversive character of the ideal that bound the conspirators together. Yet we should also give proper weight to this kinship, which was openly embraced as such, and to asking why Babeuf was so enthusiastic about his two predecessors. The question remains, of course, to what extent the legacy of Morelly and Mably goes beyond a simple common allegiance to a vague ideal of community of goods, and whether the status of utopia in his predecessors' works did directly inspire the people's tribune Babeuf when he elaborated his own political objectives.

So, our aim is to set a key moment in the history of utopia within its proper dynamic, and to do so without the theoretical and, above all, ideological preconceptions that have long overdetermined the narrative on these visions of human community. The first of these preconceptions consists of reading these Enlightenment utopians as 'precursors', essentially as heralds of the 'scientific socialism' that was to come; a second, mirror-image one, condemns them as the harbingers of totalitarianism, some two centuries ahead of time.[11] In contrast to these teleological

---

8   'Défense générale de Babeuf devant la Haute-Cour de Vendôme', quoted in Victor Advielle, *Histoire de Gracchus Babeuf et du babouvisme*, Paris: Éditions du CTHS, 1990, vol. II, p. 52.
9   Ibid., p. 48.
10 Ibid., p. 58.
11 Almost all works relating to these three authors bear the mark of such ideological overdetermination. Nevertheless, we can only agree with Abdelaziz Labib that 'Mably

preconceptions, we will attempt to retrace, step by step, the evolution of a genre which, through these three authors, finally led, during the Revolution, to the collective formulation of an insurrectionary project that carried a radical message of innovation. As we will try to show, it was through this project that utopia now believed itself directly possible – and sought to equip itself with the means for its realisation.

Dismantling the myth of the precursor – whose work is one-sidedly grasped as already pregnant with concepts that only take on their real significance at some later point – is a necessity if we are to avoid emptying the authors' thought of its own proper substance. However, this does not prevent us from identifying, in these Enlightenment utopians, beyond their variations on the ideal of a community of goods, a certain kinship in the way they pose particular problems related to this ideal. Doubtless, these questions, and certain aspects of their treatment, can be found also in later authors, who could not have posed them in the same way if it were not for their predecessors. In this sense, we can still *identify antecedents*, even while taking care not to distort our analysis of the texts by placing too much emphasis on looking for evidence of the 'real' idea that was still to come. Obviously, this can be done only insofar as we can plausibly establish a legacy which is maintained through successive utopias. This is what we propose to do here, through the analysis of these three authors' major works. This will allow us to both fully render the specificity of their philosophical-political production and set it in its proper context, but without neglecting the part played by lines of descent and subsequent appropriations. So, without denying the connection between a work of reconstruction such as this and one of establishing a genealogy of socialism, we will try to avoid the familiar pitfalls.

Moreover, it seems that the link between Morelly, Mably, and Babeuf has deep roots. Without wishing to take away from the significance of each man's approach, the fact remains that these three, whose works followed in succession throughout the Ancien Régime's final crisis, had to get to grips with ever sharper social strife, in parallel with the growing number of reform projects among their contemporaries. Each of them, like Thomas More in his day, could claim direct participation in political

---

and Morelly would have remained forgotten, if deep ideological crises had not intermittently awakened the memory of them in posterity' (*La critique utopiste de la société civile au XVIIIe siècle en France: les cas de Mably et Morelly*, edited by Olivier Bloch, Paris: Université de Paris I, 1983, p. 10).

activity, although unlike in More's case, their activity was more a matter of opposition to the monarchy than of serving as counsel to the king.[12] The first of them, Morelly, seems to have led a secret career as the Prince de Conti's éminence grise, carrying out various diplomatic missions on his behalf. His works are thus the writings of a discreet member of the opposition to Louis XV.[13] The second, Mably, published not only philosophical-political treatises, but also texts directly intervening in the current affairs of his time: his text *Du gouvernement et des lois de la Pologne*, written in 1770 at the request of Count Wielhorski to help him with reform efforts in Poland, is a prime example of this attitude.[14] In fact, Mably ceaselessly worked to influence the political situation: 'he tried to drive attempts at social and institutional reform in France, Poland, the United States and other countries', writes one of his greatest students.[15] His work is thus inseparable from his desire for social transformation. Finally, Babeuf's theoretical development was intertwined with his progress as a young reformer, and then as a political activist during the French Revolution, with such constant participation in events that it would ultimately cost him his life. Along the way from Morelly to Babeuf, the direct involvement in contemporary political life grew, more often than not in opposition to the mainstream.

Here, we will thus hypothesise that these three authors' personal involvement in the theoretical and political debates and struggles of a

---

12   On Thomas More, Sheriff of London, Speaker of the House of Commons, and then Lord Chancellor of England, see in particular Karl Kautsky, *Thomas More und seine Utopie*, Stuttgart: Dietz, 1888; more recently: Bernard Cottret, *Thomas More: la face cachée des Tudor*, Paris: Tallandier, 2012, and Antoine Hatzenberger, 'De More à Bacon, vers une théorie pragmatique du conseil', in L. Bove and C. Duflo (eds), *Le philosophe, le sage et le politique, de Machiavel aux Lumières*, Saint-Étienne: Publications de l'Université de Saint-Étienne, 2002, pp. 75–94.

13   Guy Antonetti, 'Étienne-Gabriel Morelly, l'écrivain et ses protecteurs', *Revue d'histoire littéraire de la France*, 1, 1984, 19–52.

14   See on this point Jacques Lecuru, 'Deux consultants au chevet de la Pologne: Mably et Jean-Jacques Rousseau', Marek Blaszke, 'Projet de réformes pour la Pologne par deux adversaires : Mably et Le Mercier de la Rivière', and Marek Tomaszewski, 'Les inédits de Mably sur la Pologne ou le constat d'échec d'un législateur', in P. Friedemann, F. Gauthier, J.-L. Malvache, and F. Mazzanti-Pepe (eds), *Colloque Mably. La politique comme science morale*, Bari: Palomar, vol. I, 1997, pp. 115–29, 131–46, and 147–59; and Marc Belissa's introduction to Mably, *Du gouvernement et des lois de la Pologne*, Paris: Kimé, 2008, pp. 7–129.

15   Introduction by Peter Friedemann to Mably, *Sur la théorie du pouvoir politique*, Paris: Éditions Sociales, 1975, p. 24.

period characterised by optimism in reformist projects can, at least partially, explain their increasingly marked orientation towards a direct use of the utopian ideal, ranging from polemical intervention in ideological disputes to the attempt to promote its practical realisation. So, when we look at Morelly, Mably, and Babeuf, we are dealing with the growing incursion of utopia into the political arena, at least partly as a result of an exceptional context. From this point of view, analysis of their work offers a striking example of the way in which a historical event transforms thinking itself.

Babeuf's writings seem especially amenable to a methodology that places texts within their ideological context of enunciation – that is, by considering them as acts aimed at producing particular effects in this specific context.[16] But such an interpretative method must necessarily be adapted to the exceptional conditions of the enunciation of Babeuf's discourse, namely the conditions of the French Revolution. From this perspective, Babeuf's trajectory seems particularly telling of what the revolution does to the concept: it allows us to see how certain categories of political theory become inoperative, and are changed, or disappear, while others emerge and become levers for action. As Georges Labica writes, for all the actors of the period,

> this meant thinking the Revolution at the very moment in which it was happening, at the moment when, sometimes groping its way forward, sometimes with lightning speed, it strove to master its acts intellectually, by inventing its terminology from scratch.[17]

Captured in live action, the phenomenon can be seen and analysed through texts that differ greatly from the philosophical treatise. These include such texts as personal correspondence, newspaper articles, pamphlets, and legal pleas. The evolution of Babeuf's ideas as his

---

16 This method is not unrelated to the one embraced by Quentin Skinner, *The Foundations of Modern Political Thought*, Cambridge: Cambridge University Press, 1978, Vol. 1: *The Renaissance*, pp. xiii-xiv: 'For to understand what questions a writer is addressing, and what he is doing with the concepts available to him, is equivalently to understand some of his basic intentions in writing, and is thus to elicit what exactly he may have meant by what he said – or failed to say.'

17 Georges Labica, *Robespierre. Une politique de la philosophie*, Paris: La Fabrique, 2013 [1989], pp. 41-2.

utopia metamorphosed over these decisive years will be taken as a paradigmatic case, in this exceptional moment, of the new relationship between the real and the possible, between the real and the ideal. For a long time to come, utopia would believe itself a realisable possibility. Babeuf's path shows how much the French Revolution is to be credited for this radical development. As Miguel Abensour writes:

> How can we account for the extraordinary blossoming of utopianism in the nineteenth century, if not with reference to the 'miraculous' character of the French Revolution, which – by opening up the field to what could be other than it currently is – upset the boundaries of possible and the impossible.[18]

This was also recognised by contemporaries themselves. Babeuf was the first to be aware of such a transformation, writing in early 1796:

> I would dispute the view that it would have been more advantageous for us to have come into the world less belatedly, in order to accomplish the mission of disabusing men of the so-called right to property. Who can disabuse me of the idea that the present time is precisely the most favourable one? . . . *the French Revolution has given us proof after proof that abuses, however ancient, were not ineradicable.*[19]

An analysis of the current of thought embodied by these three authors – from its Enlightenment foundations to its developments during the Revolution – thus has to do with a properly philosophical issue. The latter lies in grasping the theoretical implications of the confrontation between a certain discourse and history, captured in the heat of the moment. It makes it possible to give philosophical dignity to authors ignored by the academic tradition, which is likely too narrowly focused on the 'great' philosophers.

Through their active involvement in the ideological and theoretical struggles of this period, as well as through their general orientation, Morelly, Mably, and Babeuf represent a current in the Enlightenment which has its own particular consistency, notwithstanding their various

---

18 Abensour, *Utopiques*, p. 15.
19 *TP*, 37, II, pp. 134–5.

differences. This can be characterised as a radical Enlightenment current, in a different sense from that which Jonathan Israel has identified in his characterisation of the evolution visible in Europe between 1650 and 1750.[20] Indeed, *this* radicalism is not particularly expressed at an ontological or religious level: none of the three authors displays a new materialist or atheist approach. On the contrary, Morelly and Mably refer to Providence as the major explanatory principle of the world's course; each man explicitly rejects materialism. As for Babeuf, despite an obvious atheism in his last journalistic production in 1795–6, in his hopes for social change he tends to return to the promises of millenarianism, an approach which seems quite alien to the reasoning of a d'Holbach or a La Mettrie.

Rather, we can call these authors Enlightenment radicals in terms of their proposed solutions to the problem of inequality, of social injustice, and the moral depravity of a society based on property. In this sense, though they stood outside the materialist current, they took part in a movement that sought humanity's reappropriation of its fate and its history. Through the original connection which they established between theory and practice, and through their utopias' complex relationship with reality, they embodied a significant form of political thought in the eighteenth century. Through this form, the theoretical and moral conditions of possibility were gradually prepared for what would not long afterwards be called socialism. As such, their study deserves to be broken out of its usual *historical* confines – however valuable and important the insights from this discipline may be – and be addressed in a manner that pays particular attention to the concepts used, and to the internal coherence of the discourse as well as its possible tensions. In short, this means dealing with them *philosophically*.

So, without attributing these authors a 'communist' project that was not their own, here we will strive to pay attention to the real intentions that inspired them. These intentions are obviously not unconnected to the socialism, or rather the socialisms, and the utopias of the nineteenth century, but they should not be confused with the latter.

---

20 Jonathan Israel, *A Revolution of the Mind: Radical Enlightenment and the Intellectual Origins of Modern Democracy*, Princeton, NJ: Princeton University Press, 2010.

This is the perspective from which we will examine the operation of the utopian ideal in these three figures. Taking each in turn, we will grasp its role precisely by understanding its evolution, and the part it played in the development of thinking that gradually turned towards the objective of radical social change. Indeed, the most obvious feature of the writings of these three figures is that we find utopia . . . in all its forms. If Morelly did not shy away from using the novelistic form to portray the ideal society, the novel in question – *La Basiliade* – broke with most of this genre's usual canons; and, in any case, he then abandoned this form in favour of the singular construction of the *Code de la Nature*. In Mably, as in Babeuf, we no longer find a novel, but allusions and sketches of the ideal society, which pose the questions: on what conditions can we still speak of a 'utopian' ideal? What justifies the continued use of this label?

A second remarkable feature of these three authors is that each tries to root his social ideal in a conception of man that makes him naturally inclined to such an ideal. In each case, our working hypothesis is that they took up an ad hoc anthropology, indeed one with a deep connection with the utopia of the community of goods. Without attempting to settle the – surely irresolvable – question of whether utopia or anthropology takes precedence over or determines the other, we will try to show that these authors conceived man in such a way that his very essence justified and gave substance to the social ideal. This remains the case even though the ideal itself varies significantly from one author to another. Contrary to a conclusion which we might too hastily reach, the ideal of community is not identical in Morelly, Mably, and Babeuf, nor is their conception of man. So, in each case, there is an original anthropology, and here we will examine how far this anthropology fits with what each of the three men conceived as a state of bliss for humanity.

A final line of approach consists of examining how each of these three utopians sought, in certain instances, to give their utopia a historical grounding. Such an integration was in fact a new fact in the history of utopia, which became 'temporalised' in the second half of the eighteenth century. This itself made it possible to use utopia politically. This question in fact encompasses several others: can we detect a specific conception of history linked to each of the three utopias? Do these utopias belong to humanity's past, or to its future? How far do the authors define procedures of action directed towards these utopias' historical realisation – or, failing that, at the advent of a situation that approaches this? Here, we will aim to show that, in each case, the specific characteristics of the utopia allow us to account for the way in which the utopian imagines his own place in time and in action; in other words, how, from Morelly to Babeuf, we move from the *utopian novel* to a *politics of utopia*.

In essence, we are proposing a rereading of Morelly, Mably, and Babeuf's work, in the light of utopia. Starting from its expressions and particular features, we will examine the deeper way in which this utopia shapes each author's image of himself and his fellow men, as well as the historical role that he attributes to them. This will show how far we can truly say that utopia, through the Conspiracy of Equals in 1796, became a political programme. It will tell us how the philosophers had already set out to change the world, and not just to interpret it.

Morelly: The Many Farewells to the Novel

According to Pierre-François Moreau, in the opening lines of *Le récit utopique* (*The Utopian Narrative*), Morelly's works represent a break in the history of utopias: '[the] eighteenth century would multiply such journeys before seeing the genre change in the pair formed by Morelly's *La Basiliade* and *Code de la Nature*'.[1] This diagnosis is confirmed by Albert Soboul and Irmgard Hartig in a major article published in 1976. Their attempt to periodise the 'history of social theory and utopian invention' in the Enlightenment identifies three main stages, embodied respectively by the priest Meslier, by Morelly, and finally by Babeuf.[2]

Soboul terms the innovation found in the very writing of a text like the *Code* 'revolutionary'. The utopian diptych constituted by *La Basiliade* and the *Code de la Nature*, first of all, represents a formal break: never before had a utopian taken his work back to the drawing board for a second attempt, significantly changing the key characteristics of his plan for an ideal society. Moreover, his second version no longer took on the guise of a novel; rather, he presented it as the conclusion of his philosophical reflection on the nature of man and societies. It is thus worth

---

1 Pierre-François Moreau, *Le récit utopique*, Paris: PUF, 1982, p. 7.
2 Irmgard Hartig and Albert Soboul, 'Notes pour une histoire de l'utopie en France au xviiie siècle', *Annales historiques de la Révolution française* (*AHRF*) 224, 1976, pp. 161–79, at p. 171.

analysing in detail the developments from one project to the next, which mark a first turn in the history of utopia, as it moved towards political theory. Here, we shall seek to demonstrate how the construction of an ideal model of society is related to the desire to make it, if not more achievable in practice, at least more credible in the eyes of its reader. We will thus try to determine what, in the structure and the very justifications of the ideal described, allowed for the remarkable fate of this text, which would, a few decades after its writing, serve as a revolutionary breviary for the Babouvists.

1

The Critical Utopia of *La Basiliade*: Introduction to an Atypical Utopia

Le Naufrage des îles Flottantes, ou La Basiliade du célèbre Pilpai (*The Shipwreck of the Floating Islands, or the Basiliade of the Famous Pilpai*) was published in 1753; as a sign of its only relative success, there was apparently no second edition. A first approach to this text reveals that the author played rather freely with the codes of the utopian tradition. Before examining the meaning of the distance he thus kept from this tradition, it is worth defining the main aspects of this text.

First of all, if this novel does indeed contain a travelogue, it is not that of a European who, through his adventures, discovers the shores of an unknown land with ideal social institutions. Rather, the story is told by a representative of a society presented as perfect – the young Prince Zeinzemin – who is abducted by invaders and astonished to discover the corruption of the civilisations flourishing in the 'Floating Islands': societies based on property, which are allegories for Europe. By presenting its heroes as representatives of an unknown continent, *La Basiliade* inverts the classical relation between the reader's world and the utopian society. By way of comparison, Thomas More's *Utopia* had described how Utopus, king of Utopia, began by separating his country from the rest of the continent: 'he had a channel cut fifteen miles wide where the land joined the continent, and thus caused the sea to flow around the country'.[1] Utopia was thus accessible only through a passage known to

---

1 Thomas More, *Utopia*, Cambridge: Cambridge University Press, 1989, p. 44.

the Utopians alone, whereas the continent that harbours the ideal society in *La Basiliade* is readily accessible. Similarly, in contrast to the policy of conquest and colonisation pursued by the Utopians when they lack sufficient space for all their citizens, the population of the blessed continent welcome Europeans who have washed up on their shores and wish to mingle with them at the end of the novel.

Morelly thus refuses to enclose the model society within narrow boundaries and cut it off from the rest of the world. Quite the opposite: it symbolises unity and reunion, whereas the Floating Islands are presented as both unstable and separate from each other. These images counterpose, on the one hand, the lies and errors that cause fragmentation and isolate men, and, on the other, the truth and goodness that bring them together. Since the islands are themselves former pieces of the continent, separated from it by the wrath of the gods when faced with the corruption of men, the principles of the model society also appear as the original matrix of all social organisation, while these scattered remnants represent the distortion of these principles.

The image of the blessed continent is also owed to Morelly's paradoxical effort to give a sense of realism, albeit through a work presented as an oriental tale originally written by a famous Indian sage, Pilpai, which the anonymous author has merely translated. The demonstration provided by the narrative is in fact coupled with a reference to the reality of a past and geographically remote – but nevertheless really existing – civilisation: that of the Incas of Peru. In his work on Morelly, Nicolas Wagner has pointed to the inspiration that this eighteenth-century author might have drawn from Garcilaso de la Vega's *Royal Commentaries of the Incas and General History of Peru*, published in 1633 and reissued several times in the eighteenth century.[2] Many episodes in Morelly's story are clearly reminiscent of the discovery of the Americas by the Spanish Conquistadors, even though here the action is portrayed from the standpoint of the inhabitants of the discovered continent.

The allusion to this real history is quite explicit in the 'Letter to the Sultana', which embeds the main narrative in a second story, that of the anonymous translator of the tale who addresses himself to an unknown

---

2 Nicolas Wagner, *Morelly, le méconnu des Lumières*, Paris: Klincksieck, 1978, p. 174.

oriental noblewoman. This mysterious translator writes, at the end of the account of his own adventures:

> The whole action [of the] poem [of Pilpai] proves the possibility of a system which is not imaginary, since it turns out that the customs of the peoples governed by Zeinzemin largely resemble those of the peoples of the most flourishing and best-policed Empire that has ever existed: I mean that of the Peruvians.[3]

The author thus intertwines literary procedures and historical allusions in order to convince the reader of the truth of his utopia, of the suitability of its characteristics in relation to the actual possibilities of human societies. This is why the novel combines two different voices. There is the voice of the storyteller, who recounts the adventures of Prince Zeinzemin, and at the same time the history of the ideal country; and that of the so-called translator, who comments on Pilpai's words in the footnotes, most often to support them with arguments or examples.

The first organising principle of this society is the absence of private property: this is repeated twice. The first time, it is in allegorical form:

> Pitiless Property, mother of all the crimes which flood the rest of the world, was unknown to them: they looked upon the Earth as a common nurse who indistinctly offers her breast to whichever of her children feels pressed by hunger.[4]

Significantly, this vivid presentation is commented on in the following note: 'Pilpai rejects the false or misunderstood principle of most Moralists, who have stuck their *cuique suum* where there should be neither yours nor mine.'[5]

By this, Morelly indicates his main target, and the function of *La Basiliade*: it seeks, above all, to attack the moralists and the dominant morality, which is based on the idea of property and thus harmful to men. The introductory letter already announced: 'Pilpai seeks to show

---
3   *LB*, I, p. xli.
4   Ibid., pp. 5–6.
5   Ibid.

what would be the happy state of a society formed according to the principles of his excellent morals.'[6]

La Basiliade thus sets out to describe the social conditions that correspond to the 'principles of an excellent morality', which alone can lead men to the happiness that nature promises them. This aim provides a first explanation for the fact that Morelly devotes more of his argument to an *ethical* legitimisation of the ideal society than to describing how its politics or institutions might operate. In this first utopian text, he seeks, above all, to develop a critique of the existing society and what he considers its perverted moral foundations: this criticism occupies the greater part of the 'cantos' of *La Basiliade*. The author seeks to counterpose the real social order to the evidence of its unnatural character, thinking that, in so doing, he can prove that there is a possible alternative way of organising the community.

Yet, in this vein, if the first of the conditions of collective happiness is the complete abolition of private property, its justification is in its fundamental intuition remarkably close to that identified by Thomas More in the first part of *Utopia*. Like Morelly's 'Letter to the Sultana', it introduces the properly constructive passage in this philosophical-political work. In the 'Letter' the Utopian writes – as against the other poets who paint the virtues of Princes in a false light: '[They] teach them the art of palliating the evils and vices of an ordinary society, but not the means of cutting them at the root, nor the secret of perfecting their economy'.[7] In More's *Utopia*, Raphael Hythloday used similar terms to tell his interlocutors of this refusal of half-measures and half-solutions to social ills. He does this when he comments on possible measures to limit social inequalities, such as the sharing of land or the prohibition of excessive wealth:

> Laws of this sort, I agree, may have as much effect as poultices continually applied to sick bodies that are past cure. The social evils I mentioned may be alleviated and their effects mitigated for a while, but so long as private property remains, there is no hope at all of effecting a cure.[8]

---

6   Ibid., p. xl.
7   Ibid., p. xv.
8   More, *Utopia*, p. 40.

So, again, the aim is to cut at the root of evil, and do so through the community of goods. The utopian discourse is presented as one that 'assigns an overall causality to evils'.[9] In this respect, it is similar to the position adopted by Rousseau at the beginning of the second part of the *Second Discourse*, which sees in the establishment of the ownership of fields the sole cause of 'crimes', 'wars', 'murders', 'misfortunes', and 'horrors' of human societies.[10] But utopia proposes a solution to these evils: simply eliminating the cause which has thus been identified. This radicalism, in the etymological sense of the term, in the field of political theory is one of the most constant characteristics of utopias. In its own way, it prefigures the logic of Karl Marx's reasoning.

As we can see, on this important point, Morelly followed in line with the mode of utopian construction heralded by More's work. Such an approach consists in contrasting the dominant political and moral principles with the irresistible logic of a model that fully eradicates social ills because it digs down to their original source. So, Europe's morality contradicts the foundation of the social bond such as it is described in the first pages of the novel: namely, the common working of land that belongs to all, and the depositing of the products of this labour in the common stores of this 'toiling republic'.

Where natural equity reigns, says Morelly at the beginning of his novel, 'authority [is] no more than a voluntary concession of peoples' love'.[11] Hence peoples admit a royal family and a monarch whose 'good deeds [are] the only title of nobility'. The king descends from the original family of which the whole people are the offspring: he is thus bound to his people by truly paternal ties. The novel allows the classic paternalistic metaphor of the monarchy to be spun in a narrative form in which, once again, both this paternalism and its full consequences are taken seriously. Indeed, true kinship – making only natural the pooling of resources and the collective organisation of the various aspects of life – would alone enable the individual members of the community to be bound together by the bonds of affection and mutual aid necessary for happiness. Here, we find a negation 'in actuality' of the contractualist

---

9   Moreau, *Le récit utopique*, p. 20.
10 Jean-Jacques Rousseau, *The Social Contract and the First and Second Discourses*, edited by Susan Dunn, New Haven, CT: Yale University Press, 2002, p. 113.
11 *LB*, I, p. xii.

principle which forcefully rejects the model of paternal government. It is these family ties, extended to the whole community, that allow for a spontaneous submission to the authority of a beloved and benevolent monarch; and here the monarch's functions are reduced to supervising social activities, indicating 'both the times, and what [it is] appropriate to do for the common good'.[12]

Housing, meals, and harvests are thus all in common – as 'among the Peruvians', as one note specifies.[13] The main details of this society's economic organisation are contained in a single long note by the 'translator'; in the intervals between the harvests carried out by the whole social body, each man exercises a particular craft or trade, the products of which are also brought to the common store. This division of labour is sufficient to provide for all the community's needs – without excessive fatigue for anyone. Work can thus be a pleasure enjoyed in common, like meals and other festivities. The 'reciprocity of aid' between production units is the general rule, as is the moderation of work. Morelly specifies: 'The Provinces of different states communicate to each other what they have in over-abundance . . . by simple or mutual gifts.'[14] This material solidarity between the different parts of the utopian city is also found in More, as a marker of the utopian social bond: 'the whole island is like a single family'.[15] As for Morelly, he explains that: 'If [two people] happen to meet, they love each other because they know that they have rendered services to each other, without knowing each other.'[16] Mutual aid is thus presented in both cases as the foundation of the social bond – as opposed, once again, to contractual obligation.

The political organisation of the island is reduced to its simplest expression. It is condensed in the virtuous king – that is, before his abduction, which is at the centre of the novel's plot. In his absence, he is replaced by an assembly of 'a hundred wise elders' who suffice to order the collective life of a whole continent. The social body knows no laws other than the laws of nature; it does not need to write them down, for they are transmitted from generation to generation as a spontaneous consequence of the way of life of the inhabitants of this blessed

---

12 Ibid., p. 41.
13 Ibid., p. 105.
14 Ibid., p. 108, note.
15 More, *Utopia*, p. 62.
16 *LB*, II, p. 17.

continent. Coercive measures and prisons are unknown because they are unnecessary. In this respect, the form of government in *La Basiliade* lives up to the principles of the good Zamé, the beneficent despot of the island of Tamoé in the Marquis de Sade's *Aline et Valcour*. Like Zeinzemin, Zamé believes that 'establishing good arrangements' for society will prevent crime and make criminal legislation superfluous. The explanation which he offers his visitor Sainville could equally be put in the mouth of one of the kings of the lineage of the blessed continent, upon addressing a traveller from the Floating Islands:

> With equality of property, there is no theft . . . Since equality of property brings union, and the gentleness of government leads all subjects to cherish their system equally, there are no state crimes, no revolutions . . . Internal divisions are prevented by equality of rank and property, all sources of murder are extinguished . . . Be just: tolerate crime, since the vice of your government leads to it; or if crime harms you, change the constitution of the government that gives rise to it; make it impossible for the citizen to commit it, just as I have done.[17]

Common to both texts is the belief in the goodness of man's nature, which means that he will commit crimes only in a social context in which they find, if not their justification, at least objective motivations. There is no such thing as an endogenous criminality, which can be attributed to the individual alone independently of the social conditions in which he is immersed. It is assumed that 'laws wise enough, gentle enough to accord with nature, would never be violated'.[18] Once self-interest, greed and ambition are cut at the root, crimes become 'impossible', in all logical rigour. While purely symbolic punishments, public indignity foremost among them, are maintained in Tamoé, they are sufficient to amend the still minor offences that are, according to Zamé, 'the only ones possible in our nation'.[19] Contrary to *La Basiliade*, and without much concern for consistency, letter XXXV of *Aline et Valcour* thus maintains – despite the statements just cited – a range of punishments, albeit ones much milder

---

17 Marquis de Sade, *Aline et Valcour*, in *Œuvres complètes*, Paris: Gallimard, 1990, vol. I, pp. 387–1109, Chapter XXXV, at pp. 653–4.
18 Ibid., p. 668.
19 Ibid.

than those used in the real world and imposed incrementally according to their social utility. Morelly, who follows the logic of man's natural goodness to its full conclusion, is more consistent than Sade in abolishing all penal law.

Utopian ways of organising society thus seem to do without the need to repress certain behaviours. From this perspective, it is no surprise that, in *La Basiliade*, spontaneity and tolerance are the rule in matters of religion, in addition to a natural deistic cult: 'Never did this diversity of opinion [on the posthumous fate of the soul] excite quarrels among them; incorruptible common sense told them that each mortal is free to make whatever conjecture he pleases about his future fate.'[20] Tamoé does not have religious tolerance. Rather, religion has been reduced to a single, simple expression: a deistic cult without priests or ceremonies. The simplification and abolition of this institution should put an end to all religious 'sects' and 'horrible dissensions'.[21] This time, the rather more compelling comparison is with the positions attributed by More to the Utopians, albeit not at the level of spontaneous opinions but at that of concerted legislation: 'it is one of their oldest rules that no one should suffer for his religion.'[22] On this point, like others, Morelly seems to translate into an entirely naturalised, spontaneous, non-institutional mode principles that other utopias present in the form of positive laws and explicit regulations.

The last striking feature of Morelly's utopia worth mentioning is the celebration of free love, such as it is supposedly practised in the blessed continent:

> Oh, love! These peoples gave themselves up without fear and without crimes to your delicious transports; the other nations pay homage to their furious divinities by shedding the blood of victims; these ones honoured the generating power of the Universe by increasing the number of its admirers.[23]

So, from the very first pages of the book, Morelly merrily details the various aspects of a natural sexuality, free of any hindrances and thus of

---

20 *LB*, I, p. 13.
21 Sade, *Aline et Valcour*, p. 629.
22 More, *Utopia*, p. 99.
23 *LB*, I, p. 17.

any vices. This means the possibility of a premarital sex life, the choice of a partner exclusively according to personal inclination, the right to separation, and a flexible family structure: the children from a first marriage are welcomed by the second husband as a blessing. Even incest between brothers and sisters is allowed for. Only the union between parents and children is ruled out, and this for purely physiological reasons, since the parents would rather 'see these cherished offspring form other stems, and trace back to them the pleasures of their first years, than graft them again onto a trunk already weakened by the passing of time'.[24] All these elements – with the possible exception of the rehabilitation of incest – would also be found in Diderot's Tahitian utopia, the *Supplément au voyage de Bougainville* – another 'savage republic', to use an expression from Hans-Günter Funke, according to whom this text is directly inspired by *La Basiliade*.[25] In both cases, the descriptions militate in favour of the exculpation of the sexual act, which is celebrated by the community as a festival: just as Morelly's young lovers mate under the watchful eye of their parents, and conclude this first experience surrounded by the whole community in jubilation, the Tahitian girl

> [accepts] without fear or shame, in our presence, amidst a circle of innocent Tahitians, to the sound of flutes, between dances, the caresses of him whom her young heart and the secret voice of her senses [designate] to her.[26]

In both cases, the omnipresence of the social gaze on the couple presents the same ambiguity: this ultimate concession to the utopian ideal of transparency, in all the gestures of daily life, suggests a benevolent but unavoidable form of control over what nonetheless remains its most intimate dimension. The obligatory publicity of any love affair contrasts with the lack of restraint claimed for these 'children of nature'. Love freed from the absurd constraints and taboos of the real world does not

---

24 Ibid., p. 33.
25 Hans-Günter Funke, ' "La République sauvage": Anarchy als Utopie in der französichen Literatur des 16. bis 18. Jahrhunderts', *Romanische Forschungen* 98: 1–2, 1986, pp. 36–57, at pp. 54–5.
26 Denis Diderot, *Supplément au voyage de Bougainville*, in *Œuvres*, Paris: R. Laffont, 1994, vol. II, pp. 541–78, Chapter II, at p. 549.

emancipate itself from the social logic of the ideal community. The only limit placed on freedom of love bears this mark: if incest between parents and children is undesirable, this is the case exclusively from the standpoint of reproduction, which is, ultimately – in Morelly as in Diderot – the true justification of sexual morality. For evidence of this, we need only recall the arguments with which the young Thia begs the host chaplain of the Tahitian family to grant her his favours:

> Stranger, honest stranger, do not rebuff me! Make me a mother; make me a child with whom I may one day walk in Tahiti ... [a child] of whom I shall be proud, and who shall be part of my dowry, when I pass from my father's hut into another.[27]

In a society whose organisation sees in men themselves its only riches, it would seem that free sexuality 'is subject to the rules of a utilitarian morality put at the service of populationism'.[28] Thia's discourse is in harmony with that which parents have of the young lovers they have spied in their lovemaking: 'You are now among the co-citizens; from you will come the cherished tokens of your tenderness; may your posterity grow to the point of being able to take on the sole care of society.'[29] Integration into the community is thus conditioned on a real duty that individuals must fulfil. The wish here expressed is highly indicative of the fundamental purpose of the sexual act: to have offspring who can 'take on ... the sole care of the community'. Love is part of the necessary social rules because it ensures the perpetuation of the community and because it also strengthens the ties between individuals, which unite them as a self-sufficient whole. In this respect, even incest can be interpreted as 'economic autarky transposed to the domain of genital sexuality'.[30] In these conditions, it is hardly certain that we can still speak of a 'free sexuality'.

---

27   Ibid., p. 553.
28   Funke, '"La République sauvage"', p. 56.
29   *LB*, I, p. 22.
30   This is, at least, the interpretation offered by Franck Lestringant: 'L'utopie amoureuse: espace et sexualité dans La Basiliade d'E.-G. Morelly', in F. Moureau and A. M. Rieu (eds), *Eros philosophe*, Paris: Honoré Champion, 1984, p. 94.

Continuities and Ruptures in *La Basiliade*

So, as a general rule, we can say that Morelly's utopia draws some of its essential characteristics from More and from the wider utopian tradition: the community of goods, agricultural work done in common, the division of craft activities according to the preferences of each person, public stores, a collective way of life, a political hierarchy based on the virtues and benefits of superiors, solidarity among the provinces, and religious tolerance. Yet there are two important aspects that distinguish Morelly. On the one hand, there are the repeated allusions in the 'translator's notes' to the Peruvian example, thus connecting the narrative to a real-life reference point. On the other, there is the absence of written laws and of a real government, a much more surprising feature in a utopian tradition rich in pernickety regulations. It gives the society thus described the appearance of a dream, or rather of a myth, an impression reinforced by the author's frequent use of personifications and allegories such as that of Interest, Envy, and so on. This 'anarchistic' dimension – according to Funke, making the community in *La Basiliade* into a 'savage Republic' – locates this text at the limits of the utopian genre itself, on the edges of the golden age.

This impression is reinforced by the fact that nature is discussed in a way that does not confer any special position upon man. In More's *Utopia*, the goodness of Utopian institutions is related to the fact that they allow for the fulfilment of man's nature, which is considered not in its connection to other beings, but, rather, in its essential superiority: 'The pleasures of sound, sight and smell they also pursue as the agreeable seasonings of life, recognising that Nature intended them to be the particular province of man. No other kind of animal contemplates with delight the shape and loveliness of the universe, or enjoys odours.'[31] The Utopians are also distinguished by their zeal to 'do all the things farmers usually do to improve poor soil by hard work and technical knowledge'.[32] They clear forests and take special care to cultivate their minds and improve their virtues. They also cultivate their own nature by emphasising its difference from that of the rest of the universe. This effort contrasts with the immediacy of the relationship that the citizens of *La Basiliade*

---

31 More, *Utopia*, p. 78.
32 Ibid.

have with their environment: they need only 'light cultivation'[33] to make the Earth bear fruit, and their harmony with the world even forbids them from eating meat from animals. Their happiness seems to be the fruit of a communion with the rest of the natural universe, not that of the production of a human specificity.

Upon a first approach, this mythically hued exaltation of communion with nature does not fit well with the historical reference to the real Inca society. In fact, the way it is formulated, the allusion to the Incas is akin to the 'utopian denial'[34] typical of most works in this tradition, with the utopian not willingly acknowledging that his text belongs to a genre relegated to the territories of fantasy without consequences for the social world. By noting the resemblance of the Zeinzemin people's morals to those of the Peruvians, Morelly provides tangible, historical proof of the feasibility of his social and political plans.

However, in the text, we can find a second 'denial', stated as follows:

> All this is true in speculation, but impossible in practice. This objection falls by the wayside, if we take into account the fact that this philosopher's aim is only to show the provenance of the contradiction between the truth of his speculation and the falsehood of ordinary practice, based on vulgar morality.[35]

In other words, another form of argumentation in favour of the utopian society emerges. The presentation of another possible social world does not portray it as a reality, in the past or present, or even as a possibility, but as 'true': it is cast in terms of the superiority of theoretical knowledge over the error said to be embodied in existing practices because of their false moral underpinning. *La Basiliade* is the presentation, in narrative form, of a true morality, based on nature and reason, like most utopian morals. But this morality is itself based on a reality of superior essence. Its point of reference is in the last instance metaphysical in its essence, and the rules that govern the communal society are true because they are appropriate to 'the beauty, order, and harmony that reign in this

---

33   *LB*, I, p. 4.
34   The expression is Bertrand Binoche's: 'La dénégation utopique de Bacon à Condorcet', unpublished.
35   *LB*, I, p. 108, note.

admirable Whole' – that is, the universe in general.[36] The utopia of *La Basiliade* is thus a human-scale modelling of the universal order, with which Zeinzemin's people live in harmony: this explains, among other things, the scrupulously observed rule of vegetarianism, which in the text is a condition for nature or the divinity never to appear as an evil power. The description of the peaceful and gentle character of the inhabitants of the blessed continent, forbidding them to shed the blood of animals, is explicitly linked to the innocence that dispenses with any fear of divine punishments:

> The terrible crash of thunder, which everywhere else brings dread, and spreads fear among guilty hearts, was listened to, not as the voice of an irritated power, but as the majestic accents of a beneficent Sovereign who sometimes makes his greatness manifest.[37]

In other words, *La Basiliade* draws on two wholly different registers of justification: on the one hand, it bases itself on a historical reference point, which can be seen in the 'translator's notes'; on the other, it rests on a metaphysical conception of the natural and divine order, which seems to make the story itself a long mythical allegory attributed to the wise man Pilpai. In this second aspect, in particular, the outline of an ideal society is once again situated at the limits of the utopian genre, whose usual codes it upsets by its imprecision and its rejection of any legislative codifications.

La Basiliade seems, in fact, to adopt – as much if not more than the characteristics of the tradition initiated by More's work – those of Bétique, the land described by Adoam to Telemachus during one of his adventures in François Fénelon's didactic novel. Like those of *La Basiliade*, its inhabitants 'are almost all shepherds or toilers';[38] although they are a more rustic people than the former, building no buildings and rejecting all the arts, they still resemble them in the absence of any real political organisation: 'each family is governed by its chief, who is its true king'.[39] Like them, they share their goods and 'love each other with

---

36　Ibid., p. 82.
37　Ibid., p. 9.
38　François Fénelon, *Les aventures de Télémaque*, Paris: Classiques Garnier, 1987, p. 263.
39　Binoche, 'La dénégation utopique de Bacon à Condorcet'.

a brotherly love that nothing will disturb'.[40] They leave their gold and silver mines abandoned and use iron only for peaceful ends. Finally, they share with the people of Zeinzemin their rejection of seafaring, which exposes travellers to the corrupt customs of the surrounding nations. In this sense, the distinctive feature of Morelly's work lies in the fact that he endeavours, as with the elements drawn from More's work, to invert Fénelon's perspective: just as the artificial and closed island of Utopia becomes the natural and open continent, the description of Bétique, a story with mythical notes that precedes that of the more realistic reforms undertaken by Mentor in the city of Salento, is taken up and transformed by Morelly into a peerless model.

What thus remains to be established is the exact status of this model, which has no real political structure, but has an ethical and metaphysical dimension hypertrophic in relation to both the epic tradition and the utopian tradition of which it is part. *La Basiliade*, as we can see, is a myth, but this myth, unlike most, is not a narrative which seeks to explain to the members of the social community the place they occupy in the world, by showing them its provenance. Rather, it is a critique of the place Morelly's contemporaries occupy in the world, mounting an essential challenge to it, in keeping with an essential function of the utopian genre.

Integrated into a deeply religious conception of the universal order – a reflection of divine wisdom – the social organisation described in the text becomes the site for the reconciliation of the destiny of men and the will of God. In this respect, *La Basiliade* takes great liberties with the utopian tradition, which makes only distant reference to the divine order. But the fundamental novelty of Morelly's approach, as compared with myth, is that it poses this conciliation not as the human race's definitively bygone past, in the manner of an original Paradise or one from the first times of humanity, or even as the result – set in an indeterminate future – of a Christian-style Last Judgement. Rather, it appears as the imaginary reverse of the 'Floating Islands' that represent Europe – in other words, as a critical model that is valid in the here and now, even if in a novelistic mode. To give such a model an active role in deconstructing a certain conception of society is also to bring it into the arena of discussion about the best possible form of society, contrary to

---

40   Fénelon, *Les aventures de Télémaque*, p. 266.

the initial function of the myth. In so doing, Morelly extends the critical gesture of previous utopias in a new way, and with new discursive means.

With *La Basiliade*, myth is thus somehow inscribed within the human present. By characterising Morelly's gesture as 'the characteristic heresy of all the insurrections of the enlightened', Nicolas Wagner suggests that, on the theoretical level, this author's approach crosses paths with the much more practical and political approach of the millenarian movements of centuries past. Here, myth, far from justifying the world order by giving it meaning, instead has a function of symbolically tearing down this same order.[41] However, because Morelly encapsulates his vision within the confines of a novel, it retains the appearance of a contemplative ideal. If the aim is indeed to portray the image of exemplary human relations – exemplary because they are devoid of property ownership – such relations can only serve as a counterpoint to those of the perverted society. Their respective descriptions in the allegorical terms of the novel serve to radically differentiate them, to distance them from each other, thereby preventing any thought as to the possible pathway between them, of mediations that would allow the latter to be amended in the direction of the former.

Morelly's first utopian work thus obviously pursues a paradoxical project. On the one hand, it clearly intends to propose a radical counter-model of society, rejecting not only the principle of private property, but also the constitutive principles of any known society: written laws, instituted government, armed force. By exalting love as the foundation of the social bond, it even distances itself from the utopian tradition and the description of precolonial societies in the Americas, and arrives back at an origin myth.

On the other hand, although this is only roughly sketched out, this work seems to borrow certain elements of its economic organisation from More's novel. Moreover, while taking liberties with its sources, it also draws on the reported realities of the people of Peru. Finally, it does not forsake the motive of well-understood self-interest in order to explain why its ideal people acts as it does. Morelly sets up a double system of justification, both immanent and transcendent, for human action in the model society, much as he provides it with a double set of evidence, both empirical and imaginary. He makes no decision between myth and

---

41 Wagner, *Morelly, le méconnu des Lumières*, p. 193.

utopia, between metaphysical and social criticism. This oscillation in his general orientation seems characteristic of an approach whose critical will is embodied in the pure and simple inversion of the principles of the existing society, though it cannot be reduced to this negative or satirical register alone. The features of the good society, as are barely sketched out by Morelly, express an anthropological optimism, a refusal to consider our world as the only possible one, even if the author seems little-concerned with granting this society a model status. Significantly, Morelly never directly asks the question of whether the principles of the model society could replace those that govern the organisation of European societies, even to answer in the negative. More, however, did do so: as we know, he ends his novel with these words: 'I freely confess that in the Utopian commonwealth there are very many features that in our own societies I would wish rather than expect to see.'[42]

The problem would be posed in very different terms in the *Code de la Nature*. But, before that, the absence of such a line of questioning sheds light on an important aspect of *La Basiliade*'s project: its primarily critical purpose. This means that the constructive dimension of this work is not merely hazy, but rather deliberately reduced to those features that best highlight the absurdity of Europe's institutions, to the detriment of any other possible political use. In a way, it can be said that, in *La Basiliade*, critique has almost entirely absorbed utopia, and that the desire to exonerate human nature from the faults attributable to property-based society makes it appear in a light that has almost nothing human about it, given that it is so much an ideal. In this sense, the social 'model' proposed in this novel is not so much intended to be applied to European society as to be counterposed to it.

From the Model to Its Anthropological Justification

Any imaginary construct of an ideal city demands its justification, even a limited and allusive one, in the nature of man and of the social bond. For the utopian, this means showing that the proposed model is in harmony with both human nature and reason, allowing for the authentic, rather than superficial and artificial, blossoming of individuals. A

---

42 More, *Utopia*, p. 113.

characteristic feature of utopias based on the community of goods and labour thus lies in the negation of any possible discord between individual and collective interests: the individual is not required to give up providing for his needs and desires, but only to satisfy them by simultaneously working for the common happiness. But how can such presuppositions be reconciled with the selfishness plain for all to see in human behaviour? How can a society operate on any other anthropological basis than the constraint of the individual's own needs and desires, which rouse them from their torpor – perhaps even from their natural laziness – and drive them to act? The question is as old as the utopian genre itself.

As several important commentators have noted, the common answer in the utopian tradition is naturalistic in essence.[43] It is to show that, contrary to how things may seem, there is no discrepancy between the satisfaction of personal aspirations and social harmony: the spontaneously good and altruistic man will easily find his interest in benevolent collaboration with others. Classically, this possibility for man is asserted rather than deduced. In More's *Utopia*, in particular, instead of a true demonstration of its naturalness, we find a description of the concrete social organisation of the island, and of the way of life that it entails, such that it actually conditions individual behaviour in the desired direction. As Pierre Macherey writes, with regard to the institution of collective meals, the details of collective practices 'have been painstakingly worked out in order to establish the daily life of the citizens of Utopia, a life that consists of the tireless repetition of the same gestures performed in common'.[44] In *La Basiliade*, the organisation of collective life is not the artificial feat of a legislator; it is almost entirely left up to the spontaneous initiative of the members of the community. The essential justification of the principle of community of goods, and the conviction of its superiority over any other form of social organisation, is thus rooted in a characterisation of the nature of men themselves, and in the structure which Morelly gives it. From this perspective, the novel's anthropological dimension takes on unprecedented importance: it is

---

43 See Pierre Macherey and Pierre-François Moreau in the works cited above, as well as Peter Kuon, 'Utopie et anthropologie au siècle des Lumière sou la crise d'un genre littéraire', in H. Hudde and P. Kuon (eds), *De l'utopie à l'uchronie: formes, significations, fonctions*, Tübingen: Gunter Narr Verlag, 1988, pp. 49–62.

44 Pierre Macherey, *De l'utopie!*, Le Havre: De l'incidence éditeur, 2011, p. 137.

one of the most original aspects of the text, and one of the most decisive. It is aimed at showing that human nature, left to itself, is sufficient to produce the desired happy effects. Given such an outlook, *La Basiliade* suggests a quasi-physical spontaneity of social harmony: 'The mechanism of this admirable society regulated itself without effort, without difficulty and almost at the first signal, so perfect was the arrangement of all its energies.'[45] But on what individual 'energies' can such a mechanism supposedly rely?

Following many others, Morelly bases his demonstration on the idea of men's naturally social being. However, he reverses the expected relationship of the causes and effects of this sociability. Here is how he describes the causes of human sociability in the very first pages of *La Basiliade*:

> God ... created many men only so that they could help one another. If, like trees and plants, he had made them to be separated from all society ... Providence would not have left them wanting for anything; the son would not need the father's help, and the father would not feel for the son those tender affections which nature suggests.[46]

As Morelly tellingly takes the relationship of father to son as a model, he indicates that what is primary is not the self-interest that drives the individual to seek the cooperation of his fellow human beings, but, rather, the parental love that motivates care for the infant. Necessity alone would leave him to die, if it were not for the aid which is given to the child at first without immediate counterpart. In other words, in *La Basiliade* – and this is remarkably original – love, not for oneself but of others, has an anthropological primacy in explaining the relationship that binds the individual to the community. It is because the human infant receives loving care that he will develop the desire to do the same for his peers. Significantly, love is always presented in the novel as the most spontaneous feeling between beings, which needs no artificial nourishment.

Thus, *La Basiliade* presents a highly unique variant of Defoe's *Robinson Crusoe*. In a mythical account of the origins of society on the

---

45 *LB*, I, p. 48.
46 Ibid., p. 6.

continent, appearing in the second canto, we learn that the islands on which property-based society survives were originally separated from the blessed continent in a deluge, itself caused by the goddess Truth's anger over the vices of the degenerate human race. The islands were thus detached from this continent, carrying a corrupted humanity far away with them, and leaving only a brother and sister to survive. Left alone on an entire continent, instead of being stranded far from home on a deserted island like Robinson, from the outset they begin to form a small society. Its solidarity, emphasised by the author, is surely necessary for survival, but is above all cemented by the love they have for each other. A footnote specifies:

> Robinson, cast onto a desert island, draws from his stranded vessel the help which the author was embarrassed to keep him alive without; our Indian [Pilpai] has two children, who are deprived of everything, ingeniously discover the first elements of the arts necessary for life. I believe that this philosopher wanted to develop all the circumstances, all the natural and fortuitous encounters that could lead a nascent society, from experiment to experiment, to the inventions of everything that furnishes, so to speak, the human race.[47]

The aim of the story is clear: to show how the first men were able to survive and develop the techniques that gave rise to later societies. The 'counter-Robinsonade' demonstrates – in the narrative form typical of the novel – the primacy of human social ties and the inconceivability of a man surviving alone. The community, however small, necessarily precedes any isolation.

In the species' adventures, love, as symbolised by the bond of brotherhood that unites the characters, and which soon develops into a true love affair, plays the primary role. It is the real driving force behind the activities useful for survival and progress. Morelly writes of the original couple: 'Occupied with the care of making themselves truly happy, their industrious affection each day taught them something new.'[48]

Here, as in the rest of the novel, incest appears as an expression of self-sufficiency, made possible by the bonds of affection that bind together

---

47   Ibid., p. 63.
48   Ibid., pp. 65–6.

the members of the society – from the most restricted, when it comes to its origins, to the most extensive, when it comes to the blessed continent. Love, as the natural and fundamental motor of human actions, makes the community self-sufficient. From this perspective – and here lies the singularity of *La Basiliade*'s theses – self-love is inseparable from the love we have for others, as shown by the lesson the original couple gave to their children: 'No one can dispense with contributing, with all his power, to his own happiness; and it is to encourage us all to do so, that she has inseparably attached it to that of our brothers.'[49]

It is striking to note, here, that it is self-love that must be 'encouraged' and stimulated, and that nothing can better serve as encouragement than the consideration that this is tied up with the happiness of our 'brothers'. This is why love, as the natural foundation of social ties and the principle of all activity, is radically opposed to the 'interest' that characterises property-based societies, rooted in the attraction that the individual has above all to himself and his own preservation. This is seen as a vice that creates a rift in the community:

> Each individual is then bound to human duties only because he does not feel strong enough alone to crush all other men; his cruel heart would happily see the whole world perish, if he could alone collect its spoils.[50]

Self-interest is thus incompatible with love for others. It is radically opposed to it. Love is, therefore, not only the natural motor of human actions, it is the only possible bond for the community, which without it is threatened with dissolution at any moment. Ultimately, it is also the only true motive for human activity:

> It can be shown that the community of all goods, of all succour . . . can rouse men more effectively than the sad motives of particular interest which keep them subject to frivolous fears, to blinkered views and hopes . . . these torments discourage them from working, because of the little that they can expect from it.[51]

---

49 Ibid., p. 72.
50 Ibid., p. 56.
51 Ibid., p. 73.

The meagre gains that can be expected from individual work are thus 'discouraging', in contrast to the abundance that results from collective labour. Here, social harmony is thus justified by the very nature of man. The role attributed to love is at the heart of the demonstration of this harmony, a demonstration which is, essentially, the very object of *La Basiliade*. The community of goods appears, in this sense, as the translation of this conception of man, at the level of the organisation of his material survival. Just as private property is the social expression of the passion for personal self-interest, the community is the expression of love.

Natural Harmony and Political Order

If love is the principle of beings' mutual attraction, the king is the principle that gives order to these affectionate impulses: all he does is 'regulate the movements of an ever-constant unanimity'.[52] The ideal society needs a leader to regulate the smooth running of its activities. The main quality required to play this role is that of being loved by all. Morelly says of the ruling prince that 'the art of captivating hearts was his entire policy'.[53] This ability is granted him by virtue of the benefits he bestows upon the community: the king brings concrete improvements to social life by presiding over the organisation of the necessary collective works (for example, road building),[54] or by driving certain innovations (the training of horses, the domestication of oxen).

In accordance with the theory of love as the basis of the social bond, the king's heart is 'the centre and motive of all the others',[55] because his soul, which is made to govern, extends its capacity for love further than that of other mortals, beyond the circle of immediate familiarity to the whole of his people. Similarly, the affection that the members of the community have for each other is here a socially indispensable complement to that which they have for their king.

So, despite the 'equilibrium of perfect equality'[56] that characterises

---

52 Ibid., p. 41.
53 Ibid., p. 39.
54 Ibid., p. 104.
55 Ibid., p. 81.
56 Ibid., p. 37.

the relationship between the members of this nation, there may still be distinctions among them. Wisdom motivated by love deserves rewards, even if social esteem, the recognition of others, is the only possible gratification. Thus, Morelly's conception of equality emphasises a principle of compensation, with each person receiving from public judgement the share of esteem that corresponds to their qualities, and to their capacity for love – a principle that justifies some of them rising above the common lot.

The love described in the novel is of a very particular kind. Morelly portrays it as follows:

> Love is the vivid impression of a divine flame, which Nature alone has the power to kindle through the eyes, without the object that excites it having any indicators other than its own presence: some qualities may, it is true, feed and maintain this fire; I even admit that without them it would soon languish; but *it burns already before the torch provides it with matter*.[57]

In other words, it seems that love here becomes a self-sufficient passion, which spontaneously springs from the being, as a necessary characteristic of its essence, without needing to be fed and rewarded. This love, the core of the social bond, can then extend to the universe itself:

> Friendship has only one object of pleasure; love has the whole universe. The beauty, the order, the harmony which reign in this admirable whole, which enliven its parts, make life precious to us only because it places us amidst so many wonders; Nature wanted man to find the principle of his Being in this all-powerful attraction.[58]

From being the guiding principle of social relations, love then becomes the principle of a metaphysical relationship to the world in general. The love that men have for each other, so long as their nature is not thwarted by the institution of property, is a first step towards the love that man must have for the order of the universe in general, as the dispenser of happiness. Better still, it reveals this love. Following Wagner, here we

---

57   Ibid., p. 143, emphasis added.
58   Ibid., p. 82.

can only note the similarity between this principle and Fénelon's doctrine of 'pure love',[59] as a beneficent inclination sui generis, as a contemplative and blessed relationship to the order of the world. This is why utility, in the form of interest, is banished from the blessed continent. And if the love among men in the perfect society leads us back to love for the order of the world, ultimately it leads to love for its Creator: 'Oh, man! Can you make the slightest movement without feeling the presence of a Divinity? Your recognition, your love for this ineffable Being, are as inseparable from yourself as the breath of life.'[60] So, to some extent, we can draw a connection between Morelly's theses concerning the motives of human action in the ideal society, and the mystics' state of passive contemplation described by Fénelon in his *Explications des maximes des Saints sur la vie intérieure*: 'The passive state . . . excludes not peaceful and disinterested acts, but only activity, or anxious acts hastening after our own self-interest.'[61] From this mystical-religious background, Morelly was able to draw elements for his psychology of unperverted human relationships: the dynamism of love, unconditional generosity, happiness freed from all the sources of anxiety linked to self-love. The ideal collective life described in *La Basiliade* overlaps with the ideal life of the mystics. Morelly, in essence, is simply extending the language of individual disappropriation to social relations. Indeed, it is undoubtedly in this mystical disappropriation that we must look for some of the factors that lead him to the critique of private property as such. However, the particularity of this principle, here, is that it is set up as a principle of collective life, and is placed in service not of a passive acceptance of the world order, but rather a critique of it. Morelly pushes the logic of 'pure love' beyond the simple conversion of the individual. He draws on it to imagine a utopia of the dissolution of political and religious power, one of natural social relations broken from individual property and self-interest. He makes this into a universal anthropological and social principle. If his inspiration is Fénelonian, his conclusions are his own.

In this first utopia, for the sake of seeking legitimacy for a society free of all property, Morelly thus pulled off the tour de force of imagining a

---

59 Wagner, *Morelly, le méconnu des Lumières*, pp. 189–95.
60 Ibid., p. 15.
61 Quoted in ibid., p. 192.

human nature almost entirely free of personal interest. In contrast to the entire century, which almost unanimously recognised self-love as the basis of human activity, he imagines a society whose relationship of internal harmony and accord with the universe is guaranteed by love of the other and mutual recognition.[62] The break with the existing social world could not be more radical. But this in itself surely condemns utopia to a sterile confrontation with the existing order, so unthinkable does the transition from one to the other appear to be. Its kinship with the contemplative ideal of pure love essentially leads to a disengagement from the world. It is, therefore, unsurprising that the author felt the need to comprehensively rework this utopia's various aspects in his *Code de la Nature*.

La Basiliade or the Utopian Negation of History

According to the historian Reinhart Koselleck, the eighteenth century saw a crisis in the previously dominant regime of historicity, a collective relationship to time that essentially viewed the past as a reservoir of inspiring and edifying examples (*historia magistra vitae*). The crisis of this model saw the emergence of a new historicity, in which 'a consciousness of time and the future begins to develop . . . sustained by an audacious combination of politics and prophecy. There enters into the philosophy of progress a typical eighteenth-century mixture of rational prediction and salvational expectation'.[63]

The main attributes of this new perception of temporality were, on the one hand, the feeling of an acceleration of time, emptying past experience of its durability and thus of its exemplary value; and, on the other hand, a new awareness of uncertainty, faced with a future now known not to resemble the past, and thus to be partly unpredictable. It would

---

62 As Béatrice Guion writes: 'The philosophers of the Enlightenment agreed in refusing to condemn *amour-propre*: we may see this as their lowest common denominator, the point on which they agree, whatever their disagreements elsewhere. For them, self-love is the motive for all human acts' ('L'amour-propre bien ménagé: des ruses de la Providence à la morale de l'intérêt', in J. Dagen and P. Roger (eds), *Un siècle de deux cents ans? Les XVII et XVIII siècles: continuités et discontinuités*, Paris: Éditions Desjonquères, 2004, pp. 56–87, at p. 64).

63 Reinhart Koselleck, *Futures Past: On the Semantics of Historical Time*, New York: Columbia University Press, 2004, p. 21.

now be up to human reason and practice, as forces of invention and creation, to try to tame the future by putting their own stamp on it. And it was in the space opened up by the growing dissociation between the experience of the past and the expectation of the future – or, to use Koselleck's vocabulary, between the 'field of experience' and the 'horizon of expectation' – that philosophies of history and major political projects would henceforth be written. The idea of progress would be at the heart of these theoretical developments as well as of these practical projects.

Upon a first approach, we may be inclined to envisage a tension between the idea, typical of utopia, of an ideal for society applicable at all times and in all places, an unchanging image of the happiness of the species, and, in contrast, that historicity which dominates modernity, instead marked by the projection of man's hopes into a future that is destined to constantly outgrow itself. The indefinite character of progress does not fit well with the static character of the model society, frozen once and for all in a perfection that is itself constructed in opposition to a historical time that brings the human race catastrophes and misery. Jean-Marie Goulemot states in this regard – with a perhaps excessive systematising ambition, albeit one that despite everything seems well able to encompass a large number of utopias:

> The whole utopian device tends ... in various forms, to prevent time from becoming history and destruction ... When it ceases to be a simple repetition of days, a kind of immobile duration, time is, as in all the traditional representations of historical becoming, defined here as misfortune ... Thus utopias have no history.[64]

Utopia is not absolutely silent about history, such as it really happened. Despite the split between the model presented and the known sequence of events – a break materialised in the geographical distance that separates the blessed island from the world of the narrator and his reader – the texts rarely fail to offer, in some more or less long passage, a recollection and interpretation of the past and present episodes of this world. These are, evidently, presented in a negative light: the text relates the

---

64 Jean-Marie Goulemot, *Le règne de l'histoire: Discours historiques et révolutions, XVII–XVIII siècle*, Paris: Albin Michel, 1996, p. 274.

violence, wars, and misfortunes from which the members of the imaginary country have escaped. Opposed to this sad picture is the parallel history of the utopians, which is often rather meagre in significant events and which, like the social organisation itself, plays the role of a model history. It is most often a history without history. The time before the foundation of the perfect city is not always elided. However, once the foundations of collective happiness have been laid by the good care of the virtuous legislator, all that remains for the inhabitants is to live out their days in peace under the best possible legislation. As Pierre Macherey writes:

> In the world of utopia nothing happens, or at least nothing other than the endless repetition of the laws that sustain the system: in fact, once the system has been set in motion, it opposes any kind of initiative that would compromise its regulated functioning.[65]

Thomas More's text settles the question of the origins of Utopia in a few pithy sentences:

> They say (and the appearance of the place confirms this) that their land was not always surrounded by the sea . . . [Utopus] conquered the country and gave it his name (for it had previously been called Abraxa). After winning the victory at his first assault, he had a channel cut fifteen miles wide where the land joined the continent, and thus caused the sea to flow around the country . . . the project was finished quickly, and the neighbouring peoples, who at first had laughed at the folly of the undertaking, were struck with wonder and terror at its success.[66]

Thus, as Bronisław Baczko has pointed out, utopian history 'is neither the one we might hope for nor even the one we have missed', because 'we have neither past nor future in common with it'.[67] Almost no real events are common to the two worlds before the narrator's discovery of the ideal country, and, a priori, they are not destined to have a common

---

65   Macherey, *De l'utopie!*, p. 67.
66   Thomas More, *Utopia*, p. 44.
67   Bronisław Baczko, *Utopian Lights*, New York: Paragon House, 1989, p. 117.

history even in an indeterminate future. The history of the utopian island, portrayed as transparent and rational, essentially allows the values conveyed by real history to be put into question, as well as the justifications for the present social order that derive from it.

From this point of view, *La Basiliade* follows in line with the utopian novels that preceded it, even if the aforementioned inversion of the customary relations between the – usually isolated and insular – utopia and the location of the real world (for Europe is here metaphorically represented by an archipelago of unstable 'floating islands') leads to certain innovations. The imaginary place is, as we know, a free transposition of the society of the Incas of Peru, described by Garcilaso de la Vega. In this respect, it represents a fictionalisation of real elements of history, which are cast in such a way as to embody a state of unalterable happiness for humanity. It can thereby be said that Morelly makes a selective and edifying use of history, although the history in question is here that of non-European peoples.

But, in other respects, the land of Zeinzemin is the metaphorical site of the origins of humanity. As early as the second canto, in fact, comes the story of the break with depraved humanity and the rebeginning of human history through the original fraternal couple, who – spurred on by their 'industrious affection' – invent the techniques that define the real history of men. With reference to the discovery of fire by the brother–sister couple, Morelly comments in a note: 'it is probably in this way that the first men could be instructed in this important practice'.[68] Through such an account, the author thus puts sociability and love at the foundation of social bonds and the survival of the species, although it must be emphasised that the account of the genesis of human societies takes on a novelised, non-historical form.

Yet, strictly speaking, this both is and is not an origin myth, for, at the moment it takes place, humanity has already split in two, between those who, depraved by the spirit of property, have been cast away from the shores of the continent, and those who, miraculously spared this fate, can recommence a human history preserved from all moral blemish. It seems possible to read it on two levels: on the one hand, being placed at the beginning of the novel and tracing the probable technical stages of the first ages of humanity, it says something about the necessary fraternity

---

68   *LB*, I, p. 64.

which, according to Morelly, must have reigned among the members of the first societies in order to ensure their survival. In this sense, he intends to convey something of a real past, of interest in that it reveals the fundamentally moral characteristics of the species. In so doing, he conveys a truth about human nature that is not so much historical as atemporal. But, on the other hand, he provides an imaginary account of the origins of the utopian continent, whose history, without any significant events until the beginning of the novel, is supposed to have taken place in parallel with the history of our own climes. It introduces an entirely imaginary history whose main task is to underline the extent to which real history, as we know it, has gone 'wrong', both literally and figuratively. This is why the pages concerning the story of the Floating Islands in the eighth canto should be read with its utopian counterpoint in mind, for this is what conveys its true meaning.

It is no coincidence that the history of the islands that represent Europe comes in the second part of the book, through the intercession of the story of Fadilah, a wise man from these sad domains who seeks refuge with Zeinzemin. The aim is both to show its secondary character, in relation to the species' originally communal past, and to explain it from the point of view constituted by this very origin.

Very few concrete elements are brought into a history that is nevertheless rich in events and 'revolutions'. For, as Fadilah says, 'mores, customs, or rather vices, are everywhere almost the same'.[69] There is, therefore, no picture of universal history, no specific description of nations' past. The approach does not consist of inferring from real facts the deeper meaning of the sequence of events, but, rather, of giving an overall interpretation of them, which grants to the facts themselves a value that is at most revealing of a meaning that pre-exists them. Here, again, the story begins in the form of a myth; but this time the myth is charged with signifying error and deviation; it reflects the way in which human history has lost its meaning. Thus, its protagonists are not humans, but supernatural and monstrous beings: they are the goddess Property, the wife of Arbitrary Power and then of Fate, mother of Interest and stepmother of Indigence, who established her son's power by consecrating idols representing him in the temples of men.

---

69   *LB*, II, p. 33.

This striking image can be read in several different ways. On a first level, it is a metaphor for the moment when, as said later on, in the eighth canto, 'men took it into their heads' – a notion that would bring them misfortune – 'to divide among themselves the countryside, the forests, the pastures, the domestic animals, even the rivers, and the lakes'. But, in so doing, it contains the symbolic or moral meaning of this division: the erection of an 'idol' – that is, a false deity – as the supreme value to be revered. Men make themselves miserable by ascribing value to a reality that is artificial from the point of view of nature and harmful in practice. The price they wrongly put on private property, thereby committing a grave error of reasoning, is the source of the moral faults that cannot fail to result. The fetishism of self-interest is thus at the origin of a chimerical social reality where, as Zeinzemin remarks, 'everything is false',[70] starting with the values that it carries forth.

This is indeed the starting point from which Morelly reconstructs the successive appearance of conflicts between men, of social values, of statuses, and, finally, of laws. The overall logic is simple: the emergence of property leads to competition for wealth and hence to the worst violence among men. The latter, realising the destructive nature of this situation, seek to escape from it by adapting their morals; and this is how morals and 'social virtues' are born. They are erroneous because they are based on the belief in the fundamental wickedness of man and motivated by conscious self-interest alone, hence the better regulation of the relations between rich and poor, which leads to the recognition of their respective situations through the establishment of 'ranks, dignities, grandeur'.[71] But, since this illusory morality is weak by nature, and constantly threatened by the more powerful motive of self-interest, more solid barriers are soon needed to the violence that men are constantly tempted to do to each other, hence written laws and the establishment of public authorities to ensure their application.

The main character of Morelly's reconstruction is the chain of errors: a false idol leads to the emergence of false values, which produce illusory social distinctions and ultimately bad laws. Men are led to moral evil not by their nature, but by the contingent institution of property, which alone produces all men's misfortunes, according to a fatal and

---

70 *LB*, II, p. 201.
71 Ibid., p. 46.

implacable logic. The fault is not moral in origin; it is based on a wrong representation of reality, for, as Morelly points out, it is 'prejudice' that makes passions 'impetuous and harmful'.[72] This single false and harmful starting point literally nullifies all subsequent events, and thus empirical history can be essentially dismissed. As Morelly summarises: 'The inconstant vicissitude of all these motives of the human heart ... produces the most unexpected events, revolutions, the strangest catastrophes, accidents that most men attribute to blind fatality'.[73] History does not need further explanation, or even to be set into a narrative: since its essential driving force lies in an original error, it is itself nothing but accidents and wanderings, which are of no intrinsic interest once we have grasped their fundamental principle. It is for this reason alone that Morelly criticises Voltaire's *Le siècle de Louis XIV*, in a footnote. Tellingly, the reason for the utopian's indignation is Voltaire's invocation of historical fatality to explain political revolutions. It is important to attribute a precise cause to the misfortunes that have occurred in history, essentially in order to exonerate human nature and place the blame on the institution of property; but when it comes to the details, it matters little whether these misfortunes are the result of the 'whim of a monk, a mistress, a favourite, a minister'.[74] Contrary to what the observation of empirical reality may lead us to believe, concrete events are to the idyllic and fictitious history of man-without-property what non-being is to being, for nature and truth are at a higher level than anti-nature and error. As Fadilah summarises: 'since man, seduced by the lures of property, abandoned the stability of the principles of nature, he has been drifting without any other guide than error and lies'.[75]

The history reconstructed in broad strokes in the eighth canto of *La Basiliade* is thus, more properly speaking, an anti-history, indeed in several respects. On the one hand, of course, because it rejects the narrative of events. On the other hand, more deeply, because it invalidates in advance any novelty, and denies that the irruption of some historical phenomenon, present or future, can be of any interest to analysis. The explanatory principle, set once and for all, dispenses with the study of the facts themselves,

---

72 Ibid., p. 27.
73 Ibid., p. 51.
74 Ibid.
75 Ibid., p. 77.

since it simultaneously reveals that history is condemned to produce error and evil. It is therefore easy to understand the disdain that the author of *La Basiliade* shows towards historical scholarship itself. His allegory appears in the twelfth canto, in the following terms. History is

> slave to prejudice or interest; it is never allowed to tell the truth or to reveal it; it praises or blames men's actions according to what has been attributed credit among the different nations by opinion or error; it can only speak of the past according to the fables that are told about it, and it is forbidden to tell the present as it is.[76]

The narrative-of-history – a product of property-based society – is here, in contrast to the previous dialogues, the object of an outright critique, indeed one which cuts against Morelly's contemporaries' interest in empirical facts.[77] Nothing good can come of such a history, and this is because it serves the institutions that derive from the fetishism of interest, which it is responsible for legitimising. It is its edifying function – that is, the moral lessons it allows us to draw – that is denounced here as 'fable' and prejudice.

History as a reasoned account of the past is thus nowhere to be found in *La Basiliade*. The demystifying discourse on the past of the property-based societies leaves aside the facts in order to focus on the primitive and unique cause of all subsequent errors; history as a narrative is mercilessly criticised as mystifying. There is nothing worth drawing from a close familiarity with the facts; hence why no harm is done if the people of Zeinzemin does without books. If they were to acquire writing one day, one book would suffice: the one containing the principles of their excellent morality, together with some knowledge useful for the 'conveniences of life'.[78] This shows how the events of empirical history are not

---

76 Ibid., p. 231.
77 As Diderot wrote, in the eighteenth century more than ever before, 'history is facts' (Denis Diderot, 'Système des connaissances humaines', preceding the *Encyclopédie*, in *Œuvres*, vol. I, p. 225). In many respects, the scattered events of the past were left to be contemplated and set in relation by the historian, after the discrediting of the great religious teleologies, first and foremost Bossuet's. (On this question, see Bertrand Binoche, 'Montesquieu et la crise de la rationalité historique', in C. Spector and T. Hoquet (eds), *Lectures de l'Esprit des lois*, Bordeaux: Presses Universitaires de Bordeaux, 2004, pp. 35–63).
78 *LB*, II, p. 207.

worth recording, even as a safeguard against possible temptations to leave behind the state of social happiness.

From the Denial of Past History to the Rejection of Present History: Social Critique in *La Basiliade*

However, if *La Basiliade* dismisses the narration of the past, this does not prevent Morelly from 'telling the present as it is', or rather as it appears through the prism of utopian critique. The eighth canto thus provides the setting for a metaphor of the social structure of the Ancien Régime, as spun by Fadilah, which reveals an analysis in some respects comparable with the one which Saint-Preux offers of unequal society, through the view of the Parisian world provided in the second part of Rousseau's *New Heloise*. In this sense, we find in Morelly's novel a similar move to Thomas More's in the first part of *Utopia*, railing against enclosures and their catastrophic social consequences.

In many ways, the character of Saint-Preux is to Jean-Jacques Rousseau what Fadilah is to Morelly. Saint-Preux's quality as an observer of the social circles into which he is introduced is due to his position as an outsider: a stranger to both the aristocracy of blood and that of wealth, and a provincial to boot, he himself conceives of his spell in Paris as a moment to explore the recesses of the human soul. He writes to Julie: 'My objective is to get to know man, and my method is to study him in his several relations.'[79] This fruitful marginality to the world which he finds himself immersed in thanks to Milord Edward's mediation, is not unlike that of Rousseau himself. For Baczko:

> This situation, defined by the lack of social integration, is valued by Jean-Jacques as a privileged place where the discourse on man in general is formed and which, at the same time, calls into question the social structures that confine man to states that stand in a hierarchy.[80]

[79] Jean-Jacques Rousseau, *Julie, Or the New Heloise*, Lebanon, NH: University Press of New England, 1997, translated and annotated by Philip Stewart and Jean Vaché, Letter XVI, p. 199.
[80] Bronisław Baczko, 'Rousseau et la marginalité sociale', in *Libre*, no. 5, Paris: Payot, 1979, p. 68.

Similarly, Fadilah, a wise man living among the madmen in the Floating Islands until his meeting with Zeinzemin, is described as marginal. His conduct is remarkable in that it is entirely 'different from the other' navigators who land on the blessed continent. 'Free in the midst of slavery itself',[81] he is not imbued with the prejudices of his compatriots, and in this respect he is a choice witness for describing the corrupted society. Here, too, there is an unmistakable proximity to Morelly's own self-understanding.

The distortions generated by Saint-Preux's point of view – owing to his youth and his gradual contamination by Parisian society[82] – are softened in the effort to describe them to his love, who is free of all corruption: 'Let me therefore', he writes, 'incite myself to the pure zeal for truth by the tableau of flattery and lies.'[83] As Laurence Mall has observed, 'from the deceptive object, the subject derives a truth which is itself guaranteed by the addressee'.[84] Saint-Preux's description of this society betrays the illusions it conveys and the denaturing of man which it produces. Similarly, in Morelly, it is the account of the vast social lie orchestrated by property-based society that conveys the truth of this world.

Saint-Preux and Fadilah thus undertake, each in their own way, to describe to an inhabitant of uncorrupted climes (Rousseau's Julie, Morelly's Zeinzemin) the privileged observation post that Paris offers of Ancien Régime social relations. For the French capital is indeed hidden behind Fadilah's description of 'one of our main moving islands',[85] which, in fact, turns out to be an interlocking of islands, each separated from the next 'by broad and deep waters, which spread around'. At the centre of this enmeshment is the small island that houses the palace of the

---

81   *LB*, II, p. 28.
82   Saint-Preux himself writes to Julie: 'forced to attribute a value to fantasies . . . I drift from whim to whim, and my tastes being constantly enslaved to opinion, I cannot a single day be sure what I will love the next' (Rousseau, *Julie, Or the New Heloise*, p. 210).
83   Ibid., p. 200.
84   Laurence Mall, 'L'intérieur et l'extérieur: étude des lettres parisiennes dans La Nouvelle Héloïse', in O. Mostefai (ed.), *Lectures de la Nouvelle Héloïse*, Ottawa: Association nord-américaine des études Jean-Jacques Rousseau, 1993, pp. 163–73, at p. 167.
85   *LB*, II, p. 55.

'Sovereign Power'.[86] These concentric islands embody the different strata of society: as one approaches the centre, they become more elevated, more fertile, and less populated. On the outermost island, the inhabitants 'are miserable, and the most arduous work provides them with a very meagre subsistence each day', while the fate of the inhabitants of the islands nearer to the centre is much 'happier'. Similarly, Saint-Preux describes the overall structure of the capital of the kingdom: 'this is perhaps of all the cities on earth the one where fortunes are most unequal, and where the most sumptuous opulence and the most deplorable misery prevail at one and the same time'.[87] For this reason, Fadilah explains, the inhabitants of the outlying island are constantly trying to cross to a more clement one. However, the bridges are 'without parapets, extremely narrow and dangerous to cross'; the fear of 'falling back into their first condition' gnaws at those who do manage to cross them; and, finally, a first stage of success does not bring contentment, but gives rise to new desires that drive them to seek even greater social elevation. Fadilah thus paints a vivid but striking picture of the 'perpetual competition to change places of residence'[88] that characterises the inhabitants of this archipelago, who engage in a fierce and perpetual struggle to this end. Mobility from one social stratum to another is described as extremely difficult, eminently desirable but often unsuccessful; the violence of the social relations engendered by this competition is symbolised by the struggle between the assailants on each of the parapets separating the islands, thus producing a 'horrible confusion' in the whole social body.[89]

Although Saint-Preux's perspective is, by his own admission, limited to the upper echelons of Parisian society, his observations overlap with Fadilah's on some points.[90] Even among these privileged strata, he can clearly see the competition inherent in Ancien Régime society: 'as each person is mindful of his own interest, no one of the common good, and as individual interests are always at odds with each other, there is a

---

86 Ibid., p. 57.
87 Rousseau, *Julie, Or the New Heloise*, p. 191.
88 *LB*, II, p. 56.
89 Ibid., p. 57.
90 He writes: 'Moreover, I frequent only those assemblies into which Milord Edward's friends have introduced me, and I am convinced that one must descend into other estates in order to learn the true manners of a country, for those of the rich are almost everywhere the same' (Rousseau, *Julie, Or the New Heloise*, p. 193).

perpetual clash of cliques and factions'.[91] Social advancement is not considered from the standpoint of real attempts at it, as in Morelly. Rather, it is portrayed in terms of the false pretences it generates, given each person's desire to assume the appearance of a higher standing than their own – for want, that is, of being able really to enjoy its prerogatives: 'The Jurist's airs are cavalier, the Financier's are lordly . . . even the mere craftsman incapable of assuming a tone other than his own dresses in black on Sundays, to look like a man of the Palace'.[92]

At the same time, this shows the distance between Saint-Preux's viewpoint and Fadilah's. The latter, who 'had the strength [to] shake off the yoke [of prejudice]'[93] and is thus definitively free of it, enjoys a synoptic view of the social body, which is presented as objective. That is, he sees everything, from the efforts of the humblest people to achieve greater comfort, to the cabinets where the king's ministers strive to conceal from the sovereign the truth about the state of his kingdom and the fate of his subjects. Saint-Preux's assessment, on the other hand, is based on an empirical discovery of the Parisian salons, carried out through the prism of a subjectivity that is negatively affected by this immersion in this corrupt and corrupting world, and that seeks the truth concealed behind the appearances of things.

The comparison highlights what is distinctive about Morelly's analysis: despite its novelistic form, it is not presented as a situated and subjective view of the social world, as that of a novel's hero might be. Rather, it appears to be a truthful diagnosis. Just as the myth in *La Basiliade* carries a greater truth about the past of property-based societies than the historical knowledge emanating from these societies could ever produce, the metaphor of the concentric islands makes it possible to go beyond the self-image of the present and to propose a vision of it stripped of all illusions. Here, again, reality is referred to as a simulacrum, since hopes of rising socially often end in tragedy. The kings themselves are described as 'slaves to flattery and a vain shadow of authority possessed by the Great and the Insubstantial Ministers': supreme power is a sham, just like everything else.[94]

---

91 *LB*, II, p. 192.
92 Ibid., p. 193.
93 Ibid., p. 27.
94 Ibid., pp. 61–2.

2

The *Code de la Nature* and Its Constructive Utopia

The *Code de la Nature* took a fresh approach to the construction of a utopian model. By the author's own admission, its aim was to defend the theses previously advanced in *La Basiliade*, which had been attacked by the critics from two newspapers of the time, the *Nouvelle Bigarrure* and the *Bibliothèque impartiale*.[1] The criticisms in the latter publication, which extensively cited Morelly's work with regard to moral, political, and religious issues, mainly revolved around two questions. One was the free love advocated in *La Basiliade*, which the critic feared 'would do more to sully morals than to purify them'. The other was the community of goods, on which he remarked:

> We well know how much distance there is between the finest speculations of this order, and the possibility of their execution ... The project of equality is, in particular, one of those which appear most repugnant to the character of men; they are born to command or to serve, a middling state is a burden to them.[2]

In a sense, Morelly's *Code* did take on board the criticisms appearing in this first article, as he returned to more conventional ideas on love and

---

1 *Bibliothèque impartiale*, Leiden: Imprimerie Elie Luzac, November 1753, vol. VIII, 3rd part, pp. 401–15 and *Nouvelle Bigarrure*, The Hague, with Pierre Gosse Junior, November 1753, vol. IX, pp. 145–50.
2 *Bibliothèque impartiale*, pp. 407–8.

marriage. On the other hand, his opponents' disdain for the very possibility of realising the principles of *La Basiliade* led him to persist in his 'utopian denial' and to find new arguments to support his claims as to the natural character of the ideal society. In so doing, he arrived at tones close to Thomas More's, as he wrote that:

> It is as a result of these blunders of our first teachers of morals, that the moral in *La Basiliade* seems absolutely impractical to the learned scribes of the *Bibliothèque impartiale* and the *Nouvelle Bigarrure*. I will agree with them and with all those who will object; but only in our time would such an excellent legislator as the hero of this poem go entirely unheeded.[3]

Tellingly, Morelly here presented the ideal that appeared in his utopian novel not as a social model, properly speaking, but rather as a 'moral'. This choice of terminology confirms that the evanescent institutions of the blessed continent, and its king lacking all powers of compulsion, serve as elements of a social parable clearly intended for the personal edification of the reader rather than the actual reformation of society. Morelly's admission of the non-actual character of this morality is reiterated later in the text, in connection to the programme of ideal legislation that he proposes to the reader in the *Code de la Nature*: 'I give this outline of laws as an appendix, and as an hors d'oeuvre, since it is unfortunately only too true that it would be as if impossible, nowadays, to form such a republic.'[4]

Unlike his assertions in the previous work, Morelly thus here shows himself aware of the currently unbridgeable gap between existing social reality and the outline which he proposes. But, paradoxically, his reservations over the immediate applicability of the project, again reminiscent of More in his day, go hand in hand with a greater theoretical effort regarding the foundations of the ideal social organisation, its modus operandi, and even the links between this ideal form of organisation and the real history of humanity. The shift in the centre of the author's interest – from the critique of the dominant morality, presented as standing in contradiction with man's nature, to the conditions of

---

3 *CN*, pp. 63–4.
4 Ibid., p. 148.

possibility for a society that really does uphold another morality – pushes him to deepen his investigations. Ultimately, this new theoretical attitude also produces radical changes of both form and content. Indeed, in the *Code de la Nature*, instead of a novel, the reader finds a composite work, in which explanatory 'dissertations' sit side by side with purely 'pamphleteering' sections and, finally, one passage which is especially innovative in its presentation: a 'Model of Legislation' which sets out, in no less than 117 laws broken down into twelve divisions, the different aspects of life in a community which has been rid of all major social vices. The status of this new work, and of the utopian ideal described therein, is thus problematic: the change in the mode of presentation and the significant differences in the argumentation mark a shift in its theoretical and political function.

Variations on Utopia in the *Code de la Nature*

Even before tackling the famous legislative plan that makes up the final part of this work, Morelly imagines a first utopia, in a sense that would here have to be defined. In the second part of the *Code de la Nature*, entitled 'Particular Defects of Politics', he portrays a 'truly wise legislator'.[5] The latter heads to meet the primitive American peoples in the northern part of the continent – deemed to be living in the 'natural state' of humanity, and therefore ignorant of property – in order to bring them laws which will supposedly perfect their mode of organisation. The general idea of the passage seems to be twofold. On the one hand, as in *La Basiliade*, Morelly undoubtedly intends to back up his argument with concrete examples of human groups whose current social organisation is, to his eyes, able to demonstrate their permeability to utopian projects such as his own. But, on the other, it appears that through these examples he is seeking to head back to before the biggest mistake in human history – the establishment of private property – and to the era of the primitive and universal community of goods. In making this move, he can examine how a far wiser direction of operations could have allowed a very different path to be taken, one much more consistent with nature.

---

5 Ibid., p. 70.

The wise legislator of the hunter-gatherer people, which has been preserved from this baleful development in the human adventure, is careful not to teach them the fatal distinction between thine and mine. Rather, he begins by teaching them 'the cultivation of the land and the upkeep of herds'.[6] Seeing as the move to new production methods demands a more complex set of regulations, he must define the quantity of objects necessary for the satisfaction of all. He must divide work and jobs among the members of these small societies, in order to adapt the efforts demanded to the needs of society and to the capacities of each person:

> Finally, he will regulate the ranks of each individual not on the basis of chimerical dignities, but based on the natural authority that the benefactor acquires over he who receives the benefit, based on this gentle authority of kinship, friendship, experience, skill, industry and activity.[7]

Here, we recognise the same principles which govern the organisation of the community in *La Basiliade*. Indeed, these principles are also called to mind in a note, the sole difference being the emphasis that this passage of the *Code* places on the necessary but gentle subordination to the most intelligent and skilful. The most important change introduced here lies in the turn from the epic fable to what might be called a thought experiment: Morelly is no longer dreaming up a fictional plot within which he inserts a social model, distantly inspired by past realities but fixed in its perfection. Rather, in the *Code*, he attempts to provide 'experimental proofs of our principles'[8] by searching for peoples who have not yet been corrupted by property-based society and trying to imagine how they would react to the introduction of forms of progress compatible with the community ideal. But, in fact, by evoking the 'ancient Scythians, who were like the nursery of other nations'[9] – and whose social organisation, according to Morelly, was like that of the Native Americans, devoid of any notion of private property – the author

---

6   Ibid., p. 70.
7   Ibid., p. 72.
8   Ibid., p. 68.
9   Ibid., p. 83.

extends the thought experiment to all humanity. In his view, there always existed the possibility, by respecting natural principles, of offering everyone eternal bliss – that is, enjoying the benefit of technological progress without the drawbacks of a system of property ownership. The details of the application of such measures would then be a purely technical issue, a 'simple matter of counting things and people'; operations for which the human genius has already proven itself competent many times over.[10]

The community of goods thus appears as the simple and definitive solution to all political and social problems. In Morelly's eyes, it is this 'which would ensure the stability of empires' by avoiding the turmoil that republics, aristocracies, and monarchies all run into.[11] Curiously, in this section of the book, Morelly, in open polemic with Montesquieu, challenges the three 'principles' which, according to the author of *De l'Esprit des lois*, respectively underpin these three types of regime. For the utopian, neither virtue, nor moderation, nor honour can ensure lasting stability for a regime built on property rights. Interestingly, at this stage of Morelly's thinking, the principle of community can authorise any of the three types of legitimate regimes – democracy, aristocracy, or monarchy – without particular preference for either one of them: 'Lay down this excellent principle [of the community of goods] . . . there will then be only one constitution, only one mechanism of government under different names.'[12]

Here, utopia is thus generalised as the Other of all social organisation, past, present, and future. This renders even more striking its character as a pure thought experiment, which does not seem to entail any more properly political reflection on the mediations that need to be built in order to move from the existing state of affairs to the projected goal. 'Lay down this excellent principle', writes Morelly, just as all of his predecessors were content to 'lay down' the principles of their ideal city in writing. Utopia thus appears to be a purely theoretical resolution of problems that are nonetheless real. Moreover, the constructive elements of the model put forward in this part of the *Code* seem to be as vague on institutional questions as the ones in *La Basiliade*: taking up the ideas of

---

10   Ibid., p. 88.
11   Ibid., p. 103.
12   Ibid.

social organisation based on mutual aid, the distribution of tasks on a voluntary basis, and the recognition of the value of the most competent, the author seems to fully entrust human nature with regulating all details or local particularities.

However, faced with the objections he reports from his opponents – concerning, among other things, man's natural idleness – Morelly mentions for the first time the possibility of 'a severe authority which tames these first dislikes, and which obliges, a first time, duties whose exercise renders undemanding, and which the evidence of their usefulness will then make beloved'.[13]

This remark contrasts with the general impression that emerges from the descriptions, both in *La Basiliade* and in the first pages of the *Code*, of interpersonal relations and relations with authority. In *La Basiliade*, in fact, 'no one thought himself exempt from a labour that concert and unanimity made pleasurable and easy'.[14] Similarly, the second part of the *Code* begins by refusing to consider the possibility that the American populations might baulk at the wise legislator's benevolent injunctions: 'instead of finding men indisposed to his arrangements, all will applaud them'.[15]

The severity here invoked for the first time is found in the final part of the work, the 'Model of Legislation Consistent with the Intentions of Nature', which offers Morelly's most advanced elaboration of a scheme for a utopian society. In this model, the classical building blocks of a utopian city are much more clearly present than in the earlier work. However, a notable particularity of this model lies in the status which Morelly attributes it: that of an 'outline of laws', a 'form of appendix' and 'hors d'oeuvre'. If the term 'outline' is itself surprising, considering the wealth of detail that the author provides in his code of laws concerning all aspects of individual and collective life, the word 'appendix' suggests that it is not essential to the general meaning of this work. In contrast to the utopians that went before him, whose audacity – as in the cases of Thomas More or Tommaso Campanella[16] – consisted precisely in their description of the rules of the ideal society, Morelly seems to play down

---

13   Ibid., p. 79.
14   *LB*, I, p. 7.
15   *CN*, p. 79.
16   Tommaso Campanella, *The City of the Sun*, translated with introduction and notes by Daniel J. Donno, Berkeley, Los Angeles: University of California Press, 1981.

the real scope of his model. From this perspective, this final part should be considered inessential to the general economy of the work: it was perhaps added in the final phase of writing or composition. But such a hypothesis does not seem to fit well with Morelly's thoroughness in writing this legislative excursus.

Even so, the most problematic term used here is 'hors d'oeuvre', which is also incompatible with the idea that this text is an 'appendix'. If this term suggests that Morelly is making only a first approach to the issue, what does he imagine ought to come after it? Should we expect a more substantial theoretical production to follow – albeit one which would never see the light of day? Or perhaps the material realisation of the principles set out in its pages? Morelly immediately makes clear that his role is not to 'purport to reform mankind' but only to 'speak the truth'.[17] At the theoretical level, he also seems to consider the proofs put forward in the previous essays sufficient to 'fulfil [his] object'. Whatever follows this 'hors d'oeuvre' thus seems left up to posterity, depending on how receptive it is to this utopian's lessons. In any case, it is enlightening to note the many points on which this 'hors d'oeuvre' completes, but most importantly adjusts, the main lines of the form of social organisation that appears in La Basiliade. Indeed, they have much to tell us about the function which the author allotted to this new utopian construction.

Model of Legislation

The first striking feature of the Code, as has been said already, is the great number of written laws governing the life of the republic, and their precision. This contrasts sharply with the total absence of such laws from La Basiliade but also marks a considerable innovation with respect to earlier texts in the utopian tradition, notably those of More or Campanella. The various regulations are supposed to do no more than specify and concretise the basic principles of three 'fundamental and sacred laws'.[18] The first abolishes all private property, with the exception of objects of immediate use for 'needs', 'pleasure', and

---

17   CN, p. 148.
18   Ibid., p. 148.

'everyday work'. So, the abolition of property does not lead to asceticism, but, rather, allows a certain hedonism. Moreover, it immediately leads to the assimilation of the tools of the craftsman to the objects necessary for life, suggesting that this would be the status of each individual in the society thus described. The second law guarantees the citizen the right to live, for 'his upkeep . . . is to be at the public expense', but also the right to work, since it is society's responsibility to 'occupy him'. The third is the counterpart of the duties of society towards the individual, since the latter must 'contribute his share to the public good' by his own means.

Morelly's legislation thus centres the concerns of the ideal community on the satisfaction of the needs of each individual and the synthesis of individual and collective interests. It expresses the reciprocity of the rights and duties of the citizen and the community. By generalising and formalising in three preliminary rules what the other utopians had each described in a particular and imaginary form – and indeed by specifying that these rules would 'cut the roots of the vices and all the evils of a society'[19] – Morelly surely intends to give them a universal and timeless scope.

All the other laws are supposed to logically follow from these fundamental precepts, by applying them to the different aspects of social life. Naturally, the first area concerned is that of economic production and distribution. In contrast to *La Basiliade*, the *Code* reveals a clearly thought-out organisation of the territory: while this earlier work had pointed towards a federation of production units whose interconnection remained unclear, the abstract logic of the 'Model of Legislation' is divided, according to Ancient Greek terminology, into families, tribes, cities, and provinces, based on the decimal system. The basic economic unit is the city, which makes all its members participate in agricultural and artisanal work. As in More, agriculture is a compulsory job incumbent upon the younger generation: in Morelly, a special service must be performed by everyone between the ages of twenty and twenty-five, that is, for five years as opposed to only two in Utopia. In the city, on the other hand – and this is an original feature in Morelly – the citizens are divided into hierarchically organised classes of labour: each boy begins a trade apprenticeship at the age of ten. He lives on the premises until

---

19 Ibid.

the age of fifteen or sixteen and receives a technical education, then returns to live in his father's house, practising his trade as a simple labourer. After agricultural service, he could return to his first trade and become a master craftsman, or he could choose another trade and thus delay his entry into this role. The masters organise the labourers' work and report to the head of the given profession, who changes every year. At age forty, citizens are freed from all labour subject to corporate regulations and can do whatever work they please. In accordance with every utopian organisation up to and including *La Basiliade*, the products of labour are taken to the common shop, and their distribution is supervised as necessary by the tribal chiefs.

The state provides for the needs of the sick, the infirm, and the elderly, whose public housing is integrated into the architecture of the cities (Police Law no. VI). A major difference from *La Basiliade* is the enshrinement of individual marriage; in the Model of Legislation it is subject to strict regulations, in contrast to the Zeinzemin people's seeming freedom in matters of love and relations. In accordance with the rules of *La Basiliade*, divorce is allowed, but it is surrounded by administrative hurdles. Adultery is even punishable by one year's imprisonment. But this punishment remains less severe than that of More, whose *Utopia* punished adultery with 'the strictest form of slavery'.[20] Unlike the arrangements set out in *La Basiliade*, the domestic economy is not entirely absorbed into collective life: children are fed and brought up in their father's house until they enter the educational home aged five, and come back after their apprenticeship, before they reach the age of agricultural service. The family, almost dissolved in the universal affection of the utopian novel, in meals and more generally in communal life, thus becomes to a certain extent the basic social organisation again. After all, while it does not constitute a single unit of economic production as in More, it does to some extent take on the education of children, which is only partly collective. However, it is in the educational homes that children are introduced to the rules of morality and the laws of the state, at the same time as they gradually begin to be taught the rudiments of a trade. In these houses, tellingly called 'public academies', moral, religious, and professional education are thus linked.[21] Contrary to the

---

20   Thomas More, *Utopia*, Cambridge: Cambridge University Press, 1989, p. 83.
21   *CN*, p. 168.

prescriptions of More's or Campanella's utopias, very few children have access to the study of science and art. The main aim of education is stated unambiguously: 'that the defects of childhood, which might tend to the proprietary spirit, may be wisely corrected and prevented'.[22]

From this perspective, vocational education, which can render the individual useful to the community, supplemented by morality, as well as by vague rudiments of religion very close to those of *La Basiliade*, all deduced from, or in conformity with, the fundamental laws, will more than suffice. Surprising, even so, is the distrust towards human nature – which childhood embodies par excellence – revealed by these proposals. It seems to contradict not only the arguments expounded in *La Basiliade* but even those of the first parts of the *Code*. The 'Laws of Study' that build upon the educational precepts follow along the same lines; they are meant to restrain 'the wandering of the human mind' by permitting complete freedom of research only in the fields of 'speculative and experimental sciences, whose object is either the investigation of the secrets of nature, or the perfection of arts useful to society'.[23]

In other words, all that finds the author's favour is pure objective knowledge and those techniques likely to improve material comfort. No progress is foreseen, or even authorised, in the common morality, philosophy, or religion, which are forever frozen in their unsurpassable goodness.

Some commentators have rightly emphasised the anti-asceticism that emerges from these and other passages in the *Code de la Nature*, arguing that few utopias emphasise to such an extent the role of technical and scientific progress in continuously improving the everyday lives of the members of the dreamt-of society. In itself, this position represents an evolution in the utopian's thinking. In *La Basiliade*, indeed, Morelly had seemed in part to echo the theses of Rousseau's *Discourse on the Arts and Sciences*, writing, 'most of those who have worked to divest Peoples of their barbarism, far from bringing them closer to Nature, have only substituted invented vices for brutal vices'.[24] It is true that Morelly had already tempered this assessment at the end of the novel. When

---

22 Ibid.
23 Ibid., p. 170.
24 *LB*, I, p. 201.

Zeinzemin reached the Palace of Beauty, the commentary had read: 'When the Arts and Sciences begin to polish and perfect these good qualities [of the people of Nature], it is then that the barriers that kept these Peoples in ignorance of beautiful Nature disappear.'[25]

With these two passages, Morelly had seemed, in essence, to qualify Rousseau's judgement, granting that the society based on private property can only make a poor moral use of science and art, while keeping open the possibility that a fraternal community like that of the people of Zeinzemin might find therein new reasons to admire nature. In short, there Morelly's optimism regarding the possibility of a social alternative for humanity had led him to envisage an ethical function for science and art, which the citizen of Geneva had rebuffed in his first *Discourse*.

The tone changes in the *Code de la Nature*, with a sweeping condemnation of Rousseau. He is called a 'bold sophist' for arguing that the progress of knowledge has not improved men. While still conceding that the sciences and arts 'appear in some respects to have irritated greed', Morelly argued that the fault did not lie with these products of human culture, but rather, again, with the 'poisonous principle of all moral corruption', namely avarice, a product of the establishment of private property.[26]

Rejecting Rousseau's point of view, Morelly in fact sides with the classical utopians. Had not Thomas More, first among them, said that 'the minds of the Utopians are wonderfully quick to seek out those various skills which make life more agreeable'?[27] From the birth of the genre, attention was thus focused on the interest that the progress of knowledge has in its practical use. But even more than to More, or to Campanella, Morelly's point of view brings him closer to Francis Bacon in *New Atlantis*.

As compared with Bacon's utopia, which centres on the personnel and the attributions of the House of Solomon, a college dedicated to the sciences, Morelly's views stop at very general indications for legislation. But these indications are consistent with the orientations found in *New Atlantis*. In Bensalem, as in the 'Model of Legislation', the task

---

25   *LB*, II, p. 291.
26   *CN*, p. 135.
27   More, *Utopia*, pp. 80–1.

of science is a matter of state (in Bacon, the great legislator himself, Solamona, is the founder of the House of Solomon), entrusted to the 'citizens who [have] the greatest disposition' for this type of activity. According to Morelly, as with Bacon, their number is 'fixed ... for each kind of study'.[28] Bacon's text is much more explicit and provides rich detail on the different categories of personnel assigned to each scientific task: the 'Merchants of Light' who collect information, the 'Depredators' who leaf through ancient works, the 'Mystery-men' who track down the secrets of craftsmen, the 'Miners' who develop new protocols for observation and experimentation, the 'Compilers', the 'Benefactors' who strive to make the most of new discoveries with the aim of improving living conditions, and the 'Lamps' who broaden the field of research with new experiments. There are the 'Inoculators' who assist them in this task, and, finally, the 'Interpreters of Nature' who 'raise the former discoveries by experiments into greater observations, axioms, and aphorisms'.[29]

In Morelly, as in Bacon, the search for the useful does not prevent him from being interested in knowledge as such: in the *Code*, the 'search for the secrets of nature' is put on the same footing as 'the perfection of the arts useful to society'. The same is true in Bensalem, where researchers 'look into the experiments of their fellows, and cast about how to draw out of them things of use and practice for man's life' but also 'means of natural divinations, and the easy and clear discovery of the virtues and parts of bodies'.[30] The difference between the two utopias lies only in their respective celebrations of the most illustrious inventors: Bacon imagined a vast gallery dedicated to the statues of the discoverers, while Morelly proposed paying tribute 'by eloquence, poetry and painting' to citizens who had distinguished themselves through their inventions.[31] However, by remaining silent on the type of government and social organisation that might promote such a scientific enterprise, Bacon is perhaps suggesting that any of them will do, whereas Morelly closely links the progress of knowledge and technology with the community of goods.

---

28 *CN*, p. 169.
29 Francis Bacon, *New Atlantis*, in *The Works of Francis Bacon*, London: Worthington, 1884, Volume V, pp. 347–413.
30 Ibid., p. 410.
31 *CN*, p. 170.

But another important difference can be seen in the moral and political responsibility attributed to researchers. Bacon imagines that the scholars in the House of Solomon will regularly consult each other to decide which of their inventions and experiments will be made public and which will not. They choose of their own accord to keep some of these experiments secret, thus putting the state in a subordinate position.

Bacon thus somehow politicises the question of science, as he entrusts its practitioners with the task of deciding on its social uses and admits the possibility that certain discoveries will remain under wraps. The fact that this responsibility falls on the researchers of the House of Solomon probably goes some way to explain why the author refrains from reflecting on which type of government would best serve the purposes of scientific progress. Conversely, Morelly somehow depoliticises the problem by promising researchers 'complete freedom' in their field. We may conclude that any difficulties involved have been resolved upfront, for the advancement of science cannot serve purposes other than those that fall within the limits of the philosophical and social principles set out in the *Code de la Nature*. But it seems that Morelly, unlike Bacon, did not consider the possibility that the advancement of science may in itself pose moral and political problems for the community, or challenge the pre-established ideological framework by confronting it with new questions that it could not resolve by itself. The fixedness of philosophical, religious, and moral principles is taken as a sufficient guarantee against dangers that the utopian does not even seem to contemplate.

Taken as a whole, the return to the traditional family unit, in place of free love; the narrow path set out for childhood education; and the limitations introduced in the intellectual field thus seem to bring Morelly back into the more rigid framework of earlier utopias, which tend to freeze and literally set in stone the laws that govern the ideal society. But these features introduce a tension within the work itself. Even if the laws of nature were indeed known once and for all, why should it be necessary to prescribe limits to speculation in this field, if not for fear of the vicious tendencies of those who speculated in this way? And, from such a perspective, what is the value of the assertion that fundamental, sacred laws would suffice to cut 'the root of the vices and all the evils of a society'?

Still, the most original part of the 'Model of Legislation' is its plan for the organisation of the state. It does not take up the idea, maintained in the utopian tradition since More, of electing the servants of the state. Rather, political rights belong exclusively to heads of families. From the age of fifty onwards, they are members of the Senate of their tribe; before that, they are only consulted on matters that concern their own occupations. All the members of the higher bodies of the state, tribal chiefs, city chiefs, provincial chiefs, and the head of the state, are chosen by rotation from among the heads of families. This institution already existed in embryo in *La Basiliade*, for, in the absence of Zeinzemin, the sages of each province are called upon to be each 'alternately . . . the soul of this unanimity'.[32]

The central government or supreme senate has a relatively limited function, its task being to register the decisions of the lower-level political units, the tribal senates, or to put up vetoes against them when these decisions contradict the laws of the state. This conception of the organised political order radicalises the paradox already present in More's *Utopia*, in the sense that it combines extremely democratic aspects with other, much more authoritarian ones. On the one hand, the autonomy of the basic political communities, the tribal senates, as well as their limited size, corresponds to the search for a real knowledge of everyone's wishes. On the other hand, the rejection of delegated authority and election in favour of the rotation of offices provides a definitive way of solving the problem of social distinctions, even if they may be justified by personal merit or competence. So, after the abolition of all economic hierarchy comes the abolition of all political hierarchy: from this point of view, Morelly goes further than his predecessors in utopia. Even the particularly skilful craftsman, the inventor of innovative techniques, will have to leave his post at the end of the regulatory year (Police Law no. V). The central government has only a semblance of power, since it is the mere observer of the decisions taken in the tribal senates, and the chief of the nation himself is subordinate to them (Laws on Administration of the Government no. V). In this respect, Morelly could be considered one of the first advocates of a 'total democracy'.[33] And

---

32   *LB*, II, p. 159.

33   Albert Soboul, 'Lumières, critique sociale et utopie pendant le XVIII siècle français', in J. Droz (ed.), *Histoire générale du socialisme*, Vol. I: *Des origines à 1875*, Paris: PUF, 1979, Chapter IV, pp. 103–93, at p. 133.

yet, this democracy operates within severe constraints, for 'disrespect or disobedience to chiefs or senators, to fathers of families or their parents' and even 'other lighter faults, such as a few oversights, some inaccuracies' are subject to punishment.[34] The process that prohibits a magistrate from extending their spell in office, even on account of their individual virtues, in its own way expresses the fear that the competence of the few may lead to the revival of fresh privileges.

The Status of the 'Model'

We thus move from the utopia in the second part of the *Code*, which had appeared to have the status of a thought experiment, to a utopia presented as a project for human society in general. The lack of any reference to its time and place, whether known or unknown, or of any limit to the number of inhabitants or to the size of the state, gives it an ambiguous status. The *Code* that unfolds before the reader's eyes could be that of any society that takes the trouble to apply it. That is, unless – like the outline in *La Basiliade*, or the one in the second part of the *Code* – it is only a working draft with an essentially moral scope, a purely theoretical resolution to social problems which the author does not seek concretely to end.

But, when it comes to Part IV of the *Code*, the question seems rather harder to judge than in the case of the utopian novel. 'The Model of Legislation' presents itself as a description conforming to the utopian imaginary, from its excessive richness of detail to the centrality of a perfectly rational state which governs a society able to comply with its norms without undue difficulty. But, perhaps paradoxically, its purely theoretical rather than narrative character tends to make it available for other uses. Clues scattered throughout the work allow for hypotheses as to what these uses might be. Firstly, if we return to the second part of the *Code* regarding the populations of the Americas, we can see that Morelly repeatedly uses expressions that go beyond the limits of a simple thought experiment, and almost border on a project for these climes. For instance, the use of the future rather than the conditional tense ('on his arrival he will find the families of this little society . . . he will make them

---

34 *CN*, pp. 171, 173.

see', and so on) seems all the more significant given the use in the 'The Model of Legislation' of the term 'General' to designate the nation's annual leader. Indeed, in the colonial vocabulary of the time, this same term designated the leader of a settlement in newly conquered territories outside Europe. In short, it seems conceivable that Morelly – doubtless rather vaguely – toyed with the idea of introducing onto the virgin American continent, unspoiled by private property, the model that he advocates. However, as we have seen, there are discrepancies, or at least relatively indeterminate relations, between the outline rules given by the legislator to the Native Americans – which admit, among other things, the existence of 'ranks' based on the 'natural authority acquired by the benefactor' – and the much more mechanical system of rotation of offices that prevails in the 'The Model of Legislation'. There is no obvious consistency between the one and the other, and a lack of mediation between them.

Finally, the question arises as to the scope of this model: could it concern the whole of humanity, or only one of its parts? Morelly's text remains ambiguous on this score. While some passages proclaim that leaving behind the property-based condition is necessary for all humanity, others show more modest ambitions. Economic Law no. XII provides for the nation to trade with a foreign nation through the intermediary of its representatives, either to aid this nation or be aided by it. Morelly adds even more clearly: 'scrupulous care shall be taken that this trade does not introduce the slightest element of property in the republic'.[35]

In other words, the model state is supposed to exist alongside other societies operating on completely different economic and social bases. In the author's mind, its size may vary; he envisages that it will not be large enough to compose more than one province, and even that it will be limited to a single city (Laws on the Form of Government, nos VII and XI). Perhaps this explains the surprisingly repressive and strict character of the rules thus decreed; these would have the hitherto unsuspected function of protecting the community from moral corruption arriving from the outside, a recurrent concern in the utopian tradition.

More than any other, the utopia of the *Code de la Nature* thus seems to allow for a variety of interpretations. None of these can indisputably prevail over the others; or, rather, the author seems to have had each of

---

35   Ibid., p. 151.

them in mind at some point during the writing process. Several theoretical and political aims appear to overlap in this ambiguous text. The community of goods seems to be posed in various ways across different spaces and times: in some respects, it embodies a past or even present social and political alternative, left untapped by men too little aware of the true needs of their nature, and in this sense it may be no more than the moral counterpoint of reality. But, in other respects, it presents itself as a genuine model for human society, even if the articles of its laws seem torn between their repressive character and the proclaimed confidence in human nature. Without doubt, the fact that Morelly strengthened the statist and even repressive structure of his model – as if it were meant to be applied to men endowed with the inherent defects of property-based society – can be chalked up to the attempt to get closer to the conditions of reality. But this preoccupation of the author's surely also compromises the overall coherence of the *Code*'s theses. Finally, the model also appears as a project specifically conceived for settlements distant from a Europe that has been perverted beyond repair. But again, to unilaterally attribute it such a status also raises difficulties: indeed, the model seems too universal for this use, and in any case lacks any clear statement of such a perspective.

The effort to construct utopia in the *Code de la Nature* thus seems to oscillate between different functions, none of which seems to have been clear enough to the author for him to follow it to its logical conclusions. Its internal tensions are undeniable. From this point of view, Morelly's theoretical attempts to provide a sturdier philosophical basis for the epic of *La Basiliade*, decried by his detractors, appear to open him up to further criticism for having wanted to prove too much, on too many theoretical levels at once, including the anthropological and metaphysical dimensions. The *Code* appears as a heterogeneous and internally rather inconsistent arsenal of arguments in favour of the utopian model. However, this does not strip it of its significance, which lies precisely in the effort at explanation which Morelly makes. There became clear, for the first time, the multiplicity of uses that could be made of the model of utopian construction, which had already taken on such a classic form by the time that this author was writing, notwithstanding minor variations from one author to the next, that it was, in this form, perhaps no longer able to stimulate reflection. As Alexandre Cioranescu writes: 'In the two centuries between Bacon and utopian socialism, utopia as a literary genre developed within the same literary boundaries set by More's first experiment.'[36] This genre, with its remarkably stable limits and themes, thus experienced a real revival through Morelly's works. With the *Code de la Nature*, an author who had already largely distanced himself from classical utopia with *La Basiliade* thus became a pioneer in the development of the utopian model outside of the realm of literature. He left undetermined and ambiguous the relationship of this model to the real historical process, to the past, present, and future of a human group of still ill-defined contours; in particular, we cannot tell whether this group encompasses all members of the species or only a part of them. These hesitations, this contradictory profusion of arguments, nonetheless are made available for various uses, and especially political ones.

The Anthropology of the *Code de la Nature*

The *Code de la Nature* makes an entirely original effort to theorise consistently, and present as such, an anthropology coherent with the utopian ideal at the end of the text. The first three essays are almost entirely devoted to the question of the nature of man, in connection to the nature of society. Upon a first approach, the text follows in line with the aim of *La Basiliade*: it wages war against 'moralists' and 'institutional morality', which start their reasoning from false presuppositions only to conclude that man is destined to a naturally vicious end.[37] In an effort to clarify the criticisms made in *La Basiliade*, Morelly offers the reason for this error: it lies in confusing the given with the natural, of having projected onto nature characteristics that in fact result from bad human institutions: '[The moralists] have believed that man was naturally as they found him at the birth of their projects, or that he has to be that which I prove he is not'.[38] But how to avoid such a mistake? Here, too, Morelly explains his own approach, which is not lacking in interest. He opposes the moralists' methodological error with the search 'to find a situation in which it is almost impossible for man to be depraved, or

---

36 Alexandre Cioranescu, *L'avenir du passé, utopie et littérature*, Paris: Gallimard, 1972, p. 184.
37 *CN*, pp. 50–1.
38 Ibid., p. 69.

The *Code de la Nature* and Its Constructive Utopia

wicked, or is at least minimally wicked'.[39] Using a mathematical metaphor, the utopian proposes to start from this way of posing the problem ('to find a situation') to arrive at the 'unknown' in the 'equation' – that is, 'the morality that is truly susceptible to the clearest demonstrations'. The axiom on which all authentic morality is built seems to reside in 'the self-evidence of the proposition that where there is no property, there can be none of its pernicious consequences'.[40]

This formulation, if taken seriously, provides a valuable indication as to the internal logic of the utopian's reasoning. It seems to tell us that utopia as a social model has logical priority with respect to a worked-through anthropology. For the starting point of his reasoning is, indeed, a fundamental intuition about the nature of man: it would seem that Morelly begins by assuming man to be good, and by seeing in his 'situation' the cause of his present wickedness. The source of all evils is thereby deemed to be the principle of property itself. From there, his approach appears to continue into a hypothesis, in the form of the construction of a social and political ideal based on the abolition of private property, identified as the cause of all vices. In the author's view, however, such a thought experiment is itself proof of man's natural goodness. His utopianism also reveals itself through the fact that the imaginary society is taken for a more conclusive testimony of man's true essence than the spectacle of social reality itself. Hence the first utopian ideal contained in *La Basiliade*, which portrays a society absolutely free of moral ills, and where the elements of description of human nature are scattered throughout the narrative rather than ordered into a truly reasoned theory. Secondly, Morelly, under attack by his critics, is driven to revise his own anthropological principles in order to provide a sturdier foundation to his utopian hypothesis, which is itself largely reworked. From such a perspective, the anthropology of the *Code* thus strengthens the imaginary social and political construct itself.

Yet, from these remarks, it is also clear that the fundamental theoretical objective of the *Code de la Nature* remains the same as that of *La Basiliade*. It is primarily moral: it seeks to derive, from the hypothesis of the ideal society, a true knowledge of man's nature; and this knowledge, most importantly, will allow for the rehabilitation of this nature. Hence,

---

39 Ibid., p. 50.
40 Ibid., p. 58.

the properly constructive part of Morelly's utopia may not be the main purpose of the *Code de la Nature*, but simply a moment in his argumentation against the prevalent false morality and in favour of exonerating man from responsibility for the vices into which he falls. Much as how in *La Basiliade* the critique of the existing society almost entirely absorbs the social model, in this second utopian text the essays on anthropology and morality are much longer than the plan of legislation per se.

In the *Code de la Nature*, the author provides us with the key to understanding this imbalance: utopia appears to be a thought experiment, aimed at bringing out man's true nature once rid of the defects of the existing society. It essentially provides the imaginary framework for the harmonious development of his faculties. So, properly speaking, utopia is only a moment in the demonstration of man's natural goodness. From the standpoint of the overall economy of Morelly's utopian work, *La Basiliade* would appear to constitute the most radically critical moment of the prevailing morality and anthropology, and the *Code* the moment of returning to the foundations of this critique. In both cases, Morelly fiercely attacks the 'moralists', the 'reformers of the human race', the 'philosophers'. Though he never formulates this conclusion, it may be that the utopian expected that the conversion of the latter group would bring about a radical social transformation, through the lessons that they would then be able to give to men.

The Central Role of Self-Love

The spontaneous social harmony between men is now based on self-love. In granting this primitive passion a driving role in man's actions, Morelly is in line with the thinkers of his time. As against the theses which he had expounded in *La Basiliade*, he now favours 'needs' over pure love; it is these that make man 'attentive to his conservation'.[41] When it is not perverted by property-based society, self-love consists of nothing more than: 'A constant desire to preserve one's being by easy and innocent means which Providence had placed within our reach, and to which the feeling of a small number of needs counselled us to

---

41   Ibid., p. 53.

resort.'[42] Within this conceptual system, this primitive passion is at the origin of beings' 'moral attraction' to one another. This idea of attraction was not itself new to Morelly. As Pierre-François Moreau points out in connection with the *Code de la Nature*,[43] it owes much to the 'mechanical model' of sociability, which holds that the social bond is the effect, not of individual wills or calculations, but of the needs and passions that drive man to enter into a relationship with his peers, forming a society through an exchange of goods and services which precedes any reasoned convention. Here, we have, if not a materialist (since it is an effect of Providence), then at least a realist foundation for the cooperative relations between men; conversely, we may recall that in the motivations for mutual aid in *La Basiliade*, the spontaneity of love preceded any conscious consideration of interests. Here, the bonds between men result from a mechanism prepared by Providence. The model of a star around which everything else gravitates is preferred to that of the universal attraction of bodies to one another.

Indeed, man, like physical bodies, is in a primitive state of inertia and numbness; but the need for self-preservation brings him out of this primitive indifference and sets him in motion.

It is at this point that nature sets in operation a mechanism that is 'as simple as it is wonderful', inducing a slight discrepancy between man's needs and his strengths – the former being slightly greater than the latter. This natural obstacle to the satisfaction of man's needs is what drives him to trade with his fellow men and makes each man a constituent part of an 'intelligent whole' which forms 'the most beautiful assemblage'.[44] Just as the force of attraction among physical bodies draws them closer to each other, self-love drives men to join together and cooperate. This mechanism has a twofold effect on the individual: on the one hand, 'a beneficent affection' for our peers who provide for our needs; on the other, 'the development of reason, which nature has placed alongside this weakness, in order to provide it with assistance'.[45] This general schema bears an obvious Newtonian influence:

---

[42] Ibid., p. 52.
[43] Pierre-François Moreau, 'Utopie et sociabilité dans le *Code de la Nature*', *Revue internationale de philosophie* 113, 1975, 332–47.
[44] *CN*, p. 54.
[45] Ibid.

Our weakness is like a kind of inertia within us: it disposes us, like that of bodies, to undergo a general law which binds and enchains all moral beings. Reason, when nothing offends it, further increases this kind of gravitational force.[46]

Individuals are mere agents of natural laws: they develop their emotional and intellectual faculties in a mechanical way. In the 'counter-Robinsonade' of *La Basiliade*, the legend of the original couple portrays the successive invention of the techniques necessary for human well-being, spurred on by mutual affection. Here, the analysis is centred on the development of the individual's faculties rather than on the discoveries generated by them, and the ultimate origin of this development is traced back to the heart of the individual himself. Man is thus first drawn to man for the sake of satisfying his material needs, and after that for the intellectual and moral benefits he derives from exchange with his peers.

Notwithstanding this rehabilitation of self-love, Morelly builds on these foundations in order to develop an anthropology that ultimately postulates, as in *La Basiliade*, the spontaneous goodness and altruism of the human race. The reciprocal need to give and receive assistance, and the complementarity of talents generated by self-improvement, place human beings in a gentle form of mutual dependence, through the simple, universally beneficial interplay of services which they render to each other. Social harmony, as in the model of 'unsociable sociability' found in Mandeville and the founders of classical political economy, is thus based on self-interest, albeit with the major difference that this self-interest is not expressed in property.[47] As Morelly writes:

It is indisputable that the motive or end of all human action is the desire to be happy; it is no less certain that this desire is the effect of an essential property of a being destined to know that it exists, and itself to see to its own preservation; in a word, this desire is an effect of our sensibility ... But it is from the strength, from the vehemence of this feeling, that Providence derives the principle of all social harmony.[48]

---

46 Ibid., p. 115.
47 Moreau, 'Utopia et sociabilité dans le *Code de la Nature*', p. 339.
48 *CN*, pp. 128–9.

Thus, under the effect of their own sensibility, men thus naturally relate everything else to themselves. Yet, given that men are complementary in their talents, and unable to provide for their own existence in isolation, they are spontaneously driven to mutual assistance, through a trick of nature which produces the happiness of all. The necessary mutual aid is a sui generis effect of man's essence, and not the result of some rational calculation. Thus far, we have focused on Morelly's use of the general schema of the mechanical model of sociability: it seeks, within the needs of individuals, that something which compels them to turn to others, with the effect that each person contributes to the common good by pursuing his own self-interest. Yet we must also emphasise what is unique about Morelly's use of this framework. Indeed, he reminds us of the essential incompleteness of man, who cannot provide for himself alone. Morelly demonstrates that this characteristic is a sign that the individual can only be an individual as part of a whole, within which he finds his place. Moreover, what the individuals, thus defined, 'exchange' in their relations are not so much goods, as in classical political economy, but 'assistance'. So, this is less a matter of 'exchange' than of 'mutual aid'. This solidarity, in the almost literal sense of the term, involves not only a quantitative relation between things, but also and above all, a qualitative relation between beings. Moreover, through their mutual aid, men create feelings of affection among themselves, they make agreements, and they choose to join together for some common purpose. So, here we are far from a schema in which the individual involved in an exchange remains as isolated as before, either in his objectives or in his personal attachments. The nature that presides over these relationships thus produces much more than a sphere for the circulation of goods, oriented towards the satisfaction of material needs. Rather, it generates a union of men's souls, through the mutual aid and recognition of that result.

As in *La Basiliade*, nature is thus granted a metaphysical and moral value; it appears as the vehicle of Providence, and the social mechanism as the immanent translation of a transcendent and beneficent will. Just as in the novel before it, in the *Code de la Nature* Morelly sees in 'one or more associated families'[49] the origin of humanity: again, and quite logically, it is the family bond that serves as a model for his conception

---

49   Ibid., p. 82.

of natural human relations. Once again, he clearly rejects the contractualist model. Consequently, the first form of association took the form of a 'paternal government' all of whose members were 'brothers' and 'kindred'.[50] Hence, despite the priority which Morelly now grants to self-love over the love of others, he transposes the political model of *La Basiliade* onto the origins of humanity.

Since the origins of human societies, social happiness has excluded the spirit of property ownership. Rather, the 'admirable machine'[51] functions based on the 'indivisible unity of the patrimonial fund' and the 'common use of its productions'.[52] Nature itself makes men feel their 'equality of conditions and rights', through their 'parity of feelings and needs'. Yet, at the same time, the 'momentary variety'[53] of men's desires itself allows for them to live in harmony, because it means they do not all pursue the same goals at the same time. It is these variations in their desires, together with the individual 'diversity of strength, industry, and talent', that produce what Morelly calls a 'harmonic inequality'.[54] This is the basis for a general equilibrium between the claims made by each individual and what they provide to the community over the course of time, and this contributes to the common well-being. Thus, paradoxically, the natural inequality generates equality, because it allows each person to offer to others what they cannot provide for themselves, in exchange for the same service from these others. Each person ends up with an equal and sufficient share of what they need. The author thus seems to be paving the way for an egalitarian evolution of his earlier idea of compensation, in which each person received as many services and material goods as they had provided for others.

This natural state ultimately produces an essential social virtue, the product of the inseparability of the particular interest of the individual from the general interest of the whole: this is what Morelly calls 'natural probity'.[55] Marking 'an invincible distance from all unnatural action', this probity deters us from harming others by creating an instinctive repulsion towards such acts. In abstaining from wrongdoing, man is

---

50   Ibid., p. 83.
51   Ibid., p. 55.
52   Ibid.
53   Ibid.
54   Ibid., pp. 56, 86.
55   Ibid., p. 58.

merely manifesting, in its passive form, the love of the common good. This notion of natural probity seems to be the real conclusion of Morelly's demonstration: it embodies the natural non-corruption of man in a well-formed society. In many respects, all that goes before leads to the assertion of this quality; it finally exempts man from all the defects which he owes to a society that separates the individual interest from the general interest.

However, here again, in the first essay of the *Code de la Nature*, as in Morelly's previous works, this harmonic inequality seems to justify differences in 'ranks', 'dignities', and 'honours', whose only recompense must consist, as in *La Basiliade*, in 'feelings of gratitude and shared joy'.[56] Yet Morelly's thinking on this question does not seem to be very fixed. In the second essay, these markers of consideration can earn a citizen the title of king. The author contemplates the different possible forms of government, all of which are acceptable so long as they are based on the community of goods: but he seems to consider that the greater the concentration of authority, the more 'precision, correctness and regularity are found in the movements of the body politic'.[57] Thus, aristocracy seems preferable to democracy, and monarchy to aristocracy. Such a judgement does not fit well with the plan of ideal legislation at the end of the book, where, as we have seen, all manner of provisions are made to guarantee the greatest political equality through the rotation of offices, even doing away with the principle of appointing the wisest and most virtuous. Between his old principle of compensating greater services rendered with greater social esteem, and an egalitarian tendency which finds its fullest expression in the 'Model of Legislation', between the idea of a social mechanism that encourages reciprocal service, and the introduction of a principle of authority tasked with giving order to the movements of the great machinery, Morelly does not seem to have reached any definitive choice.

For Morelly, in any case, all vice stems from the introduction of a property-based society, which disrupts the original equilibrium. The fault lies with the 'so-called wise men', the legislators, the educators, the 'clumsy machinists' of the social mechanism: by basing laws and the formation of individuals on the principle of *cuique suum* (to each his

---

56   Ibid., p. 57.
57   Ibid., p. 104.

due), they have upset its functioning. Morelly's anthropology of the true nature of man is then paired with an analysis of how this nature has been corrupted. Property is in fact responsible for the degeneration of self-love, a simple desire to be, into a desire to have, or particular interest. This dissolves all social ties, and with it 'all humanity' in man.[58] Just as a well-directed self-love is the source of all social virtues and natural probity, self-interest, that 'universal plague', is the ferment of all vices.[59] It causes naturally mild passions to burst forth, transforming them into a raging torrent as the natural instinct revolts against a state of affairs that stands deeply opposed to it. Thus, paradoxically, excesses of self-love are the product of the species' thwarted altruism. Morelly implicitly adopts the traditional metaphor of the dam which has been put up against the natural flow of a river. So long as the principle of property stands in man's way, any attempt to channel his passions will be in vain, for they have become furious and harmful. Hence the patent failure of the moralists over the centuries, leading them to their well-known erroneous conclusions.

Did Morelly here achieve his stated goal? That is, did he manage to provide a solid, reasonably argued defence of the social ideal that had earlier appeared in *La Basiliade*? Georges Benrekassa has written that the *Code de la Nature*'s attempt to give the content of the previous utopia a foundation in anthropological arguments produces a result which is

> both dismaying and very interesting. Dismaying because of the confusion and contradictions into which Morelly sinks; very interesting, because the essay reveals the lacunas that allow for utopian totalisation, the economies, the 'blanks' that allow the establishment of a fictitious economy that purports to be 'perfect' and has no justification for this claim other than the author's own word.[60]

Here, we will not again revisit the sometimes-inconsistent dimension of Morelly's theses. It seems, moreover, that such an accusation does not really attach to the anthropological dimension of his work, which is

---

58 Ibid., p. 63.
59 Ibid., p. 58.
60 Georges Benrekassa, *Le concentrique et l'excentrique, marges des Lumières*, Paris: Payot, 1980, pp. 106–7.

characterised by a fair degree of consistency. There is, of course, an exception to this: the reintroduction of repressive measures in the Model of Legislation would seem to point to a rebirth of vices, even though all the argumentation that precedes this demonstrates the automatic, irrepressible character of universal benevolence in a system based on the community of goods. Yet, while this contradiction is surely worth noting, in itself the description of the social mechanism in the first essays of the *Code de la Nature* does show a certain rigour.

On the other hand, in mentioning these 'economies' and 'blanks', Benrekassa seems to point to a fundamental aspect of the *Code*'s anthropology, which lies in its removal of conflict and violence from human relations once they are restored to their natural state. Morelly never considers the possibility that the proclaimed interdependence between men could give rise to relationships, not of equality and mutual benevolence, but of exploitation or subjugation of some by others. After all, there is nothing in law to prevent such a possibility, which would be no less mechanical than that envisaged by Morelly. The great coherence of his argument on man's nature probably even relies on this denial. Moreover, one could counter the utopian's arguments with the simple fact that competition over material interests is not the only possible cause of conflict between men. Even once property is abolished, along with all the vices and evils it causes, what could guarantee harmonious social relations? From this point of view, Rousseau's analyses in the *Second Discourse*, and especially those regarding the development of *amour-propre* engendered by the simple fact of men establishing relations, could provide the basis for a considerable objection. This vice – 'arising from [the] comparisons' that man can make with others once his relations with his peers have developed his rational faculties[61] – does not require property to exist to appear and stir up quarrels. Once individuals place their own interests above all others, their sole concern is to outdo their adversaries. Whereas Hobbes had located these symbolic rivalries in a state of war, Morelly can offer the reader the image of an angelic humanity, reduced to its instincts of sociability and affection, only by refusing to consider these conflicts as anything other than a product of the reign of property.

---

61   Jean-Jacques Rousseau, *The Social Contract and the First and Second Discourses*, edited by Susan Dunn, New Haven, CT: Yale University Press, 2002, p. 146.

Is this the price to be paid for the elaboration of an anthropology consistent with a society that is supposed to offer the image of perfection? Does the idea of a sociability based on a non-egotistical and benevolent self-love amount to a fundamental theoretical condition, if the possibility of an ideal, harmonious, and cooperative community is to be rooted in human nature itself? An interesting counterpoint in this regard is Sade's attempt to envisage an ideal society through the description of the island of Tamoé in his novel *Aline et Valcour*. Contrary to what may be imagined, the blessed island does not contravene the anthropological principles expounded throughout the work, which may even justify criminal societies. As Peter Kuon summarises: 'Sade knows no other reality than that of the egoistic individual who follows his natural inclination, without there being a universal morality that would allow vice to be condemned and virtue to be praised.'[62] The good Zamé, leader of Tamoé, confirms this in his own way, when he explains to Sainville:

> The natural state of man is the savage life . . . In taking him from there to civilise him, think of his primitive state, of that state of freedom for which nature formed him, and add only what can perfect this happy state in which he had then found himself; give him facilities, but do not forge chains for him; make the fulfilment of his desires easier, but do not enslave him.[63]

Man is thus destined by his very nature to the satisfaction of his desires, which we know can indeed be 'untamed'. Sade's anthropology truly takes the opposite view to Morelly's, in that it denies any basis for social ties other than the individual's search for the most effective way to satisfy his own needs and desires. Each person in society seeks only his own happiness – if necessary, at the expense of others. It is up to the talents of the legislator to make these desires compatible with the most harmonious possible order. But how is it possible, without falling into Butua's self-destructive model,[64] to observe the golden rule of Sadian politics, which,

---

62 Peter Kuon, 'Utopie et anthropologie au siècle des Lumières ou la crise d'un genre littéraire', in H. Hudde and P. Kuon (eds), *De l'utopie à l'uchronie: formes, significations, fonctions*, Tübingen: Gunter Narr Verlag, 1988, pp. 49–62, at p. 58.
63 Marquis de Sade, *Aline et Valcour*, in *Œuvres complètes*, Paris: Gallimard, 1990, vol. 1, pp. 387–1109, at p. 644.
64 A kingdom in southern Africa.

according to Binoche, implies that 'the civil order should only be thought of in terms of the interests of desire'?[65]

The whole challenge, in the utopian construction of Tamoé, is the attempt to preserve the possibility of a common life that is in accordance with nature, while also safeguarding it from the mortifying consequences of an anthropology marked by egoism and the law of the strongest. The author comes up against a major difficulty here: how can it be ensured that the satisfaction of one man's desire will not violently clash with another's, even to the point of threatening the social bond itself? First of all, 'equality of wealth' provides a classic means of preventing crimes caused by greed or jealousy, and thus the harm that men are driven to do to each other out of material interest. The community of goods is a first response to the destructive character of individual desire: it suppresses one of the main sources that feed its violence by making personal enrichment concretely impossible, and by urging men towards an economic cooperation which is thus made necessary for their survival.

Zamé thus counts on the understanding that social institutions can, at least partly, mould human desire by offering it other modes of satisfaction than those known to European society. In this case, the satisfaction of primary needs can take other avenues than that of private property, and the vices associated with its reign – pride, avarice, ambition – simply disappear, to be replaced by social passions consistent with virtue. But Sade does not imagine that all vices will disappear similarly easily. What is to be done, Sainville asks, with those who do evil for its own sake, for pleasure?

> There is ... a kind of perversity in some hearts which cannot be corrected; many people do evil without interest; it is recognised today that there are men who indulge in it only for the charm of the infraction.[66]

The evils caused by the form of socio-economic organisation can surely be reduced by a change in this form; but those inscribed in the

---

65   Bertrand Binoche, *Sade ou l'institutionnalisation de l'écart*, Quebec City: Presses de l'Université Laval, 2007, p. 37.
66   Sade, *Aline et Valcour*, p. 670.

complexion of certain men cannot be reduced similarly easily. As we have understood, the question here is not – as in other texts of Sade's – to establish on what conditions the libertine, who takes pleasure in criminality, can become a legislator – that is, by showing the possibility of communities that do without the basic principle of reciprocity which is the foundation of all sociability. Rather, it is about finding a viable solution, from the virtuous legislator's point of view, to the problem posed by the social existence of such libertines, which does not rely on the simple repression of their desires – a repression itself considered an offence against nature.

Zamé's response has two sides. On the one hand, it is not appropriate to expressly forbid, let alone punish by strict laws, actions that run contrary to ordinary morality. A drastic reduction in the number of laws, and an almost total abolition of repressive laws, is thus highly desirable. Such leniency is a first way of reducing the frequency of these acts, which derive their main interest, in the eyes of those who engage in them, from their transgressive effect. Passions will only be heightened by the prohibition that restrains their satisfaction; consequently, the converse must be true, and the disappearance of the prohibition itself must lead to a substantial reduction in deviant behaviours.

But Zamé's argument does not stop there: he urges his interlocutor to take up the viewpoint of the happiness of the greatest number. From this perspective, it is not right to make the victims happy by repressing and punishing their tormentors, but rather by finding a form of compensation for the suffering caused by the latter, through 'indemnities' whose nature is left unspecified. Here, Sade seems to imagine an ideal balance between the sadism of some and the masochism of others:

> Thus, the legislator must not punish the one man for seeking to make himself happy at the expense of the other, because in this he is merely following the intention of nature; but he must examine whether one of these men will not be equally happy, by giving up a small portion of his happiness to the one who is most to be pitied.[67]

Whatever we may think of this improbable hypothesis of a fair and satisfying exchange between the oppressor and his victim, it is no less

---

67   Ibid., p. 673.

striking that, paradoxically, Sade's sole attempt to reconcile potentially perverse individual egoism and the demands of social life relies on the community of goods. Indeed, in its appeal to a peaceful anarchy, it draws on principles of social organisation which appear in Morelly's work, and especially in *La Basiliade*, but underpinned by a completely opposite anthropology. Morelly's scheme for social harmony is matched in Marquis's writings by that of the balancing of human passions by a skilful conductor of men, who acts, again recalling a figure in Morelly's social theory, as a mechanic of the cogs and gears of the community. Sade's attempt to integrate libertine passions into a harmonious social order has the merit of taking into account what remains a blind spot for the author of the *Code de la Nature*: namely, the possibility that even in the heart of a society built on community, social relations marked by violence and domination may persist.

History in the *Code de la Nature*: From Counter-History to Providential History

In the *Code de la Nature*, real history and temporality gradually enter into Morelly's reflection. This begins in the second essay, through the evocation of the wise legislator who could have spared all humanity a long series of misfortunes had he only refrained from instituting private property. In this, there is already a first change of direction as compared with *La Basiliade*. In these pages, Morelly breaks the utopian ideal out of the novelistic narrative and enters, if not yet into history as such, at least into a possible alternative history that was missed because of the legislator's insufficient wisdom. This thought experiment in counterfactual history does not only serve to make real history appear as the result of an unfortunate contingency or the negligence of human leaders – of stripping away what the reader might see as its self-evident and necessary character. More than that, it grants the hypothetical 'parallel' society thus outlined the weight of the temporality which it could have had. It inscribes it in a fictitious chronology that extends from the past to the present: it makes it a direct competitor of history as it really happened. This runs contrary to the utopians' customary approach, which generally settles for evoking the history of the ideal society without establishing a connection with our own.

This counter-history constitutes the development of the purely rhetorical hypothesis that Rousseau, perhaps influenced by having read the *Code*,[68] puts forward in the opening lines of the second part of the *Second Discourse*:

> How many crimes, how many wars, how many murders, how many misfortunes and horrors, would that man have saved the human species, who pulling up the stakes or filling up the ditches should have cried to his fellows: Beware of listening to this impostor; you are lost, if you forget that the fruits of the earth belong equally to us all, and the earth itself to nobody![69]

There is a clear difference between the two authors. Yet if Rousseau, like many others, immediately rejected this possibility by declaring it incompatible with the circumstances of the point in evolution where it ought to have taken place, this was perhaps because he was thinking of the theoretical path explored by his immediate predecessor Morelly. This thread of a historical utopia parallel to real history continues throughout the second part of the *Code* and allows Morelly to judge the present as a disastrous result of errors already made in the past, which could have been avoided, and which perhaps can still be rectified, as some formulations suggest.

This last idea finds its theoretical justification in the third part of the *Code*, entitled 'Particular Defects of the Vulgar Morality'. Morelly here postulates that 'in the physical as well as in the intellectual and moral, a fixed point of integrity is established, to which beings ascend by degrees'.[70] On this general teleological basis, the utopian then evokes the image of human history as having begun with a 'golden age' of first innocence, soon corrupted because it was observed 'without reflection'.[71] This corruption is not, however, the last word in the evolution of societies: as men suffer from this state, they seek to get closer to the first state through laws that are gradually improved

---

68 Research by Richard Coe and Martin Fontius has established that the *Code* was probably in circulation as early as the second half of 1754, and there are many indications that Rousseau read and ruminated on it. See Nicolas Wagner, *Morelly, le méconnu des Lumières*, Paris: Klincksieck, 1978, p. 214.

69 Rousseau, *The Social Contract and the First and Second Discourse*, edited by Susan Dunn, New Haven, CT: Yale University Press, 2002, p. 113.

70 *CN*, p. 120.

71 Ibid.

until the purified reason has become accustomed to no longer disregarding the lessons of nature ... Having reached this happy end, the reasonable creature will have acquired all the goodness, or moral integrity, of which he is susceptible; it is probably by these degrees that Providence leads the human race to it.[72]

Morelly thus outlines, on the horizon of history, a 'fixed' stage that lies in an indeterminate but nonetheless certain future. It will be established forever and will realise the promises of nature from which men have wrongly departed; it is an exit from time at the end of immanent temporality, indeed an end of history in the strict sense. How can we not see a link, here, with the 'hors d'oeuvre' that Morelly proposes in the final part of the *Code*? The sanctity of the fundamental laws, the intangibility of the philosophical, moral, and religious principles that derive from them, are part of the fixity that Morelly calls for. One of the conjugal laws also reflects this aim:

> When the nation has reached a point of growth such that the number of citizens born is approximately equal to the number of those who cease to live, the tribes, cities, etc., will remain and be maintained almost equal.[73]

The ideal of stability and fixity – connected to that of perfect equality in the arithmetic sense, a leitmotif of the utopian tradition – can thus be linked to the arguments developed in the third part of the work, which make this ideal into a culmination of the human adventure. This link would give the 'Model of Legislation' an entirely new status in the history of this philosophical-political tradition. That is, it would seem that, almost twenty years before Louis-Sébastien Mercier's uchronia, Morelly was the first to project utopia into the future, albeit in very different theoretical terms, and even if this future, in many respects, resembled a resurgence of man's origins.[74] From this perspective, utopia becomes the specific 'fixed point of integrity' to which

---

72 Ibid., p. 121.
73 Ibid., p. 165.
74 Louis-Sébastien Mercier, *L'An 2440 rêve s'il en fut jamais*, Paris: France Adel, 1977.

men 'ascend by degrees': in other words, the proven telos of human history.[75]

Morelly adds greater definition to this general intuition, offering something of a rereading of history in light of his utopia. He hypothesises that the natural state of the community of goods was at first a spontaneous social condition and thus lacked consciousness of itself. Since men had practised their initial innocent condition 'without reflection', they were also vulnerable to losing it. Within this framework, Morelly reconstructs a genesis of property-based societies: the first 'paternal government',[76] he tells us, was unable to withstand the difficulties posed by population growth, which loosened the natural bonds of family affection that had prevailed within the first communities and forced its members to disperse or even move away. Subsequently, it is said, the already weakened 'spirit of community'[77] gradually disappeared as a result of migrations, combined with the hazards of new settlements, which produced internal dissensions through a combination of material difficulties and the thinning of social ties. Peoples thus 'consented to submit to laws' that seemed likely to put an end to their conflicts.[78] But unfortunately, we are told, those entrusted with this task made the mistake, repeated by later moralists and politicians, of 'taking ... things and people as they found them'[79] – that is, as already quarrelsome and selfish. Instead of correcting their incipient vices through wise laws, they assumed that men were inherently wicked, and authored legislation consistent with this belief, thinking it best to give each his own by establishing private property.

This explanation of the disastrous evolution of human history, this critique of history such as it happened, makes the course of history appear to be a slide into decadence. In this sense, Morelly remains in line with the arguments expounded in *La Basiliade*. As in his novel, he does not worry about recounting real facts, but reconstructs in a wholly speculative fashion humanity's past, or, rather, the only moment that directly interests him, and which represents the tipping point of history. The essential difference with this first utopian text is that this time the

---

75 *CN*, p. 120.
76 Ibid., p. 83.
77 Ibid., p. 84.
78 Ibid., p. 85.
79 Ibid.

author seeks an explanation, even a hypothetical one, for the appearance of private property, which was previously denounced without any other form of rationalisation.

But, subsequently, this critical passage is left behind or, better, reabsorbed into the narrative. Decadence then becomes progress, in the form of men's historical groping towards the best possible laws to solve the problems posed by their own social organisation. Their laws, which are at first 'highly defective', are gradually replaced by other 'less imperfect' ones; and these in turn will be improved to the point of perfection.

The conceptual basis upon which Morelly moves from describing the historical decadence of human societies plagued by private property, to the idea of an underlying but undeniable progression of laws, is the notion of Providence. We can thus see the points of contact, on this question, between the arguments developed here and those advanced by Jacques-Bénigne Bossuet in his 'Sermon on Providence' of 10 March 1662. Yet there are also points of divergence that allow us to better understand the specificity of Morelly's conceptions.

Morelly begins by addressing the question of physical evil in the universe. The latter appears to us as an evil, firstly because 'our limited view cannot perceive the order and sequence of beings; it grasps only some fragment of it, which it believes to be imperfect, being able to see this alone'.[80]

In principle, this argument, an old philosophical topos, is very close to the one Bossuet develops in the 'First Point' of his sermon on moral evil, when he compares the order of human affairs to an anamorphosis. While the first view of it 'shows you nothing but shapeless features and a confused mixture of colours',[81] a change of perspective brings out the image, which stands for the 'rightness hidden' behind the world's apparent disorder. In both cases, the confusion comes from a shortcoming in the viewer's vision, and not from any real inadequacy in the arrangement of things intended by the 'infinite intelligence that has given order to everything'.[82]

---

80 Ibid., p. 113.
81 Jacques-Bénigne Bossuet, 'Sermon sur la Providence', in Œuvres, texts prepared by the Abbé Velat and Yvonne Champailler, Paris: Gallimard, 1961, p. 1061.
82 CN, p. 118.

However, on closer inspection, differences appear in the ways that Morelly and Bossuet respectively conceive of physical evil. According to the bishop of Meaux, 'sickness is an evil; but how great a good it will be, if you sanctify it with patience!'[83]

For Bossuet, physical ailments are thus part of the category of the 'mix of good and evil', which should not be rejected as such. On the contrary, they should be faced in a Christian way, in this case meaning that they should be accepted and endured. Morelly, however, writes that physical ailments, when they are not mere errors of perspective on our part, may be 'pressing warnings, or to deliver or secure us from what may harm us'.[84] In other words, it is not necessary to passively endure illness on the grounds that it is a consequence of divine will; rather, it is to be fought by the immanent means at hand. Here, the role of Providence is limited to stimulating our activity. In this detail of Morelly's argument, there thus appears a general orientation of the *Code de la Nature*: namely, that while Providence does preside over human destinies, it does not command us to submit to the vagaries of fate, but rather to use the means it places at our disposal to shape its course.

This general idea is confirmed even more clearly in the following part of the argument. One element that Bossuet and Morelly have in common is that each projects into the future the still-incomplete perfection of the order of things. For Bossuet, 'man has something to expect' from the future, insofar as in order to see justice finally established among men, he must live 'in the midst of time in a perpetual expectation of eternity'.[85] Morelly in some ways takes up the same perspective, writing that 'moral evil is in man ... only what imperfections are in physical beings', and adding: 'I call imperfect that which is not yet what Providence intends it to be.'[86]

As in the sermon, perfection in the moral order is thus deferred to an indeterminate future for men. But, here again, an essential difference must be emphasised: the perfection which the bishop of Meaux promises for the day of the Last Judgement must, according to the utopian Morelly, be realised in the immanence of a social

---

83   Bossuet, 'Sermon sur la Providence', p. 1066.
84   *CN*, p. 113.
85   Bossuet, 'Sermont sur la Providence', p. 1063.
86   *CN*, p. 120.

organisation restored to the principles of the natural order, itself now enlightened by a full awareness of what it is and must be. In this sense, we can speak of a secularisation of the Christian schema. Instead of locating the destination of human history in its negation, as represented by the advent of the Kingdom of God on Earth and the end of time, Morelly predicts an immanent outcome which is ultimately based on humanity's capacity to learn from its mistakes and collectively overcome them by its own means. In this sense, the return to the 'natural' community of goods constitutes men's reappropriation of their own destiny.

In the *Discours sur l'histoire universelle*, Bossuet sees the sign that human history is progressing towards the fulfilment of God's will in the continuous consolidation of the Church through the succession of empires. But this theodicy only encompasses the events of empirical history up to the rule of Charlemagne. The incompleteness of the theology of history does not invalidate it, however, since in any case, 'It takes the entire duration of the world to fully develop the orders of a wisdom so profound' as God's.[87] The vagaries of history since the moment at which the *Discours* stops, and in particular the setbacks for Catholicism, cannot invalidate its fundamental hypothesis, because they only make complete sense *sub specie aeternitatis* (if they are eternally true). Morelly, conversely, locates the cipher of men's progress towards the ideal state – the one in which the views of Providence will be fully realised – in their improvement of their own legislation. This characteristic signals both the proximity between two providential conceptions of human history, and the difference between a thought in which man's task is essentially to humbly accept the world's order as willed by God, and one in which man himself is the main agent of the realisation of such an order.

It should be noted, however, that this change in the theology of history comes at the cost of removing real facts from the field of philosophical investigation. In order to be able to assert that the laws of men are approaching ever closer to the perfect state to which they are called, Morelly is led to dispense with the concrete analysis of past and present positive laws. Thus, there is not even an attempt to confirm the hypothesis that is supposed to give a direction to history. The gesture of

---

87 Bossuet, 'Sermon sur la Providence', p. 1064.

rehabilitating history as such results in the disappearance of its empirical material, which is thus never subject to serious examination.

'The Other History'

As Baczko rightly notes, in the *Code de la Nature*,

> the utopia is defined by reference to history. It is in historical time that it unveils the possibility of existence of an alternative society that would give body to what had been only the object of dreams.[88]

If only for this reason, Morelly's text represents a notable break, both in the history of utopias and in relation to his previous work. However, if utopia represents an assured, if not imminent, future and the natural moral destination of the human race, the question remains as to the future of history as envisaged by Morelly in this indeterminate future. If utopia – like Judgement Day for Christians – is the end of history, is it nonetheless conceivable that, as the immanent future of the species, it will still allow society and its members to evolve?

The first part of the answer to this question can be found in the Seventh Law of the studies on 'Model of Legislation':

> Each senate will have the actions of the chiefs and citizens worthy of remembrance written down; but it will take care that these histories are free from all exaggeration, all flattery and, much more rigorously, from all fabulous accounts; the highest Senate will have them composed into the body of history of the whole nation.[89]

The history of property-based societies is eclipsed, so to speak, by this new beginning for humanity. A society liberated from an unhappy past is led to embark upon a new history, which will have its own heroes and its own glorious deeds. Morelly brings the old model of edifying history back to the future of humanity. It is striking, in this respect, that the perspective expressed in *La Basiliade* is completely abandoned, and that

---

88   Bronisław Baczko, *Utopian Lights*, New York: Paragon House, 1989, p. 122.
89   *CN*, p. 170.

The *Code de la Nature* and Its Constructive Utopia

there is no longer any question of proposing a fabulous or mythical history for the edification of mankind. Only future events seem well-placed to provide useful lessons for the regenerated society. The rejection of the study of the past of property-based societies should not, however, mask the continuity in the function attributed to history: as a narrative, it retains its moralising and didactic function. It continues to serve the edification of the younger generations and, as such, contributes to 'social cohesion'.[90]

But history is not just about great men and great deeds. It is also the story of 'physical, mathematical and mechanical discoveries', which, unlike moral and metaphysical speculations, will continue to build in order to 'perfect' the 'conveniences' and 'amenities' of society.[91] Citizens who have contributed to these improvements are to be celebrated 'through eloquence, poetry and painting'.[92] Morelly's utopia takes up the practices of Francis Bacon's utopian island Bensalem, which exhibited 'the more rare and excellent inventions' and 'the statues of all principal inventors' in specially dedicated galleries.[93] Unlike Morelly, Bacon specified that all the great discoverers, including those from the real world, had a place in the gallery: Christopher Columbus, for example, or the inventor of gunpowder or writing. Given this, it would seem Morelly's desire for a radical break with the pre-existing property-based society does not likewise appear in Bacon's work. As Pierre Macherey writes:

> Generally speaking, Bacon's conception of temporality, which makes full use of the ideas of progress and advancement, does so by excluding anything that could be likened to a break or discontinuity . . . what distinguishes Bacon's approach [is] . . . his desire to 'go further', not to break definitively with what is customary, by proceeding *in aliud*, but, on the contrary, by proceeding *in melius*, to extend and perfect it.[94]

The comparison highlights the fact that, for Morelly, in the collective imaginary the progress of the sciences and the arts must take the form

---

90 Ibid., p. 164.
91 Ibid., p. 170.
92 Ibid.
93 Bacon, *New Atlantis*, p. 269.
94 Macherey, *De l'utopie!*, Le Havre: De l'incidence éditeur, 2011, pp. 187–8.

of a new beginning, even if the new society must inevitably draw on the knowledge and techniques of past eras.

Thus, at first sight, in the society that Morelly wishes for, there is an accepted form of progress – that of science, technology, and the arts – and a form of progress that is rejected because it is impossible: nothing can supplant, in terms of truth and social utility, the principles of natural morality and religion that are developed in the *Code de la Nature*. In this sense, the conception of history found in this text confirms Binoche's claim that

> it is certain that in France, until Condorcet, ... history would thus admit improvements against the backdrop of a nature which *a priori* forbids progress and which makes history appear essentially as the indefinite epiphenomenal modelling of the human 'dough'.[95]

In a certain sense, the new history introduced by the advent of the ideal society would not change the human race's fundamental characteristics. Rather, once humans had become fully self-aware thanks to the lessons of the *Code de la Nature*, these characteristics could flourish in full. All that would need perfecting would be the material means of happiness acquired by the community, at the cost (and at the end) of a difficult and tumultuous history. To understand how far Morelly's conception of 'perfection' differs from the idea of the continuous progress of the human race, we need only make a comparison with the terms in which Nicolas de Condorcet's *Tableau historique* presents what he calls the 'indefinite perfectibility' of man. In the 'Preamble' of 1793, it stated:

> This is the aim of the work I have undertaken, the result of which will be to show by fact, as well as by reasoning, that nature has marked no end to the perfection of human faculties, that man's perfectibility is really indefinite, that the progress of this perfectibility, now independent of those who would stop it, has no other end than the duration of the globe into which nature has thrown us.[96]

---

95 Bertrand Binoche, *Les trois sources des philosophies de l'histoire (1764–1798)*, Paris: PUF, 1994, p. 36.
96 *THP*, pp. 234–5.

Several aspects deserve highlighting here. On the one hand, there is Condorcet's emphasis on the indefinite development of all human faculties, including capacities linked to philosophical and moral progress. Unlike Morelly, Condorcet apparently takes pains not to set any limit, any point of perfection, in the various fields in which the species is to exercise its faculties. As he wrote in his 'Fragment sur l'Atlantide':

> What I have just said about the intellectual faculties can be extended to the moral faculties, such as conscience [and] freedom . . . they are susceptible to a perfectibility dependent on both that of the physical constitution and that of the intelligence. The degree of virtue which a man may one day attain is as inconceivable to us as that to which the force of genius may be brought.[97]

For Condorcet, all forms of progress go together. He seriously considers the possibility – which Morelly absolutely rules out – that virtues, like positive knowledge, might be subject to continuous improvement. This would make it possible to hypothesise as yet unheard-of moral principles superior to the ones even conceivable for an intelligence and a sensibility limited by their belonging to an earlier epoch. Humanity would then be faced with the task that the utopian believed had been accomplished for it by way of anticipation. Which is to say, the task of finding new modes of social and political organisation corresponding to this unprecedented degree of perfection.

On the other hand – again in contrast to Morelly – for Condorcet the 'facts' themselves, and not just reasoning, must serve as the basis for the demonstration. Empirical history thus makes its appearance within an overall conception that rejects the idea of man's unchanging nature, the secret of which only needs to be uncovered once and for all in order to confidently map out his destiny.[98] It replaces it with the idea of a permanent future that is both open and capable of improvement. While Morelly felt no need to show that the facts confirmed his hypothesis of the gradual improvement of legislation throughout history, Condorcet

---

97 Ibid., p. 895.
98 The *Tableau historique* does make some reference to human nature; but, in Condorcet's terms, it is essentially expressed in terms of potentials (sensibility, morality, reason), which are realised through history itself.

did this. His attitude was a direct consequence of his abandonment of the substantialisation of human nature. In fact, it was only after this theoretical decision that empirical history became the main source of information likely to tell us something about humanity. The essence of humanity could thus be read in its concrete becoming, which reveals its fundamental mutability.

But was Condorcet really finished with the idea of a point of perfection, which would mark an end to the species' capacity for improvement? That is, an idea that would bring his point of view closer to the utopian Morelly's? We may well doubt this. In discussing the future extension of life expectancy, the 'Tenth Epoch' expresses some hesitation about the meaning of the term 'indefinite':

> Indeed, this average lifespan which must constantly increase as we move further into the future, can be increased according to a law such that this [duration] continually approaches a limited extent without ever reaching it. Or it can be increased according to a law such that this same duration can acquire, in the immensity of the centuries, an extent greater than any number assigned to it as a limit.[99]

The idea of a 'limited extent' – a supposed upper limit to the possible human lifespan – seems akin to the idea of a point of perfection for life's duration, even (or above all?) if this point will never be reached. It is worth noting that Condorcet generalised this thinking to all areas of human perfectibility: if it was impossible to more precisely pin down the meaning of the word 'indefinite' in this context, this owed to the inadequacy of 'current knowledge'. The final pages of the *Tableau historique* thus reveal a certain ambiguity in the idea of progress, which Condorcet gives a sophisticated appearance, but which we find again, in a simpler and unexplained form, in Morelly's Model of Legislation for the arts, sciences, and technology. He formulates the Fourth and Fifth Laws of Study as follows:

> The sagacity and penetration of the human mind shall be left entirely free with regard to the speculative and experimental sciences, whose object is either the investigation of the secrets of nature, or the

---

99   *THP*, pp. 457–8.

perfection of the arts useful to society ... The physical and moral beauties of nature, which are the objects of science and of the comforts and pleasures of society, as well as the citizens who have made a distinguished contribution to the perfection of all these things, may be celebrated in eloquence, poetry and painting.[100]

In both cases, the notion of perfection is somehow ambivalent. Does it mean developing the 'arts useful to society' to a precise point (or as close as possible to a point), beyond which progress would no longer be possible? Or is the work of perfecting them never fully complete? The *Code de la Nature* does not answer this question. It thus leaves the future of utopian society, in terms of its sciences, arts, and technology, in a state of indeterminacy that is at odds with the clear-cut stability it promises on the political, moral, and metaphysical levels.

Throughout his intellectual journey, Morelly thus granted a merely negligible value to the narration of the past. In this sense, he maintained a distant relationship with history, in each case subordinate to the moral imperatives of edifying his reader. The *Code*'s only partial reconciliation of utopia with a real temporality is left abstract, and it bears the hallmark of the utopian tradition's rejection of the real world and its affairs. The community of goods is proclaimed to be the *future* of humanity only within a framework that sidesteps the concrete analysis of its *past* and its *present*. In this sense, utopia is temporalised but not really historicised. This would, however, be done, from a quite different perspective, by the Abbé de Mably.

---

100   CN, p. 170.

II

The Abbé de Mably's Utopian Republic

Like a number of his learned contemporaries, Mably was probably aware of the *Code de la Nature*, which went through four successive editions between 1754 and 1773. This text was the object of numerous critiques in the reviews of the time,[1] which suggests that it was a fairly considerable success, albeit on account of the scandal it raised. Certain indicators in Mably's texts would seem to confirm this awareness. Admittedly, unlike Morelly, he rejected the possibility of humanity arriving at a community of goods. However, he did make decisive use of this theme in his political reflection, which is, indeed, largely organised around it. The assimilation of the utopian ideal to a pre-existing historical model – namely, the example of ancient Sparta – allows for a synthesis between utopia and republic which is never fully completed or stated outright. In the dialogue *De la législation*, this synthesis leads to the development of a new model, which also has an unprecedented political force, since it is presented as something which could be practically applied in eighteenth-century Europe. In this way, Mably strove to 'republicanise utopia' in order to set it within history and make it theoretically and politically acceptable to his contemporaries.

---

1 According to Nicolas Wagner, *Morelly, le méconnu des Lumières*, Paris: Klincksieck, 1978, pp. 245–8.

3

Des droits et des devoirs du citoyen: Utopia in Service of the Revolution

Mably was not a utopian in the same obvious sense as Morelly. None of his works is entirely devoted to describing an ideal society rid of private property, or to the theoretical justification of such a society. Yet, this does appear as a theme in many of his major texts. The first of these, which explicitly sets out an ideal of this kind, is an unpublished text, probably written around 1758 and rich in direct political implications in the context of the time. This text is the dialogue *Des droits et des devoirs du citoyen* (*The Rights and Duties of the Citizen*). The dialogue, related as a series of letters, features an English commonwealthman called Milord Stanhope. He and the narrator discuss France's fate and the possibilities that he sees for a far-reaching reform of the French monarchy, which would allow that country's citizens to regain a long-lost freedom. The dialogue, which took place at the same time as the crisis between the Parlements and the French monarchy over the *billets de confession*, tried to use this crisis as a prompt to lay the bases for positive change.

The first four letters deal with general questions of moral and political principles. The last three attempt to imagine a scenario in which the established order comes increasingly under challenge, leading to the establishment of a permanent assembly of the nation. The utopian passage, which comes at the end of the fourth letter, is thus right at the core of this work. It seems to be the culmination of the author's reflections on the principles of political action, the conclusion he draws from his elaborations on the rights and duties of the members of the body politic.

Milord begins this passage by asserting that the ownership of property is 'the principal source of the ills that afflict mankind'.[1] This observation, he argues, should lead men to aspire to 'that much-praised happy community of goods',[2] of which he mentions a few illustrations: the writings of the 'poets', the work of Lycurgus in Lacedemonia, and Plato's *Republic*. This last reference, it should be noted, is also used by Raphael Hythloday in the first part of *Utopia*. Here, as in More, it is cited only for its emphasis on the principle of the community of goods – as Raphael puts it, 'all things are held in common'.[3] However, Milord concludes by asserting that the depravity of morals now makes this community of goods 'a chimera in the world'.[4]

This first remark calls for two comments. The first is that none of the references in question draws directly on the utopian tradition, from which the author seems to distance himself. Mably combines an entirely vague allusion to poets, perhaps the bards of the golden age such as Tibullus or Ovid, a historical reference to ancient Sparta, and a citation from Plato that is more philosophical than utopian in the strict sense, even if it did itself inspire the utopians. The second comment obviously concerns the status given to these references, which are merely nostalgic: the community of goods as a mode of social and political organisation is definitely a thing of the past.

However, Milord also returns to this model in greater detail elsewhere in the dialogue: in a description that he presents as a 'folly', a 'pleasant reverie', he confesses his desire to go to a desert island and establish a republic without property. This – very briefly sketched-out – image has characteristics more reminiscent of *La Basiliade* or Fénelon's Bétique than More's *Utopia* or even the 'Model of Legislation' of the *Code de la Nature*. Here, the product of human labour, which turns out to be the labour of the ploughman, the shepherd, the hunter, or the weaver, is brought to common stores managed by 'bursars' elected by the heads of household. The lure of profit gives way to a 'love of glory

---

1 DDC, p. 107.
2 Ibid., p. 108.
3 Thomas More, *Utopia*, Cambridge: Cambridge University Press, 1989, p. 36.
4 DDC, p. 109.

and consideration',[5] while the value placed on technical or artistic inventions gives way to symbolic rewards for citizens who have displayed the virtues of hard work and familial devotion. There is no trace here of political or administrative organisation: on the contrary, men are freed from 'that burden of useless laws with which all peoples are now burdened'.[6] In short, as Stanhope himself suggests, here we are dealing with 'that much-vaunted chimera of the golden age' rather than with a utopian construct as such.

The function of this passage seems to be, first and foremost, the pure illustration of a political principle. Here, Mably clearly wants to use Stanhope to voice his own conviction that the community of goods is superior to any other form of social organisation, essentially from the standpoint of the moral effects it would have on humankind. It would enable them to 'ennoble themselves' and to find 'happiness'. This does not mean hoping for its realisation, nor dwelling on the details of this patriarchal and agrarian design. Rather, much as in *La Basiliade*, it means denouncing – precisely in the impossibility of living under these laws in the modern world – 'this enormous point of corruption [where] extreme wisdom must seem like extreme folly, as indeed it is'.[7]

Yet, unlike in Morelly's novel, Mably does not only seem to be concerned with bemoaning this situation here. Indeed, there is surely some reason why this appears at this exact point in the text. It clearly plays a role in the development of a programme to reform the French monarchy: otherwise, it would not be found in a text as activist in spirit as *Des droits et des devoirs*. In spite of everything, this text is lacking in political mediations, and it is not easy to see the connection between the ideal that fleetingly emerges and the concrete policy that needs to be instigated. If such mediations do exist, they must be constructed on bases other than the ones explicitly set out in the text.

For one of Mably's leading commentators, Jean-Louis Lecercle, 'Apart from this page [of *Des droits et des devoirs*], there is almost nothing in the whole work on the same subject.'[8] There is no doubt that this is the

---

5 Ibid., p. 112.
6 Ibid.
7 Ibid., p. 113.
8 Jean-Louis Lecercle, 'Utopie et réalisme politique chez Mably', in *Studies on Voltaire and the Eighteenth Century* 23, 1963, pp. 1049–70, at p. 1056.

only passage in which Mably sets out to describe an ideal island society, one that conforms to human nature and is certain to lead to common happiness. If we add that, in this single instance, such a society is also unambiguously presented as an unattainable chimera, we must admit that there are rather slim pickings on the subject of utopia in this author. But it could also be objected that an author's utopianism can hardly be measured by the sole yardstick of how likely he thinks it is that his ideals will be realised. First More, then Morelly himself, expressed considerable doubts, the latter going so far as to consider it 'impossible' for the republic he describes to see the light of day.

Moreover, although Mably was not the author of utopian novels, nor of a model of ideal legislation presented as such, the theme of the community of property appears on numerous occasions in several of his texts, as we shall examine below. In any case, here we will hypothesise that the community of goods, however briefly described in the 1758 text, already played a decisive and unprecedented role in the author's thinking. Indeed, it determined his conception of human nature in general and guided his reading of temporality and historical change. In this sense, the idea of the community of goods already had full-fledged political effects.

Utopia and Natural Rights

A careful reading of the 1758 dialogue reveals a significant use of the vocabulary of natural rights, which, at first sight, seems to set Mably apart from the utopians since Thomas More. Admittedly, Pierre-François Moreau has already pointed out the historical concomitance between the emergence of classical utopia and that of the conception of man as a subject of law. It was this that gave rise to the fundamentally egalitarian legal anthropology upheld by modern jusnaturalist philosophy.[9] More

---

9 Pierre-François Moreau, *Le récit utopique*, Paris: PUF, 1982, Chapter 8. Moreau characterises the 'school of modern natural right' in terms of its way of 'thinking politics under the categories of private law' (pp. 132–3) – that is, through the fundamental thesis that any social and political community rests in the last instance on the original will of the individuals who constitute it, considered as subjects of rights and equal among themselves. Following in his footsteps, by modern jusnaturalist philosophers we will henceforth refer to those whom Michel Villey also describes as 'the builders of modern

himself makes a direct reference in his novel to the 'law of nature' by virtue of which each man has a 'right to such a waste portion of the earth as is necessary for his subsistence'.[10] There is thus a deep kinship between the man of utopian societies and the man conceived by the theorists of natural rights, in the sense that utopia conveys, in an imaginary form, presuppositions identical to those of this school of thought.

However, this does not prevent there being a sharp contrast in the consequences drawn from these presuppositions by classical utopia and jusnaturalist philosophy respectively. Classical utopia relies on the essential equality of men to conclude that fundamentally egalitarian social and political conditions are necessary, even if all hierarchy is not necessarily abolished. Conversely, jusnaturalist philosophy, having got beyond the stage of first principles, reintroduces empirical distinctions of power and wealth, which are considered to be inessential from the point of view of human nature, but are more often than not justified by considerations of an extrinsic nature, which have to do with the necessities inherent in the social order itself and in political association. Ernst Bloch sums up this difference in emphasis by interpreting in terms of complementary and not opposed aspirations. In *Natural Law and Human Dignity*, he writes:

> Social utopias and natural law had mutually complementary concerns within the same human space; they marched separately but, sadly, did not strike together . . . Those differences can be formulated as follows. Social utopian thought directed its efforts toward human happiness, natural law was directed toward human dignity. Social utopias depicted relations in which toil and burden ceased, natural law constructed relations in which *degradation* and *insult* ceased.[11]

Once again, this line of interpretation suggests, through the allusion to one 'same human space', a community of foundational anthropological

---

politics and law: Grotius, Hobbes, Selden, Cumberland, Pufendorf, . . . Locke' (Michel Villey, *Le droit et les droits de l'homme*, Paris: PUF, 2008, p. 131). These are the authors who, according to these two commentators, laid the foundations for thinking about the subjective rights of man present in the revolutionary Declarations, and it is in this guise that we mention them here.

10   Thomas More, *Utopia*, New York: The Columbian Publishing Co., 1891, p. 52.
11   Ernst Bloch, *Natural Law and Human Dignity*, Cambridge, MA: MIT Press, 1986, p. xxix.

principles spanning two different purposes. Even without immediately posing problems of internal coherence, Mably's position thus remains to be clarified further. Moreover, his anthropology, marked by the use of jusnaturalist concepts, is not exclusively legal in nature.

If we follow the line of interpretation proposed by Bruno Bernardi, the distinctive feature of jusnaturalists is to recognise essentially two qualities inherent in the nature of man, which form the basis of his natural rights: 'his right reason, which allows him to recognise his interest, and sociability, which urges him to establish ties with others'.[12] These two qualities are rooted in an exclusive passion, namely the tendency to self-preservation. Man is thus, by nature, a rational, reasonable, sociable being; this is why he is capable of committing himself (and thus of subjecting himself) to obligations by concluding a pact. However, like Rousseau in this sense, Mably (without naming it as such) points out what jusnaturalist thinking overlooks, as he complements the theory of natural rights with a theory of human passions. Contrary to what Diderot, for example, asserts in his famous article 'Droit naturel', man does not reason 'in the silence of the passions'[13] but, rather, under their often harmful influence. The questions that run through Mably's anthropology can therefore be formulated as follows: can the social order help man to tame his passions while also respecting his natural rights? Under what conditions can it enable the full flourishing of man's natural qualities? And what is the place, from this perspective, of the model of the community of goods and labour?

Jusnaturalism and Perfectionism in *Des droits et des devoirs*

From its first pages, the 1758 text draws on the full authority of natural rights, in opposition to all despotisms. The discussion on the nature of man and societies opens with a condemnation of Grotius, Pufendorf, Hobbes, and Wolff, all jusnaturalists accused – in almost the same terms as Rousseau in *The Social Contract* – of having 'stripped the citizen of his

---

12   Bruno Bernardi, 'Rousseau, une autocritique des Lumières', *Esprit* 357, 2009, pp. 109–24, at p. 116.

13   Denis Diderot, 'Droit naturel' in *Œuvres*, Paris: Robert Laffont, 1995, vol. III, pp. 43–7, at p. 47.

legitimate rights' out of self-interest.[14] They are also tellingly mentioned not in terms of their works but their respective situation as jurisconsults in the societies of their times, especially as advisors to the prince. The fundamental reason for this rejection is made explicit later on in the text: Grotius and Pufendorf, in particular, are accused of 'wanting to wait until tyrannical abuses had taken place before rising up against them';[15] thus, they draw criticism for their lukewarm attitude towards respect for man's fundamental rights, faced with the governments that violate them.

As against Grotius and Pufendorf, Stanhope claims the political heritage of Locke, who had, he explains, 'the glory of making known to us the fundamental principles of society'. His allegiance to the Lockean version of jusnaturalism surely poses problems in relation to Mably's adherence to the ideal of the community of goods. As Jean-Fabien Spitz points out, the language of rights, especially from Locke onwards, refers to a 'synthesis' characterising the human individual as a *civil* animal before being a *political* animal. This civil animal is defined by 'all the relations of appropriation and transformation that it maintains with the world of nature and things', hence by relations of exchange and trade, more than by relations of strictly political equality, in the context of each individual's participation in the civic sphere.[16]

Thus, the subject par excellence of theories of natural rights would be the property owner, concerned to secure his possessions, to ensure their protection from outside incursions, or even to expand them by means of legally regulated relations with society as a whole. For the defenders of this model, politics must aim, above all, to establish civil peace and guarantee respect for property ownership. The state would thus be reduced to an instrument for the security of individuals, who would then be free to enter into purely civil alliances and contracts with one another. From this point of view, the idea of freedom in question could

---

14   DDC, p. 17. See Jean-Jacques Rousseau, *The Social Contract and the First and Second Discourses*, edited by Susan Dunn, New Haven, CT: Yale University Press, 2002, p. 172: 'Grotius, having taken refuge in France, discontent with his own country, and wishing to pay court to Louis XIII, to whom his book is dedicated, spares no pains to despoil the people of all their rights.' It is true that the rights of the people are not the same as the rights of the citizen.

15   DDC, p. 82.

16   Jean-Fabien Spitz, 'Droit et vertu chez Mably', *Corpus* 14–15, 1990, pp. 61–95, at p. 62.

only be – to use the expression made famous by Isaiah Berlin – a negative liberty.[17] Such a freedom, unlike a republican or *positive* freedom, would not imply any need for participation in the making of the law and the direction of public affairs. Rather, it would be reduced to the possibility of conducting one's personal affairs under the protection of the common rule, free from arbitrary interventions. This aspiration – which some of the most eminent theorists of modern natural rights have asserted as a prerogative common to the whole of humanity – would thus also form the basis of a universalism opposed to the narrowness of ancient cities and their internal solidarity acquired at the price of slavery, the prejudices of civic religion, and a crude and coarse life lacking in material comforts or enriching exchanges with foreigners. But how could an advocate of the community of goods sign up to such a description of man's natural aspirations and the purpose of societies, without falling into contradiction?

In *Des droits et des devoirs*, the state of nature is never really described, nor presented as an ideal state. The first reference is to the 'first moments of the birth of the human race', when men had not yet developed their rational capacities, but obeyed the impulses of their senses. Stanhope dismisses such a period in human history out of hand, saying: 'What does this situation matter to us, when it is not our own one, and may never have existed.'[18] This is reminiscent of Rousseau's *Second Discourse* on the state of nature ('which, if ever it did, does not now . . . exist'), but there also seems to be a considerable difference, in Mably, and possibly even an implicit criticism. Indeed, according to Rousseau, we apparently do not need 'to have just notions of this earlier state in order to judge properly of our present state'.[19]

Much more important, however, is the emergence – in what appears to be a second stage of the state of nature – of the ability to 'reflect, compare and reason', which gives rise to a 'moral instinct that honours our nature'.[20] The immediate connection established between the appearance of reason and the first notions of good and evil is an explicitly Ciceronian heritage. In the foreword to the dialogue, we find a

---

17   Isaiah Berlin, *Two Concepts of Liberty*, Oxford: Clarendon Press, 1958.
18   DDC, p. 12.
19   Rousseau, *The Social Contract*, p. 82.
20   DDC, p. 13.

passage from the Roman philosopher's *De republica*, which reads in part: 'There is indeed a law, right reason, which is in accordance with nature; existing in all, unchangeable, eternal. Commanding us to do what is right, forbidding us to do what is wrong.'[21] In accordance with Stoic doctrine, nature, as expressed in human beings through the fact of reason, has thereby imbued us with a principle of justice. These premises of morality form the basis of the claim to a natural right for man: it is these premises that justify this claim. It should be noted, however, that the expression 'moral instinct' is ambiguous. For Mably has reason, which is the bearer of this 'instinct', arising from the 'experience' of the first men gradually emerging from their primitive torpor. Whatever its origin, whether innate or acquired, reason is considered the undisputed source of all human dignity, 'our most essential and noble attribute'.[22] To this first attribute, Stanhope adds its natural corollary, freedom, which is none other than the faculty of 'making use of our reason'. These two fundamental characteristics of man's nature are spontaneously directed towards the search for appropriate means of ensuring his happiness: 'the reason with which nature has endowed us, the freedom in which she has created us, and that invincible desire for happiness which she has placed in our soul, are three titles which every man may assert against the unjust government under which he lives'.[23]

This seems to be the threefold foundation of natural rights in Mably's text, a foundation which is found in the essence of man himself. Man, occupied with ensuring his own happiness, must therefore find a society ready to aid him in this endeavour: 'the citizen has the right to demand that society should render his situation more advantageous'. Even so, his moral instinct forbids him to do this at any price, and society must, here again, assist him: laws are 'made to help reason and support our freedom' in their fight against the passions.[24] The latter are part of man but risk leading him astray from his duty.

For Mably, we can deduce two consequences from this conception of the nature of man and the social bond. The first is that, even if 'the idea of good and evil necessarily preceded the establishment of society'

---

21   Translation (by George William Featherstonhaugh) here taken from *The Republic of Cicero*, New York: G&C Carvill, 1829, p. 29.
22   *DDC*, p. 21.
23   Ibid., p. 27.
24   Ibid., p. 14.

– indeed, without it the very idea of bringing society into being could not have emerged – society plays a supporting role in man's march towards virtue. His quest in this direction consists of his living up to his own nature as a rational being, by ensuring that his behaviour conforms to the rules prescribed by the faculty of reason. In this sense, 'far from degrading our nature, the establishment of society has instead perfected it'.[25] A second consequence, then, is that, contrary to Lockean anthropology, in which man in the state of nature is already equipped with his characteristics and (most importantly) his essential rights, Mably sees the pre-civil state as a prehistory of humanity itself. This is rather like Rousseau in his praise of the civil state in *The Social Contract*, which made 'a stupid, limited animal into an intelligent being and a man'.[26] A legitimate system of legislation must not only guarantee the exercise of prerogatives derived from natural qualities but also mould and improve these natural qualities themselves. It was thus necessary and beneficial to emerge from the state of nature, in the manner of the Iroquois; Mably asserts the latter's right to 'repair their foolishness and civilise themselves, when they begin to be ashamed of their barbarity'.[27] Here, Mably clearly describes natural man as a being who is essentially *in the making*, and who in the state of nature has not yet realised his full possibilities.

The 'barbarity' attributed to men in the state of nature is probably the reason why, in the dialogue, Mably does not really envisage a social contract. Instead, Stanhope speaks of a kind of perfecting, over time, of institutions that are initially imperfect but capable of improvement:

> I agree that the laws, treaties or agreements that men make when they come together in society, are in general the rules of their rights and duties, and the citizen must obey them, as long as he knows nothing wiser; but once his reason has enlightened and perfected him, is it condemned to sacrifice itself to error?[28]

This clearly points to the possibility that the first social contract will lapse and that men will be driven to rewrite it. This is not because the

---

25 Ibid.
26 Rousseau, *The Social Contract*, p. 167.
27 *DDC*, p. 24.
28 Ibid., p. 14.

rulers have badly fulfilled their mission or usurped the rights of the community. Rather, it is simply because, when the contract is first concluded, men are not fully aware of their rational and free nature and of the common laws which are best suited to the flourishing of this nature within society.

In a later work, entitled *De l'étude de l'histoire* (*On the Study of History*), Mably did away with the idea of a social pact altogether. As he put it,

> It would be too absurd to think that men who did not yet have a clear and precise idea of the good they were seeking by coming together, and who were governed by brutal passions, should have suddenly moved from the greatest independence to the most complete submission. Can it be believed that in these nascent societies there were contracts or agreements between citizens and magistrates? Surely not.[29]

Still, it has to be said that, when *Des droits et des devoirs* sets out the possibility of a gradual perfection of the original contract, this departs from the classical jusnaturalist schema. Indeed, the latter holds that the contracting subjects are in full possession of their means at the time when the pact is made. The temporality of progressive civilisation is not that of a social pact concluded on just one occasion. Mably thus leaves the people the possibility of amending the nation's fundamental laws at will, the better to improve them: 'The people, in whom sovereign power originally resides . . . is thus forever entitled to interpret its contract, or rather its gifts, to modify its clauses, to annul them, and to establish a new order of things.'[30]

So, analysing this dialogue more closely, we find an ambiguity as to the exact purpose that Mably assigns to human society. On the one hand, society has the task of perfecting man, of assisting his 'unsteady reason' by helping him to be master of himself.[31] But, at the same time, Mably follows in line with the jusnaturalist theories, particularly those of Locke, in admitting that the true end of civil association is to

---

29 *EH*, p. 49.
30 *DDC*, p. 76.
31 Ibid., p. 23.

guarantee the natural rights of the individual. Stanhope even closely echoes Locke's terms in asserting during the second discussion that 'the essential purpose of society' consists in 'preserving [citizens'] life, liberty, rest and property'.[32] And yet, while, in the one case, the aim is to ensure that man is virtuous, in the other, society must ensure that man is free to pursue his happiness as he sees fit, within the limits of the rule of reciprocity, by protecting him against any violation of his natural rights. In the first case, men do not come together in society solely in order to better protect their private independence. Since freedom is conceived as man's mastery of his own passions, it becomes a political construct in which the role of legislators and magistrates is crucial. Man is free *through* the laws, not only in the sense that the laws limit external interference with his capacity to act, but also in the sense that they combine to give his actions a particular moral quality that natural man cannot achieve on his own.

While the second objective places Mably, in Spitz's words, in line with the 'liberal-juridical inspiration',[33] the first aligns him more with what John Pocock, following the historian Hans Baron, has called 'civic humanism'. This current of thought, born in the Italian cities of the Renaissance, belongs to *humanism* insofar as it is in 'direct conversation with the ancients', and owes its civic characteristic to the fact that the 'conversation with the ancients which results in knowledge is affiliated with the conversation among citizens which results in decision and law'.[34]

The civic humanists looked to antiquity for the intellectual resources they needed to think and act as citizens in their own present. One of the major sources of reading for these intellectuals was, of course, the *Politics*: the 'tradition in question may be referred back to Aristotle in nearly every respect'.[35] The moral perfectionism elaborated by Mably does seem to have been partly inherited from Aristotle's famous text. Aristotle postulates that the purpose of political association is not mere survival; otherwise, there would be nothing to distinguish human societies from animal ones. The purpose of establishing a city

---

32 Ibid., p. 74.
33 Spitz, 'Droit et vertu chez Mably', p. 71.
34 J. G. A. Pocock, *The Machiavellian Moment: Florentine Political Thought and the Atlantic Republican Tradition*, Princeton, NJ: Princeton University Press, 1975, p. 62.
35 Ibid., p. 67.

is not reciprocal non-aggression, nor attacking common enemies, nor trade, but 'living well'. Alliances and agreements do not make a city in the strict sense, but only an association with a view to a natural end, which is to 'make the citizens virtuous and just'.[36] Political society is defined by its ability to procure happiness for its citizens, and this happiness is nothing other than the practice of virtue. For Aristotle, 'the political fellowship must therefore be deemed to exist for the sake of noble actions, not merely for living in common'.[37] Here, there is no distinction between political virtue and moral virtue. When Aristotle argues that 'any state that is truly so called and is not a state merely in name must pay attention to virtue', he means this in the sense that the human essence is fully realised only in the context of a city that sets itself the goal of moral excellence, which is its natural destination.[38] Mably is clearly working within an Aristotelian framework when he identifies, as the goal of the best constitution, the practice of virtue, trying to combine the means to ensure that the greatest possible number of citizens share in the latter.

To some degree, the perspectives of modern jusnaturalism and civic humanism converge, and impose identical requirements. They require men to maintain as much of their own dignity as possible through a vigilant attitude towards public authority. For magistrates, who must be subjected to the common rule, are always liable to abuse their prerogatives because of the power granted them. The debasement of citizens by the magistrates' abuse of power obviously undermines their freedom and, from a jusnaturalist perspective, it must therefore be combated. But in reducing citizens below the level of their legitimate prerogatives, it also makes them unfit for virtue, since the latter depends on the free use of one's reason. Despotism thus threatens not only citizens' freedom but also their virtue; in order to harden its own power it encourages the rule of vile passions: 'fear, laziness, avarice, prodigality, the love of dignities and luxury'.[39] It is necessary to combat these passions by trying to 'make even the last of men understand their dignity' through the study of natural rights, and to assert the right of resistance against tyrants. These

---

36   Aristotle, *Politics*, Cambridge, MA: Harvard University Press, Loeb Classical Library, 1932, p. 215.
37   Ibid., p. 219.
38   Ibid., p. 215.
39   *DDC*, p. 41.

offer so many ways of upholding both natural rights, from a Lockean perspective, and the virtue of citizens, from a republican perspective:

> A virtuous citizen can justly wage civil war, for there may be tyrants, that is, magistrates who claim to exercise an authority that can and must belong only to the laws and are at the same time strong enough to oppress their subjects.[40]

So, if the two objectives of virtue and freedom are to be met, this requires that the people must make laws for itself, through a system of national representation that includes all the orders of the kingdom. Political participation is at once the guarantee of liberty, of respect for individual rights, and the virtue forged therein. Thus, from the twin perspective of man's essential commitment to freedom and to virtue, Mably can defend the value of citizens' exercise of legislative power by way of their representatives. Similarly, both objectives imply that all citizens should be enlightened: 'They want the people to be ignorant; but please note that this fantasy only exists in countries where freedom is something to be feared.'[41] In Mably's view, knowledge, like political rights, is necessary for freedom and virtue. Indeed, if freedom is nothing other than the power to make use of one's reason, then an enlightened reason will necessarily make one freer. Moreover, given that virtue is nothing but our preference for the counsel of our reason over that of the passions, then making reason more enlightened will strengthen it in its efforts to direct the passions towards morally acceptable purposes. The jusnaturalist perspective is thus combined with the 'humanist' perspective to promote a lofty conception of human dignity. It implies the need for rights to be extended throughout society, in the face of governments liable to threaten them.

The Question of Property Rights

But there is one point on which it is difficult for the two perspectives to agree: the question of property rights, which is crucial to Mably's anthropological theology. As we know, in Locke, the right to property applies

---

40   Ibid., p. 69.
41   Ibid., p. 56.

Des droits et des devoirs du citoyen: Utopia in Service of the Revolution 111

even in the state of nature. Labour gives the individual a right of ownership over the land, which was initially given to mankind in common by God:

> Though the things of nature are given in common . . . man, by being master of himself, and proprietor of his own person, and the actions or labour of it, had still in himself the great foundation of property . . . Thus labour, in the beginning, gave a right of property, wherever any one was pleased to employ it upon what was common.[42]

In other words, the right to property is a natural corollary of the right to one's own life and liberty. The latter itself drives man, through the law of nature which requires him to look after his self-preservation, to transform a part of nature for his own use, making it his own by the value which he thereby adds to it. It is on these theoretical grounds that C. B. Macpherson can speak of Locke's thinking as 'possessive individualism', implying a 'conception of the individual as essentially the proprietor of his own person or capacities, owing nothing to society for them'.[43] Each individual thus owns his property in the same way as he owns himself and his freedom of action – and all this prior to his entering into any political association. Along with the security of men's lives, the untroubled enjoyment of the right to property is thus one of the main reasons for the transition to civil society. Locke describes this as consisting of 'agreeing with other men to join and unite into a community for their comfortable, safe, and peaceable living one amongst another, in a secure enjoyment of their properties, and a greater security against any, that are not of it'.[44]

Thus, according to Locke, the right to property, as the fundamental purpose of the social pact, can only be enshrined by this compact and protected with all the power of the public force. But how could Mably subscribe to such a conception of natural rights, if his own pursuit of social virtue led him to long for a community of goods? The ideal island society is presented as one governed by the legislation that would allow

---

[42] Locke, *Second Treatise of Government*, Oxford: Oxford University Press, 2016, Chapter 5, sections 44–5.
[43] C. B. Macpherson, *The Political Theory of Possessive Individualism, Hobbes to Locke*, Oxford: Oxford University Press, 1990, p. 3.
[44] Locke, *Second Treatise of Government*, Chapter 8, section 95.

the human race to 'ennoble itself'.[45] It is not presented as a lost past which is now to be lamented, but, rather, as a prospect for the future. However fanciful it may be, if realised, it would make it possible to cast off 'the prejudices and passions of Europe'. It thus appears as the means of total moral regeneration. This, moreover, sheds light on the link between anthropology and utopia in Mably's thinking. For the utopian ideal of the community of goods here appears as the means of maximising the human race's capacity for moral perfection, and, in this sense, as the highest goal of human societies, even if it is bound to remain unattainable. The community of goods thus appears as man's moral destination: 'Does not [your heart] tell you that this is the happiness for which men were made?'[46]

Mably's perfectionist anthropology tends towards this mode of organisation as its ultimate goal. Even if this ideal cannot be achieved, the best government will be the one that comes closest to it by promoting the virtue of its citizens as far as possible, through a policy that equalises rights and conditions. Mably's conception of the social bond as a force for virtue leads him to present the community of goods as the highest form of organisation to which men could aspire. Mably's presentation of the community of goods as the best of constitutions distinguishes him from other civic humanists. In particular, it separates his thought from that of Aristotle, who vigorously criticises the principle of the community of goods as defended by Socrates in *The Republic*.

Through its brief utopian passage, the text thus expresses the predominance of the ideal of virtue over the ideal of freedom in Mably's thinking. He does not specify the reasons for the privileged link between human virtue and the community of goods. But it is possible to advance a hypothesis in this regard: the community, prohibiting by nature all enrichment, and granting rewards only to 'the ploughman whose fields would be the most fertile, to the shepherd whose flock would be the healthiest and the most fecund; to the most skilful hunter', would cut out at the root the vices that Mably deplores and that foster despotism. This would instead encourage the development of 'courage of spirit', 'modesty of manners', 'a taste for frugality and hard work', and 'love of the public good' which he elsewhere describes as the virtues that society must

---

45 *DDC*, p. 112.
46 Ibid., p. 113.

nurture in man.[47] The community of goods is thus the means of achieving a perfectly virtuous and thus perfectly happy life – the only life truly equal to man's moral potential. Even if the corruption of the human heart makes this ideal state unattainable, it remains the yardstick by which any legitimate government must be judged.

But, given these premises, there is a clear discrepancy. On the one hand, we have a conception of man as the eminent bearer of natural rights – including the right to property as the logical consequence of his possession of himself and his faculties – who seeks to guarantee these rights through the establishment of the civil state. Then there is a conception of man as naturally devoted to a process of perfection that could lead him – if only his corruption did not prevent it – beyond societies based on property and towards a state of community that would be the most favourable to the exercise of individual and collective virtues. How does Mably resolve this difficulty?

In general, in the text, the author emphasises the natural rights to life and liberty rather than the right to property. In the second interview, for example, Stanhope states that there are undoubtedly 'some rights which one is not in a position to abandon, for example, those which belong so much to the essence of man and society that it is impossible to part with them seriously'.[48] Among these inalienable rights, he cites 'self-preservation'. This justifies both self-defence in the face of a robber, and stealing food when one is starving, seeing as man entered into society 'only to secure his days against violence and want'. Man would thus have the right and even the duty to steal in cases of vital necessity, just as he has the inalienable right to defend his life against some aggressor. Yet this assertion does not sit well with the statement, which comes only a few lines further on, that men join in association in order to preserve their lives, their freedom, their rest, but also their property.

Overall, Mably tends to separate property rights from the rights to life and liberty. A few pages later on, the discussion turns to the statute of limitations on the property rights that an individual may assert over an asset, a house, or an estate which he had neglected to claim over many years. The narrator then uses Stanhope's lessons to argue that the

---

47 Ibid., pp. 41–2.
48 Ibid., pp. 72–3.

law can deny this individual the exercise of this right if the property in question is used by others to satisfy their needs. But what can justify this? The fact that 'in matters of civil property, the laws of nature are silent, and . . . everything depends on the agreements that citizens have made among themselves'.[49] This statement therefore tends to support the thesis that property, unlike life and liberty, is not a natural right but only a civil right.

Another statement, a few lines later, corroborates this idea: 'You have taught me, my lord, that I do not possess my dignity as a man and my freedom in the same way as my house.' Given these premises, Mably's doctrine would appear to be the following: human dignity and freedom are inalienable natural rights that could possibly justify the public authorities interfering with the ownership of property, or legitimising such interference, in the case of vital necessity. The right to property would not, therefore, be a natural right, but a right that the public authorities regulate according to the circumstances, and with due respect for the inalienable rights to life and liberty of each individual. Thus, rather than promoting the community of goods, Stanhope examined the advisability of enacting agrarian laws, limiting the right to own land, or sumptuary laws, limiting access to luxury goods, in the context of the monarchical France of the time. The question posed has nothing to do with the *legitimacy* of such measures, which is not in question, but rather their *chances of success*, depending on the state of morals and the progress of their corruption or else their regeneration.

But then we still have to understand what Jean-Louis Lecercle considers an inconsistency on Mably's part. The commentator notes this when Stanhope says:

> I know . . . that the first societies were able to establish [private property] with justice; it is even found fully established in the state of nature: for no one can deny that man then had the right to consider as his own property the hut that he had built and the fruit of the tree that he had cultivated.[50]

---

49   Ibid., p. 86.
50   Ibid., p. 108.

Is Mably contradicting what he said elsewhere about the right to property, as a literal reading would suggest?[51] Based on the text just cited, we can propose here the following interpretation, which helps overcome the difficulty raised: in the perfectionist view of human nature elaborated by Mably, the prevalent relations in the state of nature are not the same ones to which man can legitimately lay claim in view of his essential potential. This poses the need to distinguish between the law of the state of nature and natural law properly speaking. While the right to property may be considered a natural right, in the sense that it corresponds to what might have been legitimate in the state of nature, it is not a natural right in the sense of a right indexed to an intangible human nature. Rather, in its quest for virtue, a human nature seeking perfection could abandon the right to property, to better rise to the level of a community. Given this distinction, in matters of material property, civil laws are not necessarily an extension of the legitimate customs of the state of nature. If the primitive state did allow property ownership to be considered a right, this owed to the 'the barbarity of mores', to 'the right that each person claimed to exercise over everything, and the lack of experience to foresee the countless disadvantages that would result from this division'.[52]

Hence Mably tolerates the idea of property rights only with regard to a primitive state, which will fortunately be surpassed by the establishment of the civil state. The right of the first occupant, or the right gained over one's house or one's fruit tree in the state of nature thanks to one's labour, cannot serve as a model for civil society. The latter is, therefore, quite free to legislate on property. As Abdallaziz Labib notes:

> For Mably . . . the idea of the natural moral law does not refer to a state of pure nature, but rather to a 'nature' immanent in the first truly civil societies, which were thus already developed or at least existed in embryo.[53]

---

51 In a note, Lecercle comments on this passage: 'It is hard to see how Mably can reconcile his dream of a communist society with such premises' (*DDC*, p. 108). The thesis that Mably contradicts himself on the natural right to property in *Des droits et des devoirs du citoyen* is also supported by Wolfgang Asholt: 'Mably et le travail', in *Colloque Mably, la politique comme science morale*, Bari: Palomar, 1995–7, vol. I, pp. 189–203.
52 *DDC*, p. 108.
53 Abdelaziz Labib, *La critique utopiste de la société civile au XVIIIe siècle en France: les cas de Mably et Morelly*, edited by Olivier Bloch, Paris: Université de Paris I, 1983, p. 44.

Seen in this light, Mably's text seems to make a considerable revision of Lockean jusnaturalism. It already contains the seed of all of the major themes of Mably's anthropology. Quite evidently, the fundamental aim of political association has shifted from the peace, security, and freedom of men to the development of their moral qualities. From this perspective, however, certain fundamental rights must be respected, which are themselves a prerequisite for man's moral development. They concern the life, liberty, and dignity of individuals, which are bound up with a whole series of political rights, but not a right to property. The latter is a legitimate right in the state of nature, but in the civil state it must be subject to the imperatives of the public good and individual prerogatives. Natural law understood in this way looks rather like the statement of the laws of human nature that we find early on in *The Social Contract*:[54]

> This common liberty is a consequence of man's nature. His first law is to attend to his own survival, his first concerns are those he owes to himself; and as soon as he reaches the age of rationality, being sole judge of how to survive, he becomes his own master.[55]

Similarly to Mably, Rousseau postulates that a fundamental law of all living beings is to attend to their own self-preservation, since their first good is life itself. Another law holds that man's gift of reason allows him to judge what will indeed enable his self-preservation: this is Rousseau's concept of freedom, moreover explaining that it is inalienable. *The Social Contract* sticks by Rousseau's refusal, already expressed in the *Second Discourse*, to see property as a natural right, 'the right of property being

---

54 The question of natural right and natural law in Rousseau is a subject of dispute among scholars and has given rise to the most varied assessments. Robert Derathé, for example, considers that Rousseau 'did not renounce natural right', but that 'all Rousseau's efforts are directed towards finding a political system that conforms to the ideal of natural right' (*Jean-Jacques Rousseau et la science politique de son temps*, Paris: Vrin, 1988, p. 168). Conversely, for Yves Vargas, 'it is a mistake to attribute to Rousseau a position favourable to natural right; a careful reading of the texts explains the complex but radical form of the author's refusal to make the slightest concession to this concept' ('Rousseau et le droit naturel', *TransFormAção* 31: 1, 2008, pp. 25–52, at p. 25). See also André Charrak, 'Du Droit naturel au Droit naturel raisonné', in *Cahiers philosophiques de Strasbourg* 13, 2002, 107–18.

55 Rousseau, *The Social Contract*, p. 151.

of mere human convention and institution'.[56] He adds, however, that 'every man has by nature a right to all that he needs', thus also following Mably's fundamental thinking.[57] The two men are, ultimately, in agreement on the need to guarantee private property in the civil state, since Mably considered that the state of community of goods definitively belonged to humanity's past. Of course, the fact remains that, for Mably, the community of goods remained a horizon, whereas it was not one for Rousseau.

For Mably, the rights to life and, above all, to liberty are linked to man's possibility of moral perfection. To a certain degree, his natural right encompasses a right to perfection. This objective attributed to the passage to the civil state can be compared with Rousseau's theses in *The Social Contract*, which, in Chapter 8 of Book I, stresses the remarkable moral change produced in man by his entry into political society. Rousseau observes the transformation more than he considers it a 'right'; nevertheless, he makes this moment the true birth of 'morality' in man and of the ability he gains to 'consult his reason before listening to his inclinations'.[58] If (as in the *Second Discourse*) the entry into society is considered degrading when it does not take the form of a legitimate contract, here it produces a positive change in man. As in Mably, the establishment of a political authority is the only way to offer the individual the possibility of fully developing his moral capacities, through his 'obedience to a self-prescribed law'.[59] Rousseau rooted the birth of all human morality in this foundational moment. Mably, conversely, saw it only as an opportunity to lead man into a further stage of development.[60]

So, while the public authority must scrupulously respect fundamental rights, it may have cause to impose limits on property. For it must also concern itself with the imperatives of each person's right to life and the possibilities opened up by the general state of public morals. It

---

56 Ibid., p. 130.
57 Ibid., p. 167.
58 Ibid., p. 166.
59 Ibid., p. 137.
60 Rousseau does not always remain faithful to this thesis: in the *Second Discourse*, in particular, the premises of morality are perceptible in man as early as the second state of nature, even if, as Bruno Bernardi explains, they 'must be understood in terms of love, not obligation' (*Le principe d'obligation*, Paris: Vrin, 2007, p. 288).

should not seek to browbeat depraved habits but should wait for a favourable moment to promote useful reforms. Property thus becomes a purely civil right, an institutional fact. If one of the aims of a society is to preserve individuals' property, this is true only in the context of a state of corruption in which the possibilities for the improvement of the human race have been cut short. Mably does not specify how the protection of individuals' property in the least corrupt societies can be reconciled with the right to life, which may legitimise theft in extreme circumstances. But, in any case, if Mably's conceptions still express a methodological individualism, in which the civil order must uphold the natural rights of the individual, they cannot fall under the category of a possessive individualism. Rather, we might go so far as to speak of a perfectionist individualism.

Past, Present, and Future in *Des droits et des devoirs*

Unlike in Morelly and in the works of most utopians before him, in Mably's work, history is both a major and recurring concern. Indeed, if political calamities keep happening, it appears that he exclusively attributes this to ignorance of the past: 'It is because, through indifference, laziness or presumption, we disdain to profit from the experience of past centuries, that each century brings back the spectacle of the same errors and the same calamities.'[61] If the centuries resemble one another, as the same evils return time and again, this is because human nature is immutable: 'the same laws, the same passions, the same morals, the same virtues, the same vices have constantly produced the same effects'.[62] It would seem, then, that Mably unreservedly subscribes to a vision of history that was already beginning to be called into question at the time he took up his pen: that of the *historia magistra vitae*. This means seeing history as the site of the realisation (and variation) of immutable anthropological principles, which the observer must seek out for essentially practical purposes. In a later work, Mably himself spelled out these principles: they are, on the one hand, 'natural right' – in other words, 'the origin of public power in society', 'man's duties as a citizen and

---

61   *EH*, p. 14.
62   *EH*, p. 20.

magistrate', 'the duties of nations towards one another'[63] – but they are, on the other, 'the laws that nature has established to procure men the happiness of which it makes them capable'.[64] The secrets of a policy that conforms to these laws are said to be contained in 'the follies of Plato, Thomas Morus' and a few other 'dreamers',[65] authors of legislative plans that were never implemented, and surely could never be implemented, despite their 'natural' character. Utopia and natural rights are thus identified as the two sources of the principles that ought to inform the reading and use of history.

Yet even though Mably did set out these general positions, *Des droits et des devoirs* has generally itself been considered representative of a deep change in the regime of collective historicity. This was the change that crystallised around the concept of revolution and its successive uses between 1688 and 1789, from one political upheaval to the next. As Hannah Arendt observed, the word revolution – originally an astronomical term – was used at the beginning of this temporal sequence 'as a metaphor, carrying over the notion of an eternal, irresistible, ever-recurring motion to the haphazard movements, the ups and downs of human destiny'.[66]

According to Arendt, the word was first used in connection with human affairs in 1660, at the time of the Stuart Restoration in England. She explains that the term entered general use in the context of that country's political upheavals, with reference to the natural cycles that political regimes go through. Like the course of the stars, this circular evolution of human time was initially considered independent of human will, even if it surely did influence human existence. The events in England marked the first time that individuals sought to influence the course of the cycle through their own actions, by promoting the return of institutions that might have seemed to have been surpassed. In this context, a new 'revolution' had the meaning of a renovation, or even a restoration, with both the English revolutionaries and their conservative opponents seeing their struggle as nothing more than the reclaiming of *older* rights that needed to be restored to their primitive legitimacy. The

---

63   *MEH*, p. 376.
64   Ibid., p. 379.
65   Ibid.
66   Hannah Arendt, *On Revolution*, London: Penguin Books, 1990, p. 42.

concept thus oscillated between the idea of choosing to return to (and restore) a former regime, and that of the irresistible recurrence of the eternal vicissitudes of human history. Not until the eighteenth century did a sense of historical *novelty* gradually emerge, expressed in a new sense of revolution as an active process of introducing a new freedom. The idea of civil war gradually faded, while, according to Reinhard Koselleck, 'the concept of revolution was stripped of its political rigor, and it was possible for all those utopian hopes that make intelligible the elan of the years after 1789 to stream into it'.[67]

This transition from the old to the new meaning of the term revolution, including its utopian dimension, was already at work in Mably's text. It is precisely at the point of transition between these two senses, which still coexist within it: indeed, 'in *Des droits et des devoirs*, the term "revolution" seems to enjoy several meanings'.[68] In some cases, it retains its former meaning of a chain of events beyond human control – for instance, when the author recalls the essential lessons of French history: 'Too ignorant to fear or foresee anything, [our fathers] allowed themselves to be pushed by events from revolution to revolution.'[69] Here, the idea of revolution refers to the uncontrolled chain of events in French history, caused by men's inability to take control of their own destiny. Mably's perspective, which Keith Baker terms a 'specifically political mode of thinking', includes a harsh criticism of the protagonists of the time. As we have seen, the angle of attack adopted by the author is that of a reform programme: this leads him to a representation of social relationships that necessarily values voluntary action and participation in a chosen change in the course of things. Through this prism, social life appears to be, if not entirely contingent, at least always leaving room for human intervention to build a common destiny. If we abandon ourselves to the impetuous course of history's 'revolutions' without consciously trying to influence their course, if we allow ourselves to be led by our passions without trying to curb them through the action of reason, then,

---

[67] Reinhard Koselleck, *Futures Past: On the Semantics of Historical Time*, New York: Columbia University Press, 2004, p. 49.

[68] Keith M. Baker, 'A Script for a French Revolution: The Political Consciousness of the Abbé Mably', in *Inventing the French Revolution: Essays on French Political Culture in the Eighteenth Century*, Cambridge: Cambridge University Press, 1990, pp. 86–106, at p. 95.

[69] *DDC*, p. 122.

through the passivity of which we are guilty, we are making history the site of a collective wandering that leads from feudal anarchy to absolutist despotism, without the nation ever attempting to regain control of its future by establishing ad hoc political institutions.

However, the course of revolutions is not inevitable. As Stanhope says of England and the changes that need to be made to its constitution: 'If we neglect these indispensable reforms, we shall never have anything but fruitless revolutions.'[70] The text thus points to the possibility of distinguishing between those revolutions that will bring men nothing good, and those others that may have happy effects. A revolution thus appears as a period of agitation, of disorder, which can give rise to various results depending on the will of its protagonists. In this respect, Mably's comments seem to follow in line with the meaning given to the term by the leading figures in the English Revolution, for whom it did not mean undergoing the '*fact* of the revolution, in the passive sense', but 'an *act* of revolution in the active modern sense'.[71] Here, revolution can still be interpreted as a vigorous reassertion of the rights that were once enjoyed. This is no longer the case a little further on in the text, where it is clearly a matter of 'establishing a new order of things'.[72] Mably thus had to present his own programme, which was to take the form of a 'managed revolution', bringing political order hitherto unknown in Ancien Régime France.[73] But what form should this 'managed revolution' take? And in what sense was utopia an integral part of this political innovation?

A Revolutionary Scenario

The broad outlines of Mably's proposals express a desire for a historic *coup de force* through which the French nation will regain control of 'its' time. This is to be achieved via the establishment of institutions and rules capable of replacing the uncontrolled flow of events. Seeing as this lack of control is a breeding ground for despotism, it must be replaced

---

70   Ibid., p. 47.
71   Baker, *Inventing the French Revolution*, p. 58.
72   *DDC*, p. 76.
73   Ibid., p. 161.

with a regular order governed by laws that respect fundamental rights. The 'march' of despotism is characterised by a series of invasive infringements of citizens' rights. It proceeds step by step; and this slow, unconscious progress needs to be countered by decisive and deliberate action, which institutes a new order of things, in the temporal sense of the term. Political liberty will arrive in the form of the nation imposing control over its own rhythm, in a new regularity that will bring stability and freedom. But this objective must be achieved in stages.

The first stage of this historical rupture must consist of a period of social and political 'ferment', in which men will become increasingly angered by despotism and discontent will build. According to Stanhope, this period had already begun with the confrontation between the French monarchy and the parlements over the *billets de confession*. At this decisive moment, the most advanced citizens would be wise not to give their demands the form of an overly innovative programme, but rather to call for a return to ancient national principles that had gradually fallen into disuse. They could do this by calling for the reactivation of the old practice of the Estates-General.

This defence of a 'return to principles', already presented by Machiavelli as a means of regenerating a republic in the grip of a process of corruption,[74] would seem to conform to the 'English' conception of revolution. But, as J. K. Wright points out, 'The defense of the "ancient constitution" is essentially used as a *lever* to overturn absolutism.'[75] The return to older principles was here taken up in a purely tactical key: the past served as a momentary reference point, in the more fundamental cause of inventing a new and different future. The demand to convene the Estates-General – according to an ancient privilege, a prerogative belonging to the parlements – was merely a prelude to the final stage in the process of the 'managed revolution'. It, in fact, meant giving the Estates a form and a permanence that they had never had in the past,

---

74 'Men who live together in any order whatever often examine themselves either through these extrinsic accidents or through intrinsic ones': Niccolò Machiavelli, *Discourses on Livy*, translated by Harvey C. Mansfield and Nathan Tarcov, Chicago: University of Chicago Press, 1996, p. 210. In the same chapter, Machiavelli explicitly cites the example of the French monarchy and the role of the Parisian parlement, the guardian of the institutions and the laws against the nobles' ambitions.

75 J. K. Wright, *A Classical Republican in Eighteenth-Century France: The Political Thought of Mably*, Stanford, CA: Stanford University Press, 1997, p. 137.

Des droits et des devoirs du citoyen: Utopia in Service of the Revolution

transforming them into a regular assembly of the nation invested with sovereign power:

> Thus the Estates must not separate without having published a fundamental law, a pragmatic sanction, by which it will be ordered that every two or three years, the Representatives of the nation, entrusted with its powers, will be assembled, without any reason being able to impede this.[76]

Eventually, the assembly would have legislative power, control of finances and the right to declare war. But again, this situation would not be an immediate creation but must be preceded by a transition period that would involve an awakening of political consciousness. In the interval between the convening of the Estates and their transformation into a regular, sovereign assembly, Mably foresaw a period of general ferment during which pamphlets would circulate and everyone would want to learn about the principles of politics, the errors of the past, and the prospects for the future. During this same interval, history could serve as a mine of useful information and become the school of citizenship that it ought to be. During this transitional period, any measures taken must be provisional, because such a corrupted French people could only return to freedom and equality *gradually* and must not tie their hands by rushing into hasty decisions. Only in a later phase, with the definitive establishment of a regular system of national representation, would it finally be possible to pass laws to promote equality and to rein in corruption.

In this programmatic outline, we can see Mably making a conscious shift away from recalling the practices of the past and towards the establishment of new ones. No longer did he emphasise the force of example of the earlier history of the French monarchy. This history is covered in a few lines, which hardly idealise it:

> Our fathers, as you know, brought back from Germania the freest government that men could have; but as soon as they were established in Gaul, corrupted by their fortune and Roman customs, they lost their ancient genius . . . they forgot their ancient laws, which were no

---

76 *DDC*, p. 175.

longer sufficient for them, and, knowing no other police than that of the fiefdoms, they became the most ruthless tyrants or the basest slaves.[77]

Mably here summed up in a few lines the essential lessons of the *Observations sur l'histoire de France*, which he wrote in parallel to *Des droits et des devoirs*. In this first text – which, unlike the firebrand *Des droits et des devoirs*, was published during his lifetime, meeting with some success – Mably joined in the historical-political quarrel over the origins of the French monarchy. In it, he presented an idealised and indeed democratic version of its early history, from the Frankish conquest to the rule of Charlemagne. For him, in its original moments, 'the nation, always free and forming a true republic, of which the prince was only the first magistrate, ruled as a body over the various peoples who inhabited the lands of its conquests'.[78] In this, we can identify the paradigm of 'mixed government' which had characterised thinkers in the republican tradition since Polybius.[79] In the *Observations*, Mably thus presents an account of the kingdom's origins that is largely embellished for his own needs – that is, to highlight the lack of freedom under the absolutist monarchy. The republican ideal thus permeates the account of the state's origins.

Civic equality seems to be the defining principle for the various processes that Mably, like Montesquieu, calls the 'revolutions' of French history. He means this in the sense that these revolutions seem to have been caused by changes in Frankish citizens' freedom to participate in civic affairs. Hence the first revolution corresponds to the moment when the Franks – well established in Gaul and enriched by their conquests – abandoned their once-dominant passion for freedom, in favour of the narrow pursuit of self-interest. Hence, the assemblies of the Champ-de-Mars, a site of collective decision-making, were no longer convened and the idea of the public good disappeared from men's consciousness. What

---

77   Ibid., p. 122.
78   *OHF*, I, p. 145.
79   Machiavelli considers it the best form of government: 'Among those who have deserved most praise for such constitutions is Lycurgus, who in Sparta ordered his laws so as to give their roles to the kings, the aristocrats, and the people and made a state that lasted more than eight hundred years, achieving the highest praise for himself and quiet in that city': *Discourses on Livy*, p. 13.

instead met was an assembly of nobles alone, which made 'the government aristocratic, rather than democratic as it had hitherto been'.[80] The Franks only regained their freedom under the wise government of Charlemagne, who once again taught 'the French to obey the laws, by making them their own legislators'.[81] In the *Observations*, Mably dwells at some length on the procedures which this wise prince put in place in order to re-establish a mixed government, thereby giving the nation a true education in freedom. He obligingly describes how a council of the realm's most experienced lords prepared the assemblies' legislative activity in advance, together with the king, by devising draft laws to be submitted to them. He explains how the nation's assemblies were combined with provincial assemblies supervised by the king's envoy, 'a kind of censor' in the Roman style, who directed the work of the representatives of the three Estates. Mably casts Charlemagne in a manner similar to other great legislators, such as Utopus, whose genius made it possible to give their nations stable institutions at a stroke. Indeed, Mably's account of Charlemagne's rule contains certain elements of a utopian republic. These include the foundation by a wise legislator of institutions which ensure social harmony through the political representation of the different orders and the balance among them; the entrustment of public responsibilities to the most virtuous individuals; and so on. At the same time, by imagining the representation of the Third Estate in the nation's earliest assemblies, Mably democratised the account found in Henri de Boulainvilliers at the beginning of the eighteenth century, or, rather closer to his own time, in Montesquieu's *De l'esprit des lois*.[82] The idea of equality, seen both as men's natural condition and as the state most conducive to their moral perfection, orients his reading of the French monarchy's history. It makes this monarchy appear in the trappings of a decadence that is not necessarily impossible to reverse.

---

80   *OHF*, III, p. 347.
81   Ibid., I, p. 224.
82   On the dispute over the origins of the French monarchy and its political underpinnings, which took place in the context of the ideological struggle against absolute monarchy, see in particular Elie Carcassonne, *Montesquieu et le problème de la Constitution française au XVIII siècle*, Geneva: Slatkine Reprints, 1978, and Michel Foucault, '*Society Must Be Defended*': *Lectures at the Collège de France, 1975–76*, New York: Picador, 1997.

In *Des droits et des devoirs*, the ideal of mixed government appears in the form of a national assembly which is to be made up of representatives of the different orders. However, although it takes the form here of an institution which may seem like a resurgence of the March and May assemblies of Charlemagne's reign, in reality it differs on one crucial point. For, in this case, the king is displaced from his role as the initiator of laws, a task which now falls directly to the representatives themselves. Similarly, the provincial assemblies established in order to prepare the Estates-General's legislative work between its meetings are now placed under the oversight of 'commissioners' who are no longer envoys of the king (as under Charlemagne) but – and this is telling – appointed by the assembly itself.[83] In this respect, in the 1758 text, Mably seems to be outlining a political trajectory that enshrines the transfer of sovereignty to the combined orders of the nation. From this point of view, we can understand the abandonment of the idea of 'fundamental laws' – the guarantors of liberty – which were to be dropped as soon as they had done their job of allowing the first Estates-General to be convened: 'new fundamental laws will succeed the destroyed fundamental laws'.[84]

Hence the historical model is dismissed almost as soon as it is first mentioned. The same applies to the reference to Charlemagne. Such a king, who, 'knowing the rules of justice and true glory, [only wants] to be the first magistrate of a free nation', will never return, says Stanhope.[85] Is it simply that Mably did not want to dwell on arguments that he was going to explain at length in another work?

In reality, here it seems that, while positive historical models have an undeniable influence on the form that Stanhope intends to give to the national representation, these examples are bound to be surpassed by the nation on the path to emancipation. These models are useful for awakening a corrupted nation from its political lethargy by reminding it of its ancient rights. But they become clearly obsolete when it comes to setting the nation on a new course. It will then need other examples, which are in fact essentially counter-examples that it ought to avoid: it is necessary to study 'the faults [of] the old States', 'their form and their police', and 'the general and particular causes of their decadence', in

---

83   *DDC*, p. 177.
84   Ibid., p. 76.
85   Ibid., p. 161.

order to draw up 'political maps' which, like the charts used by navigators, 'will accurately mark out the reefs, sandbanks, currents, safe or dangerous shores, harbours, etc.'[86]

'Foreign history' is also useful for a nation which seeks more knowledge of the past in order to shed greater light on its future. Paradoxically, the moment when past models seem to enjoy a kind of resurrection is exactly the point when it is no longer worth holding them up as models. The study of history is above all useful for building up a practical knowledge that can make reformers aware of the risks and obstacles that stand in their way. Knowledge of the paths that have led to failure becomes more useful than a nostalgic celebration of ideals from the past. But the lessons of the republican utopia are diffuse, to say the least, and must be made to respond to the demands of action. Here, the social and political ideal is not so much an intangible paradigm situated in a glorious past, as an institutional form which, while better than any other, is also open to rearrangement, and needs to be adapted to present circumstances so that contemporaries can embrace it as their own. When it is rigidly fixed in the past, it is unusable as a practical example and thus of doubtful merit.

Natural Rights in Revolution

The utopian's ideal of mixed government was not the only political principle that had to bend to the new demands of this exceptional situation. There were also important changes in Mably's understanding of natural rights, when he theorised it in connection to the right to resistance. Like his understanding of jusnaturalism in general, this conception owed a great deal to the Lockean heritage. Here, our key concern is the way in which the author of *Des droits et des devoirs* was driven to rethink aspects of this theory, which linked the present to the future, in terms of establishing a political order that better suited the public good than the current one. What happened to the right of resistance, faced with the demands of political innovation?

Initially, it seems that, as in Locke's case, the right of resistance draws its legitimacy from a natural right. According to Stanhope, 'the reason

---

86   Ibid., p. 173.

with which nature has endowed us, the freedom in which she created us, and the invincible desire for happiness that she has placed in our soul, are three titles that every man may assert against the unjust government under which he lives'.[87] This framing bears the mark of Locke's theory of the right of resistance, based on the maintenance of man's natural prerogatives in the state of society. The English thinker is categorical on this point: the 'obligations of the law of nature cease not in society but only in many cases are drawn closer'.[88] Instituted authority must aim for the public good, understood as respect for man's natural rights, because this is the very function that justifies its establishment. In virtue of the rights that nature confers on each individual, 'there remains still in the people a supreme power to remove or alter the legislative, when they find the legislative act contrary to the trust reposed in them'.[89] The same reason seems to lead Stanhope to the conclusion – much to the scandal of his interlocutor – that 'civil war is sometimes a greater good' when society runs the 'risk of dying of despotism'.[90] It should be added, however, that the spectre of civil war is dismissed as soon as it is raised, as according to Stanhope the circumstances in France do not require resorting to such extremes. But, on closer inspection, there surely is a difference between Locke's and Mably's theories. This results from the different relationship, in the two cases, between the right of resistance and the temporality of the establishment of legislative power. To explain this divergence, it is worth again taking a quick look at Locke's theory.

For Locke, such an institution is the fruit of the original compact by which a multitude of men, emerging from the state of nature, associate in a community which has a political will to which they each submit: 'every man, by consenting with others to make one body politic under one government, puts himself under an obligation, to every one of that society, to submit to the determination of the majority, and to be concluded by it'.[91] The community thus established decides, by an 'original and supreme act of the society'[92] – not a second contract but a consequence of the first – to constitute a legislative authority and thus to

---

87 Ibid., p. 27.
88 Locke, *Second Treatise of Government*, Chapter 11, section 135.
89 Ibid., Chapter 13, section 149.
90 *DDC*, p. 62.
91 Locke, *Second Treatise of Government*, Chapter 8, section 97.
92 Ibid., Chapter 13, section 157.

determine the form of the commonwealth, whether it is a democracy, an oligarchy, or a monarchy. The legislative power is 'the soul that gives form, life, and unity, to the commonwealth' insofar as it holds the 'supreme power'[93] to which the other (executive and federative) powers are subordinated. If it betrays the mission entrusted to it by the instituting community, or is prevented from fulfilling it, then the government is dissolved. The question then arises as to whether the compact has been broken, and whether the individuals are thereby restored to the state of nature. As Jean-Fabien Spitz[94] has observed, Locke's answer is rather ambiguous. Here is the text in question:

> When any one, or more, shall take upon them to make laws, whom the people have not appointed so to do, they make laws without authority, which the people are not therefore bound to obey; by which means they come again to be out of subjection, and may constitute to themselves a new legislative, as they think best, being in full liberty to resist the force of those, who without authority would impose any thing upon them. Every one is at the disposure of his own will, when those who had, by the delegation of the society, the declaring of the public will, are excluded from it, and others usurp the place, who have no such authority or delegation.[95]

Spitz rightly points out that such a formulation in fact refers to two distinct theses which seem incompatible with one another. According to the first thesis, the power to judge is vested in the community resulting from the compact, in a body politic which self-governs according to majority rule: there is, then, no return to the state of nature but only to the primitive political state that results from the compact. As Jean Terrel puts it, 'this thesis would make Locke a defender of the sovereignty of the people', indeed *avant la lettre*.[96] But, according to the second thesis,

---

93 Ibid., Chapter 19, section 212.
94 Jean-Fabien Spitz, 'Concept de souveraineté et politique placée sous le signe de la loi de nature dans le Second *Traité du Gouvernement Civil* de John Locke', *Philosophie* 37, January–March 1993, 39–63, and 'Les sources de la distinction entre société et gouvernement chez Locke', in Y. -C. Zarka (ed.), *Aspects de la pensée médiévale dans la philosophie politique moderne*, Paris: PUF, 1999, pp. 247–72.
95 Locke, *Second Treatise of Government*, Chapter 19, section 212.
96 Jean Terrel, 'John Locke, souveraineté ou suprématie', p. 16: online article at appep.net.

the result of this situation is that each individual is left to be governed by his own conscience. We return to the state of nature, and it is up to individuals to freely associate once more, in order to ensure respect for the law of nature.

The ambiguity that we can observe in Locke's text is in fact inherent in the inevitable difficulties that are posed by the idea of a right of resistance within a contractualist framework. How can we reconcile, as part of the same bond that binds the people to their magistrates, a right that allows this bond to be totally called into question at any time? Or can a right that only makes sense within the contractual relationship itself lead to the destruction of this relationship? And what is left of the force of a contract that can be undermined in this way by the same people who created it? Locke hesitates on this fundamental problem. He leaves it unclear whether the right of resistance is able to destroy the contract entirely, forcing it to be remade, or whether it operates within the space created by the contract, within which it merely imposes (albeit important) readjustments.

Because Mably's programme is not situated in the abstract space of contractualism but directly gets to grips with a specific historical context, it sharply cuts through this difficult tangle. Mably is driven to 'dispense with the notion – so central to modern natural right – of the contract',[97] so that the nation can have an unlimited sovereignty, defined as 'absolute independence, or the ability to change its laws according to the different conjunctures and the different needs of the state'.[98] No fundamental law should restrict the freedom of a nation engaged in a radical renovation of its institutions – something clearly distinct from what Locke terms the 'mission' that it had previously entrusted to its magistrates. For the people to accomplish this task, it must not be bound by any prior contract that would set limits on this renewal process. This is why Mably himself corrects his formulations. Tellingly, he writes that 'the people . . . is therefore eternally entitled to interpret its contract, *or rather the gifts with which it endows them*'.[99]

---

[97] Jean Goldzink, 'Le droit de résistance dans les Lumières françaises', in C. Biet and J. -C. Zancarini (eds), *Le droit de résistance, XIIe–XXe siècle*, Fontenay-aux-Roses: ENS Éditions, 1999, pp. 227–45, at p. 243.

[98] *DDC*, pp. 75–6.

[99] Ibid., p. 76. Emphasis added.

The bond that binds the people to its government is, apparently, no more contractual than the bond that binds individuals to one another and makes the multitude into a people. This conceptual device, which frees the people from any pre-existing obligation to anyone, is inseparable from the stated imperative 'to establish a new order of things'. The dynamic conception of the planned reform shatters the contractualist framework, which is too static and rigid to contain it. Precisely because the aim is to institute political power from the ground up, the idea of an original contract becomes obsolete, and the right of resistance is henceforth identified with the total and permanent sovereignty of the nation. But, in these conditions, can we still speak of a right of resistance? As Jean Goldzink points out, rather than rely on this expression, which is relatively inappropriate in this new context, Mably prefers to speak of the 'right to reform'.[100] This right to constant improvement presupposes much more than vigilance to ensure respect for individuals' natural rights. It thus implies going beyond the jusnaturalistic framework, and onto the terrain of historical invention: 'Resistance to change gives way to the right, the need to change – the right to reform as an exercise of the reason and freedom inherent in popular sovereignty.'[101] Thus, the logic of Mably's reform programme seems to take him beyond the limits that he had earlier set for the political use of history. The limits of the utopia of mixed government and natural rights have become too narrow for conceiving a future inspired by the freedom of improvement and – in the long run – the winning of rights that may have previously gone unimagined. Yet, it is exactly once Mably's reasoning has reached this point that utopia appears in a form that is new and, indeed, unique in his writings. For, here, we get to the image of an island society based on the community of goods and the virtue of its magistrates. But what does such an ideal really mean, within the economy of Mably's text?

---

100   Ibid., p. 55.
101   Goldzink, 'Le droit de résistance dans les Lumières françaises', p. 243.

'In a Free State, All Bodies Imperceptibly Find Their Proper Level'

In a way, the ideal island described in the 'fourth letter' shares the same exceptional status as *Des droits et des devoirs* in general. We have said that this is the only work by this author that proposes, for the immediate future, the scenario of a revolution that would set the whole nation in motion. Similarly, this utopian passage is the only one that refers neither to humanity's past, nor to any institution that has ever existed. Rather, it presents itself as a project for founding a new order, which, even if it is immediately cut short, at least expresses an active desire to institute such a social model. This naturally leads us to wonder whether it is possible to establish a link between these two theoretical *hapaxes* in Mably's thought. Does the island utopia, presented as the republican Stanhope's inaccessible ideal, also serve as a source of inspiration in the programme of reforms to the French monarchy?

De la manière d'écrire l'histoire emphasised the usefulness of reading the works of Thomas More and Plato for producing a worthy interpretation of history. But what can be said about their use, when it comes to thinking about concrete intervention in contemporary events? Stanhope indirectly responds to this question when he examines the desirability of maintaining hereditary dignities, the privileges of the nobility and the clergy, and even the special rights of certain provinces in the early stages of the reform process. He argues:

> If it were necessary to give laws to a society, all this surely could not serve as a model. But Plato, who would have been careful not to smear his Republic with all these vices, would be careful not to want to purge your government of them when initiating a reform today. He would feel that you need certain defects to keep your nation above the rigorous despotism that threatens it.[102]

These words would seem to mean that drawing up a programme of reforms is a completely different task to that of 'giving laws to a society'. It is less a question of building something new than of rearranging existing elements so that they will better contribute to the public good. With

---

102   *DDC*, p. 129.

this in mind, Stanhope suggests an anti-utopian procedure par excellence: that of defending certain 'defects' in the French constitution rather than wiping the slate clean. By adopting this position, Stanhope claims to be adopting the stance of a Plato who has converted to the idea of reform – in other words, of a utopian who has embraced the idea of dealing with reality such as it really is.

On this basis, a severe criticism is levelled against the Abbé de Saint-Pierre. The 'Frenchman of his time most zealous for the public good' is chided for wishing to 'crush' abuses 'under the weight of royal authority'.[103] In this manifest confidence in the king's goodwill and wisdom, which will supposedly allow a radical overhaul of the monarchy, we can recognise a traditional utopian belief in the virtue of the great legislator, and – in the attitude of the Abbé de Saint-Pierre himself – the utopian's no less traditional role as an advisor to the monarch. Equally characteristic of classical utopianism is its tendency to want to smooth over the rough edges of Ancien Régime society in terms of its orders and privileges. Here, we find this mentality's typical tendency towards equalisation and standardisation, as it seeks to bend society to its plans for the rational organisation of space, time, and the condition of each person. Stanhope encapsulates his criticisms in one terse phrase: '[The Abbé de Saint-Pierre] always puts the King in the place of the law, and yet in a reasonable plan of reforms, everything should tend to subject the King to the law.'[104]

It is worth stressing the role assigned to the law, here. At this point, there is no question of an inherently perfect law, which will legitimately impose itself on any existing magistrate. Rather, Mably is talking about an imperfect law, the law of privilege and inequality, which must nevertheless serve as a dam against the monarch's excessive claims to authority, considered the worst of all dangers. We are thus much closer to Montesquieu's *Esprit des lois* than to More's *Utopia*. The presence of laws must moderate the regime, and the intermediate powers must curb mounting despotism by defending the fundamental laws (which themselves have no substantial value). Mably seems to be repeating some of the conclusions of the *Esprit des lois* without actually saying so: 'Abolish

---

103   Ibid., p. 132.
104   Ibid.

in a monarchy the prerogatives of the lords, the clergy, the nobility and the towns, and you will soon have either a popular state or a despotic state.'[105] To protect the nation from possible despotism, the author thus seems prepared to give up on the construction of an ideal society. He repeats this in various ways throughout the text: 'the lesser evil is our greater good'.[106] He makes no explicit link between the ideal island and the projects that he outlines.

Yet the fact that the text refers to the ideal society demands some explanation, or at least a hypothesis in this regard. The relationship between the ideal island and the republic that Stanhope calls for remains ambiguous and does not, in any case, allow us to conclude that this republic is a stage in the transition towards the ideal. According to Lutz Lehmann, in order to move from one to the other, Mably is perhaps lacking a certain mediation – that is, violent intervention by the people, which he disapproved of and sought to avoid. For want of such a means of intervention, he could then hope for only minimal reforms for France, in order to reach a situation ultimately close to that of the English monarchy. On this reading, the mention of the island utopia thus has more or less the same status as the defence of the legitimacy of civil war against despotism: a pure assertion of principle without practical consequences. The separation between 'ideal principles' and 'rules of practical common sense' remains a gaping wound.[107]

Without a doubt, Mably neither wanted the poorest part of the nation to rise up, nor saw its mobilisation as part of his own plans for political reform. As Stanhope puts it unambiguously:

> There is in our modern states a crowd of men who are without fortune, and who subsist only by their industry, and do not belong in any sense to any society; all that I can do for your service . . . is to ensure that this right to reform, which is so frightening, does not become a duty for this kind of public slaves, who are condemned by ignorance, education and their servile occupations to have no will of their own.[108]

---

105   *EdL*, I, p. 139.
106   *DDC*, p. 199.
107   Lutz Lehmann, *Mably und Rousseau: eine Studie über die Grenzen der Emanzipation des Ancien Régime*, Bern: Herbert Lang, 1975, p. 157.
108   *DDC*, p. 55.

Still, we would have good reason to object to an interpretation that holds that the mention of emancipatory civil war is, like the island utopia, a pure declaration of principles with no immediate consequences. For the legitimisation of civil war plays the role of an a fortiori argument to reassure Stanhope's interlocutor that the fight for a 'managed revolution' is indeed justified. If we can legitimately take up arms to prevent society from 'dying of despotism', we should have even less fear in venturing to agitate for the convening of the Estates-General.

This consideration surely sheds new light on the reference to the island utopia. In offering an image of the ideal foundations of a new social order, it stirs the courage of the reformers of the future. It is meant to urge them toward ever-further-reaching social and political transformations. It is true that, initially, privileges have to be maintained, and agrarian and sumptuary laws rejected as inappropriate, because 'they no longer suit public and private mores'.[109] But this assessment is much less definitive than it may seem. The comment that 'in a free state, all bodies imperceptibly find their proper level' may suggest the need to work toward levelling out the prerogatives of the different orders in the newly instituted republic.[110] A few pages further on, Stanhope foresees, in an indeterminate future, the introduction of censors on the ancient model, who – following a decision by the Estates-General or the provincial assemblies – could eventually oversee an 'execution of sumptuary laws' in order 'to put limits to this scandalous luxury that impoverishes us in the midst of the greatest riches'.[111] Mably's wording suggests that such an institution could emerge only in a still distant future, once representative assemblies are up and running to a regular timetable. This is also seen as the stage when the censors will control the education provided in colleges, so that it will give pride of place to 'natural law' and 'morals' and future citizens will be made 'fit to be magistrates'.[112] Lastly – and rather tellingly – at this same stage of the argument the text positively takes up the Abbé de Saint-Pierre's proposal that the principle of election should be applied to all levels of the military hierarchy. Is the ideal island's principle of electing the 'bursars' responsible for distributing

---

109   Ibid., p. 110.
110   Ibid., p. 187.
111   Ibid., p. 199.
112   Ibid., p. 200.

food here transposed to the conditions of the new French republic?[113] Could the army be a suitable testing ground for experimenting with new political practices?

We can reach no firm conclusion on this problem here, most of all because it is likely that this ambiguity endured in the author's own mind. He was undoubtedly hesitant about the question of how far reforms could go, and, in any case, he refused to set out signposts for it beyond a certain point. From this point of view, Lehmann is right to point out the insurmountable divide between utopian talk and a rational plan of reforms. But there is likewise no doubting that there is a reason why the author refers to the perfection of the utopian model: for its existence in itself underlines the imperfection of real political life. Indeed, Mably never ceases to remind us of this. So, the comparison with the ideal, which the text invites the reader to make, can doubtless be seen as a constant urge for improvement. Above and beyond the precise analysis of concrete political measures, utopia would here constitute a permanent critical counterpoint to all the inequalities and defects of the present society.

So, in *Des droits et des devoirs*, utopia does not just play the role of a dreamlike ideal which we should be happy to fatalistically yearn after. Rather, it inchoately points to the way in which Mably sees the necessary reforms. In this sense, it sheds light on the past, not just to describe it as a process of corruption, but above all to seek within this past the seeds of a better future. In an unprecedented way, utopia inspires the content of the reform plan, while at the same time communicating to it its own force of criticism of reality and its strong aspirations for social and political change.

Mably did not put utopia directly on the agenda of his reform programme. Indeed, in *Des droits et des devoirs*, he explicitly rejected such a temptation, on the grounds that it would be impossible to overcome certain defects that mankind has developed. However, if Mably makes this concession to existing reality, this does not deny the importance of the utopian ferment in his work, which fundamentally enables him to push back the limits of political possibility. In this sense, there is probably a link between the audacity of Stanhope's proposals and his utopian aspirations. Because of their radical rejection of the existing

---

113 Ibid., p. 111.

reality, these aspirations allow him to look beyond this present state of affairs and to imagine alternative possibilities. This also allows us to venture another hypothesis. Ultimately, it was perhaps utopia itself that enabled Mably, in a century so rich in reformers, to dare to envisage a French Revolution. In this, he was quite alone. It seems that the fantasy of a social ideal, displaced to an imaginary island, paradoxically provided Mably with the means to go further than his contemporaries in anticipating what would come next in the context of France. Built on dreams, it enabled him to catch a glimpse of the future.

4

The *Doutes proposés aux philosophes économistes*: Utopia in Service of Polemics

Unlike *Des droits et des devoirs du citoyen*, the other texts in which Mably speaks at greatest length about the community of goods are not direct political interventions. Rather, they are philosophical-political works in which he sets out general principles for the happiness of human societies. Real history and temporality still appear in them, but they are reduced to a relatively more background role. Does this mean that Mably's rejection of empirical history should be compared with what we find in Morelly? The answer is much more nuanced than that, and requires us to compare several texts, some of which do not directly mention their link with the utopia of the community of goods.

The Community of Goods and the Republican Utopia

The first text by Mably after *Des droits et des devoirs* to mention the community of goods is *Doutes proposés aux philosophes économistes sur l'ordre naturel et essentiel des sociétés politiques*. In this 1768 text, Mably polemicises against one of the Physiocrats, Le Mercier de La Rivière, and his work *L'ordre naturel et essentiel des sociétés politiques*.[1] Its first

---

1 Pierre-Paul Le Mercier de La Rivière, *L'ordre naturel et essentiel des sociétés politiques* (1767), Paris: Fayard, 2001.

line of attack is the indissoluble link that Le Mercier postulates between personal property or 'the property of my person'; movable property or 'the right that I have to the things necessary for my self-preservation'; and landed property or 'ownership of my field'.[2] Mably objects: 'If I today found myself in a society that generously resolved to obey Plato's laws, whyever should my fellow-citizens and I lose the ownership of our persons?'[3]

Mably thus dissociates property ownership from ownership over one's own self. He makes a rather vague allusion to community of property, which once again links this principle to Plato's *Republic*. The claimed line of descent from the doctrine of Socrates' most famous disciple is again somewhat imprecise, insofar as Mably does not in fact cite any of the defining features of the ideal city described in Plato's text. Neither the tripartition of the city, nor the community of women and children, nor the education of guardians are relevant to understanding what Mably is alluding to here. Rather than taking up Plato's philosophy in the strict sense, this is more a kind of argument from authority that lends weight to the idea of community. It thus really appears as an important theme, rather than a model with clearly definable characteristics.

This reference is then coupled with others: firstly, to the earliest societies, as then continued in the societies of the 'Iroquois' and the 'Hurons'; but, likewise, to 'civilised [*policées*] and flourishing' societies. Mably's intention here is to reintroduce the example of ancient Spartan society, and then the 'Indian' societies established by the Jesuit missionaries in Paraguay: 'Each inhabitant is destined, according to his talents, strength and age, to a useful function; and the State, owner of everything, distributes to individuals the things they need.'[4] Criticism of the Jesuit missionaries, who are accused of enslaving the Indians for their own benefit, does not stop the author in this regard. Indeed, he replies to an objection that he has himself raised:

> but if, confining themselves to being missionaries and to giving morals to the Indians, they had taught them to govern themselves,

---

2 *DP*, p. 4.
3 Ibid., p. 5.
4 Ibid., p. 8.

and to make themselves magistrates who would be the treasurers of the republic, then who would not wish to live in this Platonic society? ... I cannot help but imagine a republic whose laws would encourage citizens to work, and would make the common heritage of society dear to each individual.[5]

Here, Mably mounts a theoretical operation already seen in Morelly's *Code de la Nature*. He combines examples of real societies – whether past or present, primitive or civilised – with hypotheses which, underpinned by such an empirical basis, are thereby made less hazardous. The result is a fictional history of what Jesuit legislators could have brought to the Indians of Paraguay, namely the rules of a social life. If this history is painted in a few broad strokes, it ultimately has the same characteristics as the brief utopian passage in *Des droits et des devoirs*. It shares both that utopian society's 'bursars' – as the earlier text calls the magistrates tasked with distributing the goods produced – and even the 'laws' supposed to promote emulation, which can be related to the reward promised to the deserving labourer or the upstanding mother.

'I cannot abandon this congenial idea of the community of goods', writes Mably; further on, he even calls this idea 'my system for the community of goods and equality of conditions'.[6] The meaning of the word 'system', with all the implications that this might have, surely deserves some qualification, here, related to the particular context of its use. Mably speaks of a 'system' above all for polemical purposes, in order to contrast his point of view with what he calls the 'system' of his opponents. The Physiocrats did not themselves use this term to characterise their doctrine, and it seems to be employed here rather loosely: it tends to suggest that Mably's ideas stand in en bloc opposition to the theses of his adversaries. Basically, in this text the community of goods appears as an idea or rather a set of ideas designed to show that this principle of social organisation better suits human nature than the system of private property, and offers the possibility of happiness. It serves as a reminder of certain philosophical and political principles, rather than a precise illustration of them in the context of a model society.

---

5   Ibid.
6   Ibid., pp. 13, 155.

In many respects, Mably seems to be following in the same vein as the first parts of the *Code de la Nature*. There, Morelly had preferred not to describe a perfect city without property, but rather to offer anthropological justifications rooted in considerations about the nature of man, as well as political ones based on the nature of societies. From this point of view, the empirical references used here – not part of the argumentation, properly speaking – appear to be more illustrations of Mably's thesis than models in their own right. As for the 'Model of Legislation', it has simply disappeared from view.

Perhaps we should conclude from this that, for Mably, the community of property remained merely a vague ideal – little but a slogan used for broadly polemical purposes. And yet such an impression needs greater nuance, particularly in view of his mentions of the community of goods established by Lycurgus in Sparta – a reference little elaborated in the *Doutes*, but which is present, and which was in fact recurrent in his works around 1765. In her book devoted to the place of the Spartan tradition in European thought, Elizabeth Rawson points out that Mably, who was by no means the only admirer of the Lacedemonian city, was nevertheless 'almost isolated' in his enthusiasm for its communitarian social structure.[7] In the *Entretiens de Phocion* (1763), Mably, through the mouth of the famous ancient sage, invokes Lycurgus' efforts to regenerate the morals of his people, who had until then been languishing in a deplorable situation. This 'divine man',[8] familiar with the secrets of nature and Providence, gave the Spartans 'a government such as Plato desired'.[9] On several occasions, Mably emphasises the quasi-demiurgic role of the great legislator, credited with turning a people incapable of overcoming its own errors into a happy and flourishing community. Lycurgus is held up as the political philosopher who studied at length the secrets of the human soul and the principles that govern societies. Mably associates Plato's philosophical work with Lycurgus' political enterprise, both of which are attributed the same perfection. The legislator is sometimes presented as the inspiration for the philosopher, and sometimes as the

---

7   Elizabeth Rawson, *The Spartan Tradition in European Thought*, Oxford: Clarendon Press, 1991, p. 248.
8   *EP*, p. 46.
9   Ibid., p. 75.

political incarnation of what the thinker had been to theory. The great man is reminiscent of Utopus, the founder of Thomas More's city, 'who brought its rude, uncouth inhabitants to such a high level of culture and humanity that they now surpass almost every other people'.[10] The comparison is all the more justified given that, in another text, Mably credits Lycurgus with inventing a great Spartan institution, namely the ephors.[11] In reality, this institution was invented after Lycurgus' magistracy, and this fact was already known in the eighteenth century. But there is no doubt as to the meaning of this confusion: Mably's aim is to cast Lycurgus as the sole and direct source of Sparta's perfectly balanced institutions. Such flawless legislative work as this could not have been the result of a gradual and collective development, which would surely have been more haphazard and subject to the vicissitudes of historical time. Perfection can only be the fruit of a singular creation, dictated by an almost superhuman wisdom that has anticipated all obstacles in advance. 'Thus the Spartan constitution can be presented as the perfect product of reason', writes Nicole Dockès-Lallement.[12]

By making Lycurgus the father of the entire Spartan constitution, Mably is, to some extent, taking his model out of history as it really happens. He gives it the contours of a utopian city, as other features of his description do even more to suggest. The more detailed description of life in Sparta follows suit. On the whole, the fundamental principle of the organisation of social life remains the same as the utopians offer: 'Each age, each sex, each moment [has] its particular occupations.'[13] The meticulous use of time, which leaves no room for either boredom or vice, is a constant feature of utopian time. Indeed, seeing as it is filled in the most virtuous and useful way, this time may be frozen in a blissful stasis. In Mably's view, this explains the exceptional longevity of the Spartan republic, which he most often estimated at six hundred years, but which – he said in another text – could just as well have lasted forever:

---

10 Thomas More, *Utopia*, Cambridge: Cambridge University Press, 1989, p. 42.
11 *OG*, p. 18.
12 Nicole Dockès-Lallement, 'Mably et l'institution de la société spartiate' in *L'influence de l'Antiquité sur la pensée politique européenne, XVIe–XXe siècle*, Aix-en-Provence: Presses de l'Université d'Aix-Marseille, 1996, p. 232.
13 *EP*, pp. 124–5.

> It is proven that the Spartans lived for six hundred years in the greatest equality; and ... you cannot deny that institutions which have endured for six centuries were not the result of some passing fashion, enthusiasm or fanaticism, and thus they could have been preserved for a million years.[14]

A people that had perfect institutions could have enjoyed eternal happiness. This is the utopian path that Mably opens up for Sparta. Indeed, he illustrated the institutional result of perfectly just laws in his 1766 work *Observations sur l'histoire de la Grèce*. Here, too, historical and utopian elements are combined in order to give Lycurgus' efforts the image of the best constitution ever laid down for mankind. Mably puts it bluntly: the legislator 'dared to form the bold project of making [the Spartans into] a new people'.[15] This perfection was achieved through the balance between dual kingship – a legacy of the past which, together with the senate, made up the executive; the sovereignty of the people, which had the power to make laws; and the famous institution of the five ephors, elected annually to prevent any abuses of executive power. Mably specifies that it was the twenty-eight senators, 'chosen by the people' from among the Elders assumed to be wise men, who acted as advisors to the king and prepared the people's assemblies. The author paints an idyllic picture of the operation of such a government, in which each order – the people, the senatorial aristocracy, the kings – is duly respected by the others. They are not held in check by a balance of mutual fear or mistrust, but instead virtuously emulate one another: 'All the orders of the state helped, enlightened and improved each other through the censure they exercised over each other.'[16] Sparta is thus the perfect incarnation of the republican model of mixed government. Moreover, it offers the model of a community of goods that guarantees the lasting virtue of its members, even if, in these last two texts, the expression 'community of goods' does not actually appear. The most recent commentators have essentially drawn from these texts the idea of a republicanism dominant in Mably. In particular, J. K. Wright comments:

---

14 *DL*, p. 66.
15 *OG*, p. 17.
16 Ibid., p. 20.

it was precisely Mably's commitment to *another* utopian discourse that blocked a full embrace of the schemes of the *philosophes utopistes*. This is of course the tradition of classical republicanism, in which the model of society is not the anarchist communitarianism of the Code de la nature, but 'mixed governments' of ancient Sparta and Rome.[17]

Mably's republicanism is beyond doubt. And yet we should also qualify such a conclusion by emphasising that this republicanism includes a strong utopian dimension, in the classical sense of the term. This dimension surely shares some of the essence of republicanism, as J. K. Wright argues; but it is not entirely the same. By no means were all the civic humanists enthusiastic defenders of the community of goods – far from it. Not all offered such an obviously idealised image of the ancient republics.

What is quite particular in Mably is that his thinking on the best political model tends towards a kind of synthesis of the two traditions – the utopian and communitarian on the one hand, the republican on the other – without this tendency ever reaching full completion. The mutually exclusive nature of the two vocabularies also seems to be a sign of a relative failure in uniting these two major inspirations in a single doctrine: when Mably directly invokes the principle of community, he generally plays down the reference to mixed government, and vice versa. The Spartan paradigm proves to be the site of the non-fulfilment of this synthesis, insofar as nowhere does Mably mention a republicanism of the community, or a mixed communitarian government, which takes Sparta as its historical model.

Doubtless the main reason for this is Mably's scepticism about such a social ideal, a scepticism that is relatively lesser when it comes to the possibility of establishing non-communitarian republican institutions. This is why Mably takes up his republicanism much more forthrightly than his communitarian utopianism. However, if the utopia of the community of goods is republicanised in his texts through the image of Sparta, we can also see that – much more clearly than in other civic humanists – his republican model(s) very often don the clothes of

---

[17] J. K. Wright, *A Classical Republican in Eighteenth-Century France: The Political Thought of Mably*, Stanford, CA: Stanford University Press, 1997, pp. 107–8.

utopia. We have already seen from the example of *Des droits et des devoirs* that the republics to be found in this work, including but not limited to Sparta, often appear with ideal traits that, in many respects, make them into little utopias. Most of them have egalitarian, if not communitarian, institutions. The texts' emphasis on the value of equality is telling in this regard.

In this sense, it seems that the theme of mixed government is also a characteristic 'idea-image' of Mablyan utopianism. It constitutes a version of utopia that its author considers more realisable. We likewise see this in the 1758 text, where utopia not only appears in the island ideal, but can also be identified in the allusions to mixed government, such as it existed, according to Mably, in the distant past of the French monarchy, and such as it ought to be in his projected future. Utopia is thus split into two distinct models, and not unified as in the Spartan paradigm, even if the link between the two versions of utopia is not clearly explained.

Moreover, Mably was likely not fully aware of the utopian features he had given to the republican social and political model; and, after all, he wanted to grant this model the status of historical reality. In any case, Mably always sought more or less clearly to deny that he was a utopian. This is a denial which we can observe in *Des droits et des devoirs* and which remains a constant in most of the political texts discussed here.

Mably versus the Physiocrats: The Anthropology of the *Doutes*

The polemic against Le Mercier de La Rivière gave Mably the opportunity to clarify his thinking on the foundation and ultimate goal of human societies and on the natural right of individuals. Indeed, Physiocratic theory made natural right the foundation of all its economic and political theses. In a major article on the subject published in the *Journal de l'agriculture, du commerce et des finances* in September 1765, the Physiocrats' leading exponent, François Quesnay, offered an initial definition: 'Man's natural right can be loosely defined as the right that man has to the things proper to his enjoyment.'[18] According to this school of thought, at a primitive

---

18 François Quesnay, *Physiocratie*, texts presented by Jean Cartelier, Paris: GF, 2008, p. 69.

level, natural right is linked to the ability of individuals to materially acquire as many objects as they can – the only limit to this being respect for the reciprocal rights of other men. From this perspective, the state of nature corresponds to the right of all men to everything. Yet, the state of pure nature, marked by the independence of each man from the rest, does not enable the greatest fulfilment of each man's natural right, insofar as in the absence of cooperation the law of the strongest will prevail. 'When [men] enter into society, and make agreements among themselves for their mutual benefit, they will therefore increase the enjoyment of their natural right.'[19] On this reading, civil society is thus nothing other than the development of natural right.[20] This establishes a point of similarity between the Physiocratic and Mablyan theories: both conceive of a well-constituted society as a site for the perfection of the species and the realisation of its natural right. But the comparison must stop there. While, for the Physiocrats, perfection is the result of a quantitative fulfilment of desires, for Mably, it is a matter of leading a dignified life in accordance with the moral rules dictated by reason. While the former conceive it in terms of *having*, the latter conceives it in terms of *being*.

We have said that, for the Physiocrats, men increase their natural right by choosing to submit to collective laws. But how is this possible? In 1767, under Quesnay's direction, Le Mercier published a fundamental text for the group, entitled *L'ordre naturel et essentiel des sociétés politiques*. It gave details on this question that were to represent the specific target of Mably's arguments in his *Doutes*, published a year later. The 'Preliminary Discourse' reminds us that man's natural state is the social state, insofar as only society really opens up man's possibilities of enjoyment. As with Mably, the state of nature as a pre-social state is seen as one in which man is not yet truly a man.

Le Mercier sets out the primitive natural right of man, as mentioned by Quesnay, through the lens of two distinct prerogatives. These are the right to provide for one's self-preservation and the right to acquire and conserve objects useful for this self-preservation, respectively called the right to personal property and the right to movable property. In his account, the multiplication of the species implies the need to find a way

---

19 Ibid., p. 75.
20 On Physiocratic theory, see Arnault Skornicki, *L'économiste, la cour et la patrie*, Paris: CNRS éditions, 2011.

to multiply the means of subsistence. The solution lies in the cultivation of the land. In his view, this cultivation is the real means of providing for human needs, and is thus a physical necessity. It demands, with the same force of necessity, the establishment of the social state. The primary aim of the social state is an essential extension of the first two natural rights, namely the right to own land.

The ownership of land follows on from the ownership of movable property, since 'each first Cultivator begins by advancing to the land the movable riches of which he is the owner':[21] it is thus his only possible guarantee that the fruits of his efforts and his initial movable property will not be alienated by some third party. Property in general and, through it, natural right, are upheld by the social state, by means of the rules it establishes to govern relations between its members, its measures to enable trade, industry and employment, and its protection of individual property against internal and external threats. The social state can do this because the three orders of property 'are thus so closely united that they must be regarded as forming a single whole, from which no part can be detached unless this results in the destruction of the other two'.[22] This is the ultimate foundation for property in general, its natural and necessary justification. The Physiocrats' assertions claim to be backed up by the despotic reign of evidence. There is nothing arbitrary about the social order, any more than there is about the economic order. It is of the utmost necessity that

> In a government that conforms to the natural and essential order of societies, all the interests and forces of the nation should come together in the sovereign, as in their common centre; they are so much his own, so personal to him, that his will alone is sufficient to put them into action.[23]

The sovereign is the eminent owner of the estates that make up the kingdom: he manages them on his own behalf, since he derives his revenues from them. He thus has no other interest, in accordance with natural right, than to increase the proceeds, thereby maximising his

---

21 Le Mercier de la Rivière, *L'ordre naturel et essentiel*, p. 31.
22 Ibid., p. 41.
23 Ibid., p. 53.

own enjoyment and that of his subjects. Insofar as he respects the rules of evidence and proprietary order as set out above, he must be an absolute sovereign, and to question his power is to reject the natural order itself. The protective power must therefore be a single whole, which unites legislative and executive power under the authority of a single individual. This is the famous theory of 'legal despotism', 'established naturally and necessarily on the evidence of the laws of an essential order'.[24]

Mably thus opposed the Physiocrats for both anthropological and political reasons. For the Physiocrats, legal despotism as a political principle was based on the right to property as the foundation of the natural order. Mably challenged both, denouncing land ownership as a policy of despotism.

Two Anthropological Critiques of Physiocracy

Mably's argument starts from a critique of the supposedly inextricable link between the three types of property. As against Le Mercier, he argues not only that the three need untangling from each other, but even that there is an opposition between them. More specifically, it is necessary to counterpose personal property – along with the resulting movable property, namely 'the right to provide for one's subsistence'[25] – to landed property. Here, much more clearly than in *Des droits et des devoirs*, Mably terms the ownership of land an 'arbitrary institution'.[26] In fact, despite what the Physiocrats claim, it is absolutely not necessary for the survival of human societies. The primitive societies of the Native Americans, like both the Spartan institutions and the Jesuit 'reductions', empirically refute such a claim.

Personal property, on the other hand, is an entirely natural prerogative. It creates identical needs in men, 'to continually alert them to

---

24 Ibid., p. 177. Despite contemporary understandings, a close study of Physiocratic theories reveals that, behind the explicit promotion of the sovereign's absolute power, things are in fact a little more complex. In *L'économiste, la cour et la patrie*, Arnault Skornicki seeks to analyse the constitutional and administrative 'political technologies' (p. 292) by which the Physiocrats intended to moderate arbitrary royal power.
25 *DP*, p. 30.
26 Ibid., p. 5.

[their] equality'.[27] Even more clearly than in his 1758 text, Mably is here theorising an individualism based on possession and not on property. Apparently unaware of the paradox, he conceived of the relationship to oneself and to the objects necessary for one's subsistence on the model of material appropriation, while denying the justification for such a relationship between man and land ownership.

Yet this idea of self-possession does not portray men as autonomous and isolated entities. Rather, it gives rise to the idea of reciprocal duties, which entail material assistance. In one passage, Mably speaks of the concrete mutual aid between the first men:

> When fortune has not favoured my quest, others will provide me with my subsistence; and when their labours are fruitless, I in turn will console them for their misfortunes; I will share with them the fruit that I have gathered, or the game that I have caught.[28]

It should be noted, however, that this mutual aid is offered in response to specific circumstances, and does not involve joint effort. For Mably, cooperation for survival did not seem necessary as a general rule. The expected effect of this sporadic mutual aid was less material than moral. The first result is to develop man's 'social qualities' – the only ones likely to bring him genuine happiness.[29] It is these qualities, developed on the basis of personal property alone, that are the true 'foundation of society', and the reason why it is important to establish and maintain this society.[30]

Mably makes explicitly clear that moral or social qualities have 'contributed much more to the establishment of society than has the need for subsistence'.[31] This surprising assertion is based on a teleological conception of human nature already outlined in *Des droits et des devoirs*. Man, an intelligent and sensitive being, is born to 'make laws'.[32] He feels this moral need when he comes together with others in society. Mably does not explicitly define what social qualities actually are, but

---

27 Ibid., p. 11.
28 Ibid., p. 32.
29 Ibid., p. 11.
30 Ibid., p. 20.
31 Ibid., p. 24.
32 Ibid., p. 26.

they include everything to do with devotion to the public good, 'justice, prudence, courage'.[33] Equality of status leads to the development of these qualities through emulation, unlike inequality, which – if sanctioned by law – will only promote vice. So, man's true nature does not become apparent in the first moments of the species' existence, but only gradually. It is only when man's social qualities are fully developed that the deeper function of society, which consists in making these qualities bear fruit in the best possible way, will become apparent. To borrow a striking expression used by Yves Vargas in an article on Rousseau, we could say that, for Mably, 'the tree of human societies would grow from the middle of the trunk and then find its roots again', insofar as it is only after a certain time and after a long development of moral qualities that human society finds its true *raison d'être*.[34] Is this not typical of all teleological thinking?

A whole part of Mably's anti-Physiocratic charge thus consists in rejecting their anthropology based on the material interests of individuals as alone capable of constituting 'the basis of all justice and virtue'.[35] To this, he prefers an anthropology that roots men's sociability in their purely moral needs. Mably does not precisely set out the series of causes that might have led men to draw closer together, nor does he explain why the full development of man's social qualities should require the writing of laws. He does not tell us exactly what led men to form a society in the first place. What we do know is that men's moral nature, stirred by the presence of their fellow human beings, gradually prepared them to receive legislation. It is not the case that agriculture comes before morals and laws. The opposite is true: men had to pose the question of the political conditions of their common existence *before* addressing the question of its material conditions. Mably thus postulated that, when the Physiocrats placed the economy at the heart of the social bond, they were confusing the principle with the effect. Agriculture is a belated consequence of social life: 'society needs to cultivate the land to multiply its subsistence, only insofar as [the society itself] becomes civilised, which is to say, its morals, laws

---

33 Ibid., p. 28.

34 Yves Vargas, 'Rousseau et le droit naturel', *TransFormAção* 31: 1, 2008, pp. 25–52, at p. 28.

35 Mirabeau and Quesnay, quoted by Skornicki, *L'économiste, la cour et la patrie*, p. 194.

and institutions are more suited to making it happy'.[36] The author of the *Doutes* uses this theoretical tour de force not only to deny that land ownership is natural, but to prove that it is fundamentally *unnatural*, since it diverts men from their moral duties and detracts from their social qualities. Land ownership is not only superfluous for satisfying human needs, but is itself damaging, in that it educates men in harmful passions. A source of inequality, it is responsible both for the 'vices of wealth'[37] – avarice, ambition, and vanity – and for the 'vices of poverty' – envy and jealousy, or else a soul stultified by misery which plunges man into a 'stupid lethargy'.[38] Its emergence is likely linked to the 'laziness' of a few parasites who found a way to make others work for their benefit.[39] Ever a cutthroat force, it starts wars for the sake of building up its possessions.

When agriculture first developed, it was thus the duty of politics 'to stifle the seed of evil' by maintaining a community of goods such as could prevent an inequality of condition from emerging. But at this point, Mably imagines the ancient legislators making their first mistake: 'Our fathers did not see the danger that threatened them; far from opposing what was preparing the ground for an inequality of conditions they promoted it by establishing landed property. Their ignorance served as their excuse.'[40] Legislation that kept the land in its original, undivided state would have been beneficial because it would have suppressed these harmful passions. If only avarice and ambition had been cut off at the root, a 'love of distinction, glory and consideration' would have developed, meaning that citizens would have had no way of proving their value other than to devote themselves to the public good. Social virtues alone can bring happiness to society. Only through the perspective of devotion to the general interest, motivated by what connects man's individual pleasure to the collective well-being, can society offer man a framework properly in keeping with his fundamental dignity. Here, moral perfectionism is thus linked to a much more developed theory of the passions than Mably had previously elaborated.

36 *DP*, p. 25.
37 Ibid., p. 10.
38 Ibid., p. 36.
39 Ibid., p. 33.
40 Ibid., p. 19.

This also tells us something about the role of magistrates in the quest for man's moral development. Their role must not be a substitute for individuals' own self-determination: Mably reminds us that, if God had wanted the will of a magistrate to take the place of my own reason, He would have made them a species apart. Since God did not decide to do this, I must be free in society, and, in that society, magistrates play the role that reason plays in the individual: directing, tempering the passions, and aiding the particular reason of each man. While Mably granted magistrates this important function, he did not thereby make individuals' capacity for self-determination disappear by subsuming it under the benevolent direction of magistrates. Such a role would have made them more like guardians of the herd than representatives of the will of the majority.

It may therefore seem surprising that, at the same time, Mably reasserts man's inalienable right to the goods necessary for his subsistence. This is presented as a foundation of the social bond, even though Mably has just spoken of the essentially moral sources of this same bond. Compared with *Des droits et des devoirs*, the issues surrounding private property are, if anything, posed in even sharper terms, and Mably's criticism is better targeted. If the 1758 text refused to condemn thieving by the destitute, in the categories of the 1768 text, it is an inalienable right par excellence, because this theft constitutes the hungry man's claim to his right to movable property. More precisely, movable property is the site of a compact between the individual and society: 'One of the main advantages I find in living in society is that I am entitled to demand that [society should] provide for my subsistence, because I agree to work for it.'[41]

Subsistence is thus said to be one of the 'main' reasons for individuals to enter into political association. There is surely a tension between this thesis and the one that we have just explained, according to which it is the development of social qualities and virtues that has brought men together and justifies their political institutions. The outlining of this new condition of social life is followed by lines that speak to the full ambivalence of Mably's thinking:

But whether [society] should take care of this concern [of providing for my subsistence] by leaving goods in common, or by dividing the

---

[41] Ibid., pp. 32–3.

public domain into landed property for each citizen, *is the most indifferent thing in the world*.⁴²

Mably is again demonstrating, despite himself, how difficult it is to reconcile the two perspectives that continue to coexist in his work. If, in a jusnaturalistic framework, I expect society to guarantee my natural rights, such as Mably has redefined them here – that is, my personal property, or right over myself, and my movable property, or right to the goods necessary for my survival – then the community of goods is only one option among others, insofar as it fulfils this function. It is striking how, in his desire to deny land ownership a natural character for the sake of his polemic against the Physiocrats, Mably also comes to deny the natural character of the community of goods, which he elsewhere terms 'the true order of nature'.⁴³ Any form of social organisation thus becomes admissible, so long as it ensures respect for my natural rights; taking things to their logical conclusion, the community of goods is only preferable insofar as it more effectively serves this purpose. But, if association has a different objective, namely the development of man's social qualities, then the community of goods is the only possible path for Mably, insofar as it alone can suppress the harmful passions. This is understood in the negative, when the author recognises the irreversibility of the transformation that took place in man with the establishment of property: 'It seems to me, in fact, that property arms in its favour a hundred passions which will always take its side, and which will never listen to reason.'⁴⁴

Property is the main fuel for these passions. Mably's moral perfectionism thus remains pessimistic in character. Society had the task of securing man a virtuous happiness, but it has irreparably failed in its mission. This undoubtedly explains the coexistence of the two perspectives. Jusnaturalism can, ultimately, be interpreted as a stopgap, a second-class goal, once the possibility of a truly harmonious development of man's social qualities has been closed off. Yet it also seems important to recognise that the author never actually establishes such a clear connection. In the texts, the two perspectives generally coexist

---

42   Ibid., p. 33. Emphasis added.
43   Ibid., p. 37.
44   Ibid., p. 12.

without Mably putting them in a hierarchy or setting them in relation to one another. Their coexistence leads to a kind of compromise: in a society now definitively marked by the regime of private property, legislators must aim to limit the damaging effects in terms of individual vice, and moreover to guarantee natural rights as best they can, within the terms of this essential constraint.

On this basis, Mably makes a twofold criticism of the anthropological foundations of Physiocratic theory. On the one hand, he criticises it for not allowing the satisfaction of basic natural rights. He thus wryly remarks on the lack of success that this doctrine and its principles are likely to encounter among real citizens:

> In a word, sir, how will you go about making men who have nothing, which is to say the greater number of citizens, believe that they are obviously in the order in which they may find the greatest possible enjoyment and happiness?[45]

The Physiocrats had neglected the social consequences of unequal fortunes. This critique falls within a jusnaturalist perspective common to both Mably and his opponents: when the Physiocrats enshrine land ownership as a cardinal principle, men will judge the value of this state of affairs in terms of its real and not merely theoretical respect for their natural rights. But the *Doutes* also stress that the passions generated by the reign of property do not make man happy, because they disturb his soul. In this sense, they contravene the goal originally assigned to society by Mably, which lies in life having a certain moral quality:

> From the comparison that every man continually makes of his own fortune with that of his neighbours and fellow-citizens, there arises that secret anxiety which constantly agitates us, and which is always prone to disturb society by disturbing families from within.[46]

Contrary to what Le Mercier suggests, even the satisfaction of material needs is not enough to make men happy, because the passions unleashed by the reign of property will throw them into endless torments. Once

---

45   Ibid., p. 39.
46   Ibid.

again, there is an obvious connection with a Rousseauian concept: in this case, *amour-propre*. Here, we can recognise the probable influence of Rousseau's definition of *amour-propre* in the *Second Discourse*, which speaks of a 'factitious' feeling that constantly leads us to worry about our situation via the 'comparisons' that it invites between ourselves and others.[47] The distinction between the two notions lies in the origin attributed to each of them: while the citizen of Geneva casts this passion as emerging with society itself, Mably roots it in the right to property. For the author of the *Doutes*, only when *amour-propre* is directed towards purely material comparisons of wealth and honours does it become harmful to the social bond. But both thinkers agree in seeing this vice as at the origin of the evils that men do to each other in society.

There is also a striking comparison between the two men in terms of their critique of Physiocracy. In his letter to the Marquis de Mirabeau of 26 July 1767, Rousseau also criticised the theory of *évidence*, namely the (self-)evident truth: 'How can philosophers who know the human heart grant so much authority over men's actions to this evidence, as if they did not know that one very rarely acts by one's lights, and very frequently by one's passions?'[48] Mably would say no different. 'Passions', he asserts, in the same vein as Rousseau's letter, 'are the soul of the world.'[49] They always take precedence over *évidence*. The first appearance of property unleashed the passions because it made personal enrichment possible. '[I]t is the hope of success that nourishes and inflames passions':[50] and, hence, they constantly find new fuel in this social order. For this reason, the 'sensitive man' within each of us, whose passions are unbridled and far removed from his true personal interest, will more often than not get the better of the 'intelligent man'. This is also why, in a society doomed to the reign of private property, the role of government can be little more than a matter of making laws 'to regulate and repress passions' by

---

47   Jean-Jacques Rousseau, *The Social Contract and the First and Second Discourses*, edited by Susan Dunn, New Haven, CT: Yale University Press, 2002, p. 109.

48   Jean-Jacques Rousseau, 'Selected Letters' in *The Social Contract and Other Later Political Writings*, edited by Victor Gourevitch, Cambridge: Cambridge University Press, 2018, pp. 261–85, at p. 274.

49   *DP*, p. 45.

50   Ibid., p. 150.

establishing 'punishments and rewards'.[51] In the absence of natural equality, a mixed government is best able to do this, in the sense that it will use the different orders of society to repress each others' passions: 'all the orders of society balance each other, impose themselves on each other, hold each other in equilibrium'.[52]

Against Legal Despotism

Mably's critique of 'legal despotism', the political aspect of Physiocratic theory, thus also has two sides to it. First, Mably criticised the Physiocrats for misunderstanding the mechanisms of the human soul, on account of their disregard for its intrinsic dignity. This dignity is exactly the reason why a nation suffering under the weight of despotism could never find true happiness. Thus, in China, which Le Mercier takes as a model:

> Everyone stays in his place, not because he is happy, but because he is stupid enough to believe that this is the place that he should occupy. The emperor himself, stultified by the general stultification of his nation, vegetates without fear or desire, because all his subjects tremble at his name alone.[53]

This also implicitly points to man's elevated moral purpose. Man's proper calling is to a free and virtuous life under the guidance of reason. The denial of his rights debases him; it reduces him to the rank of a beast, with its routine and mechanical behaviour.

On the other hand, the Physiocrats' theory of legal despotism overlooked the operation of the passions. Good government is needed to *balance* the passions of the different orders of society, rather than to *crush* them. In a society based on property, the human passions cannot be the responsibility of a monolithic form of government that imposes a static order on them; rather, they require a constant, ever-precarious rebalancing operation. As Francine Markovits writes, in Mably, 'the energies of government and a policy for the passions require the

---

51 Ibid., p. 165.
52 Ibid.
53 Ibid., p. 110.

development of a moral dynamic that runs counter to static mechanics and geometry'.[54]

Mably's theory of mixed government is thus ultimately a product of his anthropology of the passions. This type of political administration – one that tempers, regulates, and conceives a system of actions and reactions – reproduces on a collective scale the mechanisms by which the individual sustains his own reason. A policy consistent with human nature is also consistent with the structure and possibilities of human beings:

> You will note, with me, the admirable artifice with which nature has placed in each man's heart the counter-weights or counter-forces that are necessary to question and listen to his reason. Have you not had the experience, Sir, in which in order to overcome some passion you have called another to your aid?[55]

The reference to this Cartesian topos highlights the fact that Mably has refined his thinking since the time of *Des droits et des devoirs*, with regard to the passional mechanism that politics must address. This is no longer a question – either for the individual or for the government – of directly helping reason to overcome the passions. Rather, it is necessary to balance the passions against each other, to the benefit of reason. This type of analysis is more in line with Mably's idea of the purpose of government in a society based on property. The aim is not to achieve the communitarian ideal, which has now been irreversibly left behind by the way in which human societies have developed. The ambition is far more modest: rulers have the job of balancing the different orders in society, which remain structurally unequal, but whose inequality can be reduced by balancing their respective weights. It is in this perspective that we can see the need to allow everyone to enjoy the natural rights of personal and movable property.

The Physiocrats conceived man as half-beast, in that he seeks above all to maximise his material pleasures, and as half-angel, in that he submits entirely to the rational force of *évidence*. Mably counters this with a vision of man who strives to maintain himself at an intermediate

---

54 Francine Markovits, *L'ordre des échanges*, Paris: PUF, 1986, p. 234.
55 *DP*, p. 234.

level. Man is not a beast, and his individual dignity requires that his rights be respected and that his will be expressed in the institutions of society. But man is also no angel, and his passions must be controlled and channelled by a government able to counterbalance the power of some with the power of others, within a shared social context. Mixed government – with its emphasis on national representation but also its ability to treat the different social forces in a tempered way – thus appears as a necessity, well suited to man's historical condition. In the Physiocratic theory, an imaginary representation of the human being replaces analysis of his real characteristics.

It is on this basis that we can understand Mably's criticism of Physiocratic theory as *utopian*. He begins by expressing his incredulity: 'But in good faith, Sir, do you believe that all this can be arranged as easily in a state as in a book?'[56] Then he offers his cutting judgement: 'our author's entire system is nothing but a real chimera'.[57] This is all the more interesting in that it resonates with Rousseau's assessment, in his letter to Mirabeau *père*, criticising the Physiocrats for constructing systems that were good 'for the people of Utopia' and not 'for the children of Adam'.[58] The two critiques clearly converge. But it may seem contradictory, to say the least, that two authors who were both accused of having set up their dreams as political models should in turn direct this same accusation against their opponents. In Mably's case, the criticism is all the more disturbing given that the author himself described his ideal of a community of goods in the same way in *Des droits et des devoirs*, writing that it 'can no longer be anything but a chimera in the world'. So, what can such an assessment really mean?

As Blaise Bachofen notes, Rousseau – like Mably, in this sense – essentially criticises the Physiocrats less for wanting to head for Utopia than 'for not giving themselves the means to get there, for lack of sufficient lucidity about the distance to be covered and the difficulty of the journey'.[59] The Physiocrats' fault lies in their unwillingness to make the

---

56 Ibid., pp. 58–9.
57 Ibid., p. 255.
58 Jean-Jacques Rousseau, letter to Victor Riquetti, Marquis de Mirabeau, 26 July 1767, in *Correspondance complète de Rousseau*, Oxford, The Voltaire Foundation, 1979, vol. XXXIII, p. 243.
59 Blaise Bachofen, *La condition de la liberté: Rousseau, critique des raisons politiques*, Paris: Payot, 2002, p. 220.

difficult journey from existing social and political relations to an ideal state, as they instead prefer to start from an illusory representation of reality. In this case, they postulate a spontaneous balancing of the economic and political order under the mere effect of *évidence*. All that would then be needed to bring this natural order to completion would be a perfectly rational despot. If this were true, then the ideal state would not be far off, and few existing realities would need calling into question. Yet, in this sense, Mably and Rousseau were blind to the truly reforming nature of the Physiocrats' doctrine, which meant putting an end to the society of orders and separate bodies: ' "Legal despotism" did not, therefore, endorse the existing political order – that of a traditional monarchy based on separate bodies in society and the system of privileges – but represented a radical plan for reforming the kingdom.'[60]

On the other hand, both men countered what they deemed an idyllic representation of reality by instead presenting an image of conflict and passions, said to mark a considerable retreat from nature's intentions. Mably and Rousseau contrasted their adversaries' chimera – which, in their view, was ignorant of its own chimerical character – with the reality of the here and now. Conversely, their own chimeras, which were openly presented as such, were attributed a specific critical importance. For Mably and Rousseau, the counterpoint that these chimeras represented ultimately made it possible to give an uncompromising, realistic image of reality, which could itself serve as a basis for transformative action. Rousseau's state of nature and Mably's community of goods were hypotheses out of step with the times, but they served – albeit to varying degrees – as reference points for 'properly judging the present state'.[61] These states of affairs were a matter of the past or were even absolutely chimerical. Yet, they made it possible to reveal man's true nature and to blame his present misfortune on a way of organising social life that stands in contradiction with this nature. For Mably in particular, the comparison between the social ideal and the concrete conditions of human existence shines a light on the genealogy of the passional mechanisms that produce the present disorder. The images of the community of goods and the equality of conditions thus allow us, through what they

---

60 Arnault Skornicki, *L'économiste, la cour et la patrie*, p. 253.
61 Rousseau, *The Social Contract*, p. 82.

tell us about human nature, to demystify the Physiocrats' alleged illusions about both the real and the possible.

The letter to Mirabeau, like the *Doutes*, thus offers an opportunity for a critique of 'the illusion of "realism" in politics'.[62] According to Mably and Rousseau, the Physiocrats were mistaken because they imagined that they could root political theory purely and simply in a reality which they were basically satisfied with, even at the cost of a few adjustments. For the Physiocrats, an order based on property, and even a despotic one, was the only natural, and ultimately the only real one; and from this perspective, property-based society, almost such as it is, becomes all that society can be. They tell us that it is, in essence, impossible to imagine anything more perfect than the society that they are painting in a fallacious, idealised – false – light.

The polemic with the Physiocrats thus allowed Mably to clarify his thinking from an anthropological point of view. The jusnaturalism of his doctrine was enriched by the concepts – drawn from his opponents – of 'personal property' and 'movable property' as inalienable natural rights. More clearly than in *Des droits et des devoirs*, respect for what appears as the right to liberty and the right to subsistence is presented as one of the main goals of political association. This gives clearer definition to Mably's reformulation of Lockean natural law, which now clearly excludes immovable property from man's prerogatives. At the same time, the properly moral purpose of public authority is more clearly framed in the *Doutes*: it must help man to overcome the passions that society is sure to promote now that it cannot surpass property ownership. The public authority must achieve this by balancing the passions of one order of society against another, within a mixed national representation. In this way, society can allow man to be as free, virtuous, and equal to others as circumstances allow. Hence, while Mably recognises that the reign of (immovable) property ownership is here to stay, he is careful to ensure that it encroaches as little as possible not only on the individual's basic right to material subsistence, but also on his moral dignity. Both the Physiocrats' framing of natural rights and their doctrine in favour of individual despotism called this dignity into question.

It should be pointed out that Mably was not content with polemicising with the Physiocrats. A few years after the publication of the *Doutes*,

---

62   Bachofen, *La condition de la liberté*, p. 222.

his general orientation inspired another dialogue, *Du commerce des grains*, written in 1775 but published posthumously. In it, he sharply attacks the policy of liberalising grain prices introduced by the Turgot ministry in 1774 under the influence of the Physiocrats. Mably supported the peasants' tax riots, forcing the merchants to sell their goods at a 'fair price'. In his words:

> These peasants of whom you speak, who have caused disorder in the town markets, do not steal; they pay in full for what they take, and they only want to buy wheat at a good price . . . you detest riots which can shake the firmness of the ministry and overturn its system and its plans; and I can excuse them and even love them, because it is not impossible that they are the cause and the principle of a fortunate revolution.[63]

Mably's utopian critique of Physiocracy was thus far from purely Platonic. For it was inseparable from a political stance which, though set within an imaginary dialogue, was a form of intervention in the reality of the times. While it did not directly give rise to a programme, it at least conditioned Mably's assessment of events and the forces at play. It led him to unambiguously take sides. This was far from a sterile position or a merely moral posture.

---

63   Gabriel Bonnot de Mably, 'Du commerce des grains', in *Œuvres complètes*, Paris: Guillaume Arnoux, 1794–5, vol. XIII, pp. 246–9.

5

De la législation: Or, Utopia in Service of Reform

The dialogue *De la législation* published in 1776 pitted a 'Swedish philosopher' – in fact an avatar of Gabriel Bonnot de Mably – against an Englishman, Milord. The latter begins as an enthusiastic supporter of his country's commercial society and its ambitions but is then gradually won over by his interlocutor's arguments. The choice of the Swedish spokesman is due to the fact that for Mably the Swedish republic is the most typical example of mixed government. In *De l'étude de l'histoire*, where he discusses Sweden's institutions in more detail, they are still presented as 'the masterpiece of modern legislation'.[1] The combination of a diet made up of the four main orders of the nation (the nobility, the clergy, the representatives of the towns, and those of the peasants), an aristocratic senate, and a monarch who governs by consulting the senators, constitutes 'the government most worthy of the praise and admiration of politicians'.[2] In addition to this institutional balance, there is also the advantage of Sweden's sumptuary laws, the drastic limitation of foreign trade, arts, and luxury. Mably thus has Milord telling the Philosopher in *De la législation*: 'one could already compare you with the venerable Spartans'.[3] If Mably

---

1 Gabriel Bonnot de Mably, *De l'étude de l'histoire, à Monsieur le Prince de Parme*, 1778, in OEuvres, vol. XII, p. 257.
2 Ibid., p. 241.
3 Gabriel Bonnot de Mably, *De la legislation ou principes des lois,* 1776, vol. IX in *OEuvres*, Paris: Guillaume Arnoux, 1794–5, republished with introduction, bibliography and index of names by Peter Friedemann, Darmstadt: Scientia Verlag Aalen, 1977 (15 vols), p. 7.

recognises that 'equality [was] not established' in eighteenth-century Sweden, it does at least appear to him as 'this constitution in which the rights of humanity and equality are much more respected than one would have hoped for in the unhappy times in which we live'.[4] Nor does Sweden lack a virtuous legislator. The Philosopher praises the role of King Gustav Vasa who – even if he did not establish all legitimate laws in one fell swoop – should nevertheless be credited with curtailing the clergy's harmful sway over economic and political questions. Mably concludes his praise for the king in rather telling terms: 'Sweden is a great proof that nothing is impossible for a skilful legislator; he holds our hearts and minds in his hands, so to speak; he can make new men.'[5]

De la législation thus offers an unprecedented combination of two kinds of utopia: both a communal one and a republican one. Indeed, in some respects, the Philosopher may be considered an ambassador for the republican utopia, even if we should also take into account Mably's reservations over the imperfections of the Swedish government. It was surely not as ideal a model as that of ancient Sparta. By making this character the principled defender of the community of goods, Mably once again links the precepts of political equality and material equality, of republic and community. In this dialogue between an Englishman and a Swede, with a Frenchman as arbiter, it is as if the (French) reader is being placed before a political alternative. Which model, which reforms, would be best for the monarchy of Louis XVI? Not surprisingly – albeit against the mainstream of the Enlightenment – Mably rejects Anglomania in favour of the republican ideal.

Utopianism and the 'Denial of Utopia'

Mably's two characters begin with a general philosophical discussion on the nature of man and society. Soon enough, they come to the relationship between human nature and social equality: are they really compatible? Milord argues that they are not, on the grounds that a primitive equality in the division of land would inevitably produce, within a few

---

4   *EH*, p. 258.
5   *DL*, p. 168.

generations, the birth of inequalities owing to the differences in individual talents, the number of children, and so on. The Philosopher agrees: to this ineffective doctrine of equal sharing, he contrasts the idea of community of goods, which is here explicitly identified with the Spartan model. It is because Lycurgus wanted to prevent the disadvantages noted by Milord, the Philosopher says, that he made the republic itself the owner of all the land, making each head of household a mere 'usufructuary'.[6] The superiority of the community of goods over the division of land is an idea which Mably had already advanced in the *Entretiens de Phocion*. The notable difference with this text, as well as with the contemporary *Observations sur l'histoire de la Grèce*, is that, in *De la législation*, this principle of social organisation is presented as the main feature of Spartan society, which could have allowed it to last 'a million years' had it been perpetuated. It also follows from this that the abandonment of this principle is clearly presented as the cause that 'lost the republic and the laws of Lycurgus, which were devoid of resources'.[7] So, here, the Spartan city is again used as a utopian motif, while its more properly historical aspects are strongly pushed into the background: Mably tells us of a republic that could have lasted forever, tightly bound to its guiding principle as the sole source of its invariable happiness.

This dialogue thus puts the idea of the community of goods back at the heart of the conceptual schema. As in the *Doutes*, this is presented as the only possible mode of organisation for the first human societies. Indeed, the Philosopher even admits that 'far from looking upon this community as an impracticable chimera, I find it difficult to determine how we came to establish property'.[8]

Mably, like Morelly in his time, reverses the usual relationship between the real society and the chimerical one – the same relationship that he had taken for granted in *Des droits et des devoirs du citoyen*. Here, it is the model society – the one which best suits man's nature and which alone can bring him happiness – that is presented as the most 'practicable'. It is, instead, the society based on property that appears to be an alarming deviation – the product of a misguidedness of the human race whose origin is difficult to imagine given how much it contradicts our

---

6 Ibid., p. 66.
7 Ibid., p. 67.
8 Ibid., p. 71.

rationally formed image of the species' characteristics. This taking of one's distance from the real world – presented as an absurdity, because it is deeply at odds with one's anthropological postulates – is a common move in the utopian tradition. But it can be seen in particular in *La Basiliade*, and in a slightly different way in the *Code de la Nature*, from which Mably may have drawn inspiration.

Moreover, this discussion of early societies also delves into hypotheses about the details of their day-to-day life. Here, we find the major features of the previous sketches of such societies, albeit with some variations:

> I think I see the citizens distributed in different classes; the most robust are destined to cultivate the land, the others work at the lowly arts which society cannot do without; everywhere I see public stores, where the riches of the republic are kept; and the magistrates, truly fathers of the nation, have almost no function other than the upkeep of morals, and to distribute to each family the things which are necessary for it.[9]

Apart from the allusion to different classes of citizens – classes of labour no doubt borrowed from Morelly's *Model of Legislation* – here we find the same terms and ideas already formulated in *Des droits et des devoirs*. Clearly, this time around, Mably attributes the principles of a utopian mode of organisation to all of the early civilised societies, and not only to natural societies. This was, the Philosopher avers, a 'golden age' of humanity, where men had all the advantages of the political state without the disadvantages of the establishment of property. However, the status of the society thus described changes imperceptibly in the course of the dialogue, as Milord objects to this initial presentation. Indeed, he openly scoffs at it, saying: 'The only thing missing from the description of your golden age are the streams of milk that wind their way through its plains.'[10]

Such taunts are coupled with other more serious arguments, in particular claiming that the absence of selfish motivations would lead to the general rise of laziness. In this case, the Philosopher responds not by citing humanity's past, but rather by using the conditional tense: 'If men

---

9 Ibid., pp. 75–6.
10 Ibid., p. 79.

had never established property, the earth would be as cultivated and as populated as it can be.'[11] Soon, this general assumption is more specifically asserted: the Swede mentions the possibility of societies 'which would not have abandoned this situation whose passing I so regret' and which would cohabit with 'neighbouring peoples who would hasten to leave it behind'.[12] Up to this point, we may well think that Mably is still alluding to Sparta: after all, he is arguing that the obligation to defend such a homeland with arms in hand against greedy neighbours is not a source of corruption of the community's morals, but rather an opportunity to raise the courage and the value of the citizens. At the same time, here we see the return of a particular theme of the republican tradition, namely the celebration of the citizen-soldier. This, again, demonstrates the convergence of these two great influences in the author's thinking.

But, almost without us noticing it, Mably's verbs change from the conditional to the future indicative. It would appear that he is no longer just interested in glorifying the past, or even in advancing a working hypothesis. Rather, it seems that here he is envisaging the creation of such a republic in a concrete future. In any case, his wording fully allows us to suppose as much:

> Your laws, my lord, will acquire more majesty; you will see the formation of establishments suitable for making as many heroes as you have citizens ... Without supposing magistrates equal to Lycurgus, a republic will be born which is even more excellent than that of Lacedaemonia, because the principles of its government will not in any way deviate from the views of nature.[13]

So, it seems that, in his strategy of finding legitimacy for his approach, the Philosopher comes to imagine a utopian republic which could possibly be built in the future (indeed, a future which remains wholly indeterminate). In the same vein, he speaks a little further on of 'the citizens of my republic',[14] albeit without it really being possible to pin down what this expression really refers to. Indeed, a few pages later, he seems to pull

---

11   Ibid., p. 82.
12   Ibid., p. 86.
13   Ibid., p. 88.
14   Ibid., p. 90.

back from this. While he criticises Plato's *Republic* for having granted community of property only to the class of magistrates, instead of extending it to the whole of society (and this is the first time that we find such a reservation in Mably's work), he concedes: 'But let us leave Plato there, and do not fear, my Lord, that I am thinking of making a more perfect republic than his; I lack the materials to erect such an edifice.'[15] The Swede then explains, taking up an idea already present in *Des droits et des devoirs*, that no citizen of the contemporary world would accept to live under such laws. To him, the appeal of wealth and honours, the great humility of the people, and the force of habit seem to be obstacles too great to overcome. Hence, Europe is too corrupted by the harmful effects of the rule of property to hope for any such radical change. But all is not lost: 'If you want to lay the foundations of a perfect republic, I advise you ... to go and find citizens in the forests of America or Africa.'[16] The Philosopher insists on this – and supports it with arguments similar to those advanced by Morelly in the *Code de la Nature*: it is said that the 'savage' societies would be willing to accept the techniques of modern Europe, reduced to the 'necessary arts', without thereby abandoning their egalitarian form of social organisation. This model is deemed still intact among them, although more often than not it is linked to the basic production techniques of hunting and fishing. It would, then, surely be possible to propose simple 'reforms' to improve their ordinary lives without affecting their communal way of life.

At this point, it is again Milord's turn to speak. Clearly influenced by such reasoning, he makes quite a transparent allusion to George Fox, founder of the Quaker sect in England under Charles I. He suggests that, 'had an island been presented to these enthusiasts',[17] they would surely have established the community of goods there. But this time, it is the Philosopher who tempers this ardour: religious fanaticism cannot produce wise legislators, and it must be agreed that no European should claim to re-establish a condition of life that has long since disappeared in these latitudes.

So, it seems that Mably's thought, which often seems to circulate between the two protagonists in this dialogue, defies its own utopian

---

15   Ibid., p. 97.
16   Ibid., p. 102.
17   Ibid., p. 105.

De la législation: Or, Utopia in Service of Reform

tendency. Having ventured into the field of possibilities for the future, it then immediately retreats by diagnosing Europe as too corrupt to have any hope of regeneration. Having hazarded the idea of a hypothetical settlement on the American continent, it then retreats, faced with the possible candidacy of specific and actually existing Europeans who might perhaps attempt such an experiment. The author reiterates the opinion already expressed in *Des droits et des devoirs*, where his avatar rebuffs the idea of establishing an ideal community on a distant island. He does not want to fall into 'a wisdom that can only be achieved by madness'.[18] His suggestion about the Native Americans remains in the realm of a pure thought experiment, as in Morelly. His spokesman's reaction to the Quakers shows his rejection of social solutions of this kind. The final judgement leaves no room for challenge: today's Europeans must leave behind the utopia of the community of goods, which belongs to a now-unattainable past. This is why, paradoxically, the wisest position that the legislator can take is to bear in mind that 'in any state where private property is once established, it must be regarded as the foundation of order, peace and public safety'.[19] The first book of the dialogue *De la législation* thus ends with a surprising statement. All its lines of argument demonstrating the superiority of the community of goods over any other form of social organisation, and all the outlines of a utopian model based on this principle, lead to a conclusion entirely favourable to the property rights which are otherwise so decried.

However, it does not follow that the lessons of utopia are simply erased. From all the above discussion, the Swede claims, there follows a general political orientation which every good legislator must follow. This consists in seeking to destroy by all available means two of the vices that property produces – avarice and ambition – which are the bane of mankind. Mably's avatar insists that this overriding objective must be pursued above all others.

Thus, a clear and valuable lesson emerges from the path which he has headed along. Utopia is discounted from the range of achievable goals, as an ideal construction to be imitated, but it is not abandoned as a source of inspiration. In the books that follow, it appears that utopia offers the principle for a policy for which – once again, but for

---

18   Ibid., p. 107.
19   Ibid., p. 109.

somewhat different reasons – Sparta is used as a model to which one should adhere as closely as possible. Mably thus lists a series of general measures, according to the text applicable in all times and places, which should be able to cut off avarice and ambition at the root, despite the continued establishment of property. These are presented as a 'compass'[20] that should guide the legislator on the road to the public happiness of which Europe is still capable. It can thus be said that here the utopia of the egalitarian republic is the unambiguous substitute for the utopia of the communal republic. The question obviously remains as to what status should be attached to these universal political proposals, even though the author has endeavoured in the first part of his text to show the close link between the vices which they are supposed to combat and the very existence of property, which is no longer itself in question. At the very least, the maintenance of the principle of property raises questions over the relationship between the distribution of goods and the morals that it would appear to condition.

This position has clear consequences: from this point in the dialogue onwards, the Philosopher traces the outlines of a 'republic' that grants reality its due, without abandoning the lessons of utopia. Hans-Ulrich Thamer has rightly referred to this as a 'second-rate utopia', because, for its author, it amounts to a second choice.[21]

A 'Second-Rate Utopia': Republican and Utopian Political Economy

Here, we will not attempt to detail all the various aspects of the Philosopher's republican utopia. Rather, we will limit ourselves to a more specific examination of two of its fundamental aspects: firstly, its political economy, or the way in which it conceives of the egalitarian measures necessary for the best possible state of society; and secondly, the religious and educational questions it raises, insofar as they concern the essential problem of morals, important to both the republican and utopian traditions.

---

20 Ibid., p. 159.
21 Hans-Ulrich Thamer, *Revolution und Reaktion in der französischen Sozialkritik des 18. Jahrhundert*, Frankfurt am Main: Akademische Verlagsgesellschaft, 1973, p. 185.

De la législation: Or, Utopia in Service of Reform

The dialogue, as we have said, sets down the political principles which are supposed to pave the way to the happiness 'to which man is called by nature'[22] – and then shows that these are unattainable for contemporary human societies. Having reached that point, it sets out to review the various areas in which the legislator – armed with this wisdom and with the model towards which he must strive – can and must pursue his reforming endeavours. The order in which these areas are mentioned is also indicative of the way in which Mably sees their influence on each other. The book's structure thus tells us not so much about the respective *importance* of the different fields of intervention, as about how Mably conceives the strategic priorities of a plan for social reform.

Before he can even think of changing the nature of social relations, the legislator must set about reforming the state itself, as the main instrument of all subsequent transformations. This first stage clearly shows that Mably saw reform as a top-down process. Like his utopian predecessors, he believes that society must be open to the state's rationalising endeavours. But – taking their thinking further by analysing the means necessary to achieve this end – he is naturally driven to prioritise the rationalisation of the state itself above any other task. This first orientation is immediately identified with Lycurgus: it means 'reducing the state finances' by prohibiting the creation of a permanent public treasury, so as not to tempt the greed of the magistrates and to avoid their corruption from infecting the entire republic. Rather, it is supposed that a frugality in the state itself should be transmitted and spread to social relations in general.

Here again, the Sparta in question is quite obviously considered in its historical and republican aspect. Mably refers to the details of its political institutions – the two kings, the ephors, the senate – and compares it with the Swiss cantonal republics of his own era. Mably attributes the latter the same characteristics of frugal spending and moderation in the accumulation of public resources. Sumptuary laws prevent the enrichment of magistrates at public expense. This allows for state funds to be directed to their proper role in coming 'to the aid of those [citizens] who have suffered a loss'.[23] Mably thus sets out a series of principles that ought to govern the management of the public finances. The state must

---

22   *DL*, p. 1.
23   Ibid., p. 118.

avoid all luxury spending. It must limit the subsidies it demands from individuals to a direct tax on land, with the onus placed on the magistrates to always seek to reduce these charges rather than increase them. Men 'who have nothing',[24] especially wage earners, should not be subject to taxation. The Philosopher goes so far as to reject payment for magistrates, such that the exercise of public office will be a disinterested affair rewarded by public esteem alone. It is this principle that must, even more than any positive law, regulate the morals of politicians. The reference to this great principle of public life draws on both the utopian and republican traditions.

These wealth-limiting measures, which are first applied to the state itself, are then extended to all citizens. This is meant to rein in the greed which is naturally stirred by the existence of property. It is important to keep it within the bounds of preserving wealth that has already been acquired and prevent its spontaneous tendency for further 'conquest' and seeking to lay its hands on other people's property. Sumptuary laws are the linchpin of such a policy. The right to property must itself be regulated, allowing only for transmission within families and equal sharing among legitimate descendants. Citizens without descendants will have their inheritance shared among the poor families of their place of residence. The Swede also imagines that excessively large inheritances could be shared between the legitimate child(ren) and their brothers or sisters adopted by the public authorities. Finally, agrarian laws to limit the expansion of landed estates, inspired by the laws of the Roman Republic, must also maintain 'a certain equality which is necessary to unite the citizens'.[25]

It is interesting to compare these general approaches proposed by Mably with those of Rousseau, particularly in his *Discourse on Political Economy*, from 1755, and in his *Considerations on the Government of Poland and on its Proposed Reformation*, from 1772. Indeed, in 1755, Rousseau set out principles of the 'general economy' of government 'with reference to the administration of property',[26] which may in many respects appear similar to those of the author of *De la législation*. These constitute the principles of a public economy that Rousseau calls

---

24 Ibid., p. 122.
25 Ibid., p. 145.
26 Jean-Jacques Rousseau, 'Discours sur l'économie politique', in *Oeuvres complètes*, vol. III, p. 262.

'popular',[27] as opposed to a tyrannical one. This expression could just as well be used to describe Mably's recommendations on the same front. This comparison was already made by Henri Mettrier in his 1901 thesis, with this opening remark:

> Experience and induction are unknown to them. Their theory of public charges derives as a corollary from the general principles of their system ... What they are proposing, above all with regard to finance, is morality, and it is still politics.[28]

Mettrier here emphasises a common characteristic of the principles set out in both *De la législation* and Rousseau's texts. It lies in the fact that neither author is proposing measures suited to a specific government in particular circumstances, so much as setting out general rules intended as a model for any given legislature. So, any charge of idealism or unrealism would risk missing the deeper objective of both theories, which are surely not meant to be directly applicable in practice. To use Mably's expression, the concern is rather more to provide a 'compass' to the legislator, who is responsible for keeping the state on course, in the suggested direction.

Both authors start from the same principle: just as Mably decreed that the legislator should consider property 'the foundation of public order, peace and safety', Rousseau bases all his measures on the axiom that 'the right of property is the most sacred of all the rights of citizenship'.[29] This principle also leads to the conclusion that the government must provide for its own subsistence and public expenditure while laying as light a hand as possible on individuals' property. Rousseau is thus also a supporter of cheap government, which is sure 'to take more pains to guard against needs than to increase revenues'.[30] It is also from this perspective that he takes up the idea of a public domain from which the state would draw the necessary revenues for its expenses, including the upkeep of magistrates, whose payment Mably rejects. In this text, Rousseau does not yet speak of completely abolishing the magistrates'

---

27 Ibid., p. 247.
28 Henri Mettrier, *L'impôt et la milice dans J.-J. Rousseau et Mably*, Paris: L. Larose, 1901, pp. 6–7.
29 *DEP*, p. 263.
30 Ibid., p. 266.

income, but the evolution of his thinking would lead him to the same conclusions as the Swede. In *The Social Contract*, he brings in the idea, with regard to the form of government that he decrees the best – namely the elective aristocracy – that the members of the government must be able to live off their own means:

> Inasmuch as this form of government includes a certain inequality of fortune, it would be well in general that the administration of public affairs be entrusted to those who are best able to devote their whole time to it.[31]

As they developed, Rousseau's ideas on these matters actually tended to come closer to Mably's. This is further evidenced by this line in the *Considerations on the Government of Poland*:

> In short, I should like, if it were possible, for there to be no public treasury, and for the exchequer to know nothing of money payments. I feel that this can never be strictly realised; but the spirit of the government should always tend in that direction.[32]

This contrast, between the effective *impossibility* of abolishing money taxes and the preference for a 'spirit' of government which tends towards such an ideal, is a distinction that we also find in Mably. We noted that Rousseau speaks of the principles of frugal government, which aims as far as possible to reduce its needs, and even to eliminate its own financial reserves in favour of the simplest mode of functioning, least likely to entail an accumulation of wealth. To these, he adds the principles – again converging with Mably's – of a tax system which, as Mettrier rightly explains, 'tends not so much to provide revenue to the state as to correct the unequal distribution of wealth, and to bring fortunes down to a sufficient level through the possible sequestering of large incomes'.[33] The aim of Rousseau's popular public economy is to ensure the subsistence of all, by allowing each person to live a dignified existence from the

---

[31] Jean-Jacques Rousseau, *The Social Contract and the First and Second Discourses*, edited by Susan Dunn, New Haven, CT: Yale University Press, 2002, p. 203.

[32] *CGP*, p. 1009.

[33] Mettrier, *L'impôt et la milice*, p. 51.

proceeds of their work. To this end, the citizen of Geneva proposed, as early as 1755, that taxes be distributed in proportion to individuals' amount of 'superfluities'. Only in his *Considerations on the Government of Poland* did Rousseau agree with the view that individuals' land should be taxed instead of their income;[34] but, as early as the *Discourse on Political Economy*, he asserted, in agreement with Mably, that 'he who possesses only the common necessaries of life should pay nothing at all'.[35] Still, this difference surely is worth noting, insofar as it refers to a crucial difference between the two authors in terms of the value they respectively attach to property. In *De la législation*, Mably suggests that owners should be taxed as opposed to non-owners, whereas, in the *Discourse on Political Economy*, Rousseau proposes taxing those who possess more than the necessities of life, as opposed to those who have only what is necessary. This expresses Rousseau's penchant for small, self-sufficient property, exempt from taxes, which Mably does not share; after all, the Genevan's obsession with autarchy cannot much interest a defender of the principle of the community of goods. On the other hand, both authors agree in favour of sumptuary measures: Rousseau wants to establish a tax on the products (imported or not) of those 'frivolous and all too lucrative arts'[36] to which the rich remain wedded.

Yet this only makes makes the nuances between the two authors – both of whom are, we have seen, unconventional champions of what can be called a 'republican political economy' inspired by the ancients – even more instructive. Even beyond the fact that Rousseau (unlike Mably) seeks to exempt from taxation small properties that produce only the necessities of life for their beneficiaries, the Genevan's measures are on the whole less drastic than Mably's. Rather than proposing sumptuary laws outlawing luxury altogether, Rousseau advocates only taxing it. As for land ownership, he does not put forward any direct measures to limit its extent or to regulate its inheritance. Moreover, his analyses, especially in the *Discourse on Political Economy*, show a degree of concern to take into account the economic reality of his time. For example, despite his disapproval of luxury consumption, he deems it necessary to tax it in a manner not too disproportionate to the price of

---

34 *CGP*, p. 1011.
35 *DEP*, p. 271.
36 Ibid., p. 276.

objects, so as to avoid encouraging fraud.[37] This type of economic 'realism' is absent from the measures proposed by Mably in *De la législation*.

The only text by Rousseau in which he advocates measures similar to those championed by the Philosopher is a text that Mably could likely not have read: the *Constitutional Project for Corsica*.[38] Written in 1765, it would remain in manuscript form long after Rousseau's death. In many respects, this text can be considered the application of Mably's principles of political economy to a nation situated in space and time. It is worth noting that this project, whose proximity to the tradition of the 'island utopia' many commentators have emphasised, was even considered 'Rousseau's utopia' by Antoine Hatzenberger. He explains his thinking as follows:

> What makes Rousseau's text so original is that it marks a transitional moment in the evolution of the utopian form, in that it stands as an intermediate stage between the treatise on better government ... and the utopia-programmes of the socialists of the nineteenth century ... which were designed to be applied.[39]

It would thus seem that the *Project for Corsica* followed the intentions of Mably's spokesman in two senses. Not only was there agreement on a certain number of measures that were needed, but it would also seem that Rousseau's text echoed Mably's effort to distance himself from the realm of political sketches which lacked a direct grip on reality and instead strive to identify the means for the concretisation of these measures in the here and now. On this reading, it would appear that Rousseau and Mably not only agreed on principles of political economy, but each expressed a utopianism which – whatever their differences – had a common interest in real-life application. Mably's and Rousseau's utopianism would, in that case, be one which 'placed hope in the possible and

---

37 Ibid.
38 The unpublished manuscript was given to Paul Moultou in 1778, the year of Rousseau's death, and was not published until 1861. On this point, see Tanguy L'Aminot, 'La réception du Projet de Constitution pour la Corse', *Études Corses* 66, 2008, pp. 89–110, at pp. 90–2.
39 Antoine Hatzenberger, *Rousseau et l'utopie*, Paris: Honoré Champion, 2012, p. 351.

De la législation: Or, Utopia in Service of Reform

in the future, . . . insofar as this hope was motivated by the critique of a given situation.'[40]

Rousseau recommends the following principle for the Corsican people, in keeping with the theses expounded in particular in Chapter 9 of Book I of *The Social Contract*: 'Everyone should make a living, and no one should grow rich.' This is in line with the objectives put forward by Mably in *De la législation*. But translated into the terms of property relations, this objective implies the following consequence, which Rousseau had not drawn so clearly in his 1762 text:

> My idea . . . is not to destroy private property absolutely, since that is impossible, but to confine it within the narrowest possible limits; to give it a measure, a rule, a rein which will contain, direct, and subjugate it, and keep it ever subordinate to the public good.[41]

In this text, Rousseau thus goes further than ever in the social reforms he advocates and considers the possibility of establishing agrarian and sumptuary laws on the island of Corsica. In the republican tradition, agrarian law has often played the role of a bogeyman to be guarded against: it is condemned by classical authors such as Cicero and Machiavelli. But it is not totally foreign to the republican tradition, and it is notably championed by the Stranger of Athens in *The Laws*.[42]

It is worth emphasising Rousseau's moderate stance on the application of these laws. Severe sumptuary laws are appropriate only for the 'leaders of the state' and should be 'more lenient for the lower orders'. Agrarian laws should prevent the rich from accumulating further wealth, but they can hardly apply retroactively: as he puts it in the *Project for Corsica*, 'no law can despoil any private citizen of any part of his property'. The stress that Rousseau's own words place on this is eloquent proof of his respect for individual property rights, which are sanctioned by the social pact and impose a limit on the state's levelling action. The state can legitimately prevent the excessive accumulation of real estate, but it cannot challenge an already existing unequal distribution of property: this was the Gracchi brothers' mistake. Rousseau's caution in this

---

40   Ibid., p. 422.
41   *Constitutional Project for Corsica*, text from constitution.org.
42   Plato, *The Laws*, Cambridge, MA: Harvard University Press, 1926, 737c.

area therefore leads him to posit a time when it is simply too late for nations to remedy social inequalities. Indeed, it might well be asked whether a government can ever legitimately exercise the right to limit individuals' wealth. So, we can see the distance that separates Rousseau's approach to this crucial question from that of his contemporary Mably. The latter, after all, based his republican ideal on proximity to the ideal of the community of goods. In Mably's view, at least in the dialogue that concerns us here, it is always possible, if not to abolish, then at least to correct the excesses that flow from the right of ownership. In contrast to Rousseau, he does not hesitate to demand an agrarian law, not in one case but in all possible ones. The law must forbid 'owning more than one hundred acres of land'.[43]

As we have seen, from this same perspective, Mably sets out extremely specific rules on inheritance, aimed at preventing the accumulation of all property in just a few hands over the generations. In doing so, he encroaches – despite his previous assertions – on the freedom to determine one's will. This, even though the defenders of this choice most often considered it a right just as sacred as the right to property itself. On this point, it should be noted that his thinking once again tallies with Rousseau, who writes without elaborating further that: 'The laws of inheritance should all strive toward equality, so that everyone has something and nobody has too much.'[44] Hostile to the public authorities' direct requisition of rich citizens' land, the Genevan perhaps hoped to restore justice with the least possible violence or challenge by using the laws of succession.[45]

In Mably's case, his specification of the various details of succession is reminiscent of the minutiae of utopian regulations. He was probably inspired here by Plato's *Laws*. In Book V, through the mouth of the Stranger of Athens, Plato sets out the conditions of succession in the city which he has in mind, and which are meant to prevent inequalities between families becoming entrenched over the passing of the generations.[46] Be that as it may, Mably's boldness in this text is all the more striking because it is not found in other works of his, which are much

---

43   *DL*, p. 146.
44   *PCC*, p. 945.
45   Montesquieu had already demonstrated the political importance of the question of inheritance rights in Book XXVII of *The Spirit of the Laws*.
46   Plato, *The Laws*, 740b–741c.

more pragmatic. The limits placed on the right to property are tighter than in any other republican project, including those which he himself wrote.

From this point of view, the characteristics of Mably's political economy in this dialogue appear to be a compromise between a utopian ideal that he cannot completely give up on, and a republican tradition whose mainstream trend holds back from such economic and social radicalism. We can therefore subscribe to Mettrier's understanding that '[the] ideas [of Mably and Rousseau] substantially meet' only insofar as we interpret this to mean the convergence of two ways of thinking that had begun from entirely distinct starting points.[47] Rousseau's ideal for Corsica – that is, an ideal of independence – also applies to the individuals who make up his republic, who must be able to provide for themselves if they are to be full citizens. The union of citizens is desirable, but it is not the main goal. But Mably's concern is to bring the body politic closer to the communal ideal and – from this perspective – to establish equality among the citizens to better 'unite' them. This difference in emphasis, placing the accent not on independence but on union, is no mere accident. It makes it impossible to establish any total identification between the two authors' respective ideals. Mably's 'republican' view is, indeed, a diluted version of his utopian model, while Rousseau's utopia is an attempt to embody his republican economic ideals.

A 'Second-Rate Utopia' II: Education and Religion

Book IV of *De la législation* is devoted to educational and religious matters. These two fields have one key aspect in common: for they each concern the formation and maintenance of what Mably calls 'the mores' of a well-constituted republic. Morals are thus the final domain to which the legislator applies his wisdom. Still, this certainly does not imply that they are of only secondary importance. They have a complex relationship with law. Only with the help of morals are laws themselves sustainable, for if the citizens are corrupt then laws will lose all authority, and they will soon fall into disuse. Morals thus condition the efficiency of

---

47 Mettrier, *L'impôt et la milice*, p. 158.

the entire legal-political framework. Moreover, they 'make up for what is missing'[48] in the laws and protect them. They serve as a guide for individuals in situations where the law is silent, keeping them on the straight and narrow path of justice. Of course, the set of laws outlined above are themselves meant to promote virtue by combating avarice and ambition, and thereby to influence morals. However, these legal conditions are insufficient if they are not accompanied by measures that will govern the upbringing and the spiritual life of the citizen. Education and religion thus appear as indispensable complements to the laws that have been laid down. Mably no doubt remembers Montesquieu's lessons here: 'It is in republican government that the full power of education is needed.'[49]

In both these areas, the utopian and republican sources of inspiration are difficult to tell apart, insofar as the legacies of the two essentially converge. The first feature they have in common, which we find in Mably's text, is the principle of the *commonality* of education. The Philosopher thus advocates a 'public and general' education capable of giving 'common principles of union, peace and concord'. This is meant to grant all the children of a given generation 'a single spirit' devoid of 'domestic prejudices'.[50] The public and common character of youth education thus has two explicit aims: to unite the future citizenry and, on the other hand, to give this union a substance which is useful to perpetuating the city's rules of functioning. From this general perspective – and in accordance with the doctrine set out in Plato's *Republic* – young people must be subjected to physical and military training; they must be taken regularly to exercise on the 'Field of Mars', where they can be toughened up. Here, the ancient inspiration seems predominant. But it should be remembered that More's Utopians go to war accompanied by their sons, whose courage 'education and the good institutions of their society both reinforce',[51] and, indeed, that Campanella's Solarians train the young of both sexes in the art of war from the age of twelve.[52] Moreover, the military discipline in which youth must be trained

---

48   *DL*, p. 356.
49   *EdL*, I, p. 160.
50   *DL*, p. 371.
51   Thomas More, *Utopia*, Cambridge: Cambridge University Press, 1989, p. 95.
52   Tommaso Campanella, *The City of the Sun*, London: Merchant Books, 1929, p. 38.

according to the Philosopher also includes a directly political dimension, insofar as each age group is divided into companies that choose their leaders or captains. With this institution, he intends to teach both obedience and subordination, 'so necessary among men', and at the same time the ability 'to command':[53] these precepts are probably to be seen as an echo of Aristotle, who states in the *Politics* that all citizens must learn 'the duties of command and of obedience'.[54] Both qualities are indeed necessary to perform the various political duties of a free man, and Aristotle already relates the learning of these skills to military experience in the cavalry or infantry.

The training of youth must be, fundamentally, both a school of morals and an apprenticeship in equality. First of all, morality: the Philosopher demands that morality must be 'the basis of these studies',[55] in line with More's wish, who entrusts the teaching of children and the young to priests elected by the people. Here, 'instruction in morality and virtue is considered no less important than learning proper'.[56] The same general tone is found in Morelly. While he advocates a more directly vocational education, he also recommends to the 'professional leaders' of the 'public academies' that they should provide their young charges with 'moral instruction'.[57] For Mably's Philosopher, the important thing is to give children lessons in virtue, 'disinterestedness and generosity' from a young age in order to prepare them for devotion to the public good. Subsequently, history lessons designed with this edifying aim in mind will complement the education started with play at an early age. To the same end, the education of women should not be neglected, for failure to do so would lead to the maintenance of a ferment of corruption in the home of every citizen. On this question, the Swede leaves open an alternative: 'One must choose either to make men of them, like in Sparta, or to condemn them to withdrawal.'[58] Utopian education had envisaged the same kind of training for girls as for boys.

The idea common to these authors is that morality must be at the foundation of the social bond that is able to bring happiness to all. For

---

53 *DL*, p. 374.
54 Aristotle, *Politics*, Oxford: Clarendon Press, 1885, Book II, Part 11.
55 *DL*, p. 377.
56 More, *Utopia*, p. 104.
57 *CN*, p. 167.
58 *DL*, p. 375.

each of them, morality must preside over the reproduction of generations of citizens capable of leading a life worthy of man. Any bond based on other grounds, such as individual self-interest, degrades the community and its members, cuts them off from each other, and produces social unhappiness. This is perhaps the clearest manifestation of the utopian dimension of Mably's approach to reform: the institutions are conceived with an essentially moral aim in mind. In this sense, his project is radically opposed to the paradigm of the social bond based on interest or the contract. Nowhere is this more strongly expressed than with regard to education. For a discussion of this question demands reflection on the upbringing of future citizens and what they must be taught as a priority in order to make them full-fledged members of the community, worthy of the name. Here again, Montesquieu preceded Mably in the close link he established between the need to promote virtue as a 'continual preference of the public interest over one's own'[59] and the need for education in republican government.

Above all, a strong sense of equality must be instilled in youth. To this end, the Philosopher recommends the study of natural law, 'which I might call the law of equality among men'.[60] Here, he is referring to an equality of condition and of rights, and thus a political and social equality, and not an equality of talents. Indeed, the distinction of a minority justifies that some should be chosen to command rather than others, including within the youths' mock military companies. It is therefore necessary to ensure that education is the same for all and that the differences in wealth that property is bound to create between the children of each generation are erased for as long as possible. The idea of this egalitarian education is probably borrowed, once again, from the Spartan example. But, in Mably's thinking, it is perhaps also linked to the utopian tradition, as it is not found in this form and function in Plato or in other exponents of the republican tradition before the eighteenth century. On the other hand, it is present in Rousseau, who, in his *Considerations on the Government of Poland*, states with regard to citizens' children that:

---

59   *EdL*, I, p. 160.
60   *DL*, p. 379.

De la législation: Or, Utopia in Service of Reform 183

All, being equal under the constitution of the state, ought to be educated together and in the same fashion; and if it is impossible to set up an absolutely free system of public education, the cost must at least be set at a level the poor can afford to pay.[61]

Mably does not mention how the collective education is meant to be financed, and this gives us the impression that he leaves it up to the state. He thus remained faithful to the general orientation he had set for his political principles: the republic he called for must be egalitarian, and education was its foundation. This also entails, as its indispensable corollary, the need for religion. Indeed, Mably sees religion above all in terms of its effects on the social body. As the Philosopher says succinctly, 'If there is no God, there is no morality',[62] which is why religious education is what characterises it as a 'human education'.[63] Indeed, religion, through the dogmas of free will and the judgement of souls in the afterlife, is here taken for a guarantor of the trust that citizens can place in one another. This was, after all, a commonplace view in the eighteenth century, which was hardly questioned by anyone except by the materialists.[64] It was supposed that religion would hold each person to their duties out of fear of punishment; they could perhaps hope to escape such sanction on Earth, but not in the Hereafter. From this point of view, religion appears as a kind of armed wing of morality within each conscience. This is more or less how Milord translates the meaning of his interlocutor's words: 'The object which you propose in your education is that each citizen should become for himself a stricter magistrate than that which the laws establish.'[65] Hence the denial – expounded at some length – of the possibility of even a legitimate republic subsisting

---

61   *CGP*, p. 967.
62   *DL*, p. 389.
63   Ibid., p. 410.
64   Notably Baron d'Holbach: see 'Le bon sens, ou Idées naturelles opposées aux idées surnaturelles', in *Œuvres philosophiques, textes établis et annotés par J.-P. Jackson*, Paris: Éd. Alive, 2001, vol. III, pp. 221–340, p. 294: 'We are constantly told, and many sensible people end up believing, that religion is a restraint to contain men, that without it there would no longer be any restraint for peoples, that morality and virtue are intimately linked to it . . . To disabuse people of the usefulness of religious notions, it is sufficient to open one's eyes and consider what are the mores of the nations that are the most subject to religion.'
65   *DL*, pp. 385–6.

without religion. The idea, here, was that atheism, identified with a determinism which exonerates the individual from all moral responsibility, and, with hedonism, poses an imminent and lethal threat to the social bond itself. For it renders any commitment unreliable and pushes me to be constantly suspicious of my fellow man.[66]

In this dialogue, Milord again acts as the abbé spokesman for a way of thinking which is to some degree close to the Philosopher's own and compels the latter to make a reasoned rebuttal. Here, Milord echoes the viewpoint of Pierre Bayle, who in his *Pensées diverses sur la comète* hypothesises a 'society of atheists'. Bayle puts it in these terms: 'if one wants my conjecture regarding a society of Atheists, [it] seems to me that with regard to morals and civil actions, it would be quite similar to a society of pagans'.[67]

By equating the morality of a society of atheists with that of a society of pagans, Bayle wants to point out that both act according to their inclinations and interests alone, and not their principles. This is why neither a multiplicity of beliefs nor outright unbelief represents an obstacle to uniformity or even to a certain moral goodness. Indeed, since the great mainspring of human life is the fear of (material or symbolic) punishment and the hope of reward, we may well do out of well-understood interest what we ought to do out of respect for morality. The hypothesis of a society of atheists is not a project which Bayle is putting forward, nor even, strictly speaking, a utopia. Rather, it appears, above all, as an argument in his demonstration of the necessary decoupling of the principles that ought to guide politics from the principles that prevail in morality and the Christian religion. As Binoche explains, the strength of Bayle's argument consists of showing that the presence or absence of religion will not change men's behaviour: 'the effectiveness usually attributed to religion must in fact be attributed to other levels which do not imply any kind of creed'.[68] Mably, like all the detractors of the hypothesis of an atheist society, implicitly rejects this division between

---

66 This is exactly Locke's view in *A Letter Concerning Toleration* (translated by William Popple, 1689): 'those are not at all to be tolerated who deny the being of a God. Promises, covenants, and oaths, which are the bonds of human society, can have no hold upon an atheist. The taking away of God, though but even in thought, dissolves all'.

67 Pierre Bayle, *Pensées diverses sur la comète*, introduced by Joyce and Hubert Bost, Paris: Flammarion, 2007, p. 341.

68 Bertrand Binoche, *Religion privée, opinion publique*, Paris: Vrin, 2012, p. 49.

the spiritual principles of men and the motives of their actions.[69] For him, Bayle is an adversary who simply demands to be subjected to critique, insofar as he defends the idea that political society can and should be based on other foundations than a morality built on religion. The whole final part of the dialogue is aimed at instead showing how only a morality transmitted by education and sanctioned by religion allows for a social existence that conforms with human dignity. But it is especially important to refute Bayle precisely because he reaches several philosophical and political findings which he shares with the interlocutors in this dialogue. These include, for example, the rejection of superstition, but, above all, the consideration of religious questions from the point of view of their social utility. In the paragraph quoted, atheism is no worse than paganism insofar as it does not do anything more to disturb the peace among citizens.

Translated into the terms of Mably's dialogue, the question that then arises is: 'Why could a republic not survive without religion?'[70] While raising such a possibility, Milord puts forward a certain proviso: such a society would probably require stricter penal laws than societies of believers do. In addition, he also refers to travel accounts of peoples in the New World who apparently showed no sense of divinity. These examples also exist in Bayle's work, but in later works than the *Pensées diverses*, namely the *Continuation des pensées diverses* and the *Réponses aux questions d'un Provincial*. No doubt Mably had read these texts.

But the savage societies of the New World are not the real issue here. The point is to show that a society cannot 'have laws and magistrates'[71] unless it also worships a deity. In order to prove this, the Philosopher uses a procedure that is not similarly found in his opponent: he proposes that Milord imagine that, as a prince, he should grant 'one of [his] provinces to all the atheists of the world in order to establish Bayle's marvellous Republic'.[72] This thought experiment is all the more surprising because Bayle never spoke of a 'Republic', but only of a 'society of atheists'. Moreover, as Isabelle Delpla observes, 'Except for examples from travelogues, the societies of atheists described by Bayle are societies

---

69   Ibid.: 'No Enlightenment thinker would be able to do without answering Bayle and asking himself whether a society of atheists would really be possible.'
70   *DL*, p. 394.
71   Ibid., p. 398.
72   Ibid., p. 399.

within political societies.'[73] So, as in the writings of most of Bayle's opponents, his hypothesis is altered beyond recognition. The Swede purports to be applying a principle from Bayle to an entire community in order to examine its consequences. He does this by portraying, in a few satirical lines, an assembly of atheists discussing the laws to be set for their province. But in terms of legislation, only one measure is examined: one which would compel fathers to teach atheism to their own children. We are thereby meant to examine the content and foreseeable consequences of a materialistic education. According to the proposed law, children would be taught that the only valid rule of conduct is the pursuit of pleasure and the flight from pain, and that justice and injustice do not exist in themselves. Mably thus imagines that the arguments expounded by Bayle in his works would be taught as lessons to the young generations of an entire nation. He thus subjects his adversary's thinking to what might be called a utopian, or rather a dystopian, distortion.

As they are turned into legally decreed educational precepts, Bayle's ideas become lessons in collective immorality. According to the Philosopher, this atheistic education would lead each child to make their own passions the principle of their actions. It would make them indifferent to their own moral character and to that of their fellow human beings: Cato and Catilina would be placed on an equal footing. Thus, a tyrannical policy and a republican policy would have the same value. We can see that this theoretical characterisation of atheists' way of thinking has little concern for coherence. If an individual is indeed sensitive to punishments and rewards, then in all seriousness it can hardly be said that they will be indifferent to whether their government is virtuous or tyrannical. This is, moreover, what Bayle himself argued in the *Pensées diverses*. But it allows the Swede to draw an unambiguous conclusion. A society that raised its citizens on such principles would never know any rest, for it would make each person distrust every other.

This dystopian move allows Mably to emphasise the core of his critique: a republic based on such principles is not only scandalous, but unrealistic and unviable. Such a community would in fact be devoid of a social bond. Bayle's 'Republic of the Atheists' thus appears to be the

---

[73] Isabelle Delpla, 'Bayle: pensées diverses sur l'athéisme ou le paradoxe de l'athée citoyen', in E. Cattin, L. Jaffro, and A. Petit (eds), *Figures du théologico-politique*, Paris: Vrin, 1999, p. 139.

De la législation: Or, Utopia in Service of Reform

outline of a countermodel, less a dream than a nightmare. But, at the same time, it is highly revealing of the way Mably reasons here. He argues – or at least purports to do so – as if his opponent were not a philosopher engaged in a thought experiment to demonstrate the truth of a political thesis, but a utopian describing the main features of his ideal for society.

Mably's nightmare was starkly depicted a few decades later by the Marquis de Sade, when he included the famous pamphlet 'Yet Another Effort, Frenchmen, If You Would Become Republicans' in his *Philosophy in the Bedroom*. This is indeed a republic rid not only of Christianity but of religion in general, which is 'incoherent with the libertarian system'.[74] The author of this programme sketches this out before an audience who are in any case – and this is crucial – wallowing in debauchery. Indeed, the institutions of an ideal republic are here seen from the point of view of desire, which overturns all widely recognized moral precepts.[75] The beginning of the pamphlet seems to subscribe to the principles commonly accepted in a republican regime. At first, the text suggests replacing worship of divinities with the worship of the 'true principles of freedom', and the replacement of religious rites with the observance of 'heroism, capabilities, humaneness, largeness of spirit, a proven civism'.[76] Like Bayle, the author of the pamphlet stresses that 'the moral fear of hell's torments' is not effective in stopping crime. Using a perspective that the author of the *Pensées diverses* would likely himself have accepted, Sade proposes to replace religious education with one based on well-understood interest. This, after all, advises each person to be virtuous because their own happiness depends on it, and consequently teaches children to be honest out of simple selfishness. The proposed national education, while it uses means radically opposed to Mably's, thus seems to pursue similar moral and social objectives: the republican's 'only guide is virtue', even if this virtue is achieved by making individuals

---

74 Marquis de Sade, in 'Yet Another Effort, Frenchmen, If You Would Become Republicans', in *Justine, Philosophy in the Bedroom and Other Writings*, New York: Grove Press, 1971, p. 301.

75 As Binoche writes, Sadian political reflection is always an answer to the following question: 'What happens to institutions in general, and political institutions in particular, from the point of view of the one who gets a hard-on – and writes to get a hard-on?' (Bertrand Binoche, *Sade ou l'institutionnalisation de l'écart*, Quebec City: Presses de l'Université Laval, 2007, p. 39).

76 Ibid., p. 302.

realise that it is to their own advantage.[77] Mably could even have agreed with the conditions that Sade places on respect for property in the second part of the pamphlet. He could have been sensitive to the argument that punishing the thief is tantamount to condemning the sacred right to preserve one's own existence by all means.

But the call for the abolition of the punishment for theft ought to be put in its proper context. As Claude Lefort points out, the whole of the second part of Sade's 'Français, encore un effort' aims to destroy what has been built up in the first part, by studiedly perverting the language of republican virtue that was used in it. Prostitution, adultery, incest, rape, sodomy, and murder are all legitimised. In the pamphlet, Sade remarks that the 'means to the preservation' of the republic can in no way be 'moral means'.[78] He tells us that, in places of debauchery, citizens should be able to express the dose of desire that each naturally carries within them, and the measure of the despotism that constitutes its essence. And he makes the doubtless ironic assertion that 'Thomas More proves in his Utopia that it becomes women to surrender themselves to debauchery'.[79] The republican nation, it is said, can sustain itself only 'by many crimes'. As a society that respects natural rules, the republic must allow all individual tendencies to express themselves, without legal restraint.

'Français, encore un effort' rejects religion as contrary to the laws of nature and seeks to translate into civil laws the rule of 'might is right', which excludes the punishment of crimes. This is, surely, a paradoxical implementation of the principles developed in the *Pensées diverses*, a 'materialist response to Bayle's paradox'.[80] Sade seeks to show not only that a society of atheists is possible, but also that a republic is only possible if it is atheistic. However, as against the idea developed in the *Pensées diverses*, he asserts at the same time that such a republic cannot rely on the same standards of behaviour as existing societies. In his own way, Sade fully validates the criticism that had been consistently levelled at Bayle's hypothesis and at those who had sought to defend it.

But, in doing so, as Claude Lefort summarises, 'Sade exploits the philosophical-revolutionary discourse in order to bring out consequences

---

77 Ibid., p. 307.
78 Ibid., p. 315.
79 Ibid., p. 324.
80 Ibid., p. 38.

that destroy its principles.'[81] Sade's pamphlet appears to be not just the programmatic realisation of atheism and its consequences, but also the openly embraced reverse side of the republican utopia, its détournement to satirical ends. The target of the attacks seems to be, if not Mably directly, at least the republicanism that was prevalent in the eighteenth century and which permeated the Revolution itself. Thus, Sade reverses the principle laid down by Montesquieu in *De l'Esprit des lois*, according to which the republic is based on virtue. On the contrary, such a regime can only be based on corruption. Some of the themes of 'republican humanism' and the utopian tradition are directly cited and parodied in the sense of explicit praise for corruption.[82] Here, the community of women in Plato's *Republic* – linked to the need to detach the guardians from any affection that will distract them from the common good, but also connected to eugenic imperatives – turns into a generalised prostitution. The utopian need to allow spouses to see each other naked before getting married, which, in More, was supposed to be a measure to prevent adultery, becomes an argument in favour of 'debauchery'. The effort in ideological and political subversion contaminates the very nature of the social bond. Whereas the republican seeks to cement the union of citizens by subjecting their personal aspirations to the imperative of the general interest, Sade forcefully reaffirms the despotism of individual desire and the fundamental solitude of the citizen of the republic in following his own wishes. From this point of view, the exchange between Dolmancé and Eugénie that concludes the pamphlet is highly revealing: 'never listen to your heart', the libertine advises his pupil.

The pamphlet does not uphold virtue, but objects to it by defending corruption and crime; to the promotion of the common good, it opposes the pursuit of the selfish interest of the desiring subject. Sade's political 'programme', if it can be called that, is an antidote to republican utopia. It challenges it on every point. But it is important to note, finally, how much this opposition operates within the same frame of reference of concepts and arguments shared by many Enlightenment thinkers: Mably and Sade share a common interpretation of Bayle's paradox. Neither questions the presupposition – which was indeed opposed by a

---

81 Claude Lefort, 'Sade, le boudoir et la Cité', in *Écrire. À l'épreuve du politique*, Paris: Calmann-Lévy, 1992, pp. 90–111, at p. 103.
82 Ibid.

number of materialists, from d'Holbach to Sylvain Maréchal[83] – that declining belief in the immortality of the soul and in a God who judges our actions also brings moral behaviour down with it. For both, the virtuous atheist remains a chimera. This is why, in contrast to Sade's project (or its parody of one?), the Philosopher in Mably's dialogue concludes that religious education is essential if social virtues are to thrive in individuals, and that atheism, which is so ruinous, should be punished with a jail sentence that can become perpetual if the culprit persists in his convictions. This punishment, which may seem very severe, is a direct consequence of the thesis that deprives the atheist of all morality and thus makes his presence in the social body eminently corrosive.

More and Rousseau, rather like Mably, also consider religion from an essentially political angle. The former affirms the need recognised by Utopians to believe 'that there is one supreme power, the maker and ruler of the universe'.[84] To this first dogma, the Utopians add that of a Providence presiding over the destiny of the world, as well as the idea of the immortality of the soul, which implies 'that after this life, rewards are appointed for our virtues and good deeds, punishments for our sins'.[85] If anyone should dispute this, they could not 'count him as one of their citizens, since he would openly despise all the laws and customs of society'.[86] Like the atheist in the Philosopher, the heretical Utopian is thus cut off from the political community. Rousseau is of the same opinion and justifies the 'tormenting' of whoever does not believe in these same dogmas. Indeed, 'any one [who], after publicly acknowledging these dogmas, behaves like an unbeliever in them' should be put to death.[87] In a word, 'it is very important for the State that every citizen should have a religion which may make him delight in his duties'.[88] The place of religion in Rousseau's political perspective ought not to be

---

83 See Sylvain Maréchal, *Dictionnaire des athées* (1799), Paris: Coda, 2008, p. 9: 'The atheists, who were taken as such cause for fear, and who are still used to frighten women and children, big or small, are the best people in the world. They do not form a corporation like the priests, they have no propaganda; consequently, they cannot put anyone's nose out of joint.'
84 More, *Utopia*, p. 98.
85 Ibid., p. 69.
86 Ibid., p. 100.
87 Rousseau, *The Social Contract*, p. 253.
88 Ibid., p. 252.

De la législation: Or, Utopia in Service of Reform

underestimated. It is foundational to public morality and leads the believer to the true good.

From this perspective, idolatry and superstition are the subject of a certain indulgence; for however false these beliefs may be, they are not the most dangerous. The Philosopher joins the Savoyard Vicar in a common observation that the scandalous vices of the pagan gods did not lead the Roman citizens to behave badly for long: it was better that they worshipped them than worship no deity at all.

However, in all three authors, this radical condemnation of atheism – deemed incompatible with the political bond – goes hand in hand with reservations towards Christianity, as well as a measure of tolerance with regard to citizens' dogmatic beliefs. First of all, each of these authors expresses their distance towards Christianity in different ways. In More's case, it takes the form of clearly ironic praise for it: the Utopians are described by Raphael Hythloday as practising a broad religious tolerance, based on the minimal foundation of beliefs whose political utility has already been mentioned. Travellers from Europe introduce them to the mysteries of Christianity, which they welcome all the more enthusiastically because Christ, they are told, 'approved of his followers' communal way of life'.[89] Unfortunately, the absence of priests among the visitors prevent them from receiving the sacraments that offer access to the priesthood. The Utopians are thus left without a minister in the Christian faith and maintain their tolerant ecumenism.

In Rousseau, Christianity is the object of much more direct political attacks. His critique is broadly similar to Machiavelli's in his *Discourses on Livy*: the Christian religion, or at least the misinterpretation of it by its appointed representatives, values the 'humble and contemplative' virtues over the 'active virtues'. According to Machiavelli, because this identifies happiness with humility, self-denial, and contempt for earthly things, it turns the believer away from the fight for the glory and freedom of his homeland. It weakens the people and hands them over to the tyranny of the 'wicked'. This is also Rousseau's view of things, writing in *The Social Contract* that: 'Christianity preaches only servitude and dependence. Its spirit is too favorable to tyranny for the latter not to profit by it always.'[90] In Mably, the question appears to be settled in a

---

89   More, *Utopia*, p. 98.
90   Rousseau, *The Social Contract*, p. 252.

somehow more evasive manner, since the precise case of Christianity is not directly mentioned, nor any of its liturgical dogma. His treatment of the religious question seems to suggest that society could practise any kind of worship, so long as it involves collective ceremonies. He does not condemn deism in substance but insists that it should remain the wise man's own private conviction; it is not suitable for the multitude, who need public worship. Most souls remain subject to the dominant influence of their bodies and so convincing them and sustaining their conviction requires this sensory stimulation. Mably again refers to the political role of these practices: ceremonies 'unite the citizens among themselves by tangible acts and dispose them to be of one mind, and to fulfil their mutual obligations'.[91]

In a similar vein, More held that the Utopians would only worship in public in ways compatible with the beliefs of all, while reserving the observance of more individual faiths for the private space. In either case, religion remains first and foremost a way of binding citizens together, and as little as possible to do with separating them from each other. The quite particular form of tolerance that the three authors embrace is also a product of this general intuition. In each case, their tolerance applies to dogmas that might cause distinctions among the different religions which already exist in the state, which are to be tolerated insofar as they do not contradict civic duties. According to the Philosopher, such tolerance should not apply to new religions; indeed, the state must try to prevent them from flowering, so that they will not sow fresh seeds of social division. However, once established, they must be tolerated: the Philosopher draws on the authority of 'the author of the *De l'Esprit des lois*'[92] to argue that in these new circumstances persecution would prove counterproductive. The link between the spiritual and the temporal is thus conceived in a similar way by each of More, Rousseau, and Mably. The latter goes further than Rousseau in subsuming religious affairs under political authority. Indeed, he follows More in this sense: he advocates that in his republic priests, who are elected as magistrates in Utopia, should receive salaries from the state. This means controlling the (necessarily modest) income of these men of the cloth, and ensuring equality among them, in order to prevent the establishment of any

---

91 *DL*, p. 426.
92 Ibid., p. 465.

hierarchy parallel to political authority. For Mably, priests should be stripped of all temporal 'power' and confined to the purely religious domain, in order to avoid them wielding a 'tyranny'. In his mind, in accordance with enlightened opinion, the clergy is associated with absolute monarchy.

Utopia and Republicanism

Mably's dialogue ends with an exposition of these principles. Tellingly, these last lines are the place of a final 'denial of utopia'. The Philosopher concludes as follows:

> For some, my legislative principles will seem to be nothing but pipe dreams. But who really ought to be accused of revelling in chimeras? I, who seek to penetrate the intentions of nature, and who propose only the laws which the wisest and happiest peoples have obeyed? Or those profound politicians who fancy that they can subjugate nature to their whims, . . . and who hope to make us good citizens by multiplying and extending our vices?[93]

So, this final defence is mounted in the name of nature, and of the history of the wise and happy peoples of the past. This is but further confirmation of the status we have already attributed to the set of 'principles' found in the second part of Mably's dialogue. For the author, this is, indeed, a matter of 'proposing laws': a task which no utopian before Morelly had directly undertaken. But, unlike in Morelly, these proposals are picked from the real history of human legislation (or at least from Mably's image of that history) according to how far they resemble the laws and morals that would govern a state organised around the community of goods. We see this in his egalitarian tendency – which at the level of political representation takes the form of an equality between orders, not between individuals, but which elsewhere is indeed established between citizens. It appears as the second-rate political ideal that substitutes for the communal ideal, providing its closest image. Equality thus becomes the watchword that guides the legislator's entire activity. In his

---

93   Ibid., pp. 475–6.

search for models lent political credibility by their genuinely historical character, Mably naturally drew on ones from antiquity that granted their citizens the status of 'equals', which is so dear to his own thinking. If the republic that Mably calls for thus draws considerable inspiration from utopia, it is also true that, in becoming an egalitarian republic, utopia strives to be part of a future that is not just a chimera.

Here, looking through the various areas of social life considered in the course of the dialogue, we have tried to trace out Mably's republicanism. Governed by what we might call a social rather than a political radicalism, this republicanism embodies his programme for the future. This review of the different areas of social life itself links Mably's model sometimes to More's model and sometimes to the political principles of Rousseau. The latter, too, is marked by a republican point of reference inherited from his dialogue with the ancients, as well as by his reading of Machiavelli and by his knowledge of the Genevan institutions. But, above all, we have seen the convergence of the utopian and republican traditions around a certain number of crucial subjects. Hythloday already mentioned this convergence at the end of his description of the island of Utopia: 'I have described to you as accurately as I could the structure of that commonwealth which I consider not only the best but indeed the only one that can rightfully claim that name.'[94] Quentin Skinner also emphasises, in his own way, the partial compatibility of the utopian and republican traditions. He counts Thomas More among the civic humanists, heirs to ancient political thought, and casts Utopia as a 'humanist critique of humanism'.[95] In Skinner's reading, it is through More that, from the outset, utopia has built connections with the republican tradition; in a sense, it appears at one of its edges, the one most sensitive to the egalitarian aspects of the legacy of antiquity. From this point of view, Mably's thought establishes a new junction between two heritages, several of whose aspects had been close together ever since the Renaissance.

With his utopia, More achieved the synthesis of the republican idea and the idea of community of goods, in the mode of an imaginary construct. Ultimately, Mably merely combines the same elements on a

---

94 More, *Utopia*, p. 109.
95 Quentin Skinner, *The Foundations of Modern Political Thought*, Cambridge: Cambridge University Press, 1978, vol. 1, p. 343.

more directly political level: not yet that of action, but at least that of the general orientation to be given to a plan of reforms meant for the present. In so doing, in taking up the utopian model he provides it with a new function that neither More nor Morelly had granted their own social and political constructs.

Human Nature in *De la législation*

In his 1814 work 'De l'esprit de conquête et de l'usurpation dans leur rapport avec la civilisation européenne', Benjamin Constant wrote that

> Mably's work on *La législation* or the *Les Principes des lois* is the most completely despotic code that can be imagined. Combine its three principles – 1) legislative authority is unlimited; it must be extended to everything and bend everything to itself; 2) individual liberty is a curse; if you cannot destroy it, then at least restrict it as much as possible; 3) property is an evil: if you cannot destroy it, weaken its influence in every possible way – and through this combination, you will have the constitution of Constantinople and Robespierre combined.[96]

So, for Constant, indeed also reflecting his contemporaries' understanding in this respect, *De la législation* is deemed the work that best reflects Mably's views. It is taken for his philosophical and political profession of faith. In accusing him of despotism, Constant confuses Mably's attacks on the principle of property with his attacks on individual liberty in the strictly political sense. Drawing on a now-famous dichotomy, Constant indicts the author of *De la législation* for having based human freedom on the model of the ancients. Which is to say, a freedom that finds its highest expression in participation in legislative authority, to the detriment of the properly individual latitude of action said to be represented by the 'freedom of the Moderns'. On this reading, the freedom of the ancients powerfully restricts this freedom of the Moderns, since – according to an expression he used in his famous speech delivered at the

---

[96] Benjamin Constant, 'De l'esprit de conquête et de l'usurpation' dans leur rapport avec la civilisation européenne, in *Écrits politiques*, Paris: Gallimard, 1997, pp. 117–302, at p. 213.

Athénée Royal in Paris in 1819 – it implies 'the complete subjection of the individual to the authority of the whole'.[97] Through Mably and Rousseau, the more strictly philosophical targets of this accusation, the aim here is to indict the Jacobins and the Reign of Terror. The latter is interpreted as an anachronistic attempt to resurrect the now unbearable reign of the freedom of the ancients, in the conditions of modern France.

It is not our intention here to examine Constant's positions in any great detail. Rather, our concern is to determine the value of his criticism of Mably's theories. Without delving further into possible similarities between Mably's theory of sovereignty and Rousseau's – and Constant did equate them, despite his greater admiration for the citizen of Geneva – we will focus on his critique of the concept of liberty. Is it really true to say that, in Mably, and more particularly in *De la législation*, the subjective rights of the individual are sacrificed on the altar of collective decisions? Can the individual not raise some of his prerogatives in opposition to the possible demands that the public authorities might make? In fact, being 'a free people'[98] is one of the primary goals that the Swede – an avatar of Mably's – assigns to a good policy. So, we might well ask what really does constitute freedom, for Mably, and what he thinks detracts from it, based on the new conceptualisation of human nature which we find in this text.

The Theory of Passions

We can start by noting the appearance of a new concept in Mably's anthropology: *amour-propre*. This is now placed at the foundation of our being: it is presented as 'the motive of all our thoughts, movements and actions'.[99] It is rooted in man's sensitivity to pleasure and pain. It is easily blamed for all evil passions, and yet in its natural state it is 'the bond that should unite us in society'. Indeed, the Creator himself has arranged our various needs in such a way that we also need each other if we are to fulfil them. He invites us to show our 'mutual benevolence'

---

97 Benjamin Constant, 'De la liberté des Anciens comparée à celle des Modernes', in *Écrits politiques*, pp. 589–619, p. 594.
98 *DL*, p. 21.
99 Ibid., p. 28.

De la législation: Or, Utopia in Service of Reform

because of this need, as well as because of the innate social qualities that encourage us 'to draw together, to unite, to love, to relieve, to serve and to make sacrifices for each other'.[100]

Clearly, the social qualities mentioned here mark a considerable change relative to the time when Mably had written his *Doutes*. For, alongside 'love of glory' and 'emulation', new passions such as 'pity, gratitude, [and] the need to love' also appear. These are, therefore, social rather than political affections, unlike those – such as justice, temperance, and courage – which the *Doutes* cast as directly and classically civic virtues. Above all, these passions bind individuals to each other by way of their material needs, which force them to help each other: in this respect, there seems to have been a major about-turn in Mably's position since the time of his polemic with the Physiocrats. He takes much more seriously than before the need for a strong emotional bond between the members of the social collective – a bond that is formed, unlike in the previous dialogue, not by a purely moral need to exercise one's virtue among one's fellow human beings, but primarily through the need for these peers' help in satisfying one's needs. Sensitivity is foregrounded, here, and this situates moral needs as necessary consequences of this same sensitivity. So, what the 'legislators of nations' must bring to fruition is this affective bond between men ready to help each other, in the role of 'co-operators in providence'.[101] This passage raises – again, for the first time in Mably's writings – the insistent idea that Providence plays a major role in setting the disposition of human qualities. Indeed, the *Code de la Nature* probably somehow influenced this passage, however implicitly. It was, doubtless, a reading of this text that suggested to Mably the idea of purely social affections, which precede any properly civic virtue. These are, for Mably, affects that develop in the mutual aid that men are led to lavish on each other under the beneficent influence of their Creator.

So, at the beginning of the dialogue between the Swede and his English interlocutor, these social affections are presented as the 'good morals' whose flourishing the legislator must prioritise. However, 'mutual benevolence' is not likely to spring from the luxurious tastes or the trade defended by Milord. In fact – contrary to Morelly's text, which

---

100 Ibid., p. 29.
101 Ibid., p. 30.

admits a positive progress in the arts, the sciences, and the means to satisfy human needs – for Mably, the superfluous corresponds to the birth of false needs in men. These new needs are harmful to the unity of society itself; the Swede cannot imagine that they will be the prerogative of all, rather than being reserved for the few. They thus quickly pervert social affections, turning benevolence into jealousy and greed. Soon, some people will monopolise everything, leaving nothing for the rest. This is why anyone who wishes for both good morals and wealth is seeking to 'combine things that do not go together'.[102] Poverty, or at least mediocrity, is the condition that suits human equality and produces social happiness by binding individuals together. Individuals need to be freed from the attractions of superfluous goods, which will interest them in a purely material and artificial well-being to the detriment of others. Only once released from their charms can individuals devote themselves to the public good – the true good to which their nature calls them – by helping to provide what is necessary for all. As Constant claims, this is indeed a matter of depriving individuals of the possibility of personally enjoying superfluous goods. But Mably's idea, behind this measure, and in exchange for it, is to offer individuals access to moral goods that would otherwise remain closed off to them: namely, the general benevolence and the exercise of virtue.

Poverty is thus explained to be attractive insofar as it allows for equality. Nature itself attaches human happiness to this condition: only in a unanimously shared poverty can men live in harmony and in a desirable state of moral excellence. As we read in this same dialogue, 'Equality must produce all goods, because it unites men, elevates their souls and prepares them for mutual feelings of benevolence and friendship.'[103] Sanctioned by the absence of private property, and having become conscious of itself, equality provides the foundation for the intimate feeling of our own value, of our intrinsic dignity. Only once we are convinced that we are the equals of all other men can we live up to our own humanity. This consciousness, this 'inclination of the soul' is never completely stifled in man. It distinguishes him from animals. Mutual respect for one another's dignity is the condition of the happiness to which every rational being is naturally destined. This is why – unlike all

---

102   Ibid., p. 19.
103   Ibid., p. 46.

the passions that stir the human heart – the feeling of equality can never be overblown, nor can it lead to any corruption. It unites men by the only non-alienating bonds that exist, whereas inequality instead divides them. The legitimate sense of dignity is rooted in man's rationality from his first steps, and in some measure at least allows each individual to lead his own life freely.

Earlier, we saw that the social bond was attributed a two-sided purpose. Here, this purpose is reformulated in conformity with this value placed on the idea of equality. As in the previous dialogues, society is responsible for both ensuring that man's social qualities will flourish and guaranteeing the individual's natural rights. The means for achieving both ends is to create equal conditions. Thus, the Philosopher insists that the aim of society is only 'to preserve for all men the rights they hold in the liberal hands of nature', but he immediately characterises natural law in a quite telling way: 'the natural law, which I may call the law of equality among men'.[104]

While Mably here emphasises the equality of individual rights, the deeper meaning seems identical to the one that appears in the previous dialogues. Which is to say, in society men must enjoy their rights to individual freedom and subsistence, which constitute the basis of their common condition. As for the second aspect of society's aims, it can be said that the author does not abandon his moral perfectionism but assigns it a somewhat altered objective. By this point the concern is primarily to encourage mutual understanding by developing the social qualities which underpin such fellow feeling. This does not just mean ensuring that virtue should flourish, in the sense of reason winning out over the passions. Rather, it seems more a matter of allowing the affectionate passion to win out over the passions of disunity and selfishness – unnatural passions that can only come to men belatedly.

Compared with the previous dialogues, Mably's emphasis here seems to be on the need for unity between the equal members of the social whole, in line with the *Code de la Nature*. It is this union that Constant later interprets as a despotic risk. For Mably, man seems all the nobler the more helpful he is to his fellow men; in the *Doutes*, man was all the more noble the more devoted he was to the public good and the more committed he was to justice in a more abstract sense. Here, as in

---

104   Ibid., p. 379.

Morelly's text, the community is not an anonymous whole. Rather, what produces the agreement of hearts and not only of wills is a set of concrete individuals endowed with needs and who call on their fellow human beings for help.

The State of Nature, and the State of Society

In contrast to the previous dialogues, but in line with Morelly's lessons, the state of nature enjoys something of a rehabilitation in the Philosopher's remarks. This is praised as the state of 'the most perfect equality'.[105] By giving men 'the same organs, the same needs, the same reason', nature also gave them the Earth 'in common'. Taking up the notes of *Des droits et des devoirs*, Mably adds to this equality of condition a *consciousness* of this equality, which he defines as a 'feeling of a nobility, elevation and freedom'.[106] In the 1758 dialogue, man's intrinsic dignity was connected to the notions of good and evil that he discovered through the first developments of his reason. But what is remarkable in this text is that this dignity is linked to man's awareness of his equality: 'The feeling of equality is nothing other than the feeling of our dignity; it is by allowing its weakening that men have become slaves, and it is only by reviving it that they will become free.'[107] This is the first time that Mably has so exclusively linked human dignity with equality. That he would make such a statement no doubt owes something to the vigour with which Morelly dismisses any legal basis for inequality in the *Code de la Nature*. It is from this standpoint that the state of nature – the original condition which was decried in the early dialogues – can be praised as a more enviable state than the current one. The Philosopher rehabilitates the societies of 'Savages', using a tone that had not been present in the earlier dialogues. These 'Savages' spontaneously observe the social principles that he considers best suited to bringing a human society happiness:

> I find in their society, barely sketched out, the most perfect equality. It admits no distinction between the chief of the tribe and the lowliest

---

105   Ibid., p. 52.
106   Ibid., p. 53.
107   Ibid., p. 54.

head of household; he is chief only because he has given more proof of his courage, and he will cease to be so if he allows himself to be outdone.[108]

Here, it is striking to note that the dominant feature of natural societies, which justifies this high regard for them, is fully encapsulated in the idea of equality of condition, and in the resulting absence of markers of social distinction. After all, even the leading functions obey this same logic. However, while praising these primitive societies, the author does not present them as the ideal state of humanity. Mably deplores the 'ignorance' of these first societies; to these descriptions, he prefers the following characterisation of the first civil state:

> In the first situation of men, an equal education developed more or less the same talents in all, and if some citizens were distinguished by their merit, they were amply rewarded by public esteem and by the magistracies to which they were elevated.[109]

We can see that the condition described here is not only a society, but also a state in which men have already established 'magistracies' among their rank. These posts do not contradict the fundamental equality between men any more than it is contradicted by the inequalities of natural talents that these appointments also reflect. They each contribute to the unity of society. Indeed, the 'different gifts of nature' serve to 'make society flourish' by granting each individual a place that he can spontaneously occupy. If nature had made men identical, then they would not have been complementary and they would not have come together so easily. Thus, even in their 'first situation' – equal in condition but usefully unequal in talents – men renounce their independence, precisely for the sake of their natural complementarity. They make magistrates their 'proxies' for the sake of maintaining order, drawing on a 'borrowed and transient' authority.

Thus, in this dialogue, the community of goods is taken as humanity's primitive social state. This description contrasts with the line of argument set out in *Des droits et des devoirs*, where the primitive social state

---

108 Ibid., p. 103.
109 Ibid., p. 59.

involved a personal right of ownership over one's house, or one's fruit tree. The Swede points out that the community of goods persisted long after the establishment of a public authority given the power 'to punish, avenge or redress the wrongs and injustices of individuals'.[110] Indeed, the equal condition in which natural societies long maintained men kept them from the vices of avarice and ambition, which are, in turn, wholly blamed for later public ills. This equality cannot have prepared them for the appearance of social differentiation; thus, the state of community life was continued under the best political laws ever enacted.

It thus appears that Mably substitutes the jusnaturalist opposition between the state of nature and the civil state with another opposition – that between the state of primitive community and the subsequent state of property and inequality. In the primitive communal state, the civil state is preferable to the natural organisation that precedes it. Here, the Philosopher describes the gathering of forces both to form a public authority and to bring together productive labour. Clearly, this communal civil state is preferable because it involves a conscious decision on the part of its members to live according to the principles of equality.

Mably locates his 'golden age' in this early civil state, and not in the state of nature. This era is embodied both in the Spartan model and in a vaguer reference to a primitive republic built on the community of goods. In the earlier dialogues, human nature had seemed essentially readable through the prism of its ultimate perfection, whereas the state of nature did not itself provide a model for thinking about it. But, in *De la législation*, we are dealing with a more traditional schema, in which the early ages of humanity offer a picture of man in accordance with his natural destination. Through his history, man has thus misguidedly departed from his good original nature – and done so after a stage in which he had succeeded in combining the constituent features of natural organisation with the advantages of developing his moral and technical faculties. However, it was indeed his primitive nature that inspired in him, right from the beginning, the benefits of communal association. So, in *De la législation*, the chronology and logic of the birth, development, and corruption of man's nature all fit together.

This then takes Mably to the problem of the origins of corruption. As is often the case when an author has to explain how men came to give up

---

110 Ibid., p. 69.

on their state of natural happiness, the question seems difficult to deal with:

> I find it difficult to guess how property came to be established. I have only conjectures on this subject which do not entirely satisfy me; and if I did not fear disrespecting our fathers, I would sharply criticise them for a mistake which was almost impossible to make.[111]

Here, the factual reality clearly poses a problem in the internal logic of the doctrine of human nature. What can explain how man's true nature came to be lost? Mably sees two possible causes. One hypothesis is that certain members of the community were too lazy; this may have aroused the indignation of their fellow citizens, who, in turn, demanded that each be given his due by distributing the land into individual plots. But there is also a second possible explanation, that the magistrates may have become unjust or prevaricating, and thereby pushed the citizens to the same conclusions regarding the need for individual appropriation. The fact that there is more than one explanation testifies to Mably's difficulty in thinking through this problem and finding a satisfactory solution within the terms of his conception of human nature. In fact, neither of these explanations fits well with the anthropological principles that are set out elsewhere in the dialogue. From what Mably tells us, emulation and the pleasure of public prestige ought to have been enough to prevent these disorders. The Philosopher softens the apparent contradiction by stating that the latter initially presented only a small problem and could have been easily corrected by a reminder of the community's founding principles, whether on the part of the magistrates themselves or that of the wider collective. The appearance of private property thus has to be explained via the same kind of reasoning that Morelly offers in the *Code de la Nature*: it is supposedly due to an error of evaluation, a bad solution to the dissensions arising in the social body, which leads to vastly disastrous consequences. However, here an explanation in terms of the will of Providence – which in Morelly places the legislators' initial error in a teleological perspective – is missing. Men seem to owe all their misfortunes to their simple lack of foresight.

---

111   Ibid., p. 71.

Hesitations

This difficulty is also why a second, underlying form of anthropology emerges in the dialogue, which is much more pessimistic than the first. It is discussed just a few pages later, when the Philosopher notes the proximity of human qualities and vices: 'Always ready to go astray, always surrounded by traps, we continually need laws to guard us ... laws are necessary to support our faltering reason and our fragile virtues.'[112]

The responsibility for the early societies' failure is thus said to fall on human nature. On this reading, laws are not the simple expression of man's natural needs but also safeguards against the harmful tendencies contained in this nature itself. Like most utopians, and especially Morelly, Mably seems to oscillate between anthropological optimism and pessimism. His optimism leads him to deem human nature inherently destined to seek out community. He roots this assessment – following Morelly – in social qualities that spontaneously lead to mutual aid. On the other hand, his pessimism leads him to value the role of the law and civil institutions in keeping individuals on the straight and narrow. Ultimately, it is the inability of human nature to find the path of natural organisation that leads him to renounce the ideal of the community of goods in favour of a second-rate ideal in which laws regulate the various aspects of life. In this aspect of his thinking, Mably thus seems to corroborate Constant's accusation that he had sought to restrict individual freedom. Still, such a conclusion can only apply to the 'pessimistic' dimension of his thought, whereas its 'optimistic' side, which in fact dominates the dialogue, instead leads him to celebrate the spontaneous dynamism of mutual aid and a confidence in the capacities for social organisation which are inherent in human nature.

On the whole, then, it seems that reading the *Code de la Nature* contributed to a shift in Mably's conception of the nature of man and of societies. This did not mean fundamentally questioning either of the two purposes which he had assigned to society. But it probably did lead him to refocus the claim to natural rights around the notion of equality, and to refocus the assertion of man's moral destination around the notions of mutual aid and complementarity. It led him to place self-love

---

112 Ibid., pp. 85–6.

at the foundation of human actions. It helped to give the Philosopher's words a generally optimistic tone regarding the nature of man, which would disappear in the later dialogues.

But, as we have seen, equality – cast as the foundation of natural law and the moral destination of man – can no longer be unproblematically taken for the objective of political association. Rather, some nuance is needed on this point, given that the establishment of property is now an irreversible fact. Equality should thus instead serve as the regulating concept for legislative action, the yardstick against which the more or less useful character of a law can be measured. From this point of view, an analysis of Mably's anthropological principles shows us that, alongside the objective of real, material equality, he sought, perhaps above all, to re-establish the individual's heartfelt awareness of the fundamental equality of all human beings. It seems that a society that can instil in each individual a sense of their own dignity, equal to that of all others, will have fulfilled its purpose, even though it cannot re-establish the equality of condition that prevailed in the bygone golden age of the community of goods. The republican utopia, which is supposed to bring about a certain measure of equality in concrete reality, seems to be the model most likely to produce such an individual and collective awareness of the value of each person. For Mably, man is at the height of his own moral powers when he is fully aware of this. Mably's mature dialogues, *De la législation* foremost among them, are doubtless above all intended to help bring about this consciousness.

III

Gracchus Babeuf, a Utopian in Revolution

Babeuf discovered the thought of Mably, and then that of Morelly, in a chronological disorder that was partly due to his eventful intellectual trajectory. It was a trajectory disrupted halfway through by the outbreak of the revolutionary episode that was to ensure Babeuf's historical standing.

The evolution of Babeuf's ideal was, in part, closely linked to the revolutionary process itself. However, the way that he saw this process depended on the theoretical and ideological tools at his disposal, which themselves informed his thinking. These tools included an – in some measure – secondhand Rousseauianism. But the utopian inheritance figured especially prominently from the outset. What is most particular about Babeuf is the direct engagement, evident throughout his writings, between this heritage and political action. This indefatigable publicist's trajectory was not a linear one, precisely because it was so influenced by events and by the battles he waged. Babeuf offers the – perhaps paradoxical – image of a utopian who became a man of action through sheer force of circumstance.

In the course of the revolutionary process, which corresponded to Babeuf's development of his thinking, his horizons gradually broadened. A surveyor by training, he increasingly looked beyond the problems specific to his original rural milieu, and the feudal relations of domination with which he was familiar, to general questions of social organisation. These concerned not only the urban world and its economic relations, but also the political field and the problem of the state. Hence, only once Babeuf had reached intellectual maturity did he discover the dimension of the social sphere from which the classical utopians had started out, in their reliance on the public authorities to organise humans' common life down to the last detail.

Here, we will try to show how the test of events changed the ideal model of society to which Babeuf had laid claim even in the period preceding 1789. At the end of his journey, Babeuf drew a lesson from utopia that led to a decisive change in its status. Now revolutionaries by profession, Babeuf and his comrades revolutionised utopia itself. They gave it the face of a programme that ought to be implemented in the here and now.

6
Babeuf's 1786 Draft Letter: Utopia in the Villages

Babeuf soon moved to speculate on the forms of social organisation apt to significantly improve man's lot, and, in June 1786, drafted a long letter on this theme. Babeuf addressed this missive to the aristocratic Dubois de Fosseux, but eventually he did not send it, likely having been deterred by the overly radical character of its content, for which he continually offered his apologies throughout the text. The letter's primary objective was to provide a commentary on the entries to the Académie d'Arras essay contest of 1785, which asked candidates to appraise the utility of partitioning farmland in Artois province, as well as the limits that ought to be placed on this division. Here, Babeuf bemoaned the unfairness of the concentration of land – something which denied work to the poor peasant – but also criticised the parcelling of land into small strips, which he considered ineffective from the perspective of the community. Significantly, Babeuf argued:

> Believe me, Sir, that so long as the edifice ill-suited to the happiness of the generality of men has not been razed to the ground and rebuilt from the ground up according to an entirely new plan, in perfect harmony with the requirements of their free and complete development, everything will still have to be destroyed, everything will have to be remade.[1]

---

1 *OB*, p. 81.

An 'Entirely New Plan'

What, then, was this project that Babeuf vaunted as the means to ensure the 'happiness of the generality of men' – in this showing the same radicalism as his utopian predecessors? For Babeuf, it was necessary to overcome the binary between large farms run by a single wealthy individual and the fragmentation of the land into tiny plots, which would be 'more harmful than useful'.[2] This was to be achieved through the exploitation of large expanses of land by 'a group of workers proportionate to its size and bound by one same contract to farm it'.[3] With a great plethora of technical detail, he explained how the rent due to the landowner should be calculated in order to ensure the 'comfort' of those who worked the land. Without overlooking the landowner's interests, he expounded both the economic and the moral advantages of such an association for the workforce. Delving into the internal organisation of the small community, he argued:

> Necessarily, where several men come together to work towards the same goal, there is always a leadership entrusted to the most intelligent, the most experienced, the most honest; there is always mutual supervision and emulation among them, hostile to all dissipation, to all harmful distractions . . . Should any of them fall ill, nothing will suffer as a result – neither his wife, nor his children, nor the farm, for then everyone shall redouble their activity, and each shall cheerfully take on a little extra toil . . . in this fraternal community, everyone offers each other mutual assistance.[4]

Striking, in this short extract, is the presence of features corresponding to the usual themes of the utopian imaginary, even though Babeuf's plan is otherwise so marked by its pragmatism and respect for private property over the land. Such traits include the entrustment of an operational leadership role to men chosen for their above-average personal qualities, but who do not draw any material privilege as a result; the transparency of daily life, through a benevolent 'surveillance' which keeps vice

---

2 Ibid., p. 83.
3 Ibid.
4 Ibid., pp. 84–5.

away from the community; and the fraternity which produces spontaneous mutual aid. In this reference to the extra work 'cheerfully' taken on by the associated workers should one of their number fall ill, we are reminded of the descriptions of the joyous continent of *La Basiliade*, where sowing and harvesting are a collective amusement. The organisation of tasks in these ideal collective farms seems to be characterised by forward planning, diligence, and the absence of drudgery. The absorption of all families into a single merged whole, in the interests of the greater benefit of all, is the natural result of communal life: '[collective farms] would, so to speak, fuse several poor households into one well-to-do household'.[5] Although Babeuf does not venture any exact count of the number of members necessary for these communities' well-being – as Fourier, for instance, would later do – he nevertheless insists on the *need* to calculate this number. Clearly, this number is not to be calculated according to the complementary moral qualities of different human types, but rather according to the farm's productive capacity. The point is to optimise this number, in order to obtain the greatest possible productivity and the greatest comfort for each member of the community.

Lastly, Babeuf insists on the 'great modifications in the construction, distribution and extent of buildings', which are to be made for the sake of 'the morality and happiness of the inhabitants of the countryside'. The point, here, is to get them to live in collective houses, both in order to make the rural habitat more comfortable and to ensure the visibility of each person's deeds in the eyes of others – thus cutting at the root of all crime and vice. Hence there would be 'no more thieves, no more arsonists, no more gallows, no more executioners'.[6] The power of public esteem is thus increased to its fullest extent. In this sense, Babeuf seems to go even further than most of the utopians who went before him. For he offers a truly idyllic description, in which the spontaneous policing resulting from a community's own constant self-observation renders superfluous the means of repression that persist in other descriptions. A real golden age seems to begin for the community thus constituted.

The other natural result of this new form of organisation is the enlightenment of the intellect. While Babeuf does not set out any particular

---

5   Ibid., p. 85.
6   Ibid.

educational plan for these collective farms, he does nevertheless state that 'a host of prejudices and dangerous superstitions will soon disappear, for wherever men gather to live together, reason soon makes its home among them'.[7] It is clear that the ideal – characteristic of the enlightened circles of the eighteenth century – of reducing the 'prejudices' and 'superstitions' among men is here reliant not on the dissemination of knowledge by those who already possess it, but rather on community life as such.

In several respects, the utopia of the collective farm seems to be a modern and egalitarian response to another model of domestic economy which enjoyed wide renown in the eighteenth century, and whose utopian dimension has often been noted: namely, the model of Clarens in *The New Heloise*. We will not here analyse the details and the richness of 'the Clarens utopia', but just note a few points on which Babeuf and Rousseau seem to have conceived two radically different solutions to an identical problem.[8]

Both authors appear to be looking for a satisfactory answer to the question of social relations in the countryside, so as to protect the peasants from destitution and ensure the common happiness without fundamentally altering the social order. Like the collective farm, the Clarens estate is chosen by its masters 'not to obtain a larger gain from it, but to feed more men'.[9] Here, all measures are taken to maximise its members' material and moral well-being by satisfying their needs and tightening their emotional bonds. As in Babeuf, we have a shared house where everyone lives together; this is 'like their father's house where everything is but one family'.[10] Lastly, just as in the collective farms, 'the fundamental law of Clarens is a reciprocity of services which rests on

---

7 Ibid., p. 86.

8 On this point, see especially Antoine Hatzenberger, *Rousseau et l'utopie*, Paris: Honoré Champion, 2012, and James F. Jones, *La Nouvelle Héloïse: Rousseau and Utopia*, Paris: Droz, 1978. It is true that some of the most attentive commentators on Rousseau reject this definition: thus Francine Markovits, in 'Rousseau et l'éthique de Clarens, une économie des relations humaines', *Stanford French Review*, 15/3, 1991, p. 323, writes that 'Clarens is not a utopia but the theatre of another ethic'. But utopias can all, at some level, be understood as the staging of an alternative morality to that of the real world, a morality extended to all social relations. The essential ethical dimension of utopia in the work of various authors has been discussed at length in the preceding pages. Clarens is no exception in this sense.

9 NH, p. 364.

10 Ibid., p. 462.

common utility'.[11] A blessed virtue is the natural consequence of the internal organisation of the small community.

But, while the result is apparently identical, in Babeuf's case it corresponds to a horizontal organisation of social relations, whereas Rousseau sees it as the effect of their vertical structure. Whereas in the case of the Roye *feudiste* (land surveyor) Babeuf, the master is conspicuous by his absence and withdraws once the farming contract is concluded, the Genevan imagines the presence, even the omnipresence, of the de Wolmar couple, who are truly the heart of the house. All initiative, all impulse comes from their continuous, dynamic activity: they are the soul of their domain. While Babeuf imagines that emulation could derive from the egalitarian fraternity of farmers, in Clarens it is a pure product of encouragement by the de Wolmars. They give their servants a financial motive for efficiency (the so-called *prix de bénéficence*) or stir the workers' courage through the simple demonstration of Julie's 'beneficent beauty'.[12] It is not that the competent will be granted an accepted pre-eminence over the others, as their superiority gradually becomes clear to the general opinion through the accomplishment of everyday tasks. Rather, Monsieur de Wolmar and Julie's superiority over their community is *essential* – it blends into their social supremacy and is never questioned by anyone.

While, in Babeuf's case, surveillance is reciprocal and egalitarian, in Clarens, it naturally takes on an asymmetrical form. It is essentially a surveillance of the servant by the master. The lords visit their workers 'almost every day',[13] thus exerting a benevolent but undeniable pressure on their work. The de Wolmars encourage their servants to render services to each other, for the couple more readily grant the favours that a servant seeks on another's behalf;[14] they also organise the matrimonial encounters of their community, by way of the balls that they oversee every Sunday; finally, through the example they provide they are the true guarantors of collective morality.[15] They even go so far as to

---

11 Markovits, 'Rousseau et l'éthique de Clarens', p. 331.
12 *NH*, p. 366.
13 Ibid., p. 392.
14 Ibid., p. 380.
15 If it is true that the 'domestics' judgment . . . [is] the surest and most difficult test of their masters' virtue' (*NH*, p. 378) given that they are constantly in their sight, it does not follow that the relationship is reciprocal. The masters direct and guide the awareness of the servants; the servants are merely witnesses to the masters' virtue.

encourage their servants to report on one another. Despite the idyllic trappings in which this is presented, this also shows how the servants are divested of the capacity to make the slightest decision or resolve the slightest internal conflict by themselves. If, in Babeuf, the prevalent model of family relationship in the relations between community members is the fraternal bond, the model that dominates the description of Clarens is the de Wolmars' parental relationship to their servants; parents who do not seek to emancipate their children but rather to maintain them in this state. Madame de Wolmar's maxim is, indeed, 'not to favor changes of condition', but rather to 'contribute to making everyone happy in his own [condition]'.[16] So, the objective is not, as in Babeuf, to learn self-organisation within a group of equals, but rather happiness under the gentle guardianship of exceptionally benevolent lords. The author of *The Social Contract* is himself doubtless conscious of the limitations of his model, which he feels obliged to acknowledge: 'Servitude is so unnatural to man that it cannot possibly exist without a measure of discontent.'[17]

Through the Clarens model, Rousseau thus sought to pull off the feat of making inequality bearable within the framework of close and enduring social relations, softening 'institutional inequality through the adjustment of morals'.[18] As Markovits observes, the bond of kinship established between the de Wolmars and their community is the only alternative to pure coercion and conflict, in a society based on distinction by birth and private land ownership in which personal will takes the place of law. Babeuf, conversely, sought to compensate for the constraint of service not by introducing bonds of friendship and familiarity between masters and farmers – that is, by tightening the ties between the dominated and the dominant – but rather by loosening this personal bond so that they would be bound only by a regulated, material relationship: that of a rent calculated according to precise rules set in advance. A link between unequal individuals is thus replaced by a link between a group constituted as such and a third party to whom they simply pay rent. In this sense, the young *feudiste* seeks to substitute 'modern' relationships for the feudal relations between individuals,

---

16   Ibid., p. 439.
17   Ibid., p. 378.
18   Markovits, 'Rousseau et l'éthique de Clarens', p. 333.

using the introduction of a just law to dim the inequality of birth and the difference among orders.

Once the members of the farm have been freed from too close a relationship with the landowner, they can engage in other, egalitarian relationships with the outside world. Babeuf ends his description by imagining a possible aggregation of collective farms, which would join together to better provide for all their needs – and, again, offer each other mutual aid whenever necessary. In fact, he seems to come close to advocating general expropriation of the big landowners, who would make way for an association of mutually independent, collectively managed agricultural production units. But he continues:

> I did not want to question the legitimacy of the large properties and thus arrive at a radical solution regarding the large farms, whose very principle was then under attack. It is too late, or too soon, to tackle such a subject.[19]

This formulation calls for comment. It undoubtedly expresses the caution of the author, who does not want to frighten his audience but rather to persuade it of the advantages – for the 'château' as well as for the 'cottage' – of such a shake-up in the village's social structures, with its benefits in terms of productivity as well as security and morality. But it undoubtedly reveals that Babeuf's thoughts, at least, went further than his own proposals in terms of questioning land ownership itself. He returns to this question later on in his letter:

> Those who have, shall have; but would it not be more advantageous for society, as well as for themselves, if they had never had, and if each of us were to arrive, with the enlightenment acquired thus far, in a wholly new world where everything would be taken in common.[20]

Like the previous formulation, this one is immediately followed by an assertion as to the unshakeable character of the social edifice based on the principle of property. But it remains clear that, in this period, Babeuf was convinced of the superiority of a form of social organisation based

---

19   *OB*, p. 87.
20   Ibid., p. 115.

on the community of both goods and work itself. In this respect, Daline has rightly noted that, on this terrain, the Roye *feudiste* proved to be a supporter not only of a community of the distribution of goods, but also of production, clearly seeing the drawbacks of 'fragmentation' and the individual cultivation of the land. To Babeuf's mind, it would be possible to bring material comfort to all by combining the community's efforts in the work process itself. The 1786 manuscript, discovered in the archives by a Russian researcher only in the 1950s, thus allows us to refute the earlier analyses offered by the historian Georges Lefebvre, who claimed that 'Babeuf did not realise that his communism of distribution would require a communism of production.'[21]

So, despite his major concession to the existing property regime, on these questions Babeuf proceeds in the same vein as the utopians who preceded him. On the other hand, his proposals differ greatly from most of the utopias we have mentioned thus far, in one important respect: they remain completely outside the political field, leaving the organisation of the state and the major institutions such as the church and the army unchanged. Babeuf's 1786 utopia is a cooperative utopia that concerns limited groups of individuals. In this respect, his thinking is both close to and distinct from that of another autodidact whose own social extraction also made him very familiar with the realities of peasant life: Restif de la Bretonne.[22]

Indeed, in his first successful novel, 1755's *Le paysan perverti*, Restif includes in his conclusion the 'statutes of the *bourg* of Oudun'. This is the new village in which the main character – the famous peasant – settles, now cured of his moral problems caused by his spell in the city, along with his whole family and a few others forming a complete

---

21   Georges Lefebvre, 'Les origines du communisme de Babeuf', in *Études sur la Révolution française*, Paris: PUF, 1954, p. 307.

22   Restif, born in 1734 to a family of well-off peasants in the Burgundian village of Sacy, spent his childhood and youth in the countryside. He remained in touch with his homeland for many years. See on Restif: Katharina Middell, 'Egalitarismus und Kommunismus im Vorfeld und während der Französischen Revolution. Die Entwicklung der Auffassung von N. E. Restif de la Bretonne', in K. Holzapfel and K. Middell (eds), *Die Französischen Revolution von 1789, Studien zur Geschichte und zu ihren Wirkungen, Jahrbuch für Geschichte* n°39, Berlin: Akademie Verlag, 1990, pp. 121–46, and Katharina Middell, 'Babeuf et Restif: les voies du communisme utopique à la fin du XVIII siècle', in A. Maillard, C. Mazauric, and É. Walter (eds), *Présence de Babeuf: Lumières, Révolution, communisme*, Paris: Publications de la Sorbonne, 1994, pp. 67–78.

community of assets. The land, which belongs to all, is divided equally. The barn, the refectory, and the oven are shared, and the inhabitants of the village eat meals together, prepared by their wives. A very strict organisation regulates all aspects of life, from the hours of work and leisure (which are rather restricted and always collective), to the village hierarchy, dominated by the heads of the families, the twelve Elders assisted by the priest, the schoolmaster, the annually renewed 'syndics', and so on. This patriarchal – to tell the truth, gerontocratic – society rewards merit with roundels and other honorific marks, but also through the building of a personal nest egg which even allows the acquisition of land outside the village. The supreme reward, however, remains the possibility for the most deserving young men to have first choice of wives from among all the young maidens, on the understanding that 'the right to choose . . . belongs and must belong only to the man'.[23]

The small number of community members, directly connected to the peasant world's concrete way of life, is evident in the models proposed by both authors. Both are rural utopias, implying that they have a certain archaic character, especially in *Le paysan perverti*. Like Babeuf, Restif emphasises both the material and moral advantages of the village community, drawing inspiration – as his novel itself puts it – from the examples of the traditional peasant communities of the Auvergne, which were much debated in the eighteenth century, but also from the monastic communities of Eastern Europe, in particular the Moravian Brethren, which are the subject of a famous entry by Faiguet in the *Encyclopédie*,[24] and perhaps also from the Jesuit 'reductions' in Paraguay. However, despite these more original aspects, Restif otherwise takes up a rather classic utopian perspective, inserting the statutes of Oudun at the end of a novelistic narrative, whereas Babeuf, who would never write a novel, reflected more on the role of a reformer of the existing order. The latter's intellectual approach betrays a deep desire to 'raze to the ground the edifice ill-suited to the happiness of the generality of men'. As a result, Babeuf, unlike the author of *Le paysan perverti*, gives his proposals a

---

23 Restif de la Bretonne, *Le paysan perverti*, in *Œuvres romanesques*, Paris: Robert Laffont, 2002, vol. 1, p. 800.
24 Faiguet, 'Moraves ou Frères unis', in D. Diderot and Jean Le R. D'Alembert (eds), *Encyclopédie ou Dictionnaire raisonné des sciences, des arts et des métiers*, Neufchâtel: S. Faulche et compagnie, 1765, vol. X, pp. 704–6.

more than purely moral scope. Babeuf's model seems to have been thought of as a possible solution to the general problem of rural poverty – a question which would continue to preoccupy him throughout his life. But we should also remember that he only formulated his thoughts for himself, thus making his text a simple hypothesis which was probably too radical to be proposed outright.

Paradoxically, then, it is precisely the boldness of Babeuf's social theory that explains why he lagged behind most of the utopians, and, in particular, Restif de la Bretonne, on the question of private property. Babeuf was more concerned than Restif with the conditions for realising the social ideal of his imagination, and was thus more inclined to seek a form of compromise with the existing order – a compromise whose terms he struggled to find. Babeuf set the objective of a state where, in his own words, 'all are reassured of their fate':[25] this very pragmatic ideal of man's security regarding his and his family's future would continually recur in his writings. It most likely derived from Babeuf's personal experience worrying about where tomorrow's bread would come from – giving his social theory its general orientation and explaining his constant search for its means of application.

In addition, Restif remains within the terms of a very traditional organisation of rural labour. For him, while the products of the harvest were to be taken to the common stock, the harvest itself was a task to be taken on by each peasant isolated on his own patch of land. It is also worth noting that private property, which Restif would abolish within village limits, is maintained on the outside, thus leaving open the possibility for the community's most resourceful members to personally enrich themselves. Babeuf's thinking is instead more in line with the compulsory agricultural labour service of the likes of More and Morelly. As we have seen, Restif's utopia also maintains the patriarchal structures of peasant society. Babeuf, for his part, extends his reflection on collective farms by commenting on Dubois de Fosseux's analysis of the public gatherings at the Académie d'Arras, which discussed 'the natural and philosophical history of woman'. In his commentary, Babeuf proves to be a remarkable advocate of the equality of the sexes, perhaps recovering the essential

---

25   *OB*, p. 102.

intuition of predecessors in utopia such as More or Campanella. Babeuf shows no ambiguity on this score, insisting:

> Let us re-establish woman in her rights and in the liberty which belongs to her as to us; let us recognise that, if she is less favoured than we are in the matter of physical strength, she is, conversely, endowed with qualities of which we are deprived, and which would be a thousand times more salient, if, instead of their being compressed or altered in a false direction, we had known or wished to develop them in their true sense.[26]

Babeuf thus invokes a complementarity of human qualities that justifies equality of treatment. He concludes that this equality is necessary as a condition for true human progress: 'True civilisation stops and majestically fixes a level; here is marked the end of all misery, of all wailing, of all sobbing, of all gnashing of teeth.'[27] As we can see, a new dimension of Babeuf's social thought emerges, which, although relatively allusive, would remain a constant in his writing: namely, the eschatological tone of his predictions for the human race's future. Here, he expresses hope not in the gradual improvement of the female condition, but rather in the advent of a new age of emancipation, rich in still-unheard-of consequences, and which will justify 'new laws' which remain unknown. Appearing in connection with the abolition of domination over women, in Babeuf's thinking the 'chiliastic consciousness' – as Karl Mannheim put it[28] – evidently blends with more rationally enlightened hopes about the progress to be expected from providing education to women.

In reality, the eschatological relationship to social reality has a much broader scope in the general economy of this long letter. It emerges on several occasions, for example when Babeuf describes the moment when the poor peasant will realise that he is the equal of the great landowner:

> From that moment, a ray of sunlight has pierced the clouds which once obscured the intelligence of the unfortunate man, a thousand

---

26   Ibid., p. 98.
27   Ibid., p. 102.
28   Karl Mannheim, *Ideology and Utopia*, London: Routledge, 1991, Chapter 4.

and one flashes similarly come to light among his peers, one day the blindfold has fallen, and it is no longer a ray which illuminates them, but the Sun of truth which shines with all its brilliance – and all the old forms of prestige are dissipated.[29]

These are the kinds of terms in which Babeuf expresses his very high hopes for the future of the human race. Here, the faith in the progress of humanity characteristic of the enlightened circles of the eighteenth century is obviously mixed with older depictions more deeply rooted in popular consciousness, whose hope for better times the young *feudiste* relays. So, in all areas where equality can be established, the end of all misfortunes, of all that obscures individual and collective existence, is thus on the horizon of history. However, it should be noted that in this period Babeuf's hopes were still hesitant. The better times would – perhaps – come, and even then only in an indeterminate future; it was still 'too late, or too soon'. While evoking the benefits to be expected from the triumph of equality, Babeuf remained fundamentally in a condition of expectation – something again well illustrated by the fact that the letter would ultimately remain a draft.

Nonetheless, a study of this important text also brings out the most important traits of Babeuf's utopianism, which would again resurface later on. First of all, as most commentators emphasise, he had a very acute sense of reality, which led him to adapt his ideal to the concrete conditions in which it was likely to be enacted. This is what leads Jean-Marc Schiappa to remark: 'Thus it can be said of Babeuf that when his conceptions were utopian, they always bore the stamp of pragmatism, which Béatrice Didier has rightly called a "combat utopia".'[30] This unfailing pragmatism went hand in hand with an eschatological tendency which, though less marked, also represents a continuous undertow of Babeuf's utopian thinking. This characteristic has also been noted by specialists:

> What jumps out from Gracchus Babeuf is an absolute belief in possible happiness, in the universal triumph of Equality; exaltation,

---

29 *OB*, p. 88.
30 Jean-Marc Schiappa, *Gracchus Babeuf avec les Égaux*, Paris: Les éditions ouvrières, 1991, p. 33.

enthusiasm, fanaticism, proselytism, prophetism, total commitment, and even a vocation to sacrifice – all of this accompanied by an appropriate practice.[31]

It was probably the conjunction of these two tendencies that made Babeuf an active utopian. In contrast to all his predecessors, he was the first to attempt to put the conclusions of his political theories into practice – a move clearly encouraged by the unfolding French Revolution.

Babeuf's Anthropology in 1786

For Babeuf, reflection on the nature of man is always linked to the need to show in what way existing institutions are ill-suited to his full development, and how they must therefore be transformed. In this vein, Babeuf forcefully asserted, as early as 1786, the inalienable prerogatives of each individual, drawing extensively on the language of natural right. But here a difficulty arises, inherent in Babeuf's approach itself: how to deduce, from the observation of man denatured by present circumstances, the characteristics of natural man? In the jusnaturalist logic to which Babeuf's thought explicitly adheres in this first phase of theoretical development, it was necessary to reconstruct – as many others had – a genesis of humanity, starting from the hypothesis of the state of nature. But the relationship of Babeuf's thought to this hypothesis is immediately ambiguous, as the author seems to constantly be seeking – not always successfully – to do without it. But what can provide the basis for a critical conception of human nature that accounts for its 'real' characteristics, when one starts out by refusing to take a perverted human nature for the original, while also claiming ignorance as to the conditions in which the first human groups emerged? The problem is redoubled by the author's attention to the importance of temporality in the development of human characteristics: for this poses a deep challenge to the idea of an unchanging human nature, which would appear in all its purity if only it were freed from its coating of corruption.

---

31 Maurice Dommanget, 'Tempérament et formation de Babeuf', in *Sur Babeuf et la Conjuration des Égaux*, Paris: Maspero, 1970, pp. 22–59, at p. 29.

This is undoubtedly the reason why, in the 1786 draft letter, we can see a variety of methods for shedding light on the difficult question of the nature of man and human societies. Tellingly, the letter opens with two assertions, which it will be the job of the rest of the text to demonstrate:

1. Nature's 'intentions' are the following: it can only 'will human society, under the condition that each of its members may find therein the full satisfaction of the needs of life'.
2. So long as the edifice ill-suited to the happiness of the generality of men has not been razed to the ground and rebuilt from the ground up according to an entirely new plan, in perfect harmony with the requirements of their free and complete development, everything will still have to be destroyed, everything will have to be remade.[32]

With the first of these two statements, Babeuf explicitly attaches the goal of human societies to the fulfilment of nature's own concerns, which regard the satisfaction of vital 'needs'. Initially these remain undefined, but they can apparently be linked to the concerns of material conservation. With the second, he asserts the need for a radical reform, not only to satisfy these basic necessities, but to allow the 'free and complete development' of the faculties of the human race. This second demand apparently implies a conception of man as having to actualise the potentialities that his nature itself harbours. We would therefore expect his subsequent argumentation to set out not only the list of natural needs that man and thus society must necessarily provide for, but also views on the natural fate of each individual, from the point of view of the actualisation of faculties that by definition cannot be seen in every individual, especially in a society 'ill-suited' to the 'happiness of the generality of men'. Yet it turns out that neither of these two expectations can be fulfilled, without triggering tensions within the concept of human nature itself.

Babeuf's 'demonstration', if it can be considered one, consists of three moments. The first is the presentation of the collective farm project and of the advantages that the small group of associated farmers would derive from this type of organisation: material well-being, the

---

32 *OB*, p. 81.

entrustment of operational direction to the most capable, overall moral improvement through the transparency of everyday conduct, and so on. The important thing is that, having provided this idyllic description, Babeuf attacks something which is nevertheless destined to remain part of the framework of his system of collective farms, namely large-scale property. Affecting to disavow such a stance, he insists that he does not want to question their 'legitimacy', nor does he want to arrive at a 'radical solution'[33] on this issue. Yet, 'to the philosopher's eyes', he writes, large-scale property is de facto delegitimised, on account of its very origin: for more often than not this is due not to 'work', but to the cunning of the forefathers of the present large landowners who 'had the skill to benefit themselves, to the prejudice of their fellow men', by depriving others not only of the right to 'enjoy in equal portions the great common inheritance of the earth', but also of their 'freedom': 'thus iniquity and tyranny were founded and supported one another reciprocally'.[34]

In this critique of large landholdings for stripping the majority of their right to necessities and their natural freedom, it seems we can make out a trace of Rousseau's developments in the *Second Discourse* – which, we know, Babeuf was familiar with by this period. In the second part of the *Discourse*, Rousseau describes the situation of the rich at the end of the state of nature as the result of 'usurpations' most often achieved by force. Like Babeuf, Rousseau refers to the case where the rich accumulate their lands and possessions through their labour, and contrasts the legitimacy of such appropriation with that conferred upon others by their need for what 'you have too much of'.[35] In any case, the rich man has no right to deprive his fellow men of what they need by extending his ownership over that which would allow them to live. It is, indeed, 'natural law' itself that is contrary to the interests of the rich man, in that the rich – as Rousseau sees things in this passage – forbid taking from the common subsistence more than what you 'needed for your own maintenance'. As Blaise Bachofen writes: 'Those who pull up the stakes of the fences formulate a jusnaturalist statement, since they

---

33 Ibid., p. 87.
34 Ibid.
35 Jean-Jacques Rousseau, *The Social Contract and the First and Second Discourses*, edited by Susan Dunn, New Haven, CT: Yale University Press, 2002, p. 124.

define the limits of a legitimate property even though no positive right yet distinguishes yours from mine.'[36]

Babeuf thus seems to take the first idea from Rousseau's *Second Discourse* – namely, a natural right to enjoy the products of the Earth, up to the amount necessary for individual subsistence. A second idea, only appearing in outline form in Babeuf, is the conjunction – sealed in Rousseau by the 'leonine' (deeply unequal) contract between rich and poor – between the material usurpation of the natural right to live and the destitution of natural liberty. If Babeuf merely suggests the link between 'iniquity' and 'tyranny', Rousseau is much more explicit about how the rhetoric of the rich – mobilising the energies of the poor in the constitution of public authority and common laws – ends up destroying 'natural liberty' and subjecting the whole human race 'to labour, servitude, and misery'.[37] However, at this stage in the development of his thinking, Babeuf had not yet moved on to properly political considerations, and he did not take up his predecessor's idea of a contract establishing a civil society and laws. He more likely had in mind the local tyranny exerted by lords and large farmers, the injustices of which were directly known to him through his experience as a surveyor.

But, at this stage, these views were asserted rather than demonstrated in such a fashion as to properly root them in the nature of man and the social bond. Babeuf would therefore need to revisit these issues in a different way. Thus far, he had sought to show by example the possibility of another mode of organisation, the mere presentation of which would serve to delegitimise the iniquities of current reality. The nature of humans' rights was thus revealed by way of a thought experiment, which intended to show that these rights were not only just, but also possible and even favourable to all. Seen through this prism, the real thus took on the appearance of a perverted and ineffective system. It is thus remarkable that, unlike Rousseau's demonstration, which deduced humanity's fundamental rights from 'conjecture' as to its supposed origins, Babeuf's approach is, above all, rooted in an effort of the imagination, which immediately extracts itself from reality the better to contrast it to a critical counterpoint. Paradoxically, man's nature is

---

36 Blaise Bachofen, *La condition de la liberté. Rousseau, critique des raisons politiques*, Paris: Payot, 2002, p. 112.

37 Rousseau, *The Social Contract*, p. 125.

deducible not from what he may have been in the distant past, and still less from what he is in the present, but from what he could be in circumstances imagined by the utopian. It is this very particular theoretical effort that offers the reader a first image, still in the form of a sketch, of man and his fundamental rights.

The Female Condition and Its Anthropological Significance

However, clearly this effort is not alone sufficient, and Babeuf was not satisfied with it. After providing an illustration of a small imaginary society functioning on bases different to those of the prevalent society – a vision also bearing a strong critical charge against large property – Babeuf engaged in a further case study. This time, he highlighted not man's natural right to the satisfaction of his basic needs, but rather his intrinsic capacity for development and 'perfection'.

In contrast to Morelly and Mably, in whose work the female question is entirely marginal, Babeuf dealt at length with the nature of women, setting them up as paradigmatic of the whole species' potential.

Here, again, Babeuf's theories intersect with Rousseau's. This, not because the two men's opinions of the status of women converged, but rather because in a certain sense Babeuf retains Rousseau's lesson about the nature of man by transposing it onto the nature of woman. From this point of view, Babeuf's reflection on female nature is highly revealing of his way of approaching the anthropological question in general.[38]

Firstly, on a methodological level, it is notable that Babeuf's approach to female nature overlaps with the one Rousseau indicates in the Preface to the *Second Discourse* with regard to man in general. We know that the human soul, 'like the statue of Glaucus', has been so 'altered' by the moral and material achievements of civilisation that it has become almost unrecognisable.[39] As Binoche writes, such statements harbour

---

38 Here, we will not enter into the contemporary debates on Rousseau's legacy for feminism. We will confine ourselves to proposing an interpretation of Rousseau's discourse on women as it appears in Book V of *Émile*, by comparing it with that of Babeuf in the draft letter of June 1786. For a summary of the debate within contemporary feminism, see Céline Spector, 'Au prisme du féminisme', in *Au prisme de Rousseau. Usages politiques contemporains*, Oxford: Voltaire Foundation, 2011, pp. 227–61.

39 Rousseau, *The Social Contract*, p. 81.

an implicit warning against the spontaneous prejudices of the human observer:

> If, therefore, it is still appropriate to deduce genetic origin from human nature, it is clear that the accessibility of the latter is no longer self-evident and that one cannot continue to identify men 'as they have been made' with man as nature had made him.[40]

But Babeuf also formulates a similar warning, directed against the author of the *Histoire naturelle de la femme*:

> In proposing to write the *Natural History of Woman*, Mr. Dr. Taranget has in my view adopted a bad starting point. He has studied woman bent, folded, dulled, enslaved, entirely metamorphosed almost from the cradle, with a view to ensuring that the law of our miserable superiority should reign.[41]

Whereas Rousseau pointed to a multiplicity of factors responsible for the unrecognisable features under which contemporary man appears, Babeuf is interested in only one of them, namely oppression, which is, in turn, held responsible for a single effect: the diminution of individual qualities and the existential narrowing of the female condition. Babeuf takes from Rousseau and applies to women the idea that the first observable effect of denaturation is the development of an inequality that did not exist at first sight. Speaking of the condition of men in general, the citizen of Geneva wrote:

> It is easy to perceive that it is in these successive alterations of the human constitution that we must look for the first origin of those differences that distinguish men, who, it is universally allowed, are naturally as equal among themselves as were the animals of every species before various physical causes had introduced those varieties we now observe among some of them.[42]

---

40 Bertrand Binoche, *Les trois sources des philosophies de l'histoire (1764–1798)*, Paris: PUF, 1994, p. 25.
41 *OB*, p. 98.
42 Rousseau, *The Social Contract*, pp. 81–2.

In both authors, inequality is thus the most striking effect of the denaturation of individuals. The entire reasoning of both the *Second Discourse* and the draft letter consists of bringing out what has long remained under the carpet, namely the intrinsically equal qualities of individuals. While Rousseau is perfectly conscious of the difficulty of this task, claiming to venture onto this slippery slope only by way of 'conjecture', Babeuf seems much less concerned with pre-empting objections than with the chimerical nature of his assertions. But in both cases, the approach is similar – it is to show that

> the corruption being denounced is not a curse whose mark each individual must fatally inherit, but a collective corruption which reproduces itself through social mechanisms from which the individual can be freed, so long as it is done in time.[43]

Using a perspective common to both authors, it is therefore possible to liberate the individual (or nations: and this is the meaning of the *Constitutional Project for Corsica*) from harmful, denaturing influences. This becomes possible through an education that, far from seeking to 'rectify' spontaneously perverse tendencies, must instead strive to let elements of good nature flourish.

Logically, from such a perspective, Sophie's education – which takes place in Book V of *Émile, or Education* – could be presented as a 'natural' education which enables her to escape corrupting social determinations and offers her the freedom that constitutes the species' very essence. But this is not the case, and, here again, it is interesting to examine the parallel between the education that Rousseau and Babeuf respectively propose for women. It appears that Babeuf's answer, unlike Rousseau's, is an extension of his doctrine of human equality and thus, again unlike Rousseau's, brings out characteristics common to the whole species.

---

43 Binoche, *Les trois sources des philosophies de l'histoire*, p. 27.

Childhood, for Each of the Sexes

In both Rousseau and Babeuf, the first moments of childhood are moments of non-differentiation, but this non-differentiation has a different nature and function for each of them. The author of *Émile* states that, 'Up to the age of puberty children of both sexes have little to distinguish them';[44] but this indistinction is merely an 'external resemblance' and serves only to highlight the difference that separates them: 'But for her sex, a woman is a man ... Yet where sex is concerned man and woman are unlike; each is the complement of the other.'[45]

This physiological differentiation is prolonged and amplified in the progressive formation of the personality: while boys are called upon to develop their faculties, producing profound transformations, girls 'never lose this resemblance':[46] they remain in a sense children all their lives, and can thus be considered as imperfect men. Time does not have the same evolutionary effect on them that it has on boys; it is as if the nature of women were given once and for all. In particular, they prove lacking in self-love, indifferent as they are to its first fundamental characteristic, the judgement of others. On the contrary, it is as if, in many respects, they were ready-made women from the start, imbued with the marks of sociability: 'Even the tiniest little girls love finery; they are not content to be pretty, they must be admired.'[47] Unlike the natural man, who is indifferent to how he is seen, girls seem instinctively driven by the *amour-propre* which subjects them to the judgement of others. In this sense, they are, paradoxically, morally women even before they have grown up: 'A woman's judgement develops sooner than a man's; being on the defensive from her childhood up, and intrusted with a treasure so hard to keep, she is earlier acquainted with good and evil.'[48] Although nature destines women to the immutable role of nurturing mother, they are always already marked by the characteristics conferred by social life, which subject them to the tyranny of opinion. This stands in contrast to man, who

---

44 *E*, p. 172.
45 Ibid., p. 321.
46 Ibid., p. 172.
47 Ibid., p. 329.
48 Ibid., p. 360.

'has no one but himself to consider, and so long as he does right . . . may defy public opinion'.[49]

The position of women, who must above all preserve their reputation, and whom some texts even set up as guardians of the reputation of others, thus gives them from infancy a very different destiny to men's. As Yves Vargas writes, woman is not a natural being in the sense of being likely to develop according to the successive ages of life, like man; rather, she is 'transtemporal', simultaneously both a little girl who is already a woman and a woman who is an eternal child, both 'naturally premature' and 'naturally immature'.[50] We can see how radically the portrait of the woman distinguishes her from the image of the natural man that emerges from *Émile*. Since, paradoxically, unlike men, women are social beings, their entire education must henceforth consist of adapting them to the requirements of their role within the group.

Babeuf provides a completely different analysis of the early life of the two sexes. For him, childhood is the age of the undifferentiated manifestation of a typical characteristic of man in general: the blossoming of 'friendship and pity', a natural impulse of the heart that expresses humanity's spontaneous tendency towards fraternity: 'The feeling of fraternity is innate in the human heart, and for it to be removed it is necessary that education should come along to suffocate it.'[51] Thus, Babeuf completes the first elements of his anthropology, first illustrated by his description of collective farms, with an observation of childhood, which is supposed to be closer to nature because it is not yet corrupted by education. In this primitive situation, there surface the most spontaneous manifestations of human nature, residing in the tendency to love one another. The first fault of perverted education consists precisely in its teaching of social distinctions and the attitudes of domination and servility that go with them:

> But soon, in the name of two inequalities which nature did not create, which it is even ignorant of – rank and fortune – the nobles are

---

49 Ibid., p. 328.
50 Yves Vargas, 'Rousseau et le droit naturel', *TransFormAção* 31: 1, 2008, pp. 25–52, at p. 28.
51 *OB*, p. 96.

inspired with harshness, with haughty airs, the rich are inculcated with the arithmetic of the basest interests.[52]

This is how society instils the habit of docility and submission in the minds of the poor, and the habit of arrogance and self-importance in the minds of the rich and noble. The original fraternity that Babeuf attributes to humans immediately engages men and women in egalitarian relationships that Rousseau's theory expressly rejects.

Both Babeuf and Rousseau raise the question of the limits inherent to female education, but they draw opposite assessments. Babeuf describes his view of female education in the following terms: 'She grows up in shackles of every kind, her education moulds her from the earliest age for the domination of a master to whom she will have to constantly yield everything, even in her most innocent games.'[53] It is striking that Rousseau evokes the same kind of 'shackles', but in a tone which is far from critical, but rather prescriptive:

> All their life long, they will have to submit to the strictest and most enduring restraints, those of propriety. They must be trained to bear the yoke from the first, so that they may not feel it, to master their own caprices and to submit themselves to the will of others.[54]

For Rousseau, the 'perpetual struggle against self' for which a woman's education prepares her for life is considered 'just', insofar as it is 'only fair that woman should bear her share of the ills she has brought upon man'.[55]

Remarkably, Rousseau here seems to take Eve's original sin in the original Paradise as an argument for consigning woman to a form of perpetual punishment. The immanent good nature that Rousseau sought to uncover in man, as he strove to free him from his coating of socially produced corruption, contrasts with a spontaneously dangerous female nature. Her secondary nature compared to man, cursed by her origin, condemns this sex to exhibit what would constitute 'defects' for a

---

52 Ibid.
53 Ibid., p. 95.
54 *E*, p. 332.
55 Ibid.

man. Yet, one should not seek to 'destroy' these, but only to prevent them from 'degenerating into evil',[56] because the defects of women are their qualities, so long as they are kept within their proper limits. There is no better way to present women as an eternal germ of corruption that education has to channel, insofar as this very corruption paradoxically makes up her entire charm, and the secret of the rule of the feminine over the masculine. Thus, little girls are attributed, as spontaneous and beneficial characteristics, attitudes that were rejected in little boys, such as the taste for finery, the art of pleasing, which the little girl exercises first of all by looking after her doll. The relationship between the two sexes is fully a mirror image. Female attitudes, far from being harmful, prepare the child to be a source of joy for the virtuous man who will become her husband.

Babeuf makes a diametrically opposed judgement on these feminine habits, which he insists are by no means the result of nature, but are entirely imposed on her:

> She is forbidden anything that might contribute to her attaining the degree of health and skill that she is apt to acquire ... No science for her, no art, nothing serious, nothing the product of reflection; all is frivolity or futility; all is dissipation, or sad misery.[57]

It is true that Rousseau also condemns the exaggerated 'delicacy' in which the little girl is raised – she cannot jump or run or shout, in a word 'be her natural, lively, little self'.[58] But, in his writing, this criticism is correlated with the end to which the citizen of Geneva destines women, namely motherhood. If they are to have any strength, it is so that the men born to them will inherit it. Babeuf, on the other hand, denounced this debilitating education as a deliberate enterprise in 'oppression'. Fundamentally, he converged with Mary Wollstonecraft, who opposed Rousseau's views in the following terms:

> If [women are] really capable of acting like rational creatures, let them not be treated like slaves; or, like the brutes who are dependent on the

---

56   Ibid., p. 327.
57   *OB*, pp. 96–7.
58   *E*, p. 329.

reason of man, when they associate with him; but cultivate their minds, give them the salutary, sublime curb of principle . . . Teach them, in common with man, to submit to necessity instead of giving, to render them more pleasing, a sex to morals.[59]

From the Reign of Force to the Exercise of Talents

In the last analysis, the inequality between men and women finds its ultimate justification in the inequality of strength between the two sexes. As Élisabeth Badinter summarises, 'The first inequality in fact and in law is physical: women are weaker than men, and from this all the other inequalities, both moral and intellectual, are deduced.'[60] However, physical inequality is not only presented as a fact, but, above all, as a necessity: 'The man should be strong and active; the woman should be weak and passive; the one must have both the power and the will; it is enough that the other should offer little resistance.'[61] This imperative distribution of roles is due, once again, to a biological reality: it is the maternal function of the woman which requires her subordination. As *Émile* tells us, 'She to whom nature has entrusted the care of the children must hold herself responsible for them to their father.'[62] The social role of the woman stems from this double determination. It confines her to the observance of her domestic duties, both sexual and maternal, and to strict submission to the head of the family, the man. This status instils in the woman a complete dependence on her husband. Certainly, by the time Émile and Sophie meet, they have become mutually necessary to each other. But this complementarity does not at all mean equality. For Rousseau, woman is and must remain relative to man. As he summarises:

---

59 Mary Wollstonecraft, *A Vindication of the Rights of Woman*, New Haven, CT: Yale University Press, 2014, pp. 61–2.

60 Élisabeth Badinter, 'L'éducation des filles selon Rousseau et Condorcet', in R. Thiéry (ed.), *Rousseau, l'Émile et la Révolution, Actes du colloque international de Montmorency, 24 septembre–4 octobre 1989*, Montmorency: Universitas, 1992, pp. 285–92, at p. 287.

61 *E*, p. 322.

62 Ibid., p. 324.

> Men and women are made for each other, but their mutual dependence differs in degree; man is dependent on woman through his desires; woman is dependent on man through her desires and also through her needs; he could do without her better than she can do without him.[63]

A male autarchy is thus matched by a female heteronomy – and, in a way of thinking in which autonomy is set up as a primary objective, this is the marker of a manifest imperfection and inferiority. This characteristic is asserted as a natural rule: it is 'by the very law of nature' that women 'are at the mercy of men's judgement' – that is, subject to rules that do not derive solely from their own reason and needs. In reality, the relationship between male and female is caught up in a dialectic that is much more complex than would be implied by the simple submission of one sex to the other, since woman's 'relative' character with respect to man nevertheless confers on her – if she knows how to keep to her proper place – an absolute 'kingdom' over men:

> But the woman who is both virtuous, wise, and charming, she who, in a word, combines love and esteem, can send them at her bidding to the end of the world, to war, to glory, and to death at her behest.[64]

However, the woman's realm is limited to the domestic sphere. An exemplary mother, a chaste wife who nevertheless satisfies her husband, she reigns over her family, but without leaving her home. Although she is the guardian of morals, she never participates directly in political life, which is always outside her jurisdiction. This is what leads the American philosopher Susan Moller Okin to say that '[Rousseau's] inflexible attachment to the patriarchal family results in a philosophy of woman that, in all its most important respects, contradicts his philosophy of man'.[65] For Babeuf, conversely, inequality of strength cannot be the basis of any right, and he vigorously denounces the right of the strongest. The heart of this critique lies in his comparison between the reign of force,

---

63 Ibid., p. 328.
64 Ibid., p. 356.
65 Susan M. Okin, *Women in Western Political Thought*, Princeton, NJ: Princeton University Press, 1992, p. 123. Quoted in Spector, *Au prisme de Rousseau*, p. 235.

which seems to justify male domination, and the exaltation of warlike values, which legitimises domination by the nobles:

> If we go back to the roots of the family tree of our great houses, what we find at the top of the line is usually a warrior whose entire merit consisted in the immense superiority of his physical strength ... The supposed superiority of men over women and the despotic authority they arrogate to themselves have the same origin as domination by the nobility; in each case there is a usurpation of rights and the consecration of a prejudice that led our fathers to worship physical strength.[66]

The female condition is far from being, as in Rousseau, the radical other of the male condition. Rather, for Babeuf, it constitutes a paradigm of human oppression in general, broadly comparable to social oppression. The latter is conceived on the model of feudal domination, which is based on the cult of violence through the warrior values that underpin the seigneurial rights of which Babeuf, as a surveyor, was particularly well placed to study the functioning and spot the abuses. Seigneurial domination and the male domination which constitutes its counterpart at the level of inter-individual relations find their justification in the framework of a humanity governed by the law of the strongest. But, for Babeuf, the reign of such a right corresponds to a bygone stage in the species' history: '[Woman] is physically less strong than man, but for her what does strength mean? Since gunpowder and firearms were invented, strength even in man has lost much of its value.'[67] Paradoxically, therefore, Babeuf goes further than Rousseau in his denunciation of the right of the strongest as far as women's condition is concerned, even though, as we know, such a right is dismissed even in the very first chapters of *The Social Contract*. Even if Rousseau sees the domestic reign of the strongest as only apparent ('the stronger party seems to be master, but is as a matter of fact dependent on the weaker'),[68] the fact remains that these very appearances, with what they presuppose from the point of view of social laws, are fully legitimised, whereas Babeuf sees in them only the mark of the most repulsive archaism.

---

66 *OB*, pp. 97–8.
67 Ibid., p. 97.
68 *E*, p. 323.

Babeuf does not, however, particularly criticise strength as a source of oppression, as if counterposed to other qualities that would be worthier of man or better able to justify the superiority of some over others. Technical progress, which causes the holder of physical superiority to lose his advantage over others, is only good in that it creates 'one less inequality'. Babeuf then asserts an anthropological thesis that is fundamental to all his thought: 'Progress is, I believe, only levelling.'[69] This statement introduces a certain parallel between his thought and that of Mably, who writes in *De la législation* that the feeling of equality is at the heart of the individual's awareness of his own dignity. But the author's assertion in the draft letter of 1786 places equality not at the origin of the human condition, but rather on the horizon of its progressive development. The relativisation of the rule of force through technical innovation is a step towards equality, and 'this is how it will be with each advance of humanity, until all inequalities have disappeared'.[70] This leads to the conclusion that the nature of man is not entirely observable in his original condition. This is less a matter of tracing a genesis, as in the *Second Discourse*, than of making an optimistic forecast of the possibilities that equality of conditions will inevitably bring to fruition. Again, as with his thought experiment regarding collective farms, here Babeuf envisages the species' authentic nature not on the basis of what it may have been, or of what it is, but of what it could be and will surely become in an indeterminate future.

In this respect, it is interesting to note that the young *feudiste*, moving away from Rousseau, converges – no doubt involuntarily – with the thought of Condorcet. In his *Discours de réception à l'Académie Française*, delivered on 21 February 1782, the latter states in a note (this, in an edition revised by the author):

> Has nature placed some differences between men and women? Undoubtedly women are weaker, and what proves this is that among all the rough peoples they have been oppressed. But physical strength depends on muscles, whereas it is highly doubtful that the strength of the mind or soul depends on them.[71]

---

69 *OB*, p. 97.
70 Ibid.
71 Jean-Antoine-Nicolas de Caritat Condorcet, 'Discours prononcé dans l'Académie Française', Thursday, 21 February 1782, introduction by Keith Baker, in *Studies on Voltaire and the Eighteenth Century*, 1977, vol. CLXIX, note L, p. 56.

A few years before Babeuf, Condorcet's remarks aimed to deflate the value of physical strength in relation to other human qualities such as strength of mind or soul – areas in which women had, in his view, given ample evidence of their abilities. For both men, the progress of the Enlightenment must put an end to the reign of force, and goes hand in hand with the blossoming of egalitarian relationships at all levels of social relations, from the most intimate to the most political.

However, the young *feudiste* is led to seek some anthropological basis for these possibilities. Would the talents that came to develop in a setting free of oppression be the same in men and women? In *Émile*, Rousseau postulates a complementarity of qualities in which men have the theoretical part and women the practical one. Despite the outward appearance of reciprocity ('All the faculties common to both sexes are not equally shared between them, but taken as a whole they are fairly divided'), what instead emerges is a subordination of women's knowledge to the knowledge in the possession of men, of which they only cede part: 'They should learn many things, but only such things as are suitable.'[72]

In essence, women's knowledge is only an application of principles that it is up to men to find, or consists of observations that men will have to generalise. Works of genius are 'beyond a woman's grasp' and the exact sciences require too much 'accuracy' and 'attention' for them. Here, again, it is man's 'strength'[73] and his supposedly greater capacity to act that marks him out for understanding the laws of nature. So, the complementarity that Babeuf sees between men and women is fundamentally different from Rousseau's line of reasoning, even if it may appear similar: 'From one sex to the other the faculties are equal in number, and if taken one by one they do not always correspond as equals, on the whole they are balanced.'[74] At this point, one could conclude that the qualities of men and women are complementary, similar to what Rousseau advocates. But Babeuf specifies: the faculties of men are also found in women, and above all 'they apply to the same objects, but for many of them differently'. Contrary to the citizen of Geneva's reasoning, there is no domain reserved for men such as would

---

72 *E*, p. 327.
73 Ibid., pp. 349–50.
74 *OB*, p. 99.

confine women to what it is 'appropriate for them to know'. The paths of artistic creation, like the discovery of nature's secrets, must be open to women. If in the arts the respective genius of the two sexes remains different, women must not settle for trying to produce 'man's works', as women artists contemporary to Babeuf's text did. Instead, woman must develop the genius of her sex and honour the entire species with a new order of works:

> Woman would not have taken refuge in these sad imitations, if her genius had not been killed: there would then have been a women's literature, a women's poetry, a women's music, painting and sculpture, comparable and equal to the genius of man; the genius of woman would have risen up with its own proper character, and the two sexes would have been able to admire and charm one another.[75]

This text expresses an egalitarianism that does not shy away from differentiating among the faculties of men and women, though they are also *equivalent in value* and ought to produce a mutual attraction between the two sexes. Babeuf's text thus tends to refute Élisabeth Badinter's conclusion that 'the philosophy of gender difference always generates inequality, particularism and even exclusion'.[76] For Babeuf offers an example of a thought that, while conceiving the creativity of the two sexes as different in a number of areas, does not conceive this difference in hierarchical terms, but, in the context of a complementarity enriching for the human race in general. Indeed, contrary to the Rousseauian mechanism, here attraction is based on identical mechanisms on both sides. Each sex is charmed precisely by the fact of finding in the other the same capacities, applied to the same objects, but according to distinct modalities. This does not stop Babeuf from restricting this differentiation to areas that do not rely solely on rational procedures: science, on the other hand, 'cannot have a sex'. Consequently, women, whom Rousseau excluded from knowledge of the laws of nature, rediscover their right to devote themselves to an activity in which, Babeuf bets, they will make as much headway as their male counterparts.

---

75 *OB*, pp. 99–100.
76 Badinter, 'L'éducation des filles selon Rousseau et Condorcet', p. 291.

Condorcet expressed a similar opinion in his *Cinq mémoires sur l'instruction publique*, calling for women to have the same access to education as men. Like Babeuf, he did not believe that the fields of application of human reason would require different access routes simply on account of the gender of the rational being in question:

> Indeed, since all instruction limits itself to exposing truths and expounding the proofs for them we cannot see how the difference between the sexes would require any difference in the choice of these truths, or in the way they are proved.[77]

From this perspective, Condorcet's educational proposals for women represent an extension of Babeuf's analyses from 1786. It can even be said that this author lags behind the young *feudiste* in his stance in favour of gender equality, insofar as, unlike the latter, he questions the creative capacity of the female sex in the field of science and the 'first-order discoveries which demand a long meditation and an extraordinary strength of mind'.[78]

The denunciation of the current female condition thus gives rise to a conception that, unlike in Rousseau, can be extended to the entire species. The latter appears in Babeuf's writings as essentially in-becoming, its array of qualities less visible through empirical observation than through the imagined progress of equalisation and its effects. But experience is not dismissed entirely, and Babeuf repeatedly draws on observable 'examples' of women writers, politicians, or artists to support his demonstration.

But these cases do not form the basis of his argument, which focuses on the mechanisms of despotism exercised against women, interpreted as a veritable 'conspiracy of one half of the human race' against the other, whose very violence gives hope for great changes when it comes to an end. 'Levelling', which was to be so decried by the liberal tradition, is seen as positive in that it actually lies in the end of the domination blamed for compromising human potential.[79] What would they become,

---

77 Jean-Antoine-Nicolas de Caritat Condorcet, *Cinq mémoires sur l'instruction publique*, presented by Charles Coutel and Catherine Kintzler, Paris: GF, 1994, p. 96.

78 Ibid., p. 97.

79 See in particular De Tocqueville, *Democracy in America*, Indianapolis: Liberty Fund, 2012, pp. 8–9, 14: 'As soon as citizens began to own the land in ways other than by

were they free to develop? Babeuf, despite his belief in a continuous progression of individual capacities, admits his ignorance on this score. Insofar as a 'woman's education' was never provided and never thought of, 'it becomes impossible to say with certainty what the destination of woman is, since knowledge of this destination can only result from a knowledge of the natural propensity of each woman's faculties'.[80]

Looking at things from this perspective, the destiny of the human species can be seen, through the example of women, as an open process. Here, again, Babeuf's thinking is similar to that of Condorcet. Women may, indeed, be included in the hopes that the latter expresses regarding the progress of the human mind in general:

> However, is there not a point at which the natural limits of our mind make all progress impossible? No, gentlemen: as enlightenment increases, the methods of instruction are perfected; the human mind seems to grow greater, and its limits recede.[81]

This confidence in the ineluctable progress of human knowledge and capacities clearly prefigures Babeuf's argument – albeit with one qualification. In Babeuf's case, progress, although unfinished, is not presented as *indefinite*: it stops, as we have seen, at the exact point when equality reigns among men: 'True civilisation stops and majestically fixes itself a level; there is marked the end of all misery, of all wailing, of all sobbing, of all gnashing of teeth.'[82] Babeuf thus offered no precise predictions regarding the human race's future. But he did set the criterion which he saw as likely to define, if not the end of history, at least 'the goal of society': namely, the equalisation of conditions. At this stage in the logic of his argument, this equalisation means nothing other than the end of all

---

feudal tenure, and as soon as personal wealth, once known, could in turn create influence and confer power, no discoveries were made in the arts, no further improvements were introduced into commerce and industry, without also creating as many new elements of equality among men. From this moment, all processes that are found, all needs that are born, all desires that demand to be satisfied, are progress toward universal leveling ... The entire book that you are about to read has been written under the impression of a sort of religious terror produced in the soul of the author by the sight of this irresistible revolution.'

80 *OB*, p. 99.
81 Condorcet, 'Discours prononcé dans l'Académie Française', p. 18.
82 *OB*, p. 102.

servitude. Does this limit to *social* progress also set an endpoint for progress in the fields of scientific knowledge and artistic achievement? Babeuf does not provide any more specific answers on this point, but there is nothing in the text which would point against a constant development of the entire species' creative potential.

In Condorcet, and more precisely in the 1793 preamble to the *Tableau historique des progrès de l'esprit humain*, the perfectibility of man in general – and thus also of woman – is clearly said to be indefinite. Here, we can get the measure of the polemical, anti-millenarian charge carried forth by such a line of reasoning. The perfectibility which can be inferred from the *Tableau historique*, starting from the origins of man, is characteristic of humanity as a species; not in that it is the only perfectible species, but in that it possesses this quality in proportions far superior to any other. Hence, the 'more extensive, easier perfectibility, attached to his species, has separated him from the rest of organised beings'.[83] The progress that has been accomplished already makes it only reasonable to extrapolate further progress for the future. This means that no one can set limits to the accumulation of knowledge, and that man 'can become ever more learned, happy and virtuous'.[84] But the anticipation that this author ventures into in the Tenth Epoch of his *Tableau historique*, after having traced the historical stages of the development of the human mind, seems to obey an intuition that is – taken as a whole – rather close to that of the young *feudiste*. Allusive and referring to general tendencies, as Bertrand Binoche writes, Condorcet 'limits himself to painting in very broad strokes what a world of equality and abundance could be'.[85] Yet he also gives no sign of doubts. What is confidently presented by the *Tableau historique*'s author not as a hypothesis, but as a true 'doctrine', makes it possible to trace out future perspectives for the human race which, although not certain, are presented as the most probable ones.[86] As in Babeuf, this is a future due to see the advent of 'de facto equality,

---

83   *THP*, p. 499.
84   Bertrand Binoche, 'L'historicité du Tableau historique', in B. Binoche (ed.), *Nouvelles lectures du Tableau historique de Condorcet*, Québec: Éditions du CIERL/Presses de l'Université Laval, 2010, pp. 11–42, at p. 34.
85   Ibid., p. 37.
86   *THP*, p. 392.

the final goal of the social art'.[87] The specificity of Condorcet's prediction, as compared to Babeuf's, lies essentially in the fact that the former sees equal access to education as the major condition for the equalisation of men's material conditions: 'If education is more equal, there is greater equality in industry, and hence in wealth, and equality of wealth necessarily contributes to equality of education.'[88] In 1786, Babeuf did not explicitly establish this link; rather, he separated his proposals for social reform from his hopes for the progress of egalitarian education for the two sexes. However, this idea would not long remain alien to his thinking: a few years later, in 1789, he in turn insisted on the role of education in the fight against social inequalities. As with Condorcet, it was the Revolution, with the prospects it opened up for the institution of a real public education provided by the state, that triggered a more programmatic thinking on the establishment of a school for all. Yet, as we shall see, Babeuf's confidence in the progress of the human race thanks to an egalitarian education was a long-standing concern, which had a certain influence right from his earliest writings.

As an emblem of man's oppression by man, the figure of the woman thus also symbolises the species' capacity for perfection through the progress of equality. And what is true of the education of women also applies in the case of the education of the poor. Babeuf thus asserts both immutable characteristics of human nature – since there are indeed 'natural dispositions to each sex'[89] and equality itself, like fraternity, is presented as a fact of nature – and potentialities whose development is impossible to predict with certainty, both because of theoretical ignorance as to 'the natural propensity of each [of] the faculties'[90] and the practical impossibility of observing their stages of development under a situation of domination. Human nature is thus defined in temporal terms, since it unfolds along the course of the progress of equality, while, in other respects, it remains immutable, since equality and fraternity themselves constitute the substratum on which Babeuf relies to critique all oppression. The notion of a deep human nature, covered up by the

---

87 Ibid., p. 430.
88 Ibid., p. 441.
89 *OB*, p. 98.
90 Ibid.

effects of centuries of domination, thus coexists with that of a gradual conquest of new characteristics for the species, which will, however, have unprecedented effects on human societies:

> What would be the consequences of this emancipation; what new laws would become indispensable, so that it should have only salutary effects? These are questions that I am not in a position to answer; but one day we will have to think about them.[91]

Strikingly, this splitting of human nature into an unchanging nature and a historical one is found in 1793 in the *Tableau historique*, which postulates the human race's (including women's) sentient, moral, and reasoning nature as the foundation of its perfectible historical nature.[92] As Binoche writes:

> This overlapped combination of two natures ... undoubtedly refers epistemologically to a cumulative conception of progress which presupposes the conservation of what is to be perfected: man can only be perfected if he remains sentient, reasonable and moral.[93]

But it should be noted that, in Condorcet, this theoretical move does not give rise to any kind of harking back to the primitive state of man. For the natural characteristics of man make him a 'waiting table' susceptible to receive the imprint of increasingly perfected theoretical and moral knowledge. Human nature is to be understood essentially as a set of aptitudes, potentialities, which need the time of history to be actualised. This is why the *Tableau historique* shows no nostalgia for the earliest societies, until then considered closer to an origin which Condorcet now denied any privileged link to man's essence. Thus, in the conclusion of 'Première époque' we find him offering this telling assessment:

91　Ibid., p. 102.
92　The demand for equal rights for all, men and women alike, is rooted precisely in this unchanging human nature. See the 'Fragment sur l'Atlantide': 'I have established elsewhere that a complete equality of rights between individuals of both sexes is a necessary consequence of their nature, that these rights are the same for all sentient beings, endowed with the faculty of reasoning and of having moral ideas' (*THP*, p. 897).
93　Binoche, *Les trois sources des philosophies de l'histoire*, pp. 74–5.

Revenge and cruelty towards enemies as virtues, the opinion that women are in a kind of slavery, the right to command a war considered as a family prerogative, finally the first ideas of the various kinds of superstitions – such are the errors which distinguish this time; and whose origin and motives must be sought and elaborated upon.[94]

From the perspective of a continuous process of progression, the first ages necessarily appear as less advanced along the path of perfectibility than the periods that follow. Hence, they are necessarily barbaric ages, which man has happily left behind. For Babeuf, however, the social relations of the species' origins have an essential morally positive aspect, and progress consists partly in reviving these relations. Thus, in the same progressive movement, two distinct regimes of temporality are blended together: on the one hand, the return, to a certain extent, to the original equality and friendship, visible in the first movements of the children of either sex; on the other, the onset, through this return itself, of an unprecedented situation which Babeuf foresees will give rise to new laws, a new order of things. The utopian sets out no plan for this new order; he contents himself with setting a first milestone, rather than an ideal of egalitarian legislation. From this point of view, the draft letter of 1786 is consistent with what Binoche calls the 'utopian' tone of Condorcet's *Tableau historique*: anticipation implies an irreducible prophetic dimension, since it is indeed a question of predicting the future. In this sense, Babeuf's prudence and his obvious reluctance to specify the exact nature of the progress that could be made is, no doubt, part of a desire not to succumb to the siren songs of the 'philosophical dream', in which the thinker gives free rein to his most optimistic fantasies.[95]

But the opening to the future is not one-sidedly the site of a radical novelty. It is also a resurgence of the original human condition. The primitive equality and fraternity are to be rediscovered on a higher plane than that of the species' past history, and this will also produce unprecedented effects on the level of individual and collective achievements. The dominant concern for the equalisation of conditions explains why, unlike Condorcet, Babeuf sets an at least major, if not

---

94   *THP*, p. 248.
95   Ibid., p. 874.

exclusive, goal for the progress of the human race, as embodied by the 'levelling' able to equalise the condition of all humans. This distinguishes him from the author of the *Tableau historique*, who instead insists on the idea of an evolution that remains forever open. In so doing, Babeuf postulates the idea of a 'goal for society' – inscribed within the very nature of man, in the generic sense of this term – whose premises are visible in childhood, but whose realisation lies in the future and which presents still unknown aspects. The future of humanity is thus both anticipated and left open, determined in its ultimate purpose and indeterminate with regard to the consequences of that achievement.

The 'Right to Life'

However, Babeuf was not finished with his considerations on the nature of man: after the model of an imaginary society, after the denunciation of all forms of oppression in the name of equality and man's capacity for self-improvement, the analysis somehow systematises the conclusions his argument has arrived at by giving a positive content to the idea of human equality. This means determining what prerogatives derive from the status of human beings themselves and what society's corresponding duties towards individuals are. From a logical point of view, this statement of principles ought to have preceded the two lines of elaboration which we have just analysed, because in fact these principles derive from them. The model of collective farms represents the application of the precepts that Babeuf develops in this passage, in the sense that it proposes a social organisation that fulfils the conditions induced by what he considers to be man's natural right. Similarly, Babeuf's elaborations relating to the status of women are fully based on what he considers to be the inalienable right of every human being. It is obvious that – in what is, we should remember, a draft – the author's thinking becomes clearer as he moves forward, the principles arriving after the fact to provide theoretical support for types of discourse that can be seen as their own implementation: a model of social organisation, or a case study of one form of oppression that exposes all the others. Practice (though it is still imaginary at this stage) gives rise to theory, rather than the other way round.

Babeuf thus took up the question of the 'principles of natural and political law' after reading the speech given by a member of the Académie d'Arras, a copy of which had been sent to him. Babeuf was not persuaded by this speech and criticised its approach: he saw it as getting lost in conjectures about the origins of the species, in order to then determine the rights that correspond to man's nature. His critique was both methodological and axiological. Firstly, from a methodological point of view, Babeuf questioned the very possibility of reconstructing humanity's distant past: 'What do we know of the first family? What do we know of the first people and their dispersion?'[96] At this point, we may well think that this was a simple empiricist objection: the absence of concrete data forbids us from piecing together the species' distant past. But more profoundly, the criticism is targeted at the value for contemporary humanity that any account of its origins can have. Given what is actually known about the past, the early ages are not, as such, a model for the human race, and present customs should not be measured by the yardstick of past ones:

> If you go up the scale of the ages of mankind, at each rung there is some more error; if you go down the scale, at each rung there is some less error ... Looking back on our era, you see only alternatives of barbarism and civilisation mixed with barbarism.[97]

Babeuf thus warns his reader against nostalgia for a bygone golden age. The starting point of an enquiry into the natural rights of man cannot be carelessly confused with an enquiry into his origins, which would inherently reveal many 'barbarian' features. Rather, it is necessary to have some criterion that offers a frame for analysing these early ages and make it possible thus to produce a narrative useful to men the better to judge their own present. It would only be possible to derive some useful understanding of man's origins by breaking them out of the covering of brutality that necessarily surrounds them. Babeuf thus seems to indicate the need for a selection of past events, which alone would make it possible to derive some useful principle for the present time. But what yardstick is there for such a selection? For Babeuf,

---

96 *OB*, p. 104.
97 Ibid., p. 105.

nothing could be simpler. Rejecting all reasoning, all genealogies, he appeals to the self-evident:

> The natural right of man! But it is a thousand and one times too clear; it is the most striking of all self-evident facts ... The self-evident cannot be proven or disputed: it is felt, heard, touched. It is a ready-made and permanent experience.[98]

What is striking, here, is how long Babeuf puts off this moment of stating such a right. He is obviously seeking to make the reader feel spontaneously the nature of this right which will serve as the pivot of the whole of the reasoning that follows. The right to life – since this is what we are talking about – would henceforth constitute the principle that will make it possible to reconstruct an image of the origins of the species, knowledge of which could be useful to contemporary humanity. This right, which has long been present in the jusnaturalist tradition, here has the status of a true political *cogito*: it emanates from an intimate, intangible certainty that founds and justifies the actions of the individual and regulates his relationship to society as a whole. It is inherent in the self-consciousness of the being who is both sentient and thinking, and it is within his immediate reach. It needs no justification; rather, it constitutes the principle that justifies all other rights. Formulated as such, it is close to its expression in *Émile*:

> The first law of nature is the care of self-preservation ... Everyone must live. This argument, to which everyone gives more or less force, in proportion to his greater or lesser humanity, seems to me to have no reply for the person who makes it, in relation to himself.[99]

As Bachofen observes, each human being's right to appropriate the means necessary for his subsistence is also, in Rousseau, natural right 'taken in its only absolutely indisputable sense'.[100] In spite of all the limits that can be seen in this author, in terms of the relevance of the reference to nature in thinking about the human condition; in spite of the

---

98   Ibid.
99   *E*, p. 467.
100   Bachofen, *La condition de la liberté*, p. 112.

historical and contingent character of most of the inclinations of civil man – this right alone marks the persistence of the primitive demands of authentic nature – that is, those of physical sensitivity. It plays the role of a prior condition for all subsequent claims. It may justify even extreme expedients to ensure its satisfaction: 'Everything is permitted by [nature] to anyone who has no other possible means of living.'[101] Babeuf takes up the same idea, giving it an even more central place, an even more decisive importance: despite all the progress to which civilisation is called, bringing with it new aspirations for the human race (think, for example, of the creativity which women are called upon to have in future times), this is based on the intangible foundation of primary needs to be met. These take precedence over the respect of all other forms of rights: 'The right to live implies, in an absolute way, fighting all that in one way or another harms or opposes the exercise of this right; in that case, attacking is only self-defence.'[102]

In both Rousseau and Babeuf, the simple fact of being human thus leads to a right to everything that satisfies basic needs. In Babeuf, this right has a counterpart: 'the law or obligation of labour'.[103] Work is thus presented as the only legitimate way of exercising natural right. In Rousseau, conversely, labour only comes into play at the stage of appropriation of land. It is even inseparable from it. In the *Second Discourse*, the savage owns nothing, and does not work either. He sleeps at the foot of a tree or in a natural shelter which he abandons in the morning; he feeds on whatever he finds, and keeps nothing as his own:

> His moderate wants are so easily supplied with what he everywhere finds ready to his hand, and he stands at such a distance from the degree of knowledge requisite to covet more, that he can neither have foresight nor curiosity.[104]

Living from day to day, deprived of the capacity for reasoning and technological elaboration, the savage does not have the necessary means to pursue a labour process, which requires the investment of specific efforts

---

101   *E*, p. 467.
102   *OB*, p. 107.
103   Ibid., p. 106.
104   Rousseau, *The Social Contract*, p. 97.

towards some objective whose satisfaction is deferred. It would take all subsequent evolution – and, in particular, the progress of socialisation, with the development of human faculties inherent to it – for man to conceive the idea of producing with his hands objects that belong to him. The formation of families leads to the introduction of a 'kind of property' – that of the huts, the first lasting product of human labour, in which the first, the strongest, and the most skilful housed their wives and children. Moreover, both labour and the appropriation of its fruits are individual processes from start to finish. Rousseau specifies that at this first stage of development, with each man applying himself to 'such works only as a single person could finish', men remain in a relationship that he calls 'independent intercourse'.[105] It is only after the appearance of metallurgy and agriculture that men become interdependent, indeed to the species' great misfortune. At this point, it is possible for a man to own not only the fruits of his labour, but also the asset that produces them, namely the land. Labour is then designated – with a mild reworking of Locke's famous theory – as the foundation of a future of complete individual appropriation: 'It is impossible to conceive how property can flow from any other source but work; for what can a man add but his labor to things which he has not made, in order to acquire a property in them?'[106] Thus, in the process Rousseau describes, individual property and labour are linked. This is not the case in Babeuf. Revisiting the first ages of humanity, no longer by looking for what would supposedly constitute men's natural rights, but rather by starting from the prior affirmation of the right to live, he envisages the ways in which this right might have been exercised in times when needs were necessarily limited and when 'there was still no exaggerated or depraved egoism'.[107] He discerns three parameters – ones we surely also find in identical form in Rousseau – that render possible the universal satisfaction of the right to live: in addition to the limited extent of individual needs, the small number of individuals on Earth and the fertility of nature place its exercise within reach of all. But Babeuf draws different consequences from the Genevan, and indeed Locke, who had already before him linked the

---

105   Ibid., p. 120.
106   Ibid., p. 121. Indeed, it should be noted this, at this stage of Rousseau's analysis, property is still only 'nascent': it is not yet a fully enshrined right, which it will only become with civil status.
107   *OB*, p. 106.

Babeuf's 1786 Draft Letter: Utopia in the Villages

questions of labour and appropriation. The young *feudiste* formulates the hypothesis of a state where the products of labour are amicably distributed among the members of the nascent humanity.

In contrast to Morelly, Babeuf defends the idea that every normally constituted man 'has been endowed in general by nature with more strength than he needs to sustain himself'.[108] The 'social instinct' placed in man's heart by nature commands him to offer to society the surplus which his efforts have produced, such that it may meet the needs of those who – like children, the sick, and the elderly – cannot provide for their own subsistence. Obviously, the model on which this conception of the social bond is based is the family: nature itself is a 'mother' who orders men to consider each other as 'brothers'.

Babeuf thus supports the idea that the species displays a spontaneous altruism in the state of nature. The social instinct, which corresponds to the friendship and pity seen already among children, is part of man, just like the experience each person has of his right to live. If men are driven to help one another, it is not because each individual needs the others to survive, as in the *Code de la Nature*, but simply because the working capacities of the majority of them allow it, and their natural benevolence towards their fellow men commands it. The social instinct seems to be unevenly developed among men. However, he who fails to fulfil the obligations which it imposes – either by withholding for himself the surplus which ought to accrue for society, or else by taking without working and without necessity from the surplus resources produced by the work of others – is thereby deprived of his right to live. For Babeuf, such an offence is the only one which, in a 'sovereignly equitable, sovereignly fraternal society', should be punishable by death by 'abandonment'.[109]

To give up the right of one's fellow man to live is to give up one's own right. This shows how much the right to life is essentially conceived in connection to a counterpart due to the social whole; to Babeuf's mind, at least, this right only applies insofar as it is linked to the negation of egoism and the obligation to help one's fellow human beings. Taken in its fullest sense, the right to live is less an individual right than a right of humanity as a whole. It takes effect only as a right of all.

---

108 Ibid., p. 107.
109 Ibid.

It implies the need not only to not take more than one requires – as in Rousseau – but also to consider, in production, the needs of one's fellow human beings. As Guy-Robert Ikni writes in an article on Babeuf's relationship to natural right: 'The acquisition of freedom by natural law can only take place within the limits of the common needs of all men; this reciprocity is the basis of the universality of natural right'.[110] In his conception of natural law, Babeuf thus emphasises its universal and reciprocal character. This gives it a different tone from that of Rousseau's texts, but also from that of his jusnaturalist predecessors, such as Hobbes or Locke, who cast it as a strictly individual right. This is the basis on which Babeuf returns to the question of property, on which he had already said a few words at the beginning of his letter, postulating a natural right for men to 'enjoy in equal portions the great and common inheritance of the earth'. In this first characterisation, he put forward the idea of an equal right to the enjoyment of the Earth's products, thereby essentially setting a limit to what some could appropriate at the expense of others' needs. But Babeuf had not clearly and positively defined the limits of legitimate appropriation. Indeed, does the much-vaunted right to live imply that mankind must radically renounce all forms of ownership of the land and only take its fruits, or is there some form of appropriation which is indeed compatible with this right? The question is to be posed with regard to not only Babeuf, but also the ambiguities of Rousseau's theory. After all, how can Rousseau proclaim the right of each person 'to all that he needs',[111] praise the fence puller at the beginning of Book II of the *Second Discourse*, and at the same time assert that labour provides the basis for a legitimate appropriation of the land itself? On this crucial point, Babeuf's and Rousseau's responses converge, although there are distinct reasons to lead each of them to their respective conclusions. Both agree that there is some right of ownership: for Rousseau, it is a product 'of convention and institution';[112] for Babeuf, it is legitimacy that comes with some conditions.[113]

---

110   Guy-Robert Ikni, 'Autour des luttes agraires picardes: Babeuf et les droits de l'homme', in *Grandes figures de la Révolution française en Picardie, Blérancourt, Aisne, 17 et 18 June 1989*, Tergnier: Imprimerie Dupuis, 1990, pp. 59–71, at p. 61.
111   Rousseau, *The Social Contract*, p. 167.
112   Ibid., p. 130.
113   *OB*, p. 107.

One first characteristic shared by both lines of reasoning is the distinction made – in the words of the title of Rousseau's *Discourse* – between the origin and the basis of property. Blaise Bachofen has illustrated that such a distinction makes it possible to explain the apparent contradiction between the fence puller's rejection of property, and its justification by labour. Labour provides property with, if not a foundation in nature, then at least an objective basis: it can potentially grant it legitimacy and some measure of its dimensions, even if it does not provide a 'natural' right. But the real origin of land ownership is out of step, or even in contradiction, with that which could and should have constituted its foundation. It is presented as opaque and a usurpation, either because it has been acquired by dishonest means or because it has been erected at the expense of the needs of others and without authorisation from 'the human race'. For Rousseau, for property to be fully legitimate, it should be based on two foundations: it should be rooted in the labour of the owner, as we have already said, and fulfil a real need on his part, but it should also be the subject of an agreement between men, which would ensure that the property of some does not encroach on the needs of others. *The Social Contract* formalises this:

> first, the land must not yet be inhabited by any one;
> secondly, a man must occupy only the area required for his subsistence;
> thirdly, he must take possession of it, not by ceremonial statements, but by labor and cultivation, the only mark of ownership which, in the absence of legal title, ought to be respected by others.[114]

Need, on the one hand, and labour, on the other, both sanctioned by convention, constitute the legitimate bounds of individual property. Property, as really established among men, is indeed a usurpation which the fence puller had every legitimate reason to rebel against; but it is possible to envisage a basis for it which no one could contest.

It is notable that, in his draft letter, Babeuf makes this same distinction between the origin and basis of property rights. Unlike Rousseau, his account of origins takes on a much more concrete and historical

---

114   Rousseau, *The Social Contract*, p. 168.

aspect, since, as he points out: 'In my capacity as a commissioner-*feudiste*, I could not be unaware of how most of the great properties were formed and came into the hands of those who possess them.'[115]

Babeuf then offers a rapid overview of the 'enormous iniquities' and 'ferocious spoliations' that governed the establishment of large landed estates. But, as in Rousseau, this is not the main purpose of his argument: 'Let us look for a less odious origin for property', he quickly adds. The analysis then turns to the legitimate basis for the right of ownership. Babeuf speaks of the rigorous climatic conditions under which man, forced to think about stocking up on food for himself and his livestock, decides to settle on land that he cultivates. This creates a legitimate property, 'the daughter of foresight and work'. As in Rousseau, but also as in Locke, the right of the first occupant finds its full confirmation in those efforts which – undertaken within a group constituted by the different generations of the same family – constitute the basis of a hereditary right. In this passage, Babeuf seems to reduce to the family unit the demands of material solidarity that he had earlier extended to the whole of humankind. The right to live is indeed a collective right, but in this first period the collective is reduced to its most immediate form. So, here he proposes a more individualistic version of the right to live, of which small property represents a 'simple translation', limited as it is to the necessities of subsistence. These criteria make it possible to distinguish a 'modest property', which is legitimate, in terms of natural right, from 'ambitious property', which extends far beyond what is necessary, is the product of excessive desire, and, as for Rousseau, is eminently condemnable. That is, it is condemned not so much as property per se, but rather because, within the framework of limited natural resources, it deprives others of the enjoyment of their right to live.

We would more properly distinguish two moments in Babeuf's reconstruction of the history of humankind. The first moment lasted 'as long as the soil was free and at the disposal of the first occupant'.[116] In this moment, men would opt – as per their preference – for a sedentary and proprietary life, for a nomadic life of hunting and fishing, or else for the life of a tradesman. In this natural state, the right to live was fulfilled in different ways and did not necessarily find concrete expression in

---

115 *OB*, p. 108.
116 Ibid., p. 111.

property ownership. This was a time of fair exchange without the need for any public power to regulate it. A 'tacit contract' bound together men whose mutual needs regulated economic relations. According to Rousseau, this stage, in gradually tightening the ties of dependency among men, marked the beginning of the cycle of inequalities:

> From the moment one man began to stand in need of another's assistance; from the moment it appeared an advantage for one man to possess enough provisions for two, equality vanished; property was introduced; labor became necessary; and boundless forests became smiling fields, which had to be watered with human sweat, and in which slavery and misery were soon seen to sprout out and grow with the harvests.[117]

In Rousseau's analysis, interdependency is the primary cause of the growth of inequalities. Indeed, for him, autarkic independence is the primary norm. Natural inequality, which makes one person more skilful than another, faster at producing, or hungrier in his needs, is of no consequence so long as each person endeavours to provide himself with the necessities of life. But, as soon as men enter into a process of exchange, through the course of commercial relations the most skilful accumulate wealth at the expense of the rest: this is what the citizen of Geneva calls the inequality 'arising from men's combining',[118] governing the appearance of a wealthier class within the state of nature itself. Babeuf can draw on no such conceptual arsenal. He settles for observing the accumulation of wealth in the hands of a minority with the appearance of money, which soon allows 'the traffic in landed property'.[119] Here, again, we can only be struck by how close Babeuf's arguments are to those of Chapter 5 of *The Second Treatise on Civil Government*.[120] However, the author of the draft letter attributes this harmful change to the rise of 'passions', of an unlimited desire to possess which drives the

---

117 Rousseau, *The Social Contract*, p. 120.
118 Ibid., p. 122.
119 *OB*, p. 112.
120 'This partage of things in an inequality of private possessions, men have made practicable out of the bounds of society, and without compact, only by putting a value on gold and silver, and tacitly agreeing in the use of money' (from section 50 of Chapter 5).

richest to pursue a boundless monopolisation of material goods. Then begins the second moment in human history: the moment of the spoliation of large-scale property, which monopolises most of the cultivable land and encroaches upon the right to live of the many.

This stage brings the reconfiguration of the relationship between the right to live and the right to property. Whereas, in the first stage of history, the right to live could legitimately be sanctioned by a necessarily limited right to property, and only entail duties for the individual in the family sphere, everything changes with the reign of 'ambitious property'. In a context where land resources are limited, men – be they owners or non-owners – must now all become 'associates', in the interests of the survival of each individual. This is the perspective of the collective farm project. It comes to express the subordination of the right to property to the right to live, which implies that large landlords make the essential concession to humanity of allowing their farmers to take from the land they allocate to them 'all that is necessary for human organisation constantly to have what it requires'.[121] The process of human history thus reflects a moral extension of the duties of the individual, linked to his right to live. If, in a first moment, this natural right only entailed duties towards one's immediate surroundings, henceforth it implies being part of a wider organisation of production. According to Babeuf's conceptions, the circle of men's dependence on one another is bound to gradually widen, without this necessarily leading to increasing inequality, as in Rousseau. On the contrary, he foresaw that this could lead towards an ever more generalised cooperation. As we can see, Babeuf's anthropology remains closely linked to his utopian hopes and his belief in the possible progress of the human race.

Moreover, Babeuf does not imagine the possibility of human labour becoming more productive. Yet, if 'one day the population were to be so formidably increased that those who could still have some superfluous things ... would no longer have even their full right to live', the difficulty would have to be solved by increased cooperation.[122] The association of collective farms would then have to be succeeded by a society of the human race as such. This society, 'the only true one', could then envisage distributing the world's population over the entire surface of the globe, as far as this is possible, and with a view to extending the areas used for

---

121 *OB*, p. 111.
122 Ibid., p. 116.

cultivation. Clearly, here again, the right to live takes precedence over all other considerations of property, be they individual or national. In this final hypothesis, Babeuf asserts the right to life of all the world's inhabitants, as a fraternal and united whole. Natural right would then reach its maximum extension. Striking, in the whole development of Babeuf's argument, is that he is concerned not only with the anthropological foundations of natural rights – that is, its very possibility – but also with the concrete conditions of its exercise. Remarkable, from this perspective, is the absence at this stage of any properly political reflection. Babeuf still conceives of social relations only as direct relations between the members of the species, without going via the mediation of a public institution that produces legal rules.

Difficulties

In the draft letter of 1786, natural rights thus prove, albeit retrospectively, to be the ultimate justification for the utopian construction of collective farms, and even serve as the basis for the hypothesis – in the form of a quick sketch – of the idea of a society of the human race. From Babeuf's perspective, its foundational status comes from its obvious and immediate character, linked, in his first characterisation of it, to man's primary needs:

> [The natural right of man] is written in our own organisation at all times: from the moment we were called to life we have felt it; it has been revealed to us by all the needs of this organisation which must be fully satisfied in order that it may reach the fullness of its development and preserve itself to the end free from suffering through the deprivation of what is indispensable to it.[123]

By such statements, Babeuf clearly seems to see the right to live also as a right to the satisfaction of physiological needs, such that the 'organisation' of the body will develop in conformity with its nature. In this way, he is clearly trying to give natural law an unquestionable objective foundation. However, a little further on, he adds:

---

123   Ibid., p. 105.

> The right to live is the right par excellence ... To live is to proceed freely through the cycle of life, giving to all the periods of which it is composed what is appropriate to our both physical and moral organisation.[124]

Here Babeuf significantly alters the implications of the right to live by giving it not only a physical, but also a moral content. Though he does not seem to realise it, this extension of the right to live makes it problematic: it implies determining moral needs supposed to be as natural to man as his physical needs. But what could they be – and what would justify calling them natural? The answer comes a few pages later: the 'native idea' by which the human brain feels all that is due to it, goes as follows: 'Freedom to think, freedom of will, freedom to express one's thought, freedom of action.'[125] Freedom is presented as the right to live from the viewpoint of the 'brain' and considered a need analogous to that of the 'stomach'. Up to this point, natural rights as defined by Babeuf seem quite close to what Rousseau describes at the beginning of *The Social Contract* as the law that derives from man's nature, and which consists both of the duty of self-preservation, and the requirement to be 'one's own master'. But Babeuf does not stop there. He postulates a third fundamental need, entailing a third right, that of the heart: 'Speak, the brain tells him, love and feel freely, your inclinations do not deceive you, all men are brothers, all men are equals.'[126] This brings a radically new element to thinking on natural rights: a right to universal brotherhood, a right to mutual affection considered as an essential human need. The difficulty with this right, however, lies in its indeterminacy. It does not appear to have made itself heard in the early history of mankind, when the circle of relationships seems to have been narrowly constructed around the family. Should family affection be considered the first manifestation of a right that expands as the mutual dependence of men develops? If so, should we contemplate an extension of natural rights through society? Babeuf says nothing on these questions.

Indeed, we can detect an ambiguity in Babeuf's thinking in this period, between what is properly man's nature and what comes from the

---

124 Ibid., p. 106.
125 Ibid., p. 113.
126 Ibid.

relationships generated by social life. Babeuf does not conceive of a social contract, except when he vaguely refers to a 'tacit contract', concerning the exchanges among men during the early days of the species. Reading him, we get the impression of a gradual transition from a family-centred sociability to a broader one. No mention is made of the establishment of public authorities. These omissions relieve him of having to detail the transformations that men owe to the establishment of a civil status. However, in the text, we also find the following remark: 'It goes without saying that it is up to society to measure the right to live and to decree its equitable standard, either according to the totality of general resources, or according to the nature of local resources.'[127] What does the term 'society' mean, here? Does it refer to all people, to their representatives – and who might they be? Above all, what is to be said of the supposed 'naturalness' of a right which society is responsible for measuring and ultimately establishing? This text does not allow us to answer these questions. There is thus a notable hesitation between defining fundamental human rights as either natural or social in character. This is a sign of the unresolved problems in the Babouvist thought of this period, which would resurface with the continuation of attempts at theoretical elaboration of these philosophical and political problems.

The Hope of Progress and the Reform Programme in the 1786 Draft

Through the case of the 'natural history of women', in the 1786 text human time is generally envisaged as continuing along a line of progress that manifests itself through the successive disappearance of all kinds of inequalities. The text thus asserts not only a vision of history as progressive, but also a gradualism in progress. In Babeuf's words, inequalities disappear one by one, with the overcoming of each of them hailed as a partial, but certain improvement of the collective lot. Thus, Babeuf tellingly endorses *mésalliances* – marriages between two youngsters belonging to different social orders: 'From all these so-called *mésalliances*, society can only gain in equality, in good harmony.'[128] In other words, it

---

127 Ibid., p. 110.
128 Ibid., p. 93.

seems that the author's strategy in this period was to promote, as far as possible, any progress – however small, however purely individual – in favour of equality. This, as a means of achieving a happiness which still lies far from the reach of the human race. However, as has already been pointed out, progress in the status of women, while desirable, remained relatively indeterminate. How could women's rights be advanced in concrete terms? What steps could be taken in this direction? Babeuf's text does not allow us to answer these questions with any certainty, even if equal rights in marriage and the reform of female education are mentioned as eminently positive measures. The same cannot be said of the question of improving the material lot of the inhabitants of the countryside, an issue for which Babeuf had a real battle plan. It is interesting to return to this point in order to clarify how the text articulates the relationship between the past, the present, and the future.

The present state of the countryside obliges Babeuf to return to the origins of land ownership in general, in order to account for the present. The past, on this question, is then the subject of two successive descriptions, one in the mode of concrete historical reconstitution, the other in the mode of jusnaturalist genesis, the two being separated by this remarkable formula: 'But let us look for a less odious origin for property.'[129] The first is a narrative – one which Babeuf allows himself 'in his capacity as a *feudiste*-commissioner' – of the 'enormous iniquities' and 'ferocious spoliations' held to be solely responsible for the creation of the large feudal estates which still existed at the time of his description:

> This is the law made with a sword and a torch to peasants, men of toil who, in order to save their lives, handed their own persons – which they no longer knew what to do with – up to these spoliators, along with the soil they had cleared.[130]

Feudal ferocity is thus the primary cause of the 'deplorable social state', which has continued relatively unchanged up to the present day.[131] It explains the bleak picture in the contemporary countryside, and it

---

129 Ibid., p. 108.
130 Ibid.
131 Ibid., p. 87.

mortgages the future, if nothing is done to put an end to these abuses. Through such a description, we see both what linked Babeuf to the *Encyclopédiste* current and what distinguished him from it. While he agrees in seeing this as a dark and barbaric period, he describes it less as a phase of eclipse of reason[132] than as the site of violence directed against the poor masses of the countryside, which the present century must now remedy.

This indignant account is coupled with the aforementioned reconstruction of the legitimate origins of property as a 'mere translation of the right to live'. Clearly, Babeuf's aim is to contrast the factual history of usurpation that leads up to the present with the earlier account of a more legitimate genesis of property – thus bringing out still more forcefully the scandal of the spoliation that followed. Thus, this genesis does not enter into competition with real history, but precedes it as a reminder of the rights that were subsequently lost. The counter-position of legitimate genesis and illegitimate history, of right and fact, is expressed in terms of the genesis falling into history as a result of events that Babeuf briefly tries to reconstruct. These have as their central cause the greed of a few wrongdoers, which leads them to overstep the bounds of legitimate property to appropriate land far beyond what is necessary, to the point of causing a shortage to the detriment of everyone else.

However, Babeuf does not conclude that it is necessary to recover this limited right to property. Instead of this claim, he proposes a succession of steps that should make effective the respect of the right on which it is based, namely the right to live, which appears to be more fundamental, and ultimately more legitimate. Indeed, Babeuf explicitly rejects the idea of a new division of land, deeming this an 'absurd operation' which 'could only be carried out in blood following a dreadful upheaval'. This, moreover, would be incapable of ensuring subsistence for everyone because

> it would require the union of forces and wills to fertilise [the soil], and to crumble it into equal parcels among all individuals is to reduce to

---

132   See for example Jean Le Rond D'Alembert, *Essai sur les éléments de philosophie*, Paris: Fayard, 1986, p. 13: 'Looking at the picture [of past centuries] that we have just presented, it seems that reason has rested for more than a thousand years of barbarism, only to manifest its awakening and action by repeated and powerful efforts.'

nothing the greater sum of resources which it would give to combined labour.[133]

The agrarian project was thus rejected for two main reasons: the first of these, the desire to avoid bloodshed and general upheaval, confirms that Babeuf, at this time, stood far from the radical solutions he would adopt during the Revolution. The second is focused on the effects of 'combined labour' – that is, the presumed technical superiority of the production-community, which is better able to feed the whole rural population. It is striking that, unlike Mably or even Morelly, Babeuf does not situate the model of mutual aid in labour in humanity's past, but rather in a desired future. From this point of view, he is not talking about reviving a community of production lost in the mists of time, but of innovating by imagining social relationships that had never before been experienced.

In what framework could such a community of labour be achieved? We have said already that Babeuf's preference at this time was for his project of 'collective farms', in which several associated families would become the tenants of an area of land allocated by a big landowner so as to provide for the material well-being of all. But it is interesting to note how Babeuf foresaw this project coming to fruition.

A first step would be to divide the farms into plots each large enough to support a family's subsistence. This first step would involve big landowners ceasing to entrust their land to large-scale farmers who then reduce their own farm labourers to destitution. According to Babeuf, this change could come about through the big landowners being aware of their own interests:

> The rich, if they managed to understand their own interest better, would certainly endeavour to alleviate a state of affairs which causes the poor to reflect too much on the injustice of their lot; they would be keen to guard against the future demand for redress.[134]

These statements are rather ambiguous. Did they amount to a veiled threat, and were they directed towards the addressee of the letter, who, it should be remembered, was a descendant of a great noble family from

---

133   *OB*, p. 114.
134   Ibid., p. 87.

Artois? Did Babeuf hope to bring the discussion to the Académie d'Arras, of which Dubois de Fosseux was the secretary, in order to accelerate awareness; or did he now imagine that such an awareness would come naturally to the great landowners in the near future? As we shall see, only by taking the text as a whole is it possible to rule on this question.

But the transition from the division of farms to the establishment of collective farms is hardly a self-evident process. Why should the fact of allocating sufficient plots of land to small farmers spontaneously lead to the idea of combining these plots in order to work them on a common basis? Here, again, Babeuf is relatively evasive:

> I make no presumption to believe that the system of collective farms will soon be adopted; it is too far remote from accepted practice, and there is too much opportunity to convince oneself that a habit is little short of an incurable disease. However, any idea that is intrinsically good ... eventually comes under serious consideration, and there comes a time when the demonstration of its goodness becomes so self-evident that the only resistance comes from the false-minded or those overly imbued with preconceived notions.[135]

This is a remarkable passage. How are we to interpret the advent of this 'moment' upon which the rational power of the right idea will convert all minds? Should we trust in the power of truth and justice alone, or should we rely on the advice that the fear of revolts will eventually counsel to the rich and propertied? Babeuf is not clear on this point. Rather, the passage related above points to the notion of a peaceful progress of the most reasonable idea among men. This idea can be found in the enthusiasm which seizes Babeuf, when he reads a speech given by a new member of the Académie d'Arras, to thank him for his admission to its ranks. Babeuf saw the academies as 'hotbeds of enlightenment' through which the whole nation became enlightened, with the light gradually reaching the most deprived strata of society. He states:

> Around every academy, the thickest shadows will give way to clarity, and ... they will eventually disappear entirely. Then the whole world

---

135   Ibid., p. 89.

will be illuminated. This is a revolution that must be foreseen and that will infallibly arouse the wrath of the ancient initiates of science who are irritated at no longer being alone.[136]

Again, in this short passage, an ambiguity emerges: when Babeuf points towards the peaceful spread of enlightenment by way of the academies, he asserts his confidence in a change (the next 'revolution') that will bring understanding within reach not only of the already enlightened, but of all. Knowledge is thus already considered, like material wealth, a prerogative monopolised by some and which must be disseminated among those who remain deprived of it. The point, then, is not only to persuade the propertied, in whom the power of decision rests in the last instance, to accept the reasonable option of dividing up the farms. For it is also necessary to spread, among the uneducated, an awareness of the iniquity of the present state of affairs and the illegitimate origin of large property, much to the displeasure of the current bearers of enlightenment. Ultimately, underneath Babeuf's ambiguous formulations, we can see the idea emerging that the disinherited will be able to access a full knowledge of their rights and of the causes of the present state of affairs, and that this will lead to a compromise that is more forced than agreed upon, and to a more equitable distribution of resources, which the propertied would surely not alone have committed themselves to. Once again, in the text, we see the threat that inequity poses to social peace: 'Property will understand how dangerous it would be for it not to take measures such that its existence can no longer be considered an enormity, incompatible with the natural rights of all.'[137]

Throughout the text, we can sense the hope in this 'moment' – which, as we have said, has a distinctly eschatological ring to it – when justice will prevail and preside over a radical social change. Babeuf was, moreover, aware of the boldness of his own words: on several occasions, he begs for his interlocutor's patience: 'If I happen to hurt your convictions, I ask for your indulgence in advance.'[138] He concludes his letter by hoping that Dubois de Fosseux will not hold the length of his letter 'and above

---

136   Ibid., p. 104.
137   Ibid., p. 115.
138   Ibid., p. 92.

all the ideas it expresses' against him.[139] Once again, it should be pointed out that the author would finally give up on any idea of transcribing and sending this letter, and that this clearly showed his fear of provoking a split. Indeed, this was not yet a call to revolt, but only an appeal to the reason of the propertied, based on the fear that the poor will, one day, violently demand a settling of accounts. From this point of view, it can be said that Babeuf translated the eighteenth century's hopes in the progress of justice into the terms of the – still more or less latent – confrontation between antagonistic social layers. This marked an original, both social and millenarian, version of the faith in the advent of enlightenment and the power of reason. From this perspective, however, a question arises: for the Babeuf of the time, did collective farms constitute – as Maurice Dommanget asserts, when speaking of his proposal for the division of farms[140] – a transitional institution that tended to call into question private property in general? Surely, the idea of the community of goods did at this time bear an undeniable power of attraction for Babeuf. Yet, clearly, unlike in the case of the project for collective farms, the utopia of the community of goods had no specifiable future at that time. While collective farms may have seemed less remote from present reality, the community of goods was, at best, a distant hope. This is best illustrated by the fact that Babeuf, who was already thinking about the steps that would lead to the establishment of collective farms, nowhere explicitly ventured beyond this aim in terms of setting out reform projects. We can thus distinguish two modalities of the future in this author's discourse and thinking: one of them outlined the image of a future marked out by the stage of the division of farms and leading, finally, under the patronage of the propertied, to the establishment of collective farms; the other, hard to distinguish from a mere wish, would lead to the definitive abolition of property and to the community of goods. It does not seem possible to link the two by asserting that Babeuf clearly planned to move from one to the other at the end of the hoped-for series of progressive measures.

---

139   Ibid., p. 108.

140   Maurice Dommanget, *Sur Babeuf et la conjuration des Égaux*, Paris: Maspero, 1970, p. 94: 'Thus he suggested that the division of farms, a wholly peaceful measure advocated by philanthropists, but which he considered to be a combative demand of the victims of "tyrannical barbarism", was the first link in a chain running through the agrarian law, of which communism is the end result.'

7
Babeuf in 1789: The *Cadastre perpétuel* and the 'Preliminary Discourse'; Utopia in the Assembly

The first months of the Revolution found Babeuf occupied with the publication of a curious text, which he had busied himself with since at least 1786, entitled the *Cadastre perpétuel*. This work was closely linked to his job as a land surveyor, since its stated aim was to present a concrete programme for the territorial census, which outwardly intended to serve as a means of reforming the tax base in the direction of greater equity. It sought 'to restore happiness to an infinite number of unfortunate people who groan under the tyranny of arbitrary apportioning'.[1] The measurements were to be made using a device known as the 'trigonometric graphometre', invented by Audiffred, a geometrist with whom Babeuf had established contact. This was an innovation typical of a spirit of Enlightenment optimism which the author of the *Cadastre* fully shared – counting, like many others, on the progress of technology to improve men's lives. Originally, the *Cadastre perpétuel* was thus an essentially technical work for the purposes of tax reform. Delays in publication prevented it from being ready in time for the monarchy's calling of the Assemblée des Notables in 1787, and it finally came off the presses in October 1789, preceded by a 'Preliminary Discourse' which Babeuf had drafted in Paris between the spring and summer of that same year. It was thus written at the very moment when the deputies of the Third Estate proclaimed

---

1   *OB*, p. 202.

themselves the National Assembly and the Constituent Assembly began its legislative work, including the abolition of the privileges of the nobility on the night of 4 August and the Declaration of the Rights of Man on 26 August 1789. A reading of the 'Preliminary Discourse' thus provides valuable insight as to the influence these events may have had on Babeuf's view of man and his fundamental prerogatives. The *Cadastre perpétuel* was addressed to the 'Honourable Assembly of Representatives of the French Nation', by 'the citizens of France', Babeuf, and his collaborator Audiffred.[2]

Unlike the draft letter of June 1786, this was a published text, intended to win the approval of those who presided over the Nation's destiny. Babeuf's tactical sense had led him to abandon plans to send the 1786 text to its aristocratic addressee, giving up on the idea despite already having expressed reservations in its pages about the desirability of infringing on property rights. We may wonder whether a similar attitude led him to take precautions in the language used in the 1789 text, or even make more substantial changes in the hope that his proposals would be more readily accepted. The aim was indeed to propose a plan 'admissible within the existing order'.[3] These strategic restrictions did not, however, prevent utopianism from surfacing in several passages of this text.

In the earlier variant written in 1787, Babeuf had preceded the introduction to this text (the 'Preliminary Ideas') with the following epigraph taken from Louis-Sébastien Mercier's utopia *L'An 2440*:

> What advantage is there for a people that allows every citizen to think and write about political administration! Does it provide some good idea, does it give rise to some useful regulation? It is examined, discussed, adopted and perfected. Does it make a mockery of things? We laugh, and the pamphlet disappears.[4]

Thus, at first, Babeuf had set his reform project under the patronage of a famous utopia of this era. His work's goal seemed to be in the spirit of that of other utopians who – like Collignon, but also like Restif de

---

2 Ibid., p. 366.
3 Ibid., p. 373.
4 Ibid., p. 362.

la Bretonne, and many at the time – developed immense hopes upon the calling of the Estates-General. These authors expressed these hopes by addressing their works to the king or to the deputies of the Estates-General, soon followed by those of the National Assembly. The intention behind this gesture was clearly stated: the utopians hoped to attract the legislator's attention to their projects, confident as they were in their intrinsic powers of persuasion. On 26 October 1786, Collignon sent his *L'Avant-coureur du changement du monde entier* to Louis XVI and Calonne with a letter of request asking them to finance the complete drafting of his work.[5] As for Restif de la Bretonne, in 1788 he wrote the following lines at the end of his project *Le Thesmographe*, in connection with another utopian text entitled *L'Andrographe*:

> *L'Andrographe* is a complete Plan of reformation whose reading I will venture to recommend to you, illustrious and inviolable fellow-citizens. Alas! I have never aspired to the happiness of seeing it realised, except in these times of regeneration... Oh legislators! I repeat, deign to read *L'Andrographe*![6]

It was starting from these 'Preliminary Ideas' that Babeuf wrote the Discourse. What most concerns us here is the final social goal to which this programme was supposed to lead. Babeuf writes: 'we do not suppose that the adoption of the *Cadastre perpétuel* can be all that can be done for the improvement of the lot of Peoples'.[7] Babeuf goes on to deplore the fact that the reign of 'prejudices' has made for humanity's misfortune, by stripping a large number of citizens of all property, and by assigning a

---

[5] In 1786, the utopian Collignon published the prospectus for a work that was never to appear, *L'avant-coureur du changement du monde entier*, but whose snippets collected through his correspondent Dubois de Fosseux would stir great enthusiasm in Babeuf, notable in a number of his letters from 1787. We do not have the space to mention them here. See Claude-Boniface Collignon, *L'avant-coureur du changement du monde entier par l'aisance, la bonne éducation et la prospérité générale de tous les hommes, ou Prospectus d'un mémoire patriotique sur les causes de la grande misère qui existe partout, et sur les moyens de l'extirper radicalement*, Paris: EDHIS, 1966. On this little-known author see the article by A. Ioanissian, 'Sur l'auteur de *l'Avant-coureur du changement du monde entier*', AHRF 184, 1966, 1–14.

[6] Restif de la Bretonne, *Le Thesmographe*, The Hague, 1789, p. 586.

[7] *OB*, p. 372.

large number of useful trades a reputation of infamy which has led to their being paid below the needs of their practitioners. Writing in the conditional mode, Babeuf then adds:

> Without [these prejudices], all would have seen that Society is but one great family in which the various members, provided they contribute ... to the general advantage, must have equal rights. The Earth, the common mother, could have been shared only for life, and each share rendered inalienable.[8]

Estimating the available land at about 70 million acres, and the population at 24 million inhabitants divided into families of four, he concluded: 'consequently each manor would have been of eleven acres'.[9] In this passage, another image of Babeuf's communitarian ideal appears. This time, it does not concern collective work, but rather the repartition of the cultivable land belonging to the national territory. Here, the equal surface of the plots for use is calculated with a mathematical precision which recalls the precise accounting which utopians sometimes offered in their novels in order to give substance to their projects. For instance, in the aforementioned 'Statuts du bourg d'Oudun', Restif de la Bretonne set the area allocated to each family at ten arpents (almost the same area). Babeuf hypothesised that such a repartition of land would result in an 'honest mediocrity', itself generating a 'simplicity of manners' much in line with traditional utopian morality.

Babeuf thus presented a social ideal reminiscent of the one outlined by Jean-Jacques Rousseau in Chapter 9 of Book I of *The Social Contract*, according to which everyone should have something and no one should have too much of anything. The major difference lay in the fact that, in Babeuf's perspective, no one owns the land by right; however, the egalitarianism displayed here retained an individualistic tone, and only in a very general way could society be conceived of as a 'family', without the institutions seemingly pushing the citizens towards any particular mutual aid. Finally, we may note the hypothetical character of this outline plan for the organisation of society. It is presented by Babeuf as a plan that men could have taken up if they had not been blinded by

---

8 Ibid., p. 375.
9 Ibid.

prejudice. This meant indulging in a pure thought experiment. While it appears in the 'Preliminary Discourse' as a suggestion to his readers, it is at no point directly referred to as a programme to be carried out. In Babeuf's words, it is simply a matter of 'casting a few glances at the order that ought to exist'.[10] Yet the mediations standing in between what *exists* and what *ought to be* remain implicit – and what Babeuf directly proposed at this time was much less radical with regard to property.

A Rupture in Babouvist Anthropology

Nonetheless, the 'Preliminary Discourse' is a document of the highest interest for grasping the changes that the outbreak of the Revolution brought in Babeuf's anthropological thinking. In fact, the approach taken to the anthropological foundations of his Discourse is the opposite of a 'classic' mitigation strategy. Moreover, Babeuf explains this clearly: precisely in order to 'make less recalcitrant' those who would revolt against a 'very exact distribution of common burdens', it is necessary to 'examine the great principles that relate to the question of the rights of man'.[11] In other words, it is necessary to recall what 'primitive equality' had once been, without disguising or diluting it, the better to show the modesty of the claims aimed at restoring a little equity among men. At one point, this argument is even formulated as a direct threat to the powerful:

> We do not purport to reform the world to the point of seeking exactly to re-establish the primitive equality; but we do try to demonstrate that all those who have fallen into misfortune would have the right to return to [this primitive equality], if opulence persisted in refusing them honourable assistances, such as might be considered due to equals.[12]

Thus, the exposition on human nature is part of the general economy of Babeuf's argument in favour of measures which – without going as far

---

10   Ibid., p. 373.
11   Ibid., p. 372.
12   Ibid., p. 376.

as the agrarian law mentioned here in a purely hypothetical mode – tend to promote a partial redistribution of social wealth. The author warns the powerful of the risk that, if they do not commit to concessions in terms of the sharing of wealth, the 'oppressed' will claim the entirety of their superfluous possessions. From this perspective, we can see that Babeuf had broadened and politicised his views, in the sense that he now expected the necessary social transformations to come from the public authorities. The circumstances obviously explain this shift: his concern was no longer to propose the local constitution of collective farms by convincing large landowners to allocate such land to groups of farmers. Rather, it was to obtain a broadening of the tax base from the Assembly, in order to set up nothing less than a 'national education plan', free public relief for the needy in case of sickness or famine, and a justice system not reliant on financial payment.

It is thus unsurprising, from this perspective, that the notions of the 'political association', and even of the 'social pact', now emerged for the first time. Rousseau's influence is probably responsible for the use of this vocabulary, which was indeed widespread at the time, though it was not really conceptualised. Babeuf does not here develop a theory of the contract, but more devotes himself to deducing the rights of man in society from his natural prerogatives and from the nature of the bond that should unite the members of the political community as a freely consented association. The 'Preliminary Discourse' is a justification, rooted in the essence of man and society, of the material or moral goods that each person is entitled to expect from social life.

Natural Laws, Social Laws

But here a certain ambiguity appears. A careful reading reveals that the text makes a series of about-turns over the question of whether human prerogatives are natural or social in origin. This hesitation emerges from the very first words concerning the state of nature: 'in the natural state, all men are equal', Babeuf begins by stating. But he almost immediately adds:

> In order to justify the extreme inequality of fortunes in the state of society, it has been said, however, that even in the savage state all

individuals did not enjoy absolute equality, because nature had not endowed each of them with the same degrees of sensibility, intelligence, imagination, industry, activity, and strength ... But if the social pact were truly founded on reason, should it not do away with what is defective and unjust in natural laws?[13]

In this passage, the state of nature is first presented as a model of human equality, before an objection leads Babeuf to assign the social pact – and thus political laws – the task of correcting the inequalities produced by the 'natural laws' themselves. This concession threatens the coherence of the argument insofar as – also according to Babeuf – it is indeed in the name of 'primitive equality' that those who suffer the social order are justified in demanding concessions from those who benefit the most from it. Surprisingly, natural laws are presented as vehicles of inequality insofar as some are better endowed than others in the struggle for survival. The 'law of society' is thus called upon to serve as a corrective to the 'barbarous acts' by which the stronger in the state of nature can prey on the weaker. It is also the law of society that must enjoin me to 'share the advantage of my superior faculties' with he whom nature has deprived of the capacity to provide so easily for his own subsistence. Thus, it seems that the rule of sharing and altruism, which is regarded as a natural instinct in the draft letter of 1786, is here regarded as a necessary achievement of civilisation.

But it is important to remember the real status of this argument regarding natural laws, which serves as a response to the objection that men begin life unequally endowed in qualities. While this explanation surely is somewhat problematic in relation to the general economy of Babeuf's argument, it occupies what might be considered a marginal place within it. In fact, no doubt influenced by the *Second Discourse*, here Babeuf considers the state of nature as not so much a state of natural inequality as a state of autarchy of each individual, to be put on an equal footing less through mutual aid than through the absence of accumulation:

The natural man acquired only his day-to-day provisions, and thus left up to others the means of finding, just as constantly, all the things

---
13   Ibid., p. 373.

that were equally necessary to them. If things had been otherwise, and a single individual had taken on the notion of stockpiling, his companions would have thought themselves entitled to plunder his piles, in order to repress an ambition whose example could have become fatal.[14]

Strangely, the absence of accumulation is presented as a rule consciously established by the men of the state of nature, ready immediately to repress those who might contravene it. But the overall inspiration here is distinctly Rousseauian: in Babeuf's rapid description we again find the day-to-day self-sufficiency of the savage of the *Second Discourse*. In such a configuration, as in Rousseau, differences in talent cannot produce major inequality between individuals. The balance of this situation is upset by civilisation, which is above all characterised by the monopolisation of all resources by the few. The cause of this, as advanced by Babeuf, is not the same one found in Rousseau. For the Genevan author, it is due to the process of 'inequality of combination', whereby the more skilful or the faster acquire a cumulative advantage over the less skilful through the interplay of exchanges over time. Babeuf's explanation is more surprising: he attributes the cause of the unjust distribution of goods to the 'false prejudices' that have led men to exaggerate 'the merit and importance of certain professions whose utility was, in truth, in most cases merely illusory and chimeric'.[15] The rich are thus said to owe their privileges to the fact that they perform a type of social function that is highly valued in society and therefore disproportionately remunerated in comparison to other professions.[16]

As other writings from the same period demonstrate – notably including the correspondence with Dubois de Fosseux – Babeuf here particularly has his mind set on those inclined towards the 'study of laws', the 'Magistrature'.[17] Oddly, he does not mention the usurpations – the products of conquest and force – which he had, notably in the draft letter of June 1786, set at the origin of noble property. This omission is perhaps to be explained by the fact that here Babeuf addressed himself

---

14 Ibid., p. 374.
15 Ibid.
16 Ibid.
17 Ibid., p. 217.

not to nobles like Dubois de Fosseux, whom the draft of 1786 was initially meant for, but precisely to magistrates, tasked with drafting new laws for the national collectivity. He thus sought to point them back to the illegitimate origins of their privileged position in terms of wealth. This was meant to induce them towards greater restraint, and to better dispose them to grant new rights to those in favour of whom Babeuf claimed to be writing: 'the oppressed', the 'industrious Artisan', the 'Workers'. In any case, the author again drew on the notes of the *Second Discourse* in order to damn the injustice of the social order based on unequal property:

> Properties must be respected! But what if, out of twenty-four million men, there are fifteen million who do not have any kind of property, because the remaining nine million have not respected their rights enough to afford them even the means of maintaining their existence? Must the fifteen million therefore resolve to die of hunger out of love for the nine million, in gratitude for the fact that they have left them totally bereft?[18]

This exclamation is reminiscent of Rousseau's – doubtless more ambiguous – commentary on the social contract, imagined by the rich and concluded with the poor in order to place their property under the protection of the common law:

> Such was, or must have been the origin of society and of law, which gave new fetters to the weak and new power to the rich; irretrievably destroyed natural liberty, fixed forever the laws of property and inequality; changed an artful usurpation into an irrevocable right; and for the benefit of a few ambitious individuals subjected the rest of mankind to perpetual labor, servitude, and misery.[19]

But perhaps most importantly, the wording is similar to the famous 'leonine contract' found in the *Discourse on Political Economy*, which the rich man also concludes with the poor man:

---

18   Ibid., p. 374.
19   Jean-Jacques Rousseau, *The Social Contract and the First and Second Discourses*, edited by Susan Dunn, New Haven, CT: Yale University Press, pp. 69–148, at p. 125.

You have need of me, because I am rich and you are poor. We will therefore come to an agreement. I will permit you to have the honour of serving me, on condition that you bestow on me the little you have left, in return for the pains I shall take to command you.[20]

The two formulas, which refer with similar facetiousness to the debt that the poor are supposed to owe to the rich who overwhelm and rob them – contracting this debt precisely by virtue of the oppression they suffer – have an air of familiarity. This seems especially worth emphasising, given that the context in which Rousseau elaborates this reasoning is the same as we find in Babeuf. The citizen of Geneva sets these formulas in the middle of a train of argument where he deals with the question of fair taxation in a legitimate government. Admittedly, in contrast to Babeuf, Rousseau exempts land, the source of wealth, from taxation, instead preferring a tax on the income of individuals. The *feudiste* Babeuf, for his part, adopts an apparently diametrically opposed position, since the aim of his 'cadastre', or land register, is to measure the wealth of each individual in proportion to the land he owns, with a view to establishing the tax on this basis. But, on closer examination, the two men have similar views regarding the general idea that should govern the distribution of taxes. They both reject the principle of exemptions that governs the society of orders. Rousseau, like Babeuf in the *Cadastre perpétuel*, upholds the idea of a universal tax, although he nowhere clearly states its redistributive role. Even so, the criteria that Rousseau specifies for establishing the tax base are all found in Babeuf:

1. The idea of progressivity between each person's income and their tax contribution: if, in Rousseau's words, 'the person who has ten times the property of another man ought to pay ten times as much to the State',[21] the same is true of Babeuf: 'everyone must contribute in proportion to what he has'.[22]
2. The reasons for this progressiveness are to be found in the greater advantage that the richest receive from society, as compared to their poorer counterparts. For both authors, there is no doubt that

---

20   Jean-Jacques Rousseau, 'Discourse on Political Economy', in *The Social Contract*.
21   Ibid.
22   *OB*, p. 383.

society renders more services as more goods are placed under its protection, and as more interests are defended. Thus, in Rousseau: 'A third relation, which is never taken into account, though it ought to be the chief consideration, is the advantage that every person derives from the social confederacy; for this provides a powerful protection for the immense possessions of the rich, and hardly leaves the poor man in quiet possession of the cottage he builds with his own hands.'[23] Babeuf would say no different: 'As each person derives more or less benefit from this protection of property, in proportion to the greater or lesser [property] devolved to him, it is common law that each person must contribute in proportion to what he has.'[24]

3. The idea that taxation plays a role in rebalancing the respective wealth of the members of the social whole, and may – if need be – justify taking away from citizens all that they possess beyond what is necessary. Even if, tellingly, neither author goes so far as to directly demand this maximalist measure, they both mention the possibility and justify it. Thus for Rousseau: 'He who possesses only the common necessaries of life should pay nothing at all, while the tax on him who is in possession of superfluities may, if need be, be extended to everything he has over and above mere necessaries.'[25] The citizen of Geneva does not specify what is meant by the expression 'if need be' ['au besoin'], remaining ambiguous as to the cases in which it would be necessary to resort to a massive confiscation of the goods of the richest. Yet, his wording itself leaves open the possibility of such measures – and, above all, legitimises it theoretically. In proposing to tax 'superfluities', as opposed to 'necessaries', Rousseau takes the income of the simple peasant as the yardstick for the right to property: 'for a grandee has two legs just like a cowherd, and, like him again, but one belly'.[26] Rousseau's political economy thus seeks to promote a tendency towards the progressive reduction of the superfluous, in order to achieve a relative equalisation of conditions centred on the satisfaction of needs.

---

23 Rousseau, 'Discourse on Political Economy', p. 262.
24 *OB*, p. 383.
25 Rousseau, 'Discourse on Political Economy', p. 262. Translation edited.
26 Ibid.

Babeuf's demonstration takes different paths to reach similar – albeit more radical – conclusions. He asserts the inescapable need to limit everyone's income to what is strictly necessary: 'for nature, sparing of her gifts, produces only about what is useful to all the beings she creates; and some cannot enjoy a superfluity without others lacking the necessary'.[27] Such an assertion should, in all logic, lead to the radical rejection of 'superfluities' for some within the social collective. Babeuf does not go that far; here again, his reasoning on principle is only there to lead the privileged to more moderation and to a greater contribution to the fiscal effort: 'We do not purport to reform the world to the point of seeking exactly to re-establish the primitive equality'.[28] But the idea, here – more clearly than in Rousseau, if not expressed directly – is the redistributive role of taxation, which leads the 'opulent' to provide 'honourable assistance' to 'the unfortunate', with a view to equalising conditions and ensuring the subsistence of all.

At this point in our argument, one fact needs admitting: Babeuf, who, in this text, readily cites other predecessors in the theory of taxation such as Linguet, Vauban, and Condorcet, does not mention Rousseau's political economy. The similarities mentioned above could therefore be attributed to a common inspiration rather than to Babeuf's reading of Rousseau's text. Yet, if anything, this makes the theoretical proximity even more striking: their perspectives on taxation reflect a common desire to translate the equality of human needs into the social order itself.

The Twofold Justification for Equality

Even if the natural inequality of talents were a reality, it is these human needs that surely justify the demand for an equalisation of conditions. The expressions which Babeuf uses visibly refer to his theorisation of natural right as a right to live, as found in the draft letter of June 1786: 'On what grounds can those who possess nothing demand so many advantages from those who possess everything? ... On what

---

27   *OB*, p. 376.
28   Ibid.

grounds! ... But, Gentlemen, by their quality as men.'[29] Here, it is worth emphasising the force with which this principle – formulated for purely internal use in 1786 – is proclaimed as a self-evident fact, in which there echoes the Declaration of the Rights of Man of 26 August 1789. The rupture represented by the Revolution could not be expressed more clearly than in this claim, which has become imperative, incontestable, and urgent. The right to a dignified life – not a meagre existence, but one that, despite persistent inequalities, is 'suitable for equals' – is now a natural right whose universality cannot be challenged by 'defective' natural laws just because they provide unequal talents. In Babeuf's analysis, there is clearly a distinction between natural *laws* – which can be challenged by forms of social organisation that equalise conditions – and natural *rights*, which are a universal and inalienable prerogative of man.

Yet Babeuf apparently feels obliged to back up this justification of all men's access to a certain number of goods and rights, by adding in a second criterion, that of social utility: 'all states are equal when their object is the common good'.[30] It is this criterion, ultimately, that allows him to counter the argument that natural inequalities might justify an unequal distribution of resources in society:

> Not all men can be employed in the same manner; they do not have an equal aptitude for the same occupations; and it is a wise provision of nature that things should be so ordered, since it results in the effect of a thousand different productions of men's hands, which serve to multiply the common enjoyments.[31]

The problem with this criterion is that, unlike the right to life, it cannot be considered an inherently effective fact of nature. After all, Babeuf, following Rousseau, had earlier outlined the state of nature as a state of independence in which each person provides for his own needs by his own means. It is only in the civil state that the complementarity of talents can become a valid reason for giving each person a certain number of social advantages as a reward for

---

29   Ibid.
30   Ibid., p. 375.
31   Ibid.

the services he renders to the community, and that it becomes apparent that 'Society is but one great family in which the various members, provided they contribute to the general advantage, each according to their own physical and intellectual faculties, must have equal rights'.[32]

Thus, there are two sides to the system of anthropological justification for the tendency to equalise conditions in the social state. On the one hand, Babeuf continues to invoke the natural right to life, which stands prior to any social organisation. But, on the other hand, he enlists arguments that are only valid for man in the civil state: that is, the complementarity of faculties and the properly social utility of each person's work, contributing to the common production. Babeuf thus ends up going back on his initial assertions, and making man into an entirely social animal; he asserts a few pages later that 'it is impossible for each person to procure all that is physically necessary for himself', and that this has always made it indispensable for 'men to help each other'.[33] In this case, it is the social rule of collective effort that legitimises each person receiving a fair share of the product of everyone else's labour. Babeuf goes so far as to consider this share not in relation to individual needs, but as 'the share of advantages that accrue [to each person] in the ratio of the product of the country he inhabits, over the number of inhabitants of that same country'.[34] In this perspective, the constraints of the social organisation itself determine the share that each person should receive.

Fundamentally, Babeuf seems to vacillate between an individualistic anthropology, referring to natural rights, which take the isolated human being as the starting point for all reflection on the prerogatives of each person, and another anthropology which we might term – to adopt a term from sociology – holistic, in the sense that it is the totality of society, defined as a productive group, that allows us to deduce the benefits that each person is entitled to expect from it. In this second case, which Babeuf eventually adopted in the course of his argument, without, however, explicitly abandoning his first orientation, it is not man's natural right as an individual, but rather his social right as a member of the

---

32   Ibid.
33   Ibid., p. 386.
34   Ibid., p. 376.

community, that justifies egalitarian redistribution. We can thus speak of a tendency within Babeuf's text to put natural right into question, even if the challenge thus posed is evidently not clear to the author himself.

The Ambivalences of Natural Right

Babeuf was neither the first nor the only one to place natural rights in a problematic position. Rousseau himself, in his *Second Discourse*, undermined its foundations. As Bertrand Binoche shows, the difficulty in the latter text stems from the undermining of the notion of human nature itself: Rousseau refuses to infer 'the origin [of man] from human nature such as it empirically presents itself in the degraded world of artifice'.[35] Insofar as Rousseau claims in his research to 'discard all facts' and rejects any kind of recurrence, his hypothesis renders unreadable the very genesis of man that he claims to clarify. How can we find a primitive image of man if all traces of him have been erased by time – if contemporary man is totally unable to serve as a model? The idea of an unchanging human nature is nevertheless maintained, notably through the image of the statue of Glaucus that we find in the first words of the Preface. After all, this metaphor suggests that something original has remained under the layer of sediment that covers it. But, at the same time, the object of the *Second Discourse* is to describe 'how the soul and the passions of men by insensible alterations change as it were their very nature'.[36] The notion of perfectibility itself seems to clearly assign a fundamental mutability to human nature, a temporal and historical essence, which seems to run counter to Rousseau's approach to the nature of the human being. The concept of human nature is thus both maintained and dislocated. This leads the author into paradoxical claims: for example, he denies that sociability is natural to primitive man, who is instead characterised by independence, and emphasises 'the little care which nature has taken to bring men together by mutual wants, and make the use of speech easy to them,

---

35   Bertrand Binoche, *Les trois sources des philosophies de l'histoire (1764–1798)*, Paris: PUF, 1994, p. 28.
36   Rousseau, *Discourse on Inequality*, in *The Social Contract*, p. 137.

how little she has done towards making them sociable, and how little she has contributed to anything which they themselves have done to become so'.[37] But, in the letter to Philopolis, he would affirm that 'society is natural to the human species as decrepitude is to the individual'.[38] The human essence is thus temporalised; it unfolds across the specific timespan of man's genesis, following its stages from original goodness to contemporary decadence. Yet, in Rousseau's discussion, this temporalisation is inseparable from its negation – that is, in the affirmation of an immutable human nature.

A similar fate is reserved for natural rights, which is logically deduced from the idea of human nature. In the *Second Discourse*, Rousseau claims, as Babeuf would later do, to set out the true natural law and to condemn as such the false law of inequality: 'It likewise follows that moral inequality, authorized, solely by positive right, clashes with natural right.'[39]

Yet, as we have seen, natural rights are split in two. Already, in the Preface, they are divided between the original natural rights – which derive in the human mind from the principles of self-love and pity 'without there being the least necessity for adding to them that of sociability' – and rational natural rights, or 'rules, which reason is afterwards obliged to re-establish upon other foundations, when by its successive developments, it has at last stifled nature itself'.[40] What can remain of primitive natural rights in this secondary natural right, re-established 'upon other foundations' than those of man's primitive affections – ones supposed to govern the relations between men in society, when their primary nature was independence? Rousseau is even clearer in the first version of *The Social Contract*: 'But the social order is a sacred right that serves as a foundation for all others. This right, however, does not come from nature. It is therefore based on conventions.'[41] The natural right, the right of independent primitive man, is thus, following the concept of human nature, both maintained as a support for the criticism of existing

---

37   Ibid., p. 104.
38   Jean-Jacques Rousseau, 'Lettre à Philopolis', *in Œuvres complètes*, edited by Bernard Gagnebin and Marcel Raymond, Paris: Gallimard, 1964–1995, vol. III, pp. 230–6, at p. 232.
39   Rousseau, *Discourse on Inequality*, in *The Social Contract*, p. 138.
40   Ibid., p. 84.
41   Rousseau, *The Social Contract*, p. 156.

positive rights, and suppressed in favour of the right that man derives from legitimate political association, *qua* the producer of social relations based on reason and respect for the common interest. Rousseau can then assert, in *The Social Contract*, that in the civil state 'all rights are determined by law'.[42]

The right of man in the social state can be interpreted, without exception, as the dialectical re-establishment 'upon other foundations' of primitive natural rights in the social state. More rarely, it can be interpreted as the result of historical progress, as the notion of 'reasoned natural right' in the *Geneva Manuscript* seems to imply. Or, finally, at the limit, it can be interpreted as a right that is no longer natural at all, entirely re-founded on the basis of the complete de-naturing of man. In his 'Preliminary Discourse', Babeuf proposes a dual image of man – successively in his primitive independence, and in the interdependence of the social state – and a double image of man's inalienable prerogatives – seeming sometimes to be entirely natural, and sometimes to be deduced from the principles of social organisation. It thus seems that he inherited the equivocation that had never truly been resolved in Rousseau. Babeuf's right of man in society maintains an ambiguous relationship with the natural right to live. Indeed, it appears to be an emanation of the latter, insofar as it gives the individual access to the goods necessary for his development, but, at the same time, it is established on the basis of man's participation in the common effort and constitutes a corollary of this effort. As such, it no longer has anything to do with the right that man in the primitive state of equality had to procure the necessities of life through his own efforts, whether in terms of the way this right is exercised or in the goods to which it gives access. It is particularly telling that, in this social right, Babeuf includes, in addition to the right to a dignified material existence, the right to education, which cannot strictly speaking be a 'natural' right:

> It is therefore demonstrated that, in a society of men, it would be necessary for there to be either no education at all, or for all individuals to have it equally . . . Education . . . has become among us a kind of property which each person has the right to claim.[43]

---

42 Ibid., p. 178.
43 *OB*, pp. 378–9.

In the social state, the right to education – a right which makes no sense in the state of nature – becomes an inalienable prerogative. This is because it is the condition of equality between men, through the possibility which it gives to the most deprived to morally defend themselves against the attempts of the privileged to impose domination and usurpation. It guarantees, in this new state, that man can maintain his intrinsic dignity, which is the immanent corollary of natural law. It should be remembered that the right to live asserted by Babeuf is never merely a right to purely physiological survival, but rather opens up access to goods 'such as may be regarded as suitable for equals'.

It is thus necessary to grasp – in Babeuf's 'Preliminary Discourse' as in Rousseau – the ambiguity which remains nestled in the concept of natural right in society. However, this equivocation is not the work of these two thinkers alone. Indeed, it is also found in the Declaration of the Rights of Man of 1789, on which Babeuf explicitly draws in the *Cadastre perpétuel*, as he rails against seigneurial rights:

> Now that enlightenment is widespread, now that everyone knows that, according to natural right, all men, upon being born, should enjoy the same advantages; now that it is recognised that their rights are not prescribed; why do we not go back on this fraud, this usurpation?[44]

With this wording – obviously borrowed from the first two articles of the Declaration, as he alludes to equality of birth (Art. 1) and the imprescriptibility of rights (Art. 2) – Babeuf links his own claims on man's natural rights to the text of 26 August 1789. However, this text is far from free of ambiguities concerning natural rights. On the one hand, it clearly states that 'the representatives of the French People, formed into a National Assembly . . . have resolved to set forth, in a solemn Declaration, the natural, unalienable and sacred rights of man', thus implying that the Declaration is limited to stating universal prerogatives, which impose themselves on the human conscience.[45] From this perspective, the public authorities are responsible only for

---

44 Ibid, p. 386.
45 Preamble, Declaration of the Rights of Man, 26 August 1789.

promulgating, sanctioning, guaranteeing, and making effective pre-existing rights which they do not themselves determine. At the same time, however, the text continues with the idea that 'the concept of "the rights of man" can only acquire legal fullness and efficiency when mediated by laws and codes'.[46] The delimitation of natural rights by the state is not a merely formal recognition of these rights, but a real definition of them. For proof of this, it is sufficient to return to Articles 4 and 5 of the Declaration, which stipulate the following:

4. Liberty consists in being able to do anything that does not harm others: thus, the exercise of the natural rights of every man has no bounds other than those that ensure to the other members of society the enjoyment of these same rights. These bounds may be determined only by Law.
5. The Law has the right to forbid only those actions that are injurious to society. Nothing that is not forbidden by Law may be hindered, and no one may be compelled to do what the Law does not ordain.

As Stéphane Rials observes, these formulations clearly indicate that the natural rights of man have limits, which are dictated exclusively by the law. It is thus the law that finally gives form to and makes effective the very content of natural law, in particular by making it enforceable in court. Without it, while natural rights continue to serve as a reference, they are devoid of legal effectiveness: 'One cannot imagine – upon a first reading – a more radical positivism, more boldly affirming the completeness of the legal order.'[47]

---

46   Simone Goyard-Fabre, *Les embarras philosophiques du droit naturel*, Paris: Vrin, 2002, p. 325. Without claiming to draw up an exhaustive list of works relating to the problems raised by the 1789 Declaration of the Rights of Man, we can here mention Étienne Balibar, 'Droits de l'homme et droits du citoyen: la dialectique moderne de l'égalité et de la liberté,' *Actuel Marx* 8, 1990, 13–33; A. De Baecque, W. Schmale, and M. Vovelle (eds), *L'an 1 des droits de l'homme*, Paris: Presses du CNRS, 1988; Marcel Gauchet, 'La déclaration des droits de l'homme et du citoyen', *Commentaire* 43, 1988, 783–90; Claude Lefort, 'Droits de l'homme et politique', in *L'invention démocratique*, Paris: Fayard, 1981, pp. 45–83; Stéphane Rials, *La déclaration des droits de l'homme et du citoyen*, Paris: Hachette, 1988; S. Rials (ed.), *La déclaration de 1789*, Paris: PUF, 1988.

47   Rials, *La déclaration des droits de l'homme et du citoyen*, p. 354.

Yet, the expression 'legal positivism', as used in relation to the Declaration of the Rights of Man, cannot be accepted unreservedly. The nuance introduced by the commentator through the expression 'upon a first reading' must be properly recognised here. After all, one cannot seek to define or limit that which does not exist. Fundamentally, it seems to us that, here again, the ambiguity should not be dismissed, for it is consubstantial with the use of the term 'natural rights' in the Declaration. The text hesitates between jusnaturalism and legal positivism without really deciding either way, because it is based on the imprescriptible and inalienable character of natural rights, and intends to found a new political order that consecrates the reign of constitutional law. Babeuf doubtless inherited this dual preoccupation; indeed, in these first months of the Revolution, his tactical sense naturally led him to lean on texts which had already received the blessing of the political authorities, precisely in order to advance his own ideas.

Anthropology and Utopia

But in such a context, is the anthropology elaborated by the author of the 'Preliminary Discourse' particularly consistent with the utopian ideal that shines through elsewhere in the text? We have seen how much his conception of the state of nature in terms of equality-through-independence owed to Rousseau's *Second Discourse*. The state of nature is not the right place to look for the seeds of a human inclination towards a way of life marked by a harmonious sociability which provides for the common happiness. On the contrary, Babeuf identifies all the potential for a contented existence – characterised by 'honest mediocrity', 'candour', and 'invariable order'[48] – in the establishment of social laws. It is in the social state that men can compensate for the deficiencies of natural laws, by teaching each person not only that he should not feed himself at the expense of his peers, but also that he should 'share the advantage' from any superior faculties he may have. Paradoxically, the 'natural order' which Babeuf upholds, in which all form one great 'family', is only effective when 'all contribute ... according to their respective means, to provide various benefits to Society', which enables

---

48   *OB*, p. 375.

all, in law, to 'enjoy equal comfort in that society' – including even he who 'has no talents capable of putting him in a position to make more than slight offerings toward [Society]', since this 'is not his fault'.[49] With this remark, we can see how coloured by morality is the notion of social utility that Babeuf elaborates on to justify the access of each and every person to social goods: indeed, it would mean that those whose capacities allow them only to do barely effective work should enjoy full social rights, much unlike parasites who seek without legitimate reason to live off the labour of others.

On this basis, it is, paradoxically, up to society and its just laws to ensure the development of the 'natural order', just as it is the task of social rights to guarantee the natural right of each person to a dignified life. By Babeuf's own admission, the state of 'primitive equality' lies definitively in the past. He turns his gaze not towards this condition, but towards the 'order that should exist', in which the Earth is rendered inalienable and allocated to each citizen for life in an egalitarian manner. This is an order towards which it is permissible to 'cast a few glances' over and above the more moderate social justice measures that Babeuf openly calls for in his *Cadastre perpétuel*.[50]

Babeuf agreed with the ideological mainstream of his time that it was the role of government and the law to determine the legitimate relations between men and to give effective existence to the precepts of natural right. But he went further than most in considering society not just as a collection of individuals governed by a common rule, but, rather – it seems – as a community of production of wealth to which each person must contribute according to their own strength, in exchange for which they must be able to enjoy the social benefits appropriate to their dignity. Thus, the ties that Babeuf sees between the members of society are not only juridical relations or even moral constraints, but, above all, ties of concrete solidarity and material mutual aid. These ties are perverted by social laws as they currently exist, but it is the legislator's job to regenerate them. It is not clear what exact forms this solidarity should take – for, although it is made palpable through the redistributive role that taxation plays in Babeuf's programme of immediate reforms, it is not clear how it would materialise in his longer-term project of the inalienability

---

49 Ibid.
50 Ibid.

of the land. Once equal shares have been allocated in usufruct to each person, will there remain forms of redistribution according to the greater or lesser productivity of each person, such as to 'share' the natural advantages of the most skilful? If each 'head of household' is allocated a 'fine manor', how then would society still be a 'great family'? Would not everyone be concerned only with their own interests? As we have already detected, Babeuf's anthropological and social ideal vacillates between egalitarianism and community. The simple division of land between families could, in a certain fashion, reconstitute the 'primitive equality'-in-independence; here, we would have a clearly identifiable realisation of the 'natural order' on the new bases of civilisation. But it seems that Babeuf attributes men a real community of fate, which requires more of them than merely maintaining egalitarian relations. Here, again, the ambivalence is an integral part of the author's thinking, which cannot really be removed from it.

Symptoms of the Outbreak of the French Revolution in the 'Preliminary Discourse'

It is through Babeuf's relationship to history that his intellectual trajectory most clearly reflects the revolutionary rupture. As a new beginning, a break in the existing order, the Revolution flung open the field of possibilities – and, logically enough, gave fresh impetus to utopian hopes. However, in the final months of 1789, Babeuf was busy publishing the land registry project that he had already offered to the Assemblée des Notables in 1787. The rupture was thus not as clear-cut as one might expect. It is, then, necessary to analyse his words more closely, if we are to identify the growing effects that the political and social upheaval of which Babeuf was a contemporary had on his way of imagining the improvement of humanity's fate.

This evolution is closely bound to the way in which Babeuf, as both a commentator on and an actor in the period, represented the process that was now underway. In itself, in fact, the Revolution poses a certain number of problems for those who want to think about it at a historical level: if it did indeed mark the advent of a new time, this time itself needs to be characterised in a more specific fashion, through its phases and its implications. As we have seen, the eighteenth century gradually abandoned the 'restorative' meaning of revolution, instead granting it the sense of historical novelty. But, at the time of these events, this mutation was not yet complete, and from this point of view we find several regimes of historicity coexisting in the discourses of the various actors. Babeuf is no exception in this respect.

Moreover, the revolution is not a single act which in one moment brings forth the innovation it might entail: as shown by Reinhart Koselleck, in the wake of 1789, revolution became the concept 'charged with ordering historically recurrent convulsive experiences'.[51] However, the said 'order' means a succession of distinct moments: the Revolution was indeed conceived by the contemporaries of the event as a process, which unfolded against the backdrop of an acceleration of time, and which could be broken down into several successive periods. As a process of inducing changes willed, or at least produced, by the actors, 'the concept of "reform" converged here and there with that of "revolution"'.[52] Revolution can thus be understood as a series of – peaceful or violent – reforms which a given protagonist, according to his interests and viewpoint, may choose either to embrace, thus identifying himself with one or other of the phases of the revolution, or instead reject. Within this general framework, Babeuf's perception of the unfolding of events is highly indicative of the evolutions in his own understanding of the process and of the role which he strove to play therein.

It may seem odd that, even in summer–autumn 1789, as the first high point of the Revolution played out between the king and the deputies of the Third Estate in Versailles, Babeuf persisted in publishing and seeking the adoption of his tax reform project by the newly proclaimed National Assembly. This project was, after all, rooted in his activity as a land surveyor under the Ancien Régime, which had led him to produce a first version likely as early as the end of 1786. Obviously, the new circumstances of the Revolution provided him with a new opportunity to bring his project to fruition, after his failed attempt to propose it to the Assemblée des Notables in 1787. In these conditions, it is interesting to compare the two successive versions, in

---

51   Reinhart Koselleck, 'Historical Criteria of the Modern Concept of Revolution', *Futures Past: On the Semantics of Historical Time*, New York: Columbia University Press 2004, pp. 43–57, at p. 50.

52   Ibid., p. 51.

order to examine how the revolutionary events of summer 1789 (the storming of the Bastille, which he witnessed directly; the abolition of privileges on the night of 4 August; the adoption of the Declaration of the Rights of Man on 26 August, and so on) inspired Babeuf, in terms of his perception of the present time and his stance with regard to both the past and the future.

The 1787 version was preceded by the aforementioned citation from *L'An 2440*, which exalts the benefits – for public administration and politics – of the free circulation of ideas, for the sake of the dissemination of the most fertile notions and their eventual adoption. Babeuf thus rallied behind the utopian Louis-Sébastien Mercier's faith in the spontaneous effectiveness of reformist proposals based on reason. This faith also drew on an extract from Calonne's speech to the Assemblée des Notables on 22 February 1787, which immediately followed the passage from Mercier. The passage denounces the 'abuses'[53] that still tarnish the lustre of the monarchy, and whose rectification may enable it to be regenerated by 'fertilising' all its 'parts'. The cause of the 'disorders' could thus become a source of justice and prosperity. It was in this speech that Calonne made the proposal – rejected by the Assemblée des Notables – to introduce a general land subsidy, without distinction of privilege: a major fiscal reform that would have effectively ended the exemption of the higher orders. Babeuf thus closely followed the political developments of his time, as he eagerly sought reasons for hope. While expressing a certain distrust as to the real intentions of the speech's author, he comments in his 'Preliminary Ideas': 'But what does it matter where a thought is found; provided it is good, one must gather it up, and profit from it.'[54]

If the author of the *Cadastre perpétuel* sought the dual authority of Mercier and Calonne, this would seem to make sense for the following reason. In the context of the progressive political awakening of France in these decisive years of ferment, there could be a conjunction between the utopian hopes expressed in projects for reform, and the determination, among certain representatives of the monarchy, to put an end to certain overly blatant abuses – a conjunction symbolised in the text by the juxtaposition of the two quotes. In other words, this was supposed to

---

53 *OB*, p. 395.
54 Ibid.

be an especially fruitful moment for advancing proposals – and when we are talking about the draft letter of 1786, we must emphasise the moderate character of the said proposals. Babeuf, in fact, only sought to establish the proportionality of a tax whose necessity had already been recognised by the king's minister. He thus sincerely hoped to find an attentive ear among men of influence. He added:

> The adoption, by the friends of good and the protectors of order, of the principles of proportion and equality in this distribution [of public subsidies], shows how full we are today of the just provisions which I have just recalled. So, there is no longer any doubt that it is to this class of men alone that we owe the good of seeing work done to correct this host of abuses that raise the general cry of suffering humanity.[55]

This was an expression of the hope, which Babeuf shared with many others at the time, to see an era of reform under the leadership of the 'friends of the good' – and notably enough, the latter are not distinguished from the 'protectors of order'. His hopes for a more just future thus revolved around the existing powers that be.

While the new version of the *Cadastre perpétuel* was heavily reworked, it followed the same kind of perspective: although it was dated to 'L'An 1789, the first Year of French Liberty', it nonetheless placed itself under the patronage of the minister Necker. This time it reproduced an excerpt from the speech he had given at the opening of the Estates-General, which, like Calonne in his day, spoke in favour of an 'equal distribution of taxes'.[56] The juxtaposition of the quotation and the date may be cause for surprise, since by summer 1789, when Babeuf probably reworked his text by adding the 'Preliminary Discourse', the Estates-General were already a thing of the past. But Necker had become minister of finance again in July 1789, after a brief dismissal. Babeuf thus drew on the prestige of a popular minister, a supporter of tax reform; but the text is directly addressed not to Necker but 'To the Honourable Assembly of the Representatives of the French Nation'[57] with a view to making it

---

55 Ibid., p. 396.
56 Ibid., p. 365.
57 Ibid., p. 366.

'approve' the plan therein. Through this address, the *Cadastre perpétuel* acknowledged the transfer of power accomplished in these crucial months, and extended Babeuf's best wishes to the new holders of legislative authority.

The 'Preliminary Discourse', which is much more extensive than the 1787 version of the 'Preliminary Ideas', is accompanied by this eloquent subtitle:

> To serve to elaborate upon the effect of the adoption of the project, to summarise the numerous advantages which could result from it, to fix attention on the distance which, according to it, still remains to be covered to achieve the common felicity of Peoples, and on the causes which oppose the positive approach to this great goal.[58]

This time – somewhat like what he had done for his own purposes in the draft letter of 1786 – Babeuf sketched out a real battle plan to fight for the 'common felicity of Peoples', of which the tax project was only the first step. His outlook now went beyond this: the author turned his attention to the distance that remained to be covered, whose milestones he marked out with what he considered to be indispensable transitional measures. In fact, the text focuses on these intermediate stages without assigning any precise final goal to the general evolution. As we have seen, Babeuf does not present his project of the inalienability of land as the real and ultimate objective of his proposals, even if we can sense his inclination for such a definitive solution to social ills. To put the text back in the perspective of its relationship to revolutionary temporality, it cannot be considered as oriented towards this end. Babeuf replaced this objective with a series of measures that should, for now, be set in the context of a reformist project that would unfold over time.

The choice to date 1789 as the 'first Year of French Liberty' was telling: with this, Babeuf expressed the idea that a new order of things had begun, better than the old one – but it is also worth noting that the first year of French *liberty* was not the first year of *equality*. Should we see in this a simple concession to the vocabulary of the time – or rather the idea that the liberty that had just been acquired was to be followed by equality, as its desirable extension? While, with this expression, Babeuf

---

58   Ibid., p. 371.

implied that liberty had already arrived and reigned, he corrected this somewhat conventional optimism with a notable expression we find in the body of the 'Preliminary Discourse', where he referred to the present time as that of 'the happy revolution that is being prepared'.[59] This formulation seems much more revealing of the way the author of the text conceived things. In reality, for the French nation, 1789 merely opened up a new era of tasks to work towards and accomplish. In this sense, the 'happy revolution' was not a finished achievement, but remained to be done. It was still necessary to seize the opportunity to take measures to accelerate the advent of the time of 'felicity'.

The passage devoted to the 'distance that remains to be covered' opens with a list of measures that Babeuf deemed necessary: free sacraments; the establishment of a national fund for the subsistence of the poor; the creation of a system of free health care for all, with practitioners paid from the public funds; a national education plan; and free recourse to justice, again with magistrates salaried by the public authorities. Most of these measures were in line with the tax reform, in the sense that they provided for the future destination of the funds obtained through the land register. This would result in a twofold improvement in the lot of the 'toiling People'. Firstly, they would thus be relieved of the burden of taxes that they had been bearing almost alone up till that point. Secondly, they would benefit from a form of redistribution through the new institutions providing for health care, legal costs, education, and so on. This series of proposals shows, as we have seen, how much Babeuf had changed his orientation since 1786, no longer turning to the landowners to share their income with their farmers more equitably, but rather turning to the public authorities, making them responsible for proceeding with redistribution through an equitable tax. His demands for work for all were now addressed to the state and its 'Laws': 'Every man must find something to do, and the Laws must see to it that his remuneration is sufficient for his livelihood.'[60]

The ideal of usufructuary sharing of the land itself gives pride of place to political action – for it would be the nation, through its representatives, that would ultimately dispose of the plots of land upon the moment of their allocation. The author of the *Cadastre perpétuel* thus

---

59 Ibid., p. 379.
60 Ibid., p. 375.

also took a significant step forward compared to the 1787 version of this text, which had aimed only to lighten the tax burden of those who bore it. Was Babeuf now unveiling a project that he had been ruminating on all along, or was it that the revolutionary rupture gave fresh impetus to his hopes? In any case, this was the first time that these hopes, which did perhaps date back to an earlier time, found public expression and took on the sense of a demand. The land survey project itself thus changed in status: it was no longer at the centre of the programme outlined by Babeuf, but now appeared as a simple prerequisite for obtaining the 'honourable relief' that the opulent owed to those with smaller fortunes.

Among the measures advocated by Babeuf in the 'Preliminary Discourse', a central place is reserved for the national education plan. This is an important point, and not only because it is a truism to say that education has had a key role in most of the great utopias since Thomas More. Rather, it is also important because the emphasis Babeuf granted to this question is telling of how, in this period, he imagined the unfolding of the Revolution which he saw the events of 1789 as heralding.

A first observation reveals that ignorance is the primary cause of the persistence of iniquities: bad laws 'have prevailed only because men have lacked enlightenment'.[61] Ignorance of natural equality is responsible for the fact that men have believed it legitimate to use every means at their disposal to extract as much as possible from their fellow men. But the history of these unjust relationships put a few – the richest – in a position to become the 'guardians' of others, through the position of pre-eminence that property confers on them over others who lack it. Henceforth, the guardians proved to be 'unworthy': through a Machiavellian 'plan of education', they worked to give the unfortunate man 'such notions that he did not believe he should complain about [their] perfidies, such that he did not even imagine that [they] were not justified in committing them'.[62] Meanwhile, through an education of a quite different kind, they worked to form for themselves 'those hard and merciless hearts which ... make one withstand the spectacle of [one's] fellow men perishing from hunger'.[63] In other words, the inequality of

---

61 Ibid., p. 376.
62 Ibid., pp. 376–7.
63 Ibid., p. 377.

conditions in the iniquitous society is coupled with an inequality of education, which helps to reproduce these conditions. The unfortunate man is not only deprived of the knowledge of his natural rights (which is why his education is deficient), but his misfortune is redoubled in that, instead of learning his rights, he learns to submit to injustice under various pretexts ('superstitions' and 'ridiculous ideas'). Here, Babeuf is doubtless taking aim at the content of religious sermons, which preach resignation faced with the miseries of this world. For his part, the 'opulent' man possesses the knowledge that others lack; but above all he armours himself with reasoning and principles that make the spectacle of the misery of his own kind bearable – or rather, indifferent. Babeuf's analysis is in line with Rousseau's observation that pity is stifled in the rich, who are no longer able to see the poor as their peers: 'the rich console themselves for the harm done by them to the poor, by the assumption that the poor are too stupid to feel . . . We naturally think lightly of the happiness of those we despise'.[64]

However, Babeuf's line of argument postulates a symmetrical distortion in the relationship of the poor and the rich to natural rights and the idea of equality. Each of them remains ignorant of these principles, not only because of a lack of knowledge of them – itself enough to produce 'prejudices of ignorance' – but because a screen of false conceptions, conducive to maintaining the established order, is set up between these precepts and the minds of individuals. Babeuf further delves into the harmful implications of inegalitarian education as he notes that, through the deprivation of which it is the victim, 'it happens that the People is kept in a crude state, which makes it appear to be of a different nature to those whom fate has favoured with a more exact education'.[65] Thus, the people's deficient education gives credit to the fable of human inequality, since it makes it align with appearances. The fact that some people lack education reinforces the prejudices of others and maintains the illusion that their social superiority fits together with their natural superiority: the difference in education thus produces the naturalisation of the social hierarchy. The miserable state of the poor appears natural and well-founded.

Still, the central idea is that ignorance degrades the 'oppressed man'

---

64 E, p. 186.
65 OB, p. 378.

and, at the same time, makes him unable to defend his rights. This is why Babeuf seems to give education a primary role in the path to ending injustice. As a moral good, comparable to material goods – for it is 'a kind of property to which everyone has a right to claim'[66] – education alone makes individuals capable of standing up for the respect of their natural prerogatives: 'There are a host of existing institutions that an uneducated people would not put up with.'[67] Hence, universal education seems to be the first institution that ought to be established in the near future; we sense that the author of the 'Preliminary Discourse' expected that this would lead to a growing expansion of the rights of the people. As a tool of emancipation, the national education plan opens up the field of possibilities, beyond the plan presented by Babeuf. On this, ultimately, rests what turns out to be an indefinite programme for the equalisation of conditions.

---

66 Ibid., p. 379.
67 Ibid., p. 380.

8
Babeuf During the Revolution: Utopia and the Republic

We do not have enough space here to retread, step by step, Babeuf's evolution through each stage of the revolutionary process. But it is worth noting that his trajectory was far from straightforward. First, let us look at the young land surveyor's political projects. In 1789–92, he was engaged in an intense activity in Picardy as a militant for the abolition of feudal rights, with a proliferation of petitions and newspaper articles in the public arena. Between March 1790 and spring 1791, he wrote a long draft of a treatise entitled *Lueurs philosophiques* (*Philosophical Lights*). In this there is much to surprise the reader: its defence of a limited, but nevertheless irremovable, private property, and several rather radical anti-utopian professions of faith.[1] Here, Babeuf openly criticised the builders of castles in the sky, and the unreasonable desire to remake the entire social edifice, as he instead advocated an empirical and very cautious approach to political change. This is also

---

1   The manuscript of the *Lueurs philosophiques* (fund 223, no. 51, Russian Centre for the Preservation of Archives in Political and Social History (RGASPI), Moscow (henceforth *LPhi*). A total of 171 numbered pages in 8°; pp. 92–115 are missing), an unpublished text not previously consulted by any French researcher, has been the subject of a single published analysis by the Soviet historian Viktor Daline, in the volume resulting from his thesis: *Gracchus Babeuf à la veille et pendant la grande Révolution française, 1785–1794* (1976), Moscow: Éditions du progrès, 1987. Likely because of the political conditions in which it was written, Daline's work takes liberties with the text – to say the least – by giving the erroneous image of Babeuf as a lifelong collectivist. The *Lueurs philosophiques* will thus be the subject of a new scholarly study in the near future.

why we will not analyse its text in the present volume, which is, after all, devoted to the philosophical and political functions of utopia.

The Letters to Coupé de l'Oise (August–September 1791) and Republican Utopia

Given that this draft was marked by great moderation in its political and social outlook, the letters which Babeuf addressed to Coupé de l'Oise – written just a few weeks after the apparent conclusion to the drafting of the manuscript – would appear to represent a sharp reversal. Yet we can doubtless consider the evolution of the political situation responsible for such rapid changes in his thinking. The coincidence is even so clear that we may well wonder whether these events were not the direct cause of the author's abandonment of this theoretical project, which had now become obsolete. Indeed, the end of its drafting can be dated more or less to the moment of the flight of the king, who was arrested at Varennes on the night of 20–1 June 1791. This was immediately followed by the growth of a republican movement in Paris, which resulted in a flood of petitions addressed to the Constituent Assembly by popular clubs such as the Cordeliers and fraternal societies, which called for the king to be put on trial and the Republic proclaimed.[2] The mounting agitation of this sans-culotte milieu was of the greatest concern to the ruling elites of this first period of the Revolution. In these decisive weeks, a sharp opposition emerged between the Assembly, which remained resolutely monarchist, and popular Parisian opinion. The Jacobin Club suffered a split, leading to the exit of several hundred moderate members who went on to create the Club des Feuillants. The crisis flared until 17 July, when the democrats placed a republican petition on the Altar of the Fatherland on the Champ-de-Mars. The petition was declared contrary to the constitution and the law, and served as a pretext for brutal

---

2   On this point, see Pierre Serna, 'Comment meurt une monarchie? 1774–1792', in J. Cornette (ed.), *La monarchie entre renaissance et révolution, 1515–1792*, Paris: Le Seuil, 2000, pp. 417–23; Jacques Guilhaumou, *L'avènement des porte-parole de la République (1789–1792)*, Villeneuve-D'Ascq: Septentrion, 1998, Chapter 7: 'Le mouvement patriotique parisien et la formation d'un espace démocratique', pp. 155–67; Marcel Dorigny, entry 'Fusillade du Champ-de-Mars', in A. Soboul, J.-R. Suratteau, and F. Gendron (eds), *Dictionnaire historique de la Révolution française*, Paris: PUF, 1989, pp. 202–3.

repression: the Paris city hall proclaimed martial law and mobilised the National Guard against the crowd. After raising the red flag – the symbol of repression – La Fayette had his men open fire, resulting in over fifty dead. According to Marcel Dorigny, 'This drama had vast consequences: it brought an irreversible rupture within the Third Estate.'[3] Following hot on the heels of the rural movement against the vestiges of lordly rights, as well as the powerful wave of strikes that broke out in Paris in April–May 1791, this event accelerated a process which, according to Viktor Daline, tended to 'create an increasingly clear-cut demarcation between liberal and democratic circles'.[4]

Babeuf firmly belonged to the second of these two camps. In May 1791, after his release from Montdidier prison – where he had been jailed for his activities as leader of the movement in Picardy against indirect taxes (the 'aides et gabelles') – he joined the Club Populaire in Noyon. The shootings at the Champ-de-Mars made a strong impression on him. As he wrote in a draft speech in July 1791: 'This day ... will perhaps fix the most memorable period in our history, and on it may depend the eternal destinies of France.'[5] This event had thus alerted Babeuf to the differences between the liberal and moderate group, identified with the richest, and the radical democratic group, represented by the sans-culottes of the clubs and their leaders. This brought a profound shift in his thinking, which had hitherto been geared towards the search for a national consensus around the great principles of the Declaration of August 1789. This is the context in which we should understand the changes that can be seen in his two famous letters to Coupé, written between late August and mid-September 1791, just a few months after the *Lueurs philosophiques*.

Jacques-Michel Coupé de l'Oise was priest of the small parish of Sernaize, president of the directoire of the district of Noyon from 1790, and, from March 1791, also president of the Friends of the Constitution in this same location. He was a subscriber to the *Correspondant Picard*, Babeuf's newspaper during this period, and had doubtless looked kindly on the struggles that the latter had supported in the region. According

---

3   Dorigny, 'Fusillade du Champ-de-Mars'.
4   Daline, *Gracchus Babeuf à la veille et pendant la Révolution française*, p. 331.
5   Cited in ibid., p. 337.

to Maurice Dommanget, 'both read Mably together';[6] indeed, Babeuf reveals as much in a letter he addressed to him on 10 September 1791. The two men were thus very close, intellectually and politically, and Babeuf had high expectations of his friend's election to the Legislative Assembly, which was confirmed in the early days of September 1791. It can thus reasonably be assumed that Babeuf was writing to him in order to express the heart of his thought. He made this clear in the first words of his letter of 20 August 1791: 'I have a great secret in my heart and it is in yours that I feel the need to deposit it.'[7]

What, then, was the content of this 'secret', which Babeuf had likely conceived in the days or weeks before writing this letter? First of all, it concerned the author's desire to present his own candidacy – a desire he had forsaken because of the great number of enemies he knew he was surrounded by in the constituency, given his leading role in the popular movement. This did not prevent him from protesting his 'republican virtues' – thereby expressing his adherence to this political ideal, which was still in the minority, and which was evidently also Coupé's own. However, Babeuf's confession also had a political component, which lay in the revision of the constitution that he sought to advance. He wrote:

> The constitution must be a national patrimony, in which we find for the people both the bread of the spirit and the bread of the body, in which a stipulation for the complete intellectual and material life is not only clear, precise, positive, but also immediately sanctioned by setting in common all resources, indefinitely multiplied and augmented by means of a skilfully combined organisation and the wise direction of the general labour.[8]

This formulation marked the return of the idea of setting social resources 'in common' and the need for a clearly state-led organisation and direction of 'the general labour'. It was characterised by Dommanget as the 'definition of a socialist constitution'.[9] Claude Mazauric sees it as 'one of

---

6 *PCB*, p. 94.
7 Ibid., p. 103.
8 Ibid., p. 107.
9 Ibid.

the few "communist" allusions made by Babeuf during the Revolution'.[10] But are things really so clear as that? In reality, there persists a certain ambiguity. The expression 'set in common' could refer simply to social resources being placed in service of the common good by means of wise laws, without that necessarily implying the transition to collective ownership of resources. This could be the outline of an economy directed and controlled by the public authorities, of private property placed under tutelage but nonetheless maintained. Throughout his entire letter, Babeuf seems to be aiming for such a service to the common good. Rather than seeking a community of goods, it instead sets out two principles which, according to their author, tend to 'put into practice' the true 'equality of rights' such that it does not remain a dead letter, but is oriented towards 'a system of general equality'.[11] That is, equality would not only be formal, at the level of proclamations and political rights, but real, at the level of social rights. Two necessities are thus foregrounded: 'bread for all' and 'education for all', echoing the 'bread for the body' and 'bread for the spirit [*esprit*, hence also "mind"]' mentioned above. Babeuf justifies this twofold claim by adding: 'Who, then, in a village would suffer the common oven being pulled down or the filling-in of the well where everyone goes to get water?'[12]

We can interpret these lines as follows: the new political life to which France was summoned through the convening of a new National Assembly should lead to the constitution of a common good, like the common oven or the well in a village – wells or ovens that, we may note, do not totally replace the property of each individual but, rather, stand alongside it, implying an effort on the part of each individual to create and maintain them. The image is highly representative of the restricted and local scale at which Babeuf still envisaged the common good in this period. As for the national level, this common good lay in the guarantee of subsistence for all and in the implementation of a national education system. Babeuf's emphasis on education allows us to say that he did not understand equality only as an equal quantity of material goods dispensed to each person, but also as the condition through which one

---

10   Gracchus Babeuf, *Écrits*, selection of texts introduced, presented, and annotated by Claude Mazauric, Pantin: Le temps des cerises, 2009, p. 245.
11   PCB, p. 114.
12   Ibid., p. 107.

man can legitimately feel and think of himself as another's equal – and it is thus also a moral good. Education is necessary in order to enjoy this equality; it is education that provides the moral means, as Babeuf already explained in 1789, to maintain oneself at the same level as others in dignity, to protect oneself against possible attempts at domination, to exercise one's political rights, and, more broadly, to defend one's interests with full knowledge of the situation in which one finds oneself. Only this twofold aim can give real substance to the idea of equality, which will otherwise remain a dead letter. This, in turn, justifies the concrete measures that Babeuf would like to see Coupé pursue in the new Assembly. The new constitution must be a real 'national patrimony', capable of producing new men.

Thus, in his letter, bread and education were the general goals that Babeuf entrusted to the political representatives of the nation. Do such aims imply the community of goods? The following passage seems to provide some answers to this thorny question:

> You will no doubt find that I am moving forward well with my reform projects, but I am convinced that small changes will only be palliatives and that much innovation is needed, if the Revolution is to bear fruit. I have a good intuition of how far it should go, but perhaps prudence counsels that we proceed only by toothing-stones, without giving too much insight as to what the new social edifice will be. But it is very important that we seize every opportunity to move forward, one way or another, towards the true goal of the Revolution, an equality without falsehoods.[13]

Here, Babeuf points to the 'true goal' of the Revolution: equality in the full sense of the word – that is, an equality which is not limited to political rights but ensures the full exercise of these rights for all. This would demand that the minimal necessities of life are guaranteed (subsistence), that intellectual means are available to everyone (education), and that common rules are always conditioned by majority approval (sovereignty). But, while Babeuf did not want to stop at 'small change', in order to achieve this main goal he intended to move forward using 'toothing-stones' – referring to the stones

---

13 Ibid., p. 114.

through which one construction can be attached to another. Above all, Babeuf did not want to 'give too much insight as to what the new social edifice will be'. This expression would tend to confirm the assessments of Dommanget and Mazauric, insofar as it suggests that Babeuf did indeed have a plan for society that went beyond the proposals developed in the letter. But it should be remembered that at this stage – as Babeuf himself put it – he only had an 'intuition' of this plan. In place of it, he proposed measures to his correspondent which each tended towards 'equalisation' as a gradual process. To this end, he stipulated that only those amendments to the constitution that aimed at the 'extension' of freedom and equality should be adopted. Is this any coincidence? Everything seems to show that such prospects for a gradual approach towards an egalitarian ideal owe something to that developed by Mably in *De la législation*, which Babeuf and Coupé had reflected upon together. The major difference with this thinker, however, lay in the fact that the letter's author no longer considered the objective of the community of goods as part of the human past. He instead seemed to postpone it to an – albeit still very vague and hypothetical – future point towards which the Revolution 'should go'.

Here, therefore, we should acknowledge the essential change in status that the Revolution would appear – if the hypothesis inspired by Dommanget and Mazauric is correct – to have conferred on the utopian ideal of the community of goods, even if in a still very imprecise fashion. Indeed, as compared to the 1787 text, this ideal would begin to reappear in Babeuf's thinking not as a desirable, albeit distant, model, but as the final objective of the revolutionary process set underway in 1789. In such a perspective, the 'equalisation' measures advocated here should be understood as mediations interposed by Babeuf in the 'empty space' left by the utopians of the previous generation.[14] In this sense, Babeuf's thinking in this letter can be interpreted as a form of compromise between the utopian aspirations of the likes of Collignon, and the 'second' republican ideal outlined by Mably in *De la législation*. The abundance of goods for all is postponed *sine die* in favour of the

---

14 In a letter to Dubois de Fosseux in July 1787, Babeuf was enthusiastic about the ideas of the utopian Collignon, but deplored the fact that the latter 'left his means blank', and expressed the hope that he would still 'fill in' 'this empty space' (*OB*, p. 216).

immediate assurance of daily bread, but this is presented as one of the 'toothing-stones' that undoubtedly prepare a better future.

This is most clearly confirmed in Babeuf's letter of 10 September 1791. In it, he welcomed Coupé's election victory, which gave him great cause for hope. He here provides the key to the great means by which he thought it possible to achieve the real equality for which he yearned: namely, an agrarian law. These two words are repeated tirelessly throughout this long missive. The agrarian law is presented as the single goal towards which 'all the constitutions of the earth will tend, when they are perfected':[15] Babeuf had abandoned the empiricist method of the *Lueurs philosophiques*, attentive to variations in time and space, to rediscover the idea of a single way of resolving the social question for all humanity. But, for Babeuf, 'agrarian law' did not mean a simple redivision of the land. To his mind, it referred to the 'constitution of Lycurgus' – that is, to the inalienability of the soil, and to a 'new division' in each generation, which must be organised such 'that in being born each man must find his sufficient portion of [the land], as of air and water, [and] that in dying he must make its inheritor not those nearest to him in society, but the whole society'.[16] Thus, without owning the land outright, each individual would have a fund at his disposal in all circumstances, an 'unalienable resource in the face of [his] needs'.[17] Babeuf is very clear on this point: the inalienability of land is presented as a 'system which entirely destroys the objection coming from fears of the re-establishment of inequality by mutations' – that is, by changes which affect the fate of individuals from one family to another and from one generation to another, such as more or less children, or more or less developed talents in one or another person. Babeuf thus here rediscovered the ideal that he had already suggested, in a different key, in the 'Preliminary Discourse' to the *Cadastre perpétuel* in 1789, albeit with the distinction that this time he clearly presented it as an objective to be achieved. Moreover, to the demand for an agrarian law he added the – purely hypothetical – idea of an equal wage for all trades, for 'if some of them had not been assigned a value of opinion, all workers

---

15   *PCB*, p. 122.
16   Ibid., p. 124.
17   Ibid., p. 125.

would be about as rich as each other'.[18] Indeed, at the time, Babeuf intended to place not the entire economy under the regime of the community of goods, but the land alone. In the *Lueurs philosophiques*, taking up a Physiocratic principle, he said that 'in the last analysis [the land] provides everything, pays for everything'.[19] He thus counters the objection that setting goods in common would lead to a general sluggishness in production; for 'everything that is related to human industry would remain in the same state as today'.[20] By this, it should surely be understood that manufacturers and merchants could continue to conduct their business as in the past, except for the single wage that would henceforth have to be applied to all jobs. Babeuf does not elaborate on these issues, but it can be inferred from the reasoning in his *Lueurs philosophiques*, in which he had shown himself to be a fierce defender of the freedom of trade and industry. In other words, despite its radicalism, the agrarian law as such appears as a half-measure as compared to the idea of the global community of goods and work. Moreover, there is no longer any mention here of the joint working of the land, unlike in the draft letter of June 1786.

Babeuf himself claimed that he took the demand for agrarian law from Mably. But, at the time, such a demand was very much in the air. It was defended by the most radical speakers at the sans-culotte section of the Cordeliers in Paris and in certain clubs, such as the Cercle Social. The threat, made extremely concrete by the constant agitation in the countryside and the increasingly bitter struggle of the peasants against the remnants of lordly rights, would only grow during the Revolution. It eventually panicked the landowners and their representatives in the National Assembly, to the point that on 18 March 1793, the National Convention decreed 'the death penalty for anyone who proposes an agrarian law or any other law subversive of landed, commercial, and industrial property'.[21]

---

18   Ibid.
19   *LPhi*, p. 7. Babeuf must have read the famous entry 'Grains' in the *Encyclopédie*, written by Quesnay, where the following statement is made: 'It is agriculture that provides the material for labour and trade, and pays for both' (*Œuvres économiques complètes et autres textes*, edited by Christine Théré, Loïc Charles, and Jean-Claude Perrot, Paris: INED, 2005, vol. I, p. 183).
20   *LPhi*, p. 7.
21   See Jean-Jacques Clère, entry 'Loi agraire' in the *Dictionnaire historique de la Révolution française*, p. 681.

It should be noted, however, that, with this expression, the Swede of the dialogue *De la législation* had not intended – any more than the orators of the Revolution upholding this measured – to re-establish the property regime that prevailed in Sparta under the laws of Lycurgus. Indeed, he had stated that a return to such rules had become impossible. The Philosopher had instead advised that the laws of Rome be taken as inspiration, namely those 'which forbade the possession of more than one hundred acres of land', laws which were to '[hinder] the sale and alienation of property' without preventing it altogether.[22] Babeuf thus seems to have misinterpreted – deliberately or otherwise – the letter of the text from which he drew inspiration, as he turned the idea of a *limitation* of ownership rights into the *abolition* of such rights with regard to land. Thus, compared to the republican model proposed in *De la législation*, Babeuf's letter of 10 September 1791 takes a further step towards the community of goods. Such a perspective is presented by its promoter with characteristics that clearly belong to the utopian tradition. In particular, he writes: 'When we get to the agrarian law, I foresee that, like the Spartan legislator, this overly vast code will be put to the flames and a single law of 6 to 7 articles will suffice.'[23]

Here, we can recognise well-known traits, such as the assimilation of the future legislator Coupé to the great legislator who – on the model of Utopus – in just a few laws lays the foundations of the 'golden age', of 'social felicity', of a 'state of quietude extending over the whole future'.[24] But perhaps this faith in the legislator's work was also the product of Babeuf's reading of *The Social Contract*, and in particular of the famous Chapter 7 of Book II devoted to this very particular mission: 'it is neither magistracy nor sovereignty', says Rousseau.[25] In this respect, the utopian tradition here met with the doctrine of the philosopher whom all revolutionaries considered their patron. The reference that Babeuf makes to the legislator's necessary 'abnegation' is perhaps a reminiscence of the particular position that Rousseau assigns to this figure in his text, where he strips him of all constitutional power. Yet the appeal to this quality is such a

---

22   *DL*, p. 146.
23   *PCB*, p. 123.
24   Ibid., p. 125.
25   Jean-Jacques Rousseau, *The Social Contract and the First and Second Discourses*, edited by Susan Dunn, New Haven, CT: Yale University Press, p. 181.

commonplace of republican and utopian literature that it would be impossible to make such a claim. For this reason, it is difficult to say what the letter's author had truly drawn from the famous lessons of the citizen of Geneva. Yet, lacking the culture of the colleges, Babeuf probably borrowed the Spartan reference from Mably, just as he seems to have taken from him the idea of giving 'time for reflection' to the legislators, who ought to deliberate slowly in making their way towards the agrarian law.

Babeuf thus saw such a law as both the indispensable complement and the effective materialisation of the Declaration of the Rights of Man which had been proclaimed two years earlier. To his mind, this did not imply a break with the existing order, but rather the continuation of the revolutionary process towards the realisation of its principles, beginning with 'the reclamation of the first rights of man, consequently of bread honestly assured to all'.[26] In other words, with this letter, Babeuf demonstrated that he expected the institutions generated by the Revolution to fulfil the promises, if not of a utopia of abundance like the one he had found in Collignon, then at least of a more minimalist and austere version, inspired by the Spartan model via the mediation of Mably's dialogue. To Babeuf's mind, the Assembly, led by Coupé de l'Oise, could play the role of the legislator in the utopians' cities. This meant not settling for the ratification of the political rights that had now arrived, but rather assuring subsistence and, through it, the 'golden age' for all. This social ideal has obvious affinities with that of the Swedish Philosopher – even without being identical to it – and followed in line with the orientation of the 'Preliminary Discourse' to the *Cadastre perpétuel*. This position appears to have resulted from the evolution of the political situation. Indeed, insofar as it opened up greater possibilities for the realisation of reformist projects, it required their adaptation to the reality of present circumstances. Paradoxically, perhaps, the greater boldness on the practical level was accompanied by a greater sobriety in the political model proposed.

However, this letter can also be interpreted as a sign of hesitation or at least ambiguity between two social ideals. Through his ambitions for the inalienability of land and his enthusiastic reference to the laws of Lycurgus, Babeuf demonstrated his renewed attachment to a form of social community. This marked a reversal of the theses that appear in

---

26   PCB, p. 126.

the *Lueurs*, which asserted the inviolable right to property. However, other aspects of his projects show that Babeuf dreamed less of community than of equality between the citizens of the nation in revolution: wage equality, equal 'portions' of the soil allocated to each person for subsistence at birth, and equality in education. Such equality is presented as the main objective of all good policy. Compared to the common agricultural labour exalted in the utopian tradition, and even compared to Babeuf's own earlier writings, the inalienability of land here seemed to be part of a model less concerned with abolishing the distinction between yours and mine, or establishing bonds of affection and quasi-familial mutual aid between the members of a social whole forming a fusional community. Rather, it was more a matter of rendering to each person their own lot, without anyone being harmed. Here, we could speak of a 'distributive' ideal rather than a communitarian one such as we find in the great texts of classical utopia. Babeuf's social ideal in this period thus seems to be irrigated by the objectives of an egalitarian republicanism. This was surely inspired by his keen attention to the problem of subsistence, such as it was posed in the circumstances of the Revolution, but also, undoubtedly, by his reading, alongside Mably, of Rousseau, whose principles of popular political economy have already been mentioned, and indeed by his reading of the democratic Parisian press. In this period, the 'communitarian' tone dominant in the utopian tradition was not very present in Babeuf, even if it had not disappeared completely. Compared to Mably, who clearly renounced the community of goods in favour of egalitarianism, the position upheld by the letters to Coupé appears to be in tension between equality and community.

Jacobinism and Utopianism

Nonetheless, it is worth making clear that adherence to the republican ideal did not itself imply renouncing all forms of utopianism. The vocabulary of the golden age and faith in the virtuous legislator also belonged to other republicans of the same period, for instance to the Jacobin Boissel or to Saint-Just in his *Institutions républicaines*.[27] François

---

27 Saint-Just, *Institutions républicaines*, in *Œuvres complètes*, Paris: Gallimard, 2004, pp. 1085–147.

Hincker has already emphasised how much the discourse of the revolutionaries in general – of the Montagnards in particular – was imbued with utopia, and Bronisław Baczko has clearly highlighted the role of utopian 'idea-images' in revolutionary mentalities. This, even though not every republican discourse should ipso facto be considered utopian, nor even every discourse advocating the community of goods.[28]

Nevertheless, utopianism became especially influential at the moment when, with the final collapse of the monarchy, the republican idea triumphed. This idea thus naturally came to encompass all aspirations for social and political regeneration. In this period, stretching roughly from autumn 1792, with the proclamation of the Republic, to July 1794, the time of Robespierre's downfall, Albert Soboul has highlighted the flowering of more or less utopian reform projects in the sans-culotte sections, generally aimed at restricting the right of ownership and equalising fortunes and enjoyment. Thus, an anonymous pamphlet of January 1793, *Le gâteau des rois* (*The Cake of Kings*), declared the destitute to be the 'imprescriptible co-proprietors' of the rich man's property; one citizen had the Fédéré section adopt an *Essai sur les moyens d'améliorer le sort de la classe indigente de la société* (*Essay on the Means of Improving the Lot of the Poor Class of Society*), in which he imagined the sale of the former royal castles in order to provide interest-free loans for those who wished to set up a 'small establishment'.[29] The utopian aspect of all these projects lay in the fact that they expressed the desires of their author – and their imaginary reforms – without ever contemplating the method of their realisation. However, they were sometimes adopted by the sections as real projects, without any concrete action following from this. They constituted the daydreams of sans-culotterie, with aspirations

---

28 François Hincker, 'L'effet d'utopie de la Révolution française', *Matériaux pour l'histoire de notre temps* 9: 1, 1987, 2–7. This is also the view of Jean-Marie Goulemot, who writes: 'By the virtue attributed to it, the *Declaration of the Rights of Man and the Citizen* resembles the foundational gesture of a Utopus or a Sevarias. The abolition of privileges did not go without mentioning the rejection, always present in Utopia, of the errors of the past . . . It is therefore possible to locate, in the politics that became organised in 1789, the traces of the foundational Utopia' ('Utopies pré-révolutionnaires et discours règlementaires: le cas de Resif de la Bretonne', *Revue européenne des sciences sociales* 27: 85, 1989, pp. 93–102, at p. 95).

29 Cited by Albert Soboul, 'Utopie et Révolution française', in J. Droz (ed.), *Histoire générale du socialisme*, vol. I: *Des origines à 1875*, Paris: PUF, 1979, pp. 195–256, at p. 204.

towards equality rather than community, and in turn leaving an 'empty space' regarding the means for their realisation.

Moreover, several decades before Johnson Kent Wright, Soboul had already referred to the ideal of social democracy upheld by the ruling Montagnards between spring 1793 and summer 1794 as a utopia. He based this judgement on Saint-Just's famous utopian fragments written during this period, the *Institutions républicaines*. This text, which was doubtless mostly written during spring 1794, simultaneously constituted, as Miguel Abensour put it, 'an attempt to give form, before it was too late, to the conquests of Jacobinism'.[30] Even if it was not intended for publication, it can thus be read as the utopian expression of the political and social model which had been upheld by one of the main representatives of Jacobin republicanism since his rise to power.

In the republican ideal outlined by Saint-Just, it is necessary

> not to divide the fields, but to determine the maximum and minimum of the property, so that there may be land for everyone, and that the members of the sovereign, free by an illusion, may not in fact slaves of to basic needs.[31]

Here, we can observe an approach very similar to Babeuf's, in Saint-Just's desire to ensure the enjoyment of a portion of land by each citizen – in turn linked to the idea that this is the indispensable means of achieving freedom and political rights, which would otherwise remain an 'illusion'. In addition to this fundamental principle, everyone was to be obliged to work: every proprietor over age twenty-five, who had no trade and was not a magistrate, was obliged to cultivate the land until he was fifty, and idleness was to be punished. In the fields of child education, largely inspired by antiquity and particularly Sparta ('Children are rigorously accustomed to laconic speech: they must be forbidden games in which they declaim, and accustomed to the simple truth');[32] human affections ('Every man of twenty-one years of age is obliged to declare in the temple who his friends are and this declaration must be renewed

---

30 Miguel Abensour, 'La philosophie politique de Saint-Just', *AHRF* 38, June–August 1966, pp. 341–58, at p. 357.
31 Saint-Just, *Institutions républicaines*, p. 1131.
32 Ibid., p. 1101.

each year during the month of Ventôse');[33] the elderly ('Men who have lived without reproach all their lives will wear a white scarf at sixty years of age');[34] and, finally, the festivals that punctuate the year – in all this, we find the inspiration of the great utopian texts, adapted to an egalitarian ideal that leaves a limited but continued place for property. This is clearly signalled by the ritualisation of collective life, its transparency, and the emphasis on the necessary harmony embodied by friendship, here erected as a social imperative. Moreover, *Institutions républicaines* shows the essential link between the specific measures taken by the Montagnards in favour of poor citizens in Year II, and an overall political project for an egalitarian, social republic. The equal sharing of inheritances among children, aimed at ensuring the fragmentation of fortunes, passed by the Assembly in winter 1793–4; the division into small lots of immigrants' properties destined for sale, as passed on 3 June 1793; the sharing of common goods; the famous decrees of Ventôse Year II (March 1794) by which the assets of suspects were to be handed to poor patriots; the establishment of national fêtes and in particular that of the Supreme Being; and, finally, the nationalisation of assistance and the creation of free primary schools, all fit into this perspective, within the wider framework of a genuine project for the Republic.[35] To the author of this project, *Institutions républicaines* doubtless appeared to be the goal of this entire policy.

But it is no accident that this project was expressed in terms of the utopia of a natural agricultural economy – nor that Saint-Just wrote it down and kept it to himself in a moment when he was also seeing the gradual disintegration of the momentum that had brought him and his comrades to power. This had indeed led him to the observation: 'the Revolution is frozen'.[36] For Soboul, the utopia of *Institutions républicaines* is the product of the same internal contradictions of Jacobinism which also led to its failure. Torn between the ideal of the small independent producer with a mediocre fortune and adherence to the free play of economic laws, which they continued to want to maintain in commercial exchanges; between the need to legislate in favour of the

---

33   Ibid., p. 1102.
34   Ibid., p. 1104.
35   On this point, see Soboul, 'Utopie et Révolution française', pp. 222–3.
36   Saint-Just, *Institutions républicaines*, p. 1141.

fragmentation of fortunes and the inexorably inegalitarian evolution of market society – forced to choose, the Jacobins were unable to do so. In reality, the ideal of the 'egalitarian republic' stood in conflict with the embrace of the principles of the 'liberal economy'. Hence, the tension between the demands of equal rights, proclaimed in principle, and the consequences of the principle of property ownership could only be resolved in the imagination, at the level of utopia. Abensour also notes this, in his own way, when he writes in connection to Saint-Just's manuscript that ' "Utopia", in the sense of an expression of the limits of possible consciousness in a given society, is located at the point of collapse of a political action that suddenly reveals itself to its author as impossible.'[37]

It was thus the 'impossibility' of reconciling irreconcilable demands that led the author of *Institutions républicaines* to gradually replace real legislative activity with a simulacrum of regulation for a republican France, which was condemned to remain a pious wish. In this particular case, recourse to utopia should be understood as the expression of a retreat from reality, a flight of thought to a level where social and political aspirations could still find satisfactory expression. According to these two commentators, Saint-Just's utopia thus returned to the function that had been assigned to this genre in earlier times. A discrepancy opens up between the measures taken by the ruling Comité de salut public and the ideal evoked in Saint-Just's manuscript, which represents much more than their point of arrival. For, like his utopian predecessors, Saint-Just neglected to determine the mediations that would lead to it. Perhaps mounting a retreat when faced with the difficulties of a statesman, Saint-Just like others before him left 'an empty space' where his means of action should have been.

Written later on in the revolutionary process, *Institutions républicaines* nonetheless reveals an older and more fundamental tendency of Jacobin republicanism: it gives a complete and systematic picture of what had emerged in the manner of simple formulas in the speeches of 1793 and 1794, and thereby gives a sense of the decrees that were actually promulgated. No doubt written in order to clarify for the author's own benefit the true nature of his hopes, this text constitutes – despite or rather because of its utopian character – the precise plan of what would have to remain vague aspirations in the minds of certain actors of this period.

---

37 Abensour, 'La philosophie politique de Saint-Just', p. 357.

These considerations on Jacobin utopianism perhaps help to explain Babeuf's usually positive fascination with the work of Robespierre, which is particularly notable, through his correspondence from 1793 onwards, in the recurrent comparisons he makes between the Incorruptible and Lycurgus.[38] Indeed, after moving to the capital at the end of 1792, Babeuf became a 'true sans-culotte': he associated with the radical republicans of the Club des Cordeliers as well as prominent personalities or leaders of the popular movement such as Menessier, Sylvain Maréchal, and Garin.[39] It was thanks to these contacts that he obtained a position within the Paris Commune, in the administration of provisions, which he held until his arrest in October 1793, caught up in a case of forgery and the use of forgeries which had followed him from Picardy. During this period, Babeuf thus played the role of an objective and perfectly willing transmission belt – if we may be allowed this expression – of the egalitarian socio-economic policy under the Terror.

This doubtless also explains the depth and the character of Babeuf's disappointment, however fleeting, at the end of 1794, when he discovered and vigorously denounced the Vendée War and the massacres that had been committed. He offered a highly original interpretation of these developments as a perverted desire to apply his own version of the agrarian law, but through means that had become immoral. He read the decimation of the Vendéens and the parallel decimation of the

---

38 See the letter to Anaxagoras Chaumette of 7 May 1793: 'But you, however, Robespierre, who precisely defined property, who traced the limits within which this right must be tightened to prevent it from being pernicious to the great social majority . . . Come, you are our legislator. And you, Jacobins! . . . Come and stand beside our Lycurgus – you are his adjuncts and his esteemed co-operators' (*PCB*, pp. 143–4). Or again, at the end of 1794, *Du système de dépopulation*: 'Maximilian and his council had calculated that a true regeneration of France could only take place by means of a new redistribution of the territory and of the men who occupy it. They appeared convinced that the regulators of a people have done nothing stable and solid for its regeneration . . . if . . . they have not, like Lycurgus in Sparta, assured the inalienable domain of each individual and his sufficient portion of food, guaranteed on all suitable combinations, even that of the calculation of proportion between the population and the total amount of produce of the soil' (Gracchus Babeuf, *La guerre de la Vendée et le système de dépopulation*, presented by R. Sécher and J-J. Brégeon, Paris: Cerf, 2008, p. 116. However, from Mazauric onwards, there have been major reservations as to the scholarly quality of this edition.)

39 Mazauric, in Babeuf, *Écrits*, p. 50.

republican troops as a monstrous attempt to 'sacrifice' a certain number of citizens in order to combat population surplus and thus allow those who remained to finally enjoy the necessities of life. Babeuf, even in his indignation, thus understood the Vendée War as one of many steps along the road to 'drawing all property under the hand of the government', for the purposes of ensuring its enjoyment by the surviving citizens,[40] much like other measures which he listed in this passage, such as the maximum flour price or the confiscation of emigrants' property for the benefit of poor patriots. This 'egalitarian nightmare'[41] – this dystopia where aspirations for common happiness were turned against themselves – paradoxically shows that Babeuf undeniably long shared in the ideas of republican utopianism, making his own an egalitarian ideal close to that of several Jacobin leaders.

Popular Sovereignty, a School of Equality

In the 'Preliminary Discourse' of 1789, Babeuf made no reference to the events that had led to the establishment of the national Constituent Assembly. The new power was regarded as an established fact; and all he considered here was the job now incumbent upon it, in bringing forth the public 'felicity'. The text thus left aside the issue of what had made the birth of such a decision-making body possible and legitimate – a question which nevertheless conditioned the fact that decisions along the lines desired by Babeuf could now be adopted and respected. So, what kind of transition had the French entered into in 1789? Was this a new beginning, opening up an entirely new time in which all manner of innovations were permitted? Or was this a transition between the old and the new that was bound to remain gradual? And, in the latter case, what limits and deadlines were to be set? These questions concerned the source from which the new decisions could now draw their legitimacy. After, all, it was from such a source that the possible limits to the will to reform could also be deduced. Were there still institutions from the past to be respected, old regulations that had remained in force or, on the

---

40   Babeuf, *La guerre de la Vendée et le système de dépopulation*, p. 117.
41   Ronan Chalmin, 'La République populicide: relire *Du Système de dépopulation* de G. Babeuf'', *Dix-huitième siècle*, 43, 2011, pp. 447–68, at p. 460.

contrary, needed to be reactivated? The *Cadastre perpétuel* was evasive about these questions.

At the time that Babeuf wrote the 'Preliminary Discourse', the culturally dominant schema for interpreting the meaning of the establishment of a new power, and the commitments it made to those it administered (a schema that Babeuf also shared), was already a contractualist one. This is, naturally, found in this text, which made reference to 'political association' to back up the legitimacy of egalitarian demands regarding taxation,[42] and in which the 'social pact' was asserted as a means of 'tending to make disappear what is defective and unjust in natural laws'.[43] But what was the real status of such a pact? Was it past, present, or perhaps still in the future? Did the commitment that bound deputies to the nation reactivate an old contract which had been covered up by centuries of history – or did it correspond to the emergence of a new type of bond? Here again, the text remained ambiguous.

Progressively, from 1791 onwards, Babeuf made increasing reference to the principle of popular sovereignty. Although linked to the social contract, at least since its conceptualisation by Rousseau, this was nonetheless a distinct principle. But in what regime of historicity would this sovereignty unfold? In what circumstances and at what intervals should it be exercised? What was its role in the process of political innovation? Was this a principle of conserving pre-existing (because natural) rights, or did it open up new prerogatives for the people, in view of the circumstances?

We know that, in Rousseau, sovereignty appears essentially to be a means of popular control over the laws that govern their collective existence – and, when they are represented by others, over deputies who can be no more than agents of the people's will.[44] The earliest expression of this control was the permanent vigilance of the people, guarantor of respect for the social contract. This theme was taken up many times during the Revolution, where Rousseauism 'became by force of circumstance a mass ideology'.[45] But the question of popular sovereignty

---

42 *OB*, p. 372.
43 Ibid., p. 373.
44 See on this point Books I and II of *The Social Contract* as well as the *Considerations on the Government of Poland*, where the Genevan deals with the question of representation.
45 Claude Mazauric, 'Le rousseauisme de Babeuf', *AHRF*, 34, 1962, pp. 439–64, at p. 439.

concerns temporality also in other ways. One problem that conditions sovereignty, from this perspective, is that of its institution. When can and should the people's vigilance begin to be exercised? How can such practices, such habits guaranteeing that decisions live up to the principles of association, be developed and introduce a rupture in the historical process? In what precise forms can the general will declare itself for the first time? Upon an initial analysis, it first manifests itself upon the conclusion of the pact itself, under the pressure of necessity which calls for an end to the state of war. As Rousseau writes in another text, the body politic results from 'a single act of will, and *its entire duration is but the continuation and effect of a previous commitment*, the force of which ceases to act only when this body is dissolved'.[46]

The single inaugural act of the common will must, then, ensure the continuity of the period that follows it. This reveals a particular quality of the time to which the contract gives rise: for the contract must perpetuate, over the longer term, the conditions of the initial commitment. Such a time must be entirely shaped by the provisions of this agreement. But the energy that drives this new collective rhythm is not produced by the social contract itself, or at least not by it alone. In Rousseau's words, while the contract gives the body politic 'existence and life', it still lacks 'movement and will'.[47] The real institution of the people thus begins in the moment *following* the contractual moment, during which the organic laws of the state are drawn up and voted upon. The latter are, strictly speaking, 'the conditions of civil association'. As we have seen, this is the stage when the figure of the legislator intervenes.

The legislator's temporal ambiguity is immediately apparent in the fact that this figure is connected to the peoples of the past, with the evocation of great examples from ancient times (Lycurgus, Moses, Romulus), whereas the contractualist schema, based entirely on the will of the contracting parties, instead presupposes a break with tradition. As Binoche has shown, the legislator's role thus intervenes not only in the historicity of the *contract*, insofar as it alone allows the latter to produce laws fundamental to the body politic, but also in the time of *history*, which is still largely understood in terms of its edifying function

---

46 Jean-Jacques Rousseau, 'Fragments politiques', in *Œuvres completes*, vol. III, p. 485. Emphasis added.

47 Rousseau, *The Social Contract*, p. 178.

and, as such, repetitive. Finally, the legislator figure also concerns the time of *civilisation*.[48] Indeed, while the genesis of the contract introduces a discontinuity, through the moment of institutional foundation, and seems to be situated outside of history, civilisation instead defines 'the trajectory that every nation is called upon to follow in its own time, so long as circumstances . . . do not prevent it from doing so'.[49] In this sense, civilisation is progressive and continuous. It is also the legislator who civilises his people by shaping their mores by legislative means. The legislator thus derives his unique status from the fact that he superimposes at least three regimes of historicity at once:

> On the one hand, in fact, it appears in the genesis of civil society and it draws its necessity from the fact that the people is still a multitude . . . On the other hand, the Legislator is a figure of civilisation and he draws his necessity – an only initial and provisional one – from the fact that the people is still only 'being born'.[50]

In fact, upon the legislator's intervention, we discover that the people, which was thought to have emerged from the state of nature through the conclusion of the pact, is once again considered 'a blind multitude, which often knows not what it wishes'.[51] It is quite incapable of undertaking a system of legislation by itself, since it is not yet prepared for this task. The legislator must suggest laws to the people, which it is to approve, even though it is not yet in a position to grasp their true scope. He must preside over the transformation of those who – after all, and despite the pact – still lead 'the independent and physical existence which we have all received from nature' into partial beings, members of a political whole that raises them up to morality and rationality.[52] The legislator must teach the people to 'know what it wants' and enlighten its judgement. It is, indeed, through laws that the people becomes what it ought to be, and what it cannot be until these laws are established: the drafting of laws by the legislator is thus, in the full sense of the term, a

---

48 See Bertrand Binoche, 'Genèse, histoire et civilisation dans le *Contrat social* de Rousseau', in *La raison sans l'Histoire*, Paris: PUF, 2007, pp. 29–52.
49 Ibid., p. 32.
50 Ibid., p. 44.
51 Rousseau, *The Social Contract*, p. 180.
52 Ibid., p. 181.

civilising work, which is difficult to reconcile with the idea of the foundational role of the contract itself.

The sovereignty of the people, as discussed by Rousseau, is thus temporally inscribed in a second way, which stands opposed to the figure of perpetual vigilance. For this sovereignty to be established, it must pass through a phase in which it is combined with the individual action of a man (or group of men) who sees further ahead, historically speaking, than the people, for these men foresee what the Republic's future rules of operation can and must be. The moment of the establishment of the general will is, in this respect, the moment when it must be left up to itself as little as possible. This is the moment when the civilising and politicising action of he who knows how to remember and anticipate can intervene effectively. Only then can the exercise of the people's rights assume a regular and autonomous form. Here, it should be emphasised that Rousseau clearly does not see the sovereign people as a force for innovation per se; rather, on its way to the full and regular exercise of its fundamental rights, it must be guided by a founder. It is thus the latter figure who opens the people's way to its own future. But, on the whole, the figure of the legislator condenses difficulties more than it resolves them. This figure does not articulate the respective regimes of historicity of contract and civilisation, but rather superimposes them. And is it not inconsistent to consider the people mature and rational enough to enter into the contract and place itself under the direction of the general will, but too primitive to work out by itself the conditions for exercising this will?

Still, to contemporaries' eyes, the outbreak of the Revolution could legitimately be seen as a practical – historical – illustration of Rousseau's remark that

> we sometimes find, in the history of States, epochs of violence, in which revolutions produce an influence upon nations such as certain crises produce upon individuals, in which horror of the past takes the place of forgetfulness, and in which the State, inflamed by civil wars, springs forth so to speak from its ashes, and regains the vigor of youth in springing from the arms of death.[53]

---

53 Ibid., p. 184.

From this point of view, 1789 can be perfectly translated into Rousseauian terms as the moment when the people was not yet mature enough to enact laws of its own, but had reached the point of seeking a new legislation. The Revolution thus clearly posed concrete problems to Babeuf, as it did to many others, largely overlapping with the ones that hung over Rousseau's reasoning. When and how would it be possible to enlighten the general will that had begun to manifest itself? What means could lead it towards the adoption of just and good laws? If popular consent was necessary to make laws effective, how was it possible to ensure that – breaking from the habits of the past – the people would accept and embrace the new legislation?

Babeuf built on Rousseau's reflections on the adaptation of proposed laws to what the people is able to 'bear'. Right from the beginning of the Revolution, we have noted already, Babeuf introduced the idea of transitional stages between the present state and the ideal one. The problem of the right moment can thus be tackled by way of a progressive temporality. At what distance from the present state should the proposed laws be situated, so that they can secure popular approval even as they direct the people towards the other laws that must follow?

The letters to Coupé, two years after the 'Preliminary Discourse', still fitted into the perspective of a gradual improvement of legislation, relative to the work of the first assembly. Babeuf intended that the second legislature should be 'just as constituent as the first'.[54] With these words, he signalled his disapproval of the terms of the first constitution, passed on 3 September 1791. The most notable point of his argument, however, is that, contrary to what is stated in the 1789 text, it is unreservedly based on the principle of popular sovereignty:

> If it suits one generation to make itself a slave, this does not at all alter the right of the next generation to be free, . . . a people always has the unalterable and imprescriptible right to change and modify its constitution, to ratify or disapprove everything that its representatives do in its name.[55]

Throughout the letter, Babeuf's desire to set the decisions of the Assembly under a close and systematic popular control is clearly stated:

---

54 *PCB*, p. 110.
55 Ibid., p. 111.

> The people's veto is de rigueur ... The assembly must not take any decision or pass any law that cannot be annulled by the people. It is not even master of its own discipline, and the provisions of its rules must have been submitted to the people and have won its consent.[56]

This is a major shift from the *Lueurs philosophiques*, where 'the sovereignty of the people [was limited] to the power to declare its will through representatives it [chose]'.[57] The people is now called upon to systematically monitor not only the decisions of the Assembly, but also the procedures by which decisions are made. But how are we to explain such a change?

It seems that Babeuf shifted his perspective on the effects of the people's exercise of sovereignty. Instead of seeing the exercise of sovereignty as the simple expression of its immediate interests, he now imagined that the practice of sovereignty would lead the people beyond the mere assertion of its basic needs, and towards the formulation of political and social solutions to the fundamental problems it faced. He wrote: 'From this veto of the People, should we not expect that there will be demanded by its suffering part – [the one] hitherto forever exposed to this cruel feeling of hunger – an assured patrimony: an Agrarian Law?'[58] The people is thus able to move from the 'hunger' that so plagues it to what Babeuf conceives as the only social institution able to put a definitive end to this same problem: the 'agrarian law'. Babeuf means agrarian law in his own particular sense, partly linked to his utopianism. The means to ensure this transition lay in the people's broadest possible participation in political life. Babeuf foresaw that the extension to all of the right to vote and to be elected, the possibility for all to give their opinion in all assemblies, freedom of assembly, and finally the admission of all into the National Guard, would produce 'the extreme emulation, the great spirit of liberty, of equality, of civic energy' that should spontaneously lead to the demand for the agrarian law.

Thus, in Babeuf's eyes, the people is able to enlighten itself. He is so convinced of the intrinsic necessity of the solution that he proposes to social inequality that he foresees that the people, once in full possession

---

56 Ibid.
57 *LPhi*, p. 46.
58 *PCB*, p. 126.

of its political rights, will spontaneously and inevitably assert its social prerogatives in this exact form. The link that he establishes between the assertion of these new political arrangements, and the outcome he predicts for them, is the principle of equality which they underpin. Starting with the equal exercise of political rights, the people will reach the conclusion that they also need an equal exercise of the right to subsistence and the enjoyment of the soil. Equality of political rights leads in stages to 'real equality'. This idea is expressed even more clearly with regard to the need for universal admission into the National Guard. Babeuf intended the army to become a school of equality; he tellingly wrote:

> I understand how difficult it would be to secure the sudden acceptance of a general system of equality, but now that equal rights have been admitted, if they are not to be a pure deception it is indeed necessary to begin by putting them into practice somewhere.[59]

Because the army 'owns nothing' of its own and is maintained at the state's expense, and given that, in principle, equal conditions prevail among ordinary soldiers, this institution can represent an introductory school of egalitarian relations in a society where the state is the eminent owner of the land cultivated by each family. Hence the need to introduce within the army the reforms that are indispensable for it to become the wellspring of the new social relations: namely, the appointment of all leaders by majority vote and equal pay for all ranks. This is obviously similar to the idea suggested by Mably in his *Des droits et des devoirs du citoyen*. In this specific case, as in that of political rights in general, the common idea is to gradually introduce egalitarian practices, in order to gradually convert minds to equality in all areas. Within this perspective, the (again asserted) importance of the principle of universal education points in the same direction. It seeks to convince each citizen that they are the equal of any other, and to provide them with the means to move from this *conviction* as to their own dignity to the *demand* for equitable material conditions.

Not only the people needed an apprenticeship in equality; but the deputies in the Assembly also needed to be accustomed to new political

---

59 Ibid., p. 114.

habits, in order to lead them to the inevitable conclusion of passing the agrarian law. But the measures that would move them in this direction were not exactly of the same nature as those most suited to the people. Within the Assembly, it was essential to ensure that the committees were abolished, so that its debates might be followed by all, and there would be 'time for reflection' on each question. In this way, Babeuf obviously sought to allow the 'defenders of the people' among the representatives to address all the others, in conditions which would not favour 'improvisers', 'phrase-mongers', 'the absent-minded', and those 'who always speak before they think'.[60] If the object of the people's political apprenticeship must be equality, it would seem that its representatives need above all to learn to weigh their decisions, and to listen to the wisest among their own ranks. Here, again, Babeuf seems to be convinced of the persuasive power of these representatives' ideas of equality, among those who are thus fully at leisure to listen to their arguments. The triumph of the solutions he envisaged for society's future seemed assured, provided that the conditions for serene reflection were in place: the irresistible force of their rationality, and their ability to settle old and crucial problems once and for all, seemed to Babeuf to be sufficient grounds to win universal support. The optimism of the Enlightenment is here given its most fully political sense.

Babeuf's strategy had thus changed considerably compared to the writings of the period from the start of the Revolution up until spring 1791. He no longer considered that the Assembly should be the sole promoter of the new institutions under the people's watchful but unenlightened eye. Rather, he now imagined a joint evolution of representatives' legislative work and popular vigilance, which would become enlightened as it went along. Moreover, Babeuf was convinced that the eventual advent of the 'agrarian law' would be the natural conclusion of the revolutionary process; he considered that conscience of this need should come both to the people in its schools of equality – the political assemblies, the army – and to their representatives, as instructed by the supporters of equality seated among their own ranks. Babeuf was not alone among his contemporaries in this political confidence in popular intervention, or indeed in his ambitions regarding the agrarian law. His political viewpoint was, in fact, consonant with that of the Paris radical

---

60 Ibid., p. 126.

revolutionary newspapers which we find abundantly quoted in his archives, Prudhomme's *Révolutions de Paris* and Marat's *L'Ami du peuple*.[61] More specifically, in Babeuf's writings in this period, we can see the intuition – more suggested than clearly expressed – of an immanent development of the logic of the Revolution, which would progressively broaden the application of the principle of equality and finally bring it into the most fundamental domain, that of the enjoyment of land. It can thus be said that, from this moment onwards, Babeuf identified the immanent sense of the revolutionary process with that of his own struggle. In this, he went further than most of the leading actors of his time.

---

61 On this point, see Daline, *Gracchus Babeuf à la veille et pendant la Révolution française*, p. 262.

9

The Conspiracy of Equals: Utopia as a Programme

The Genesis of the Conspiracy

We have said that, up until October 1793, Babeuf was a conduit for the Jacobin policy on subsistence. His silence in prison until the end of the Reign of Terror forbids us from assessing the development of his ideas in this period. But the events following the fall of Robespierre clearly did accelerate his political evolution. His initial anti-Robespierre attitude and the hopes placed in the new strongmen of the National Convention did not last. In his *Journal de la liberté de la presse,* which became *Le Tribun du peuple* on 5 October 1794, he was the spokesman for the sufferings and demands of the Parisian sans-culottes, and became increasingly critical of the new authorities. The period would go down in history as a time of bourgeois reaction, both violently anti-Jacobin and anti-liberal.[1] The Constitution of Year III, adopted on 22 August 1795, established the property qualification for suffrage, reducing the people to political silence. More broadly, this was a time of repression of the popular movement and the enrichment of a privileged layer of the Revolution, even as difficulties in the bread supply

---

1   On this point, see Françoise Brunel, *Thermidor: La chute de Robespierre*, Brussels: Complexe, 1989; Albert Mathiez, *La réaction thermidorienne*, text presented and introduced by Florence Gauthier and Yannick Bosc, Paris: La fabrique, 2010; Michel Vovelle, *Le tournant de l'an III, Réaction et Terreur blanche dans la France révolutionnaire*, Paris: Éditions du CTHS, 1997.

threatened the very survival of the urban popular classes, particularly in Paris.

It was following a fresh jail spell between 25 Ventôse and 24 Fructidor Year III (15 March–10 September 1795) that Babeuf's social and political ideal really took a new turn. For the first time, his political trajectory broke free from the main ideological currents of the Revolution, and in particular from the strictly egalitarian aspirations of sans-culotterie and Jacobin republicanism. Babeuf took the path of radicalisation and direct action for the realisation of an *avant-la-lettre* collectivist programme, thereby taking utopia to its very limits.

This change is perceptible in the correspondence that *Le Tribun* maintained with fellow prisoners, whom Babeuf had met during this recent jail spell and who would soon become members of his conspiracy. This first and foremost meant Charles Germain, a former hussar officer who avidly read Mably, Rousseau, Diderot, and Helvétius, and who was roused by the prospect of the triumph of 'pure Equality'. This period was likely the moment of Babeuf's discovery of the *Code de la Nature*, which powerfully contributed to the transformation of the publicist's thinking.

In a letter to Charles Germain dated 10 Thermidor Year III (28 July 1795), we find entirely new ideas flowing from Babeuf's pen. The people's tribune began by speaking out against commerce, 'traffic without modesty, without entrails and without faith'; and by invoking, following his correspondent, the example of Lycurgus, who was said to have banished commerce from his republic.[2] The reference came from Babeuf's traditional arsenal, but its content did not: previously he had not taken anything from the Spartan legislator other than the agrarian reform making the soil inalienable. So, this theme was new, as was the presentation of the relationships that ought to replace commerce in the 'regenerated society'. Indeed, in the new framework that Babeuf outlines for his correspondent, 'everything must be equilibrium and compensation', which is only possible if 'all agents of production and manufacture' work 'for the common storehouse'.[3] This is Babeuf's first known mention of such an institution. If it is likely, and can be seen from other indicators, that he got the idea from Morelly, it may seem curious that he

---

2   *PCB*, p. 211.
3   Ibid., p. 210.

The Conspiracy of Equals: Utopia as a Programme

was not inspired earlier in this sense by his reading of Mably, in whom it is already present.

Let us venture a hypothesis, here: the idea of a common storehouse had not attracted Babeuf's attention up to this point because it was not linked to anything in his own professional and political experience, which had, instead, essentially confronted him with the realities of social relations in the countryside and led him to fight against lordly rights and indirect taxation. But in the meantime, in 1793, he had worked as a secretary in the Paris subsistence administration – and, here, he himself took part in the establishment of a public institution for surveying needs and supply sources, and the organisation of the requisition of flour and its transporting and distribution among a large population. This experience obviously altered and broadened his vision of social relations: it gave him the intuition of a possible use of state means in the service of the ideal of community of goods and a fair distribution of resources. This development confirms, in its own way, what Pierre-François Moreau sums up in his *Le Récit utopique* when he remarks that utopias, which tend towards the rational and meticulous organisation of all aspects of social life under the leadership of the state, are the 'spontaneous ideology of the jurist or administrator'.[4] As an autodidact learning as he went along, it was indeed by becoming an 'administrator' that Babeuf moved from an essentially rural and antiquated conception of the community of goods, limited to the community of the land, to a conception of the community liable to encompass all kinds of 'either agricultural' or 'manufacturing' industry, and to organise exchanges according to a rational survey of production.[5] Indeed, Babeuf foresaw that 'everything shall be appropriate and proportionate to present and anticipated needs according to the probable and readily ascertainable growth of the community'.[6] This remarkable synthesis of a bookish culture and a direct confrontation with political problems did not only concern the questions of the common storehouse and the distribution of resources. It is perceptible at all levels. It can be seen in Babeuf's fusion of two ideals between which he had sometimes seemed to

---

4 Pierre-François Moreau, *Le récit utopique*, Paris: PUF, 1982, p. 100.
5 *PCB*, p. 211.
6 Ibid., p. 212.

hesitate – that of egalitarianism, present both in Rousseau or Mably and in Jacobin republicanism, and that of the community, which Babeuf had encountered above all in his readings, and which corresponded to his first aspirations. From this perspective, it is no accident that to the idea of harmony or unity, specific to the utopianism of a Morelly or even a Mably, he preferred the concept of 'equilibrium and compensation'. The 'universal fraternity' is based on the following condition, stated in a striking formula: 'there must be happiness for all, equally distributed among all'.[7] Here, happiness itself is conceived as a quantifiable good that must be distributed equally among the members of the association. The ideas of the 'fusion between all professions' and a 'great national family' are constantly associated with tightly organised distribution, 'equal food', and 'perfect equality'. It seems to be a sine qua non condition of community and brotherhood that everyone should receive a strictly identical share of the overall product from the public administration. This levelling conception of the community of goods, paradoxically, goes hand in hand with the idea of the development of science, art, and industry, seeming to indicate a certain hesitation on Babeuf's part between 'economic pessimism'[8] – inspired by both a concrete situation of scarcity in revolutionary France and the republican ideal of frugality – and hopes, perhaps borrowed from Morelly, of technical progress that would spare men their hardships and bring abundance. In particular, the idea that 'if I have invented a machine, a process that simplifies and shortens the toil of my craft ... I will hasten ... to communicate it to the association and to deposit it in its archives so that no one will ever have to deplore having lost it'[9] seems taken straight from a meditation on the fourth 'law of police' in the *Code de la Nature*, which stipulates that 'in each profession, he who discovers some important secret will make it known to all in this body'.[10]

On the other hand, when it comes to the idea that 'the association' should assign young people the jobs it needs doing in order to guarantee the necessities of life for all, it is impossible to distinguish what was due

---

7   Ibid., p. 210.
8   See Jean Dautry, 'Le pessimisme économique de Babeuf et l'histoire des utopies', *AHRF* 33, 1961, 215–33.
9   *PCB*, p. 213.
10 *CN*, p. 155.

to utopian influence or else to the lessons of the administration of provisions. The obligation to work is one of the three 'fundamental and sacred laws' of the *Code de la Nature*; but the *levée en masse*, and the rapid courses the young Republic provided to train workers in the manufacture of saltpetre, may just as well have inspired Babeuf in this sense. Similarly, the care of children, the infirm, and the elderly at the expense of the community may have come from Morelly's sixth 'police law' ('The infirm and the aged will be comfortably housed, fed, and maintained in the public house devoted to that purpose').[11] But it may also result from Babeuf expanding upon the law of 22 Floréal of Year II (11 May 1794) which had nationalised assistance, opening a 'book of national beneficence' instituting medical assistance in the home, pensions for the infirm and elderly, and relief for the mothers of large families.[12]

Some of Babeuf's reflections are less ambiguous: with specific regard to the revolutionary experience itself, he argued that the *levée en masse* of Year II had shown that the Republic could withstand the mobilisation of a part of its youth without agriculture suffering as a result. Conversely, when he stated that the penal code would have no offences to punish other than 'the attack on equality through non-work', he was surely not drawing inspiration from policy under the Terror; rather, it is likely that he derived from elsewhere this idea of utopian sobriety in penal legislation.[13] More particularly, he probably drew it from the *Code de la Nature*, which wanted these laws to be 'as few as the prevarications'.[14] We can even say that, as he outlined his model of society, Babeuf was more consistent than the writer who inspired him, for he implicitly stated that crimes would disappear in such a just society. He remained aligned with the first essay of the *Code de la Nature*, which predicted that, in the society built on community, 'idleness, inaction, would be the only vices, the only crimes, and the only opprobrium'.[15] Unlike the 'plan of ideal legislation' – but in conformity with the lessons of the rest of the text – the people's tribune did not foresee the continued existence of

---

11   Ibid., p. 156.
12   See Albert Soboul, 'Utopie et Révolution française', in J. Droz (ed.), *Histoire générale du socialisme*, vol. I: *Des origines à 1875*, Paris: PUF, 1979, pp. 195–256, at p. 223.
13   *PCB*, p. 215.
14   *CN*, p. 171.
15   Ibid., p. 57.

individuals so denatured that they would kill or injure another member of the association. Lastly, it was certainly not from the experience of the revolutionary war, but rather from a utopian limbo, that Babeuf drew his hope that 'the circle of humanity' would grow 'closer and closer' and that 'borders, customs and bad governments' would one day disappear altogether.[16] To this end, he advocated that all commercial relations with other nations should be suspended, but that foreigners 'be admitted to enjoy the spectacle of our felicity so that, upon returning to their homelands, they may bring there a beautiful desire for imitation'.[17]

It is in this same design for achieving universal adherence through example and goodwill that Babeuf proposes offering other nations the 'superfluities' produced by association and accepting from them only 'what they should like to send us'. This kind of exchange of gifts is doubtless taken from Morelly, who, in his twelfth distributive law, stipulates:

> If the nation aids a neighbouring or foreign nation with the products of its country or is aided by them, this trade alone will be done through exchange and through the intermediary of citizens who will report everything in public.[18]

The new idea, in addition to what the *Code de la Nature* proposes, lies in a kind of proselytising which is no more than sketched out at the level of relations between nations, but which is discussed far more seriously within national borders. Babeuf sought to convince his correspondent, who favoured a *coup de force* to build the society of which both men dreamed in their prison cells, of the need to use other means. This raises a problem that Morelly left unaddressed, but which would represent a long-standing preoccupation of Babeuf's: how to achieve the projected social ideal in practice? Babeuf based his hopes on the force of conviction, as carried by example. He thus imagines that they would

> win over to our principles at first only a small area ... As far as possible, we seek to place ourselves in a population centre where minds are in general favourably disposed to us. Once established in this centre,

---

16   *PCB*, p. 212.
17   Ibid., p. 217.
18   *CN*, p. 151.

we have no difficulty in making our doctrines felt there. The first trials of our institutions are enthusiastically requested and welcomed by numerous ardent proselytes. They exalt them, and the inhabitants of neighbouring territories, drawn along by the example, are not slow to come to us.[19]

Significantly, this programme outlined by Babeuf is called his 'Vendée plébéienne' plan. In his *Système de dépopulation*, we have seen, the people's tribune had conceived of the Vendée as the testing ground for the Montagnards' social and political programme. It is this same case – a negative ideological symbol, but an example of the relative autonomy of a province separated by its own political choices from the rest of the country – that allows him to think of the idea of a revolutionary centre that would win over the whole country. Thus Babeuf moved from the idea of a focus of resistance to that of a centre of expanding ideological influence.

Babeuf's plebeian Vendée is the opposite of an island cut off from the rest of the world: it illustrates, in its own way, the transformation that the Revolution imposed upon utopian ideal.

In fact, Babeuf's letter opens the way for two distinct tactics. The idea may indeed have been to win over the country through propaganda and example, and to do so from a base that, although small, was firmly devoted to the cause. This is the interpretation proposed by Maurice Dommanget, who emphasises: 'Let us again note the kinship between this utopian conception and the Phalansterian and Icarian attempts that would be made a few decades later, at the time when Babeuf's wife was still alive.'[20] But it is also possible that Babeuf imagined taking power by force in a part of the country supposedly inclined to offer little resistance, and then spread this power to the rest of France. On this reading, his outlook at this point represented in outline the plan taken up by the Conspiracy of Equals, set up in Paris less than a year later. This is the interpretation suggested by Mazauric, who sees in this the prefiguration of the 'oil spot' strategy adopted by the Chinese Communist Party before the 1949 Revolution.[21]

---

19 *PCB*, p. 219.
20 Ibid., p. 206.
21 Gracchus Babeuf, *Écrits*, introduced by Claude Mazauric, Pantin: Le temps des cerises, 2009, p. 315.

So, it seems that, in this period, Babeuf was at the crossroads, in between a propagandist and proselytising road that would be taken up by the utopians of the following century (and which had already been evoked in the *Système de dépopulation*) and a conspiratorial or insurrectionary path, which would later become his own. But it should be emphasised that, at this stage, several paths still seemed open. These were each the fruit of meditation on the revolutionary experience, in its force of conviction, its capacity to achieve what had seemed impossible only a short time earlier, but also its errors and its failures.

The Plebeians' Manifesto

More immediately, upon his release from prison Babeuf seemed to take the path of conviction, or of 'evangelisation', as he put it in the prospectus of his *Tribun du peuple*.[22] In this introductory text, he declared the objective of this periodical's various issues: namely, to expound the goal of society and of the French Revolution, as proclaimed by the Constitution of 1793: the 'common happiness', an objective which he would ceaselessly uphold.

In Babeuf's writings, this expression is partly of strategic use: inherited from Rousseau, who uses it in *The Social Contract*,[23] it appeared in the first article of the Declaration of the Rights of Man in 1793 ('The goal of society is the common happiness'). In citing this article, Babeuf undoubtedly sought to confront the legislator with his responsibilities and to remind citizens of their legitimate demands, in accordance with the objective stated by the constitution in its preamble: the constitution should allow 'the people to always have before its eyes the bases of its liberty and happiness; the magistrate the rule of his duties; the legislator the rule of his mission'. More precisely, Babeuf was trying to awaken the

---

22   *TP*, 'Prospectus', II, p. 4.

23   'The better constituted a State is, the more public affairs outweigh private ones in the minds of the citizens. There is, indeed, a much smaller number of private affairs, because the amount of common happiness makes each individual more prosperous, and less remains to be sought by individual exertion': Jean-Jacques Rousseau, *The Social Contract and the First and Second Discourses*, edited by Susan Dunn, New Haven, CT: Yale University Press, 2002, p. 221, translation edited. The common happiness is here directly linked to civic devotion to the affairs of the city.

energy and the mobilising capacities of the Parisian sans-culotte milieu, among whom the memory of the social policy of Year II remained very much alive. But this expression also appears in Morelly, in the first essay of his *Code de la Nature*, in a context that has to do with social affections.[24] Once again, Babeuf seemed to blend the different sources of inspiration for his ideals, as he detailed in a few emphatic words the content of his periodical's subsequent issues: 'the comfort and happiness of all individuals, the unalterable felicity of all members of the association, a state of stable happiness, the sufficiency of the needs of all'.[25] Here, the people's tribune summons up the accents of a Collignon or a Restif; but he is no longer addressing the legislators, but the 'Plebeians', in order to commit them to the path of the grandiose social reformation he has in mind.

On 9 Frimaire Year IV (30 November 1795), Babeuf publicly revealed his project in issue 35 of *Le Tribun du peuple*, which contained the 'Manifeste des Plébéiens'. According to Babeuf, the views found therein were nothing other than those of 'democracy itself'.[26] He then used a striking expression, at a time when the call for the immediate application of the Constitution of 1793 served as a rallying point for the whole left wing of the popular movement:

> Those who believe that I am only agitating to substitute one constitution for another are mistaken. We need institutions much more than we need constitutions. The Constitution of 93 only merited the applause of all upstanding people because it prepared the way for institutions.[27]

This call for the advent of 'plebeian institutions' must be taken as prevailing even over the constitution itself. Was this a transformation of the traditional utopian theme of a small number of laws – the importance of which was now downplayed in favour of an emphasis on the well-regulated organisation of everyday life? This is most certainly the case, as the rest of Babeuf's writings would demonstrate. However, this theme

---

24 *CN*, p. 54.
25 *TP*, 'Prospectus', II, pp. 3–4.
26 Ibid., no. 35, II, p. 83.
27 Ibid., no. 35, II, p. 84.

inevitably brings Saint-Just to mind. His entire collection of fragments on the *Institutions républicaines* is devoted to this question, but he also widely publicised these concerns, for example exclaiming in his 'Rapport sur la police Générale du 26 germinal an II' (15 April 1794):

> Form the civil institutions, the institutions that have not yet been at all thought of: there is no lasting freedom without them. They sustain the love of the fatherland and the revolutionary spirit even when the revolution has passed.[28]

Abensour has shown how, for Saint-Just, the institutional project had to be understood as an attempt to go beyond the Terror and towards a positive organisation of the Revolution.[29] The goal assigned to the institutions is to 'moralise' individual and collective life in a republican manner, to substitute virtue for terror. Saint-Just thus sought to shape individual and collective psychology, to produce a 'republican way of life', to replace repressive measures by not only punishing acts, but reforming mores. Hence, in the fragments, we of course find the institutionalisation of education, which is explained in particular detail, but also that of practices such as friendship ('Every man of twenty-one years of age is obliged to declare in the temple who his friends are'[30]) as a means of maintaining the ferment of the social bond that holds the community together and, moreover, of human relations in general ('Those who fall out are obliged to explain the reasons for it before the people, in the temples').[31]

It is striking to note, in contrast, that, in Babeuf, the institutions are exclusively concerned with the improvement of everyday life and the guarantee of a sufficient material condition for that segment of the people that is deprived of them. It would seem that, as utopia became a political programme, it gave a less central place to morality. Education

---

28   Saint-Just, *Œuvres complètes*, Paris: Gallimard, 2004, p. 763.
29   See Miguel Abensour, 'La théorie des institutions et les relations du législateur et du peuple', in *Actes du colloque Saint-Just*, Paris: Société des Études Robespierristes, 1968, pp. 239–90, and 'Lire Saint-Just', introduction to Saint-Just, *Œuvres complètes*, especially pp. 88–97.
30   Saint-Just, *Institutions républicaines*, in *Œuvres complètes*, p. 1102.
31   On this question, see also Marylin Maeso, 'Réformer le peuple français: la création du citoyen révolutionnaire et les institutions révolutionnaires dans les oeuvres de Saint-Just', *La Révolution française* 6, 2014, online: https://journals.openedition.org/lrf/1093.

was indeed mentioned, but in essentially negative terms, which contrast with the more positive characterisations we see elsewhere in the writings of the people's tribune; in particular, he had approved of Michel Lepeletier de Saint-Fargeau's plan, read to the Convention by Robespierre in 1793 and strongly inspired by the public education of the ancients.[32] This was also the model for Saint-Just's *Institutions républicaines*. Here, Babeuf writes only

> that education is a monstrosity, when it is unequal, when it is the exclusive patrimony of one portion of the association . . . that social institutions must therefore lead to such a point that they deprive every individual of the hope ever of becoming richer, more powerful, or more distinguished by his enlightenment, than any of his equals.[33]

Hence, there is a shift of perspective compared to Saint-Just's utopia. If the aim were indeed to define those institutions liable to generate a 'republican way of life', this would no longer be based on a spiritualist conception of social relations that considered virtue to be the foundation of the social edifice. For Babeuf, the organisation of concrete living conditions would serve as the basis for relationships free of all subjection and oppression. The programme would thus set out essentially economic measures. The people's tribune now rejected the agrarian law: 'One would, with reason, tell us that the agrarian law can last only a day; that from the day after its establishment, inequality would again be encountered.'[34]

We can observe that, from this point on, Babeuf would counterpose the agrarian law against the 'de facto equality' experimented with in particular by the 'great tribune Lycurgus'. Notably, to this effect, Lycurgus was given the same title as the author of the Manifesto, who thereby identified himself with the great Spartan legislator. With this expression he refers to the sharing of the land, and the insufficiency of this measure.

---

32 Lepeletier de Saint-Fargeau's plan for national education, inspired by the ancients, envisaged raising all children in common in order to equalise conditions and introduce young people to the school of citizenship at an early age. It is reproduced in *Une éducation pour la démocratie, textes et projets de l'époque révolutionnaire*, presented by Bronisław Baczko, Geneva: Droz, 2000, pp. 345–82.

33 *TP*, no. 35, II, pp. 104–5.

34 Ibid., p. 82.

To ensure 'sufficiency' for all, Babeuf instead advocates a 'common administration', which implies

> the abolition of private [*particulière*] property; the attachment of each man to the talent, to the industry that he knows; the obligation upon him to deposit the fruit of [this labour] in the common storehouse; and the establishment of a simple administration of distribution, an administration of subsistence, which will keep a register of all individuals and of all things, will have these latter distributed in the most scrupulous equality, and will have them deposited in the residence of each citizen.[35]

It is worth noting the conciseness of this formulation, summarising in just a few lines the programme that Babeuf had detailed to his correspondent Charles Germain in his letter from a few months earlier. In this long article, brimming with quotations and arguments, the more strictly constructive part is extremely brief. Unlike traditional utopians, Babeuf did not elaborate on his real plans; it is as if it would suffice to outline their guiding principle. One likely reason for this is the evocative power that the expression 'administration of provisions' had for contemporaries. This term referred to the revolutionary institution of which Babeuf was one of the agents, and which was responsible precisely for realising – albeit temporarily, and only for flour – some of the tasks that the people's tribune would now like to generalise to all production across France. The author of the Manifesto spoke allusively, and did so to a readership that he, doubtless, believed had been educated, like he had, by the Revolution. This is why he writes:

> That this government, shown to be practicable by experience, since it is the one applied to the twelve hundred thousand men of our twelve armies (what is possible at a small scale is possible at a large scale); that this government is the only one from which universal, unalterable, unalloyed happiness can result.[36]

Thus, to exert his force of persuasion, it was enough for Babeuf to bring to his readers' attention the image of reality itself. The 'common

---

35   Ibid., p. 105.
36   Ibid.

happiness' would be nothing more than an extension of the institutions set up by the Revolution and rendered possible by it. This was the sense in which Babeuf's utopia was presented by its own author as a simple addition to the Revolution, a continuation or expansion of the work that had already begun.

Furthering the Revolution

In making this call for more of the Revolution, Babeuf sought to reverse the course of events since Thermidor. For the people's tribune, the evolution of the situation amounted to a 'de-revolution' process. His perspective thus amounted to going back to the crossroads represented by 9 Thermidor Year II – the date of Robespierre's arrest – in order to give fresh impetus to political and social egalitarianism. Perhaps surprisingly, this call for a further revolutionary effort is reminiscent of another formulated in the same period – that is, the one invoked by the Marquis de Sade in *Philosophy in the Bedroom*. He, too, spoke of taking another step in a revolutionary direction. Yet this similarity obviously encompasses two very different ways of conceiving the progress of a Revolution and the way in which it should be 'finished'.

There are unambiguous indicators of how far the 'effort' expected by Sade stood opposed to that which Babeuf called for. From the very first issues of *Le Tribun du peuple*, the tribune had in fact vigorously denounced the scandal of a policy decided *in the boudoir* by the Thermidorians:

> Frenchmen! You have returned to the reign of the harlots; the Pompadours, the Du Barrys, the Antoinettes are alive again; it is to them that you largely owe all the calamities that beset you and the deplorable retrogression that is killing your Revolution . . . Why keep silent any longer about the likes of Féron, Tallien and Bentabolle deciding the fate of human beings, lying limply on the eiderdown and the roses, next to the princesses?[37]

This aristocratic debauchery and luxury, denounced by Babeuf, provided the context in which the Sadean pamphlet was read, and also left its

---

37 Ibid., no. 29, I, p. 273.

mark on the ideas discussed therein. *Philosophy in the Bedroom* thus sealed the alliance between the nobility, represented by Madame de Saint-Ange and her brother Dolmancé, and the power of money, as embodied by Eugénie, daughter of 'one of the richest merchants in the capital', standing apart from and sheltered from the people. In this sense, the pamphlet is a theoretical extension of the practice of class egoism that the whole dialogue portrays. As against Babeuf's Manifesto, the text can thus, in many respects, be read as a Thermidorian utopia, given the ideological presuppositions on which it rested as well as the direction which it sought to give to French politics.

First of all, Babeuf mounts a symmetrical denunciation of the old monarchy and Jacobinism in the person of the 'decemvirs', of 'the infamous Robespierre'.[38] However, as Michel Delon reminds us, the 'Thermidorian policy was characterised by the continuation of the anti-monarchical and anti-feudal struggle at the same time as the anti-Montagnard reaction'.[39] In this text, there is no shortage of allusions to current political events, all of which supported the actions of a government to which Sade owed his escape from the guillotine. But there is more. In this pamphlet, we find the assertion of the formal equality which – as Babeuf so denounced – is perfectly compatible with de facto inequality. As an illustration of this position, Augustin, who is called upon to participate in the orgy as an underling, is excluded from the political reflection and discussion.

Moreover, we know that, in its desire to found the rules of the new economic game, Thermidorian discourse defended the 'freedom' to possess and a competition unshackled from the fetters of the system that had reigned under the Terror. Similarly, in the pamphlet, the apologia for an egalitarian but untamed liberalism – one in which the desire of each individual is legitimised with the risk of unleashing the war of all against all – spontaneously produces both dominant and dominated, indeed in the radicalised form of executioners, thieves, rapists, murderers, and their victims. When Sade calls for the softening of sentences, what is he advocating if not the limitation of state intervention in the

---

38 Marquis de Sade, 'Yet Another Effort, Frenchmen, If You Would Become Republicans', in *Justine, Philosophy in the Bedroom and Other Writings*, New York: Grove Press, 1971, p. 301.

39 Michel Delon, 'Sade thermidorien', in M. Camus and P. Roger (eds), *Sade: Écrire la crise*, Paris: Belfond, 1983, pp. 99–117, at p. 102.

relations among individuals? Essentially, we can consider Sade's programme of liberation of individual desire and libertinism – along with all that this liberation entails in terms of violence exercised against others – as the transposition onto the sexual and impulsive level of the Thermidorian liberation of economic and political relations.

The further revolutionary effort advocated by Babeuf essentially pointed towards pushing the Jacobin policy of correcting inequalities beyond its present limits, towards the radical abolition of inequality in general. But equally, 'one can only read Sade's argumentation as a move towards the limit of Thermidorian discourse', a justification of political liberalism, in which the notions of the individual and of property enter into contradiction.[40] The unlimited right of appropriation and enjoyment does away with the protection of persons and property. The utopia sketched out by the pamphlet turns into a dystopia, or, perhaps more simply, a parody. Sade's republic is doomed to the struggle of all against all, in the quest of each to sate their despotic desires. Unlike the republic which Babeuf calls for, it is devoted to permanent insurrection. It is thus consumed in an endless, compulsive, and repetitive subversion.

Conversely, Babeuf seems to think, or to want to have people think, that 'common happiness' would be at the forefront of the next popular uprising, which would also be the last. In describing it, he uses terms that betray a vision of a society that is undoubtedly much more richly textured than the few lines quoted above would suggest:

> This government will do away with bounds, hedges, walls, locks on doors, disputes, trials, robberies, murders, all crimes; the courts, prisons, gibbets, punishments, the despair caused by all these calamities; envy, jealousy, insatiability, pride, deceit, duplicity, in short, all the vices.[41]

Yet this – once again, negative – formulation no longer resonates with the tone of utopia, but of apocalypse. Here, the radical negation of all that exists must be connected to what Babeuf had foreseen a few pages earlier:

---

40   Ibid., p. 105.
41   *TP*, no. 35, II, p. 105.

It is thus revealed to us that, while new Joshua will fight one fine day in the plain, without needing to make the sun stop, several, in place of a legislator of the Hebrews, will be on the true plebeian Mountain. There they will trace, under the decalogue of eternal justice, the decalogue of holy humanity.[42]

Therefore, Babeuf did not hide the eschatological content of his hopes, which are in line with Jacob Taubes's remarks on the possible link between apocalypticism and revolution:

> If revolution were to mean only replacing an existing society with a better one, then the connection between apocalypticism and revolution is not evident. But if revolution means opposing the totality of this world with a new totality that comprehensively founds anew in the way that it negates, namely, in terms of the basic foundations, then apocalypticism is by nature revolutionary.[43]

The people's tribune presented the society that he advocated both as one of 'common administration', in accordance with the utopian tradition and the revolutionary experience, and as the radical and definitive negation of the entire old order, the essential destruction of everything that characterised the old world. This would tend to equate the revolt for which he called with a social and political Last Judgement – as he himself seemed to recognise. This tone is especially curious given that Babeuf had abjured Christianity some years earlier and had, in this same Manifesto, criticised Jesus for not having preached equality between men clearly enough.[44] This shows the resurgence within Babeuf's thinking of deep-seated tendencies of the popular revolts of the previous centuries. But it is also necessary to consider that, in doing this, Babeuf's thought enacted a 'transfer of the sacred'.[45] The advent of the new order

---

42 Ibid., p. 101.
43 Jacob Taubes, *Occidental Eschatology*, Stanford, CA: Stanford University Press, 2009, p. 9.
44 *TP*, no. 35, II, p. 191.
45 The expression is from Béatrice Didier, 'Statut de l'utopie chez Gracchus Babeuf', in A. Maillard, C. Mazauric and É. Walter (eds.), *Présence de Babeuf : Lumières, Révolution, communisme, Actes du Colloque international Babeuf, les 7, 8, 9 décembre 1989*, Paris: Publications de la Sorbonne, 1994, p. 46.

consecrates humanity itself, in its equality and finally recovered freedom. This is the advent of the religion of Equality written in the 'Book of Times and Destiny'; and in the passage just quoted, it is indeed a biblical anti-narrative that is being delivered.

Babeuf thus found himself in an ambiguous position. He reactivated the old myth of the End of Time by giving it a political, secular form. But is that not the very nature of utopia?

The Anthropology of the Plebeians' Manifesto

What conception of man corresponds to the new social and political ideal promoted by Babeuf? He gives some indications in issue 35 of *Le Tribun du peuple*. In order to back up his discourse on the authority of his predecessors, here he gives particular importance – through the sheer length of the citation – to quoting an article by the former Montagnard deputy Armand de la Meuse, which had been published in Pierre-Jean Audoin's *Journal Universel* on 26 April 1793. Clearly, he adopted its argument as his own.

In his predecessor's speech, a distinction was established between equality of rights and effective equality among men. Much like in the argument that Babeuf himself had expounded in the 'Preliminary Discourse' a few years earlier, for Armand de la Meuse, men were not equal in the state of nature. They are differently endowed 'in strength and instinct'; but these variations in natural aptitudes do not alter the equality of rights, which is 'a gift of nature, and not a beneficence of society'.[46] In particular, nature offers each person 'an equal right to the land and its produce', though it is not specified whether this 'right to the land' should be understood as a right to possession of the land or only as a right to enjoy its fruits.[47] It is thus up to the social institutions established by the pact to compensate for natural inequality, so as to guarantee each person the respect of their rights, and to artificially establish the effective equality which is, in fact, nothing other than the practical realisation of equal rights. In the state of nature, the equality of rights is only virtual, because the law of the strongest instead prevails: it is, therefore,

---

46   *TP*, no. 35, II, p. 193.
47   Ibid., p. 194.

up to society to give concrete expression to an equality among men which exists only potentially.

It is well known that those who are weak by nature will become the poor of the civil state, unless there are good laws to counterbalance the handicap that afflicts them. These laws must therefore limit the use of the right of ownership. Such rules are the condition of a legitimate civil state. To refuse to adopt them is thus to 'call men back to the exercise of the rights of nature' – that is, 'to cause the dissolution of the body politic'.[48] This was how, in 1793, Armand de la Meuse justified the insurrectionary activities of the Parisian sans-culottes as their claiming their right to existence. Such reasoning, in making equality of condition the very object of the social pact, obliges the legislator to remedy the most blatant abuses, on pain of seeing all the common rules called into question by those who find they have no personal stake in them.

It is not hard to understand how Babeuf could take up such a discourse as his own. The idea that social laws can aim to compensate for natural inequalities by limiting the claims of the strongest – or, rather, as he put it later in the article, of the most 'intelligent', who use their abilities to deceive and rob the people – was present in his writings even in 1789. In some ways, it was even present as early as 1786, when he asserted that technical progress could and should make it possible to compensate for women's physical weakness compared to men. But it should be remembered that, in these early writings, the natural rights of all had only been used to insist that the large landowners should make some corresponding offer to the community, in the form of employment or a tax contribution. At the time, there was no question of directly challenging the legitimacy of this type of property itself. Armand de la Meuse's text remains imprecise as to the nature and extent of the limitations to be placed on property rights. In contrast, in the following paragraphs of the *Tribun du peuple* article, Babeuf writes:

> We shall prove that everything that a member of the social body has below the sufficiency of his needs of every kind and every day, is the result of a spoliation of his natural individual property, made by the hoarders of common goods.

---

48   Ibid., p. 195.

That by the same token, everything that a member of the social body has above the sufficiency of his needs of every kind and every day, is the result of a theft from the other co-associates, which necessarily deprives a greater or lesser number of them of their quota of the common goods.[49]

Thus, with unprecedented clarity, Babeuf defines 'natural individual property' as the 'quota' which each person can legitimately claim 'of the common goods'. Any excess taken in relation to this share immediately leads to the deprivation of another member of the community, within the framework of a production of goods that is thought to correspond strictly to the sum of all 'undivided natural properties'.[50] This excess is therefore always illegitimate. Such a definition of natural property is very close to the one Mably gives in the *Doutes proposés aux philosophes économistes* of 'movable property', as 'the right to provide for one's subsistence'.[51] As in Mably, this makes it possible to reject the naturalness of unmovable property – that is, real estate.[52]

But Babeuf goes further than Mably, insofar as his definition of individual natural property in fact excludes any other type of property. It allows him to deny the slightest legitimacy to large-scale property, which inherently despoils others, and even to the ownership of land or any other means of producing resources in general, since all property is deemed to be 'common' before each person takes their share from it. In this sense, the community of goods appears to be the condition of the natural right to individual property. In such a system, the notion of property loses its current meaning. From being a right of appropriation, which separates the person who enjoys it from all others, it becomes a right common to all, calculated in relation to the needs of all and to all the resources produced by the collective.

---

49 Ibid., pp. 202–3.
50 Ibid., p. 203.
51 *DP*, p. 30.
52 Formulated in this way, Babeuf's definition of natural property is also close to the one given by Brissot before the Revolution: 'property is in fact only the right to make use, or the actual use, of material to satisfy one's needs; it is thus this satisfaction of needs which is the aim and the cause of the right to property itself' (Jacques-Pierre Brissot de Warville, *Recherche philosophique sur le droit de propriété et sur le vol, considérés dans la nature et dans la société*, in *Bibliothèque philosophique du législateur, du politique, du jurisconsulte*, Berlin, 1782, vol. VI, p. 277).

'The Elixir of the Social Contract'

Thus, no one has the right to take more from the 'products of nature and labour' than their personal needs require. Babeuf not only denies that property in real estate is 'natural', but also excludes the possibility that it could ever constitute a legitimate social right – an assertion which he had previously refrained from making. In saying this, the author (paradoxically) claims to be taking up what he calls 'the elixir of the *Social Contract*', borrowed from the famous note in Chapter 9 of Book I of Rousseau's text: 'For the social state to be perfected, it is necessary that all should have enough, and that none should have too much.'[53]

Thus, for Babeuf, the essential lesson of Rousseau's major text lies in an aspiration to social sharing that is comparable with, if not identical to, his own. Babeuf obviously had every interest in putting *The Social Contract* at the service of his own arguments, given the prestige enjoyed by the citizen of Geneva during the French Revolution. The reading of Rousseau's text that he here proposes is clearly a limiting one, above all because, despite its complex and contradictory character, the theory of property expounded in this famous chapter does not openly question the right to property. However, it is quite possible that some of the arguments developed in this chapter may have informed Babeuf's own rejection of property rights. The first of these is the idea that 'the State, with regard to its members, is master of all their property by the social contract, which, in the State, serves as the basis of all rights.'[54] The idea of the total alienation of each individual and all their possessions to the community may have seemed to point in the direction of a real appropriation by the public authorities of individual assets and, in particular, land.[55] Babeuf may have drawn inspiration from this argument, even though Rousseau also adds at the end of the chapter: 'The unusual feature of this alienation is that the community, in receiving the

---

53   *TP*, no. 35, II, p. 191.
54   Rousseau, *The Social Contract*, p. 167, translation altered.
55   Rousseau himself comments on this passage in *Émile*: 'If the sovereign power rests upon the right of ownership, there is no right more worthy of respect; it is inviolable and sacred for the sovereign power, so long as it remains a private individual right; as soon as it is viewed as common to all the citizens, it is subject to the common will, and this will may destroy it' (*E*, p. 425). Hence, Babeuf's solution was not incompatible with the letter of Rousseau's doctrine, but was indeed one of its possible versions.

property of individuals, so far from robbing them of it, only assures them lawful possession, and changes usurpation into true right, enjoyment into ownership.'[56] In a move quite typical of revolutionaries who drew on Rousseau's writings, even when Babeuf directly cited *The Social Contract*, he prioritised those proposals most in line with his own beliefs. From this perspective, he could also look approvingly upon the thesis that 'every man has by nature a right to all that he needs'[57] – and, of course, upon the famous note which he rather imperfectly cites, in which Rousseau denounces the 'bad governments' under which 'laws are always useful to those who possess and injurious to those that have nothing'.[58] The people's tribune thus enlists the citizen of Geneva in his fight for collective property, a move that Rousseau would probably not have endorsed, but which also reveals the difficulties of his position. His stance, seeking to establish the right to property by placing it under sovereign protection, but also to criticise its extension beyond what is 'naturally necessary' for each man, was, from the outset, open to the most opposite interpretations.

The final issues of *Le Tribun du peuple* thundered with attacks on the right to property, 'one of the most deplorable creations of human error', which gave 'birth to all the other vices, to all the passions, to all the crimes, to all the sorrows of life, to all kinds of evils and calamities'.[59] In his polemical vigour, Babeuf brings to mind the notes of the *Code de la Nature as* well as the *Second Discourse*, from which he quotes the famous formula: 'You are lost if you forget that the fruits belong to all, and the earth to no one.'[60] He thus asserted himself as the heir of the critique of property rights, as expressed in the writings of some of the representatives of the Enlightenment in the second half of the eighteenth century – but also as the first to deduce from this philosophical and moral critique the need to act on a properly political terrain, for the real abolition of this property. In opposition to the state of property, the state of community or association appears to be 'the only just, the only good one, the only one that conforms with the pure sentiments of nature'. Its 'return' – since this is indeed a return and not

---

56 Rousseau, *The Social Contract*, p. 169.
57 Ibid., p. 167.
58 Ibid., p. 169.
59 *TP*, no. 35, II, p. 237.
60 Ibid., p. 238.

a conquest – is made necessary by the very excess to which the abuse of property rights has led. Babeuf thus ended his theoretical journey with the call for the abolition of social property relations, recovering the natural rights of man through the reactivation of the original social contract. But this would only be possible if the people made recourse to its right to resistance.

The Conspiracy of Equals

The months following the publication of issue 35 of *Le Tribun du peuple* were devoted to the preparation of a *coup de force* – something that Babeuf had earlier rejected, preferring a strategy based on persuasion. The documents connected to the conspiracy are the products of collective endeavours and can only with some caution be read as a reflection of Babeuf's own thinking. However, apart from the fact that Babeuf was one of the driving forces in the group, he assumed responsibility for the contents of these papers, which were discovered in his home, at the trial of the conspirators some months later. They can thus be taken as at least indicative of his own personal views.

From this vast ensemble, we shall retain the part devoted to the project of the society of Equals in *Buonarroti's History of Babeuf's Conspiracy for Equality*.[61] Published years later, this account seems faithful to two other documents that have come down to us through Buonarroti's care: the 'Fragment of a Draft Police Decree' and the 'Fragment of a Draft Economic Decree', reproduced in an appendix to his text. These passages justify the overall assessment of Richard Coe, who, in an article on 'Morellyan theory and Babouvist practice', compares the Equals' views to the framework established by the fourth part of the *Code de la Nature*.[62] The proclamation of a community of property and labour ('There shall be established in the republic a great national community', says the first article of the economic fragment), as well as the right to be maintained 'in equal and honest mediocrity' in exchange

---

61 Philippe Buonarotti, *La conspiration pour l'Égalité, dite de Babeuf* (1828), Montreuil: La ville brûle, 2014. Published in English translation as *Buonarroti's History of Babeuf's Conspiracy for Equality*, London: Hetherington, 1836.

62 R. N. C. Coe, 'La théorie morellyenne et la pratique babouviste', *AHRF* 30, 1958, 38–64.

for the 'work of agriculture' or the 'useful crafts', depending on each person's possibilities, are not some peculiarity of Morelly's writings: they are found in the great majority of classical utopias. But only Morelly placed them at the head of his draft legislation, as the basis for all other rules.

Morelly's principle could be translated using the communist adage of the following century, 'from each according to his abilities, to each according to his needs'. But only the first of these propositions is taken up by the Babouvists. Compared to the abundance promised by this second proposition, their openly asserted frugality made more of a concession to the harshness of the times, no doubt coupled with memories of the austere egalitarianism of the Spartans. On the other hand, the Equals did draw part of their internal organisation of powers from the *Code de la Nature*. For Morelly, the ideal state is a federation of communities called 'tribes' which form small, relatively autonomous political units under the authority of the central government, which is called the 'Supreme Senate'. These political units have their own tribal senate, whose members are rotated. Small enough to ensure that each person's wishes are known, they do not in themselves represent economic units: rather, in order to provide for all the needs of their members, these basic political units must associate with each other, forming 'Cities'. The plan of legislation in the *Code de la Nature* superimposes a hierarchy of political government upon a hierarchy of economic administration, constituted in each profession by foremen who take it in turns to head the given body. The citizens are thus simultaneously divided by place of residence, with regard to political functions, and by class of work, for economic functions. In the 'fragment of a draft economic decree', this duality of powers is respected at the level of each commune. Articles 4 and 5 of the decree's section 'On common works' stipulate that, in each commune, 'the citizens are distributed by classes', to which magistrates appointed by those who compose these classes 'direct the work, ensure its equal distribution, and carry out the orders of the municipal administration'.[63] Alongside these classes, communal assemblies, and then district assemblies, remain as political institutions. As was the case for Morelly, the division of the population into work units is not a supplementary factor, but an essential one in the organisation of the

---

63   Buonarroti, *La conspiration pour l'Égalité*, p. 401.

state. The four levels defined by the Babouvists (higher administration, arrondissements, départements, communes) correspond to those of the *Code* (nation, province, city, tribe). The importance of the economic hierarchy in the two systems stems from the need to distribute work and resources properly, such that everyone might enjoy the benefits of the new administration.

Other features of the organisation of collective life represent a more diffuse inheritance of utopian literature in general: for instance, the common meals provided for in Article 3 of the section 'On distribution', which are found in More and in *La Basiliade*, but which Morelly does not have in the *Code de la Nature*. The elimination of the right to trade and inheritance, the common storehouse, the supply of deficit regions by others where abundance reigns ... all these belong to the common stock-in-trade of the utopian tradition. With regard to morals, we could also cite such ideas as the magnificence of public buildings, contrasting with the simplicity of individual homes; the suppression of money and luxury; the festivals and collective activities supposed to mould morals without imposing constraints; the clothing, whose 'different forms and colours' should serve 'to distinguish between ages and occupations';[64] and religious precepts, which exclude all revelation and which boil down to a socially useful belief in the existence of a Supreme Being and the immortality of the soul, which is liable to be rewarded or punished according to its greater or lesser devotion to the public cause. This last common decision, however, must have been the result of a compromise between those who, like Babeuf, professed atheism and more convinced believers. Buonarroti in particular, as a good Robespierrist, must have been particularly keen to maintain a belief in the Supreme Being.

More generally, the rest of the measures which we will cite here corresponded to a combination of utopian ideals, mostly inherited from Morelly's text, with the institutions promoted by the Constitution of Year II as well as the Montagnards' social policy in this same moment. This included what Coe calls the 'welfare state', which he attributes essentially to a legacy of the *Code de la Nature*;[65] provision of assistance to the old and infirm; and the establishment of a 'national, common, equal' education with an emphasis on elementary and vocational

---

64 Ibid., p. 182.
65 Coe, 'La théorie morellyenne et la pratique babouviste', p. 49.

training. This all owed much to the public educational houses of the Utopia of 1755, as well as to Lepeletier de Saint-Fargeau's educational plan and the lessons of *Émile* concerning the need to teach children a manual trade. The political aspects of this ideal constitution are a remarkable case in point: the Babouvists expected three institutions to allow the most democratic legislative activity: the 'sovereign assemblies' in each district, 'as extensive as the convenience of the meetings could allow'; the 'central assembly of legislators'; and, finally, the 'body of conservators of the national will', composed of elders charged with proclaiming the will of the sovereign and ensuring that the central legislators did not encroach on the local assemblies' right to propose, approve, or reject laws.[66] The sovereign assemblies were themselves to be flanked by a senate of elders which they would appoint. In this way, the will of the people would have the means to make itself heard, even against the despotic incursions of the central power, and to be enlightened by the experience and wisdom of individuals whose value was recognised on account of their past actions. The assemblies themselves were inherited from the Constitution of 1793. At the local level, they corresponded to the département-level 'primary assemblies' and at the national level to the Convention itself, taking over these institutions' respective functions. By adding gerontocratic assemblies, the Equals simply combined these with the Morellyan senates which, according to the first and tenth 'laws of the form of government', are composed of family fathers over fifty years of age.[67] We get the feeling that, in their fight for the popular sovereignty, Babeuf and his companions did not know how to choose between the lessons of utopia and those of the Revolution, or, rather, that they sought to add the two together. In a certain sense, they thus reproduced the ambivalence characteristic of most utopias up to Morelly. That is, the ambivalence between democratic demands and the need to impose just laws on a people which was not always enlightened enough to recognise the validity of such legislation, or even likely to undermine its durability.

To avoid the despotism of the central administrators – and, likewise, that of military tops – provision was also made for assemblies in army ranks, tasked among other things with appointing military chiefs. There

---

66   Buonarroti, *La conspiration pour l'Égalité*, p. 205.
67   *CN*, pp. 158–60.

were also to be assemblies of censure, once again directed by old men, who would judge the conduct of citizens and particularly the magistrates. Finally, there were to be assemblies of instruction, in which each citizen would be free to divulge their knowledge and opinions to the public. As can be seen, a real deliberative fever seems to have taken hold of these men, who no longer seemed to want to leave the slightest decision to individual discretion, but instead sought to regulate everything collectively, even military problems and educational endeavours.

In this model, nothing seems to remain of the old property-based order, with the notable exception of the presence of 'foreigners' – a term with which the police decree designates those who 'do nothing for the fatherland, those who do not serve it by useful work'.[68] Their presence, here, is striking in a society that otherwise seems to be entirely consistent with the Equals' wishes. To them falls the burden of all the contributions from which the citizens are exempt – contributions that are doubled each year. Thus, these 'foreigners' are powerfully encouraged to join the national community, by measures that are less persuasive than coercive. This is the sole vestige of the transition from the state of property to that of community, and seems to be a kind of anachronism which rather jars with the rest. Finally, it is to these 'foreigners' alone that the punishment of 'perpetual slavery' seems to be reserved, in cases of fraud or monetary trafficking with a member of the community.[69]

A Break in the History of Utopia

In the various aspects of their plan for society, the Equals made no great innovations: their plan simply brought the utopian inheritance together with the governmental experience of Robespierre's and Saint-Just's Committee of Public Safety. They had to therefore seek their radically new element elsewhere, in the very status that they gave to their hopes. This was the first time that such a model of an ideal society had left the purely theoretical domain and come to guide political action. The propaganda of the Equals, the means used to realise this plan – in spite of their outline character, in spite of their premature failure, even

---

68   Buonarroti, *La conspiration pour l'Égalité*, p. 229.
69   Ibid., p. 405.

before the preparations had really been completed – are the markers of this new status. Whatever motives led these men to provoke a direct and hopeless confrontation with the authorities of the Directory, and even if these motives undoubtedly had something in common with the flight from reality that led Saint-Just to write his *Institutions républicaines* a few weeks before his fall – in any case, this enterprise marks a break in the history of the utopian tradition. This break is closely linked to the French Revolution, of which it was, in some respects, the culmination. As the final onslaught of the popular and democratic movement before the ebb that ended with Bonaparte's coup d'état, it expressed its most radical transformative tendencies. A revolutionary utopia, or the furthest boundary of utopia, the Conspiracy of Equals was an episode of little significance for the history of the Revolution itself, which had already seen popular intervention recede for several months. But it is of greater importance for the history of utopia itself, on which it left its mark.

This is why the strategy adopted by the Babouvists at their trial was unable to fool anyone. In order to exonerate as many of the accused as possible, they tried to convince the jury of the non-existence of the conspiracy and attempted to disguise their group as a Club of Radical Democrats.[70] Babeuf's defence was remarkable from this point of view, in its attempts to pass off its author as a utopian in the classical sense – that is, as a 'writer', a mere 'apostle of the principles of pure democracy'.[71] As an introduction, Babeuf stated before his judges: 'I will show ... that I only adopted this system in pure speculation; that I never expected it to be established, or that the People would be disposed to accept it.'[72] The court's response to these protests of utopianism is well-known: while sparing the heads of most of the conspirators, it condemned the people's tribune to capital punishment for conspiracy against the government. In its tragic way, this sentence nevertheless did justice to Babeuf's very particular utopianism, which had pushed him out of pure hope and into action. It refused to take him for a meek dreamer, and instead took

---

70   For the details of this case, I refer the reader to my 'Un inédit de Buonarroti: la "réplique à la réponse de l'accusateur national" ', *AHRF* 370, 2012, 213–33.

71   Cited in Victor Advielle, *Histoire de Gracchus Babeuf et du babouvisme*, Paris: Éditions du CTHS, 1990, vol. II, p. 5.

72   Ibid. We can see this statement as providing a new, judicial status for 'utopian denegation'.

his attempts at social transformation seriously. Thus, the journey of this utopian-in-revolution ended in a death sentence, uniting his fate with that of the first of their number, Thomas More. The two men's shared individual tragedy would lift them to a place in posterity.

Conclusion
An Anti-School of Thought

Theory and Practice: The Politicisation of Utopia

Throughout this volume, we have covered a number of points about the relationship between theory and practice in what has been characterised as a tendency of the radical Enlightenment. We have traced the path of a *gradual politicisation of utopia*, through several converging means.

The politicisation of utopia meant, first and foremost, breaking it out of the limbo of dreams and novels and instead inserting it into the real temporality of human life. From Morelly to Mably to Babeuf, our analysis has shown that utopia was increasingly pollinated by history itself. And yet, while the author of the *Code de la Nature* was the first utopian to present his social ideal as the inevitable – if hardly immediate – conclusion of historical becoming, he did so in the abstract, without incorporating the slightest element of empirical history that was really liable to consolidate this hope for the future. From this point of view, the model of society that emerges from Morelly's novelistic vein, between *La Basiliade* and the *Code de la Nature*, does acquire a certain historical status, but this status remains largely ambiguous. Morelly never abandoned the concept of utopia as a parallel to real history, as a counter-history that men could and should have lived through if they had not strayed from the paths marked out by nature. Through his insistent reference to nature, he shifts back and forth between nostalgia for a lost past, the exploration of possibilities parallel to the present, and the call of the future. Indeed, this is well illustrated by the overlapping temporal functions of utopia in his text. With the *Code de la Nature*, as utopia becomes a universal legislative model, it is made available to history, rather than being inserted into the dynamics of historical becoming. It lacks the mediations necessary to bind it to a present, lived by men as its probable destination.

Mably's attachment to the republican tradition, along with his exaltation of the cities of antiquity, allows him to establish a first concrete link between utopia and history. In effect, Mably 'utopianises' the past by adorning the Spartan institutions – the first – with all the virtues of his own ideal. Compared to Morelly, the model loses its place in humanity's future. But what it instead gains is a place in a real past, which, though itself considered a bygone age, can nonetheless serve as a source of inspiration for modern societies, subject to certain concessions to the present. By entering into history, utopia becomes susceptible to imitation, because what has been, unlike what never was, has proven itself to be possible. We need not go so far as to assert that the republican tradition is in itself a utopian tradition. But what we can say is that Mably achieves a synthesis of the two currents of thought and effectively makes the republic, as he conceives it, a utopia. This utopia is not – or is not only – the object of nostalgic yearnings. For it is also a ferment for reforming measures: in this sense, it is the foundation of a hopeful reading of the future. Mably takes an essential dimension from the republican tradition, namely its call to action. Thus, in *Des droits et des devoirs du citoyen*, the republican utopia permeates the political project. It forms the basis of a genuine historical innovation – one that breaks with all previous institutions, however much the author may admire them.

Babeuf completes the historicisation of utopia by making it a factor in a history in the making: a political fact. With him, utopia is no longer a theoretical model but stimulates direct action as its avowed aim. Babeuf's utopia is surely open to change, as it evolves according to circumstances; he has not one but many utopias. His utopia has the flexibility of the programme of a man of action, confronted with the demands of a present that is constantly changing shape in the torrents of revolution. His reading prompts reflection on the transitional measures needed in view of the final advent of utopia – the steps that should mark the succession of time. For the historian of philosophy, this utopia is sometimes disappointing. It lacks consistency; it frustrates the reader's desire for

Conclusion

the details they would like further elaborated; it does not offer enough arguments for why it deserves to be defended in the court of reason. But it is stirred by a determination to be realised; in it, we hear the echo of the revolutionary struggle and the unprecedented hopes it raised for an entire generation, and more. Its incompleteness is, in this sense, the price of its first arrival at the level of history.

Yet, the politicisation of utopia had other consequences. It meant its entry into the terms of the philosophical and political debate of the time: for, if its message was to be heard, it had to use the words of the tribe, even if that meant changing their meaning. It was also necessary to show that the ideal that utopia was portraying did not contradict what the century (thought that it) knew about man. Corresponding to a both theoretical and tactical requirement, this is most evident in utopia's reliance on the canonical vocabulary of natural right, from Morelly to Babeuf. The author of the *Code de la Nature* makes only a few allusions to it, which have no influence on the image of man found elsewhere in this work: they seem to have a purely rhetorical role, hence this book has not delved into them further. Reflection on the natural order, in which men will seamlessly find their place if nothing interferes with this spontaneous movement, takes precedence over any consideration of what the individual should claim as his due. Radical criticism of the unnatural property-based order takes precedence over any claim to the inalienable rights of the individual.

This is no longer the case with Mably. For him, a battle is underway to ensure that man's true and inalienable rights materialise. The controversy around jusnaturalism raises the question of the essence of the individual, and of what elements of the individual a society must imperatively respect, if it is not to be an oppressive force that undermines this nature. From Mably onwards, the question of the naturalness of rights to property or subsistence became not just a philosophical issue (if it ever had been this) but also, and perhaps primarily, a political one.

Finally, we have emphasised the pivotal role of Babeuf's assertion of the natural right to subsistence, which runs through almost all of his work. The return of the vocabulary of natural right in his writings – after it was remarkably eclipsed in the *Lueurs philosophiques* – may seem strange if we were to confine ourselves to a purely theoretical analysis of the doctrinal content of his writings. Which arguments did Babeuf use to contradict some of his own assertions about the positive, social character of all law? We have no trace of these arguments; and the difficulty can only be resolved by considering the specifically political heft of the assertion of a natural right. Without doubt, it was not so much purely philosophical considerations that led Babeuf to this about-turn, as his recognition of the mobilising power of such a vocabulary, inscribed on the pediment of the Declaration of the Rights of Man. In this way, Babeuf's utopia was part of the evolution of the French Revolution as a whole, in which jusnaturalist anthropology became jusnaturalist politics.

Still, this review of the key features of the politicisation of utopia at this crucial juncture would not be complete without a word on its links with Rousseau's thought and concepts, even if they were marked by conflict. Here, we have no intention of reopening the vast debate on the 'utopianism' of the citizen of Geneva as such; but it is worth noting how often his favoured themes intersect with the thinking of our three authors, above all at a political level. Morelly is essentially in dispute with Rousseau, but, on certain points, such as the critique of property, this opposition resembles a form of competition. We have likewise seen how Mably's conception of natural right echoes Rousseau's, even precisely because of the tensions between them.[1] Finally, we noted the importance for the young Babeuf of Rousseau's denunciation of inequality, and then, during the Revolution, of the theory of popular sovereignty. Thus, Mably and later Babeuf were, in their own ways, part of a movement of thought that spanned this entire period, and which tended to make an eminently political use of Rousseau's philosophy.

From this perspective, the writings of Morelly, and, above all, of Mably and Babeuf, can be counted as part of the 'radical' reception of Rousseau's work. The specialist literature warns us against reading the *Second Discourse* and *The Social Contract* as direct proposals for social models that ought to be applied, or else as utopian texts properly speaking. But it is hardly trivial that some contemporaries did indeed consider them as such. Babeuf, in particular, questioned whether a return to the natural state – as he believed the *Second Discourse* was advocating – was

---

1 According to Luc Vincenti, *The Social Contract* contains analyses of the way in which the pressure of private property feeds into an inevitable degeneration of the body politic; from this point of view, too, Rousseau's analyses bear comparison with Mably's. See 'Rousseau et les révolutions de l'histoire', in L. Vincenti (ed.), *Rousseau et le marxisme*, Paris: Publications de la Sorbonne, 2011, pp. 135–40.

Conclusion

indeed a good thing;[2] he saw the society presented in *The Social Contract* as inspired by the institutions of Geneva, and wondered whether its forms of organisation could be applied in a bigger country.[3] Even if Babeuf offers a negative response on both counts, his reading of Rousseau is a fitting reminder that even a mistaken use of texts can be highly significant and rich in political effects.[4] The reception of Rousseauism as the bearer of a political programme was a historically important fact, and this fully belongs to its theoretical heritage. It has its own kind of legitimacy and cannot be kept at a distance from Rousseau studies as if it were a merely inconvenient error, committed by people who simply did not know how to read the texts. It demands of the community of scholars that they philosophically engage with this dimension of Rousseau's work, asking what in the literal content of the texts makes such a usage of them possible.

Variations on the Communitarian Utopia, Before and During the French Revolution

We have seen that, even though these three authors each assert the superiority of the community of goods over any other form of social organisation, they do so based on multiple (even if converging) anthropological arguments. Their claims are, moreover, based on several theories as to the place of such a social ideal in history, and as to the very conditions on which it is historically inscribed. Ultimately, we might ask if we can really speak of major conceptual transfers, in a lineage running from Morelly to

---

2 In his letter to Dubois de Fosseux of 8 July 1787, which we have not been able to analyse here, due to lack of space (*OB*, pp. 214–17).

3 In *Lueurs philosophiques*, fund 223, no. 51, Russian Centre for the Preservation of Archives in Political and Social History (RGASPI), Moscow, p. 149: 'Rousseau . . . draws everything from the little Republic of Geneva, relates everything to this Republic, and does not hesitate to set aside everything that, in more extensive governments, could not be applied to this Republic . . . Large states are unnecessary, because Geneva is squeezed within very narrow limits, and there is no way of extending them. In short, Rousseau saw only Geneva, concerned himself only with Geneva, thought, reflected and conjectured only for Geneva; and this model, barely perceptible in Europe, imperceptible in the other parts of the world, is dogmatically presented as the model for the governments of the entire human race.'

4 At least, this was the case, as far as *The Social Contract* was concerned, at the moment that Babeuf wrote the manuscript of *Lueurs philosophiques*.

Mably and Babeuf, that are able to justify the conclusion that they form a genuine school of thought.

On closer analysis, it appears that Mably probably did draw on the anthropology of the *Code de la Nature* for his own *De la législation*, but these borrowings, at most, produce an inflection in the general tone of his anthropology rather than a real about-turn. Compared with earlier texts, such as *Doutes proposés aux philosophes économistes*, or *Des droits et des devoirs*, in which the ideal of community is also present, the essential innovation lies in the introduction of the notion of *amour-propre*, whose satisfaction requires the aid of others. Combined with reason, and its demands for justice, it is this factor that pushes man to cooperate with his peers. Even if we stick to the hypothesis that Mably's innovation in this regard was inspired by Morelly and abandon the idea that perhaps the same cause – the need to justify the community of goods – may have produced the same effect – an anthropology of 'collaborative' *amour-propre* – this seems like a marginal influence on him. Clearly, Mably had no need to rely on Morelly in order to arrive at utopian aspirations, or at the idea that the community of goods was the best way to allow the free development of man's 'social qualities'. It is more that this list of qualities was enriched: individual political virtues (justice, courage, disinterestedness) were augmented through social affects (pity, gratitude, the need to love).

Mably seems to have absorbed Morelly's influence, in the sense that he adopted some of his theories, without fundamentally changing his own doctrine. *De la législation* points to the double anthropological purpose of political association; the role of the community of goods as a model which good government should tend towards, albeit without ever hoping to reach it; and to the republican character of the measures needed. Yet none of this is inspired by the *Code de la Nature*; rather, it builds on Mably's texts preceding *De la législation*. At the very most, we can hypothesise that Mably drew a certain anthropological and political optimism from Morelly, which led him, in this text, more than in his other dialogues, to propose bold reforms and consider them feasible. These measures would impose tight limits on individual property, without ever abolishing it. But it is impossible to establish with any certainty Morelly's influence in this regard.

In a sense, the same observation can be made about Babeuf, albeit with some further nuance. Babeuf drew his communitarian convictions

Conclusion

neither from Morelly – an author he likely only discovered late in life – nor from Mably. He did not become a utopian by reading either of his two predecessors, even if the actual nature and influence of his early readings (of More and others) remain difficult to establish or evaluate. This is worth emphasising, because it tells us that it is impossible to cast Babeuf as a 'disciple' of Morelly or Mably, much as it was impossible to count Mably as a 'disciple' of Morelly. The draft letter of 1786, rich in its utopian content, predates Babeuf's first mention of Mably. Even in the letters to Coupé from late summer 1791, which do bear the mark of his having read this author, an important deformation should be noted, since Babeuf did not project the ideal of the community of goods back into humanity's past, but, rather, into a distant but possible future. Even the agrarian law, which Babeuf claims to have discovered in Mably's *De la législation,* takes on a completely different meaning in his own writing, since it does not refer to the redivision of land, but rather to its definitive appropriation by the public authorities.

Morelly's influence on Babeuf surely appears greater than Mably's, insofar as the Equals did draw inspiration from the 'Model of Legislation' in the *Code de la Nature* in order to craft their image of the future society. However, this may also be seen as a loose interpretation of the utopian's message, to say the least. Morelly had not at all imagined that his views would materialise by means of insurrection. Moreover, as we have seen, the provisions set out in the *Code de la Nature* are quite considerably altered by their association with the public bodies inspired by the Constitution of Year II. It is also worth noting that the idea of the common store and a number of other institutions mentioned in the 'Model of Legislation' were already present in other utopias that preceded Morelly's, and might just as easily have been drawn from these forerunners. They are not peculiar to the *Code de la Nature,* but derive from the common heritage of the mainstream utopian tradition since Thomas More. Finally, we should note that the deeper reason for Babeuf's adherence to the utopian ideal was at least as material as it was moral. While, for Morelly, the key question was the degeneration of man under a regime of property ownership – his wickedness, his misfortune, and the means to remedy it – for the people's tribune Babeuf, the problems of subsistence surely came first (especially in the context of 1795–6), although this hardly exhausted the moral questions. The last fundamental aspect that the Equals took from Morelly was the *form* of his utopian discourse: the codification of the ideal society, which resonated considerably with the fever for legislation that gripped the builders of the regenerated society after 1789.

So, while we cannot deny the importance of Mably's, and then Morelly's, thought in forming Babeuf's thinking, this was perhaps less a matter of them directly inspiring his own conclusions than of providing solutions to problems that he had himself started from. Even then, he interpreted these responses very freely, took them out of their original context, and even twisted their meaning. In other words, it seems that Babeuf found in his predecessors, confirmation of what he already thought, as well as certain elements that he could add, with a few adjustments, to an already-formed body of thinking, rather than a source of truly new ideas. Like Mably, Babeuf developed a conception of man and history largely foreign to that which he found in the *Code de la Nature*, especially if we compare the legacy of this text with what Rousseau's writings represented for the tribune of the people. From a strictly philosophical point of view, very little was passed on from Morelly to Babeuf.

Consequently, rather than speaking of a school of thought, thus casting Babeuf (as Villegardelle did) and Mably as 'Morellystes', we should perhaps draw on the musical metaphor of variations on one same fundamental theme.[5] In this framing, the respective works of Morelly, Mably, and Babeuf, who each draw on the sources of classical utopia, present three successive versions of the utopia of the community of goods. Their different versions each have certain traits in common, above all because these traits constitute so many principled stances, related to a similar attitude to the world. Taken in different theoretical and historical contexts, and in the face of different adversaries, these stances took on particular characteristics in each author.

In this sense, these three authors' shared attachment to the utopian tradition should be distinguished from the idea that they belonged to a single school of philosophical thought. It did not involve them each embracing a theory based on precise concepts, on a clearly identifiable

---

5 François Villegardelle, 'Notice sur Morelly', in *Code de la Nature*, Paris: Delaunay, 1840, p. 8: if Babeuf and his comrades wanted 'to bear the name of their true father, they must abandon the title of Babouvistes, which reflects ... an incomplete interpretation of the master's thought, and adopt that of Morellystes'.

anthropology, or on a representation of the world whose general characteristics were fixed once and for all time. Rather, what they shared was a common rejection of the real world, based on their hatred of human suffering and depravity, and their attachment to a social ideal with certain essential features, in turn serving certain objectives. These include the reign of virtue and the happiness of the members of the community, to be achieved principally through the sharing of labour and the resources necessary for life; the common store; transparency in the ins and outs of everyday life; and several other such goals. What makes these three authors utopians is the moral nature of their revolt against the world, which justifies the need for an alternative, as well as their use of a certain type of imaginary to depict it. This is also the reason why it would be better to speak of an affinity between them than of a truly common doctrine.

In this way, Morelly sets his approach in an eminently moral perspective. Faced with the corruption of the society based on property, he seeks to demonstrate the merits of the community of goods, as the only way for human goodness to flourish. This demonstration is essentially theoretical, and no practical consequences can be directly deduced from it. As a result, the anthropology which he develops over the course of his work, despite some fundamental elements which can be immediately identified, undergoes an evolution corresponding to that of the utopian ideal itself. Indeed, the latter changes significantly between *La Basiliade* and the *Code de la Nature*. In the novel, the link between the conception of man and the social utopia seems closer than in the second text, where a discrepancy emerges between the spontaneity of generous cooperation and the severity of the code of laws. There is a contradiction, here: for the vision of a society not based on property, and the desire to root it in an original conception of man's nature, comes into tension with the description of society itself. Likewise, the providentialist conception of history, which promises a radiant future to a humanity finally freed of private property, jars with the scepticism about the forthcoming establishment of a society that fits with the principles of the 'Model of Legislation'. But, fundamentally, the objective remains almost the same: anthropology, ideal society, and conception of history converge, in a condemnation of the order based on property as unnatural, evil, and ultimately doomed to abolition. Generally speaking, it can be said that the opposition between two worlds – the one based on property, the other on community – structures the entire theory.[6]

Mably's perspective is likewise essentially ethical but also differs slightly from Morelly's. For him, the idea is not simply to make the community of goods into a counterpoint to the society of property – opposing it, as Morelly does, just as absolute good opposes absolute evil. Rather, it appears to be a point of completion, or even the situation corresponding to the full perfection of man's nature, while also guaranteeing his full enjoyment of his natural rights. If this ideal remains an unattainable horizon, and if man is henceforth incapable of fully developing his potential social qualities, it does at least give direction to a theory of political action. This, again, is in contrast to what we see in Morelly. Utopia becomes the endpoint around which judgements about individuals and situations, and plans for reform, must be organised. In this general teleological scheme, the goal (utopia) is in reality at the foundation of the conception of man and society. As with Morelly, it is starting from this goal, and it alone, that we can think about man's nature and assess his present condition. But, unlike in Morelly, utopia is no longer presented as the Other to the property-based society, at least so long as all hope of reform has not yet been dashed. Rather, it provides a compass for this society, reminding it of its deeper nature and showing it the direction to (re)discovering the path of the species' natural improvement.

Finally, for Babeuf, utopia was, from 1786 onwards, a foreseeable project. However, it underwent major changes of character between his first writings and 1796. These took the form of a gradual broadening of his views, in the light of events and his political and theoretical discoveries. In the case of Babeuf, utopia is at least as much a product of history as of the imagination. Ultimately, the republican influence joined with utopian hope in a movement that gave them new meaning by drawing on the experience of Jacobin rule. Right from Babeuf's earliest writings, utopia, as the goal of political action, is explicitly based on the natural right to subsistence. But it also corresponds to a conception of man's moral nature that is often more implicit than clearly spelled out. Its advent was thus essential both to guaranteeing the material survival of

---

6   In this respect, Morelly remains a 'classic' utopian: and this is, indeed, an opposition of the same type that we find in Books I and II of More's *Utopia*.

each person and to realising aspirations to virtue, fraternity, and – soon enough – the dignity of the species. Babeuf's path was more tentative than his predecessors' had been, both in terms of the solutions he proposed and the anthropology that underpinned them. When we seek to characterise Babeuf's ideas, the most relevant thing is not to focus on the final image of his social project, that of the 'Manifesto of the Equals', seen as 'a document that inaugurated the modern era of radical action utopias'.[7] Rather more important to keep in mind is the *movement* of a thought that is inseparable from action – one that, in each moment, adapts the utopia of the community of goods to the perceived necessities of the day, so as to make this utopia useful for practical application in the short or medium term. From this perspective, Babeuf's wavering between an egalitarian and a communitarian tendency, in his anthropology as well as in his social ideal, and the evolution of his historical diagnosis of the French Revolution and the possibilities it harbours, are an integral part of his utopia. His utopia is – fundamentally and from the outset – a programme awaiting realisation. It thus tends to mobilise history, its concepts, and its reading more with a view to the expected political effects than the demands of developing a coherent and consistent doctrine.

---

[7] Frank and Fritzie Manuel, *Utopian Thought in the Western World*, Cambridge, MA: Harvard University Press, 1979, p. 557.

Epilogue
A Post-Revolutionary Avatar of Morellysm

The fact that utopia is not a school of thought means that some of its themes and arguments can be taken up from different perspectives. This seems to be the case with Morelly's theories, which were read and praised by such diverse early-nineteenth-century socialists as Villegardelle, Dézamy, Cabet, and Proudhon.[1] Among all these names, one is conspicuously absent: Charles Fourier, the great theorist of the Ordre Sociétaire. The reason for this exception seems to have been given by the author himself: Fourier agreed with those conservatives who saw in the French Revolution an 'attempt' by the philosophers of the Enlightenment and earlier periods 'to put their ideas into practice'. On this unfortunate testing ground, Fourier said, they had 'creat[ed] as many calamities as they promised benefits' and led 'civilised society back towards a state of barbarism'.[2] The 'catastrophe of 1793', in particular – the philosophers' posthumous work – had demonstrated how far

---

1 Théodore Dézamy, in his *Code de la communauté* (Paris: Prévost-Rouannet, 1842) is openly inspired by Morelly, quoting him at many points. Étienne Cabet exclaims in his *Voyage en Icarie*: 'Listen to Diderot, in his *Code de la Nature*, or rather Morelly, the real author of this work ... See him, bolder than his predecessors, formally proposing community as possible and practicable' (*Voyage en Icarie*, Paris: Au bureau du Populaire, 1848, p. 512). Finally, in *L'idée générale de la Révolution au XIXe siècle* (Paris: Garnier Frères, 1851), Proudhon praises the *Code de la Nature* by speaking of 'the negation of government, which is at the heart of Morelly's utopia' (p. 135).

2 Charles Fourier, *The Theory of the Four Movements*, Cambridge: Cambridge University Press, 1996, p. 6.

the social sciences had gone astray. They would thus have to start again from a new beginning. The Revolution was itself the countermodel that had prompted Fourier's reflection, a negative example which called for the opening up of a new path for humanity. As he wrote, 'It was pondering this that first led me to suspect the existence of a social science of which we were still unaware, and stimulated me to try to discover what it was.'[3] It would thus seem only logical that the Fourierist utopia should be utterly at odds with the tradition of the previous century, and particularly with the utopia of the *Code de la Nature*, which was linked both to the philosophy of the Enlightenment and to the Revolution by way of Babouvism. To some extent, this is indeed true. As Pierre Macherey points out, the Ordre Sociétaire is a 'social utopia' that replaces the former classical utopia, or 'political utopia', in the sense that it no longer looks to the state to deal with the problems of collective life. This post-revolutionary utopia turns away from the need to declare the fundamental rights of individuals, which are supposed to be absolute and guaranteed by the public authorities responsible for maintaining the communitarian order. Rather, 'the social is the reality of the community considered in its changing complexity, from a perspective that cannot be reduced to a fixed schedule of rules or to a formal system of legality that the state would guarantee by exercising its authority'.[4]

Political power no longer instigates, but itself emanates from, the new modes of sociability which are now at work. The association regulates itself, without it needing any superior arbiter. Fourier's projects spoke not of a radical reform of the human race from above, but rather of a gradual progress towards the principles of harmony, through the multiplication of the *phalanstères*. The latter would prove through practical example their capacity to fulfil humanity's greatest hopes. Nor was there any question of abolishing social distinctions and private property. A member of the *phalanstères* would benefit from this association on the basis of the work they put in and the talents they brought to bear, but also from whatever financial investment they had made. In this sense, Fourier's association is not 'socialist'. It thus seems that Fourier's utopia drew essentially negative

---

3 Ibid., p. 7.
4 Pierre Macherey, *De l'utopie!*, Le Havre: De l'incidence éditeur, 2011, p. 450.

lessons from the utopias of the eighteenth century and of the French Revolution, and that it mounted a radical renewal of this genre and its typical characteristics.

Still, we would like to suggest that the relationship of this utopia to those of the preceding period and to the events of the French Revolution was more complex than Fourier himself suggests. It is not simply that he inherited the general optimism which, despite the violence of the Terror, emanated from the revolutionary process. Nor is it simply that (though this was surely true) this shaking up of all the old institutions and practices allowed such a statement as:

> We are going to be witness to a spectacle which can only be seen once in each globe, the transition from incoherence to social combination. This is the most brilliant movement that can ever happen in the universe, and the anticipation of it shall be a consolation to the present generation for all its miseries.[5]

Even beyond the fact that the Ordre Sociétaire shared in a new spirit of utopia, also obvious here is the use made of ideas strangely consonant with those of the *Code de la Nature*. One such example is the 'science' discovered by Fourier, the 'theory of passionate attraction'. How could we fail to recognise this – despite its originality and, above all, its much more developed character – as a close relative of Morelly's natural morality, which, according to Fourier, is 'as simple, as obvious in its first axioms and their consequences, as mathematics itself'?[6] Indeed, according to Fourier, the 'mathematical system of human passions' is modelled on the laws of attraction of bodies; it is based on the discoveries of Newton and Leibniz and leads to the idea of 'a unified system of movement for the spiritual and the material world'.[7] This idea is already present in Morelly's *Code de la Nature*: it is embodied in the principle of natural mechanics, which makes men depend on each other for the satisfaction of their needs, and, through the variation of desires and talents, puts them into cooperative arrangements rather than setting them against one another. Morelly

---

5 Fourier, *The Theory of the Four Movements*, p. 21.
6 *CN*, p. 49.
7 Fourier, *The Theory of the Four Movements*, p. 16.

concludes, in terms that seem to foreshadow *The Theory of the Four Movements*:

> Everything is measured with a compass, everything is weighed, everything is planned in the marvellous automaton of society; its gears, its counterweights, its springs, its effects; if we see a contradiction of forces, it is vacillation without shaking, or balance without violence; everything is driven, everything is carried towards a common goal.[8]

Morelly and Fourier agree on one crucial point: namely, that human passions are naturally good in themselves. In this view, the passions lead not to competing interests and the struggle among *amours-propres*, but to a generous and blissful collaboration. Men cannot reconcile their individual and collective happiness by turning to reason to direct or even repress the passions. Rather, they can only do this by giving the passions free rein. The whole art of society lies in bringing human organisation into line with the harmonious development of these passions. Hence, the two utopians each castigated the 'moralists' ignorant of man's true nature. The latter endeavour to repress his inclinations and attribute them malign ends – something that can only embitter them and make them all the more devastating. As Fourier makes quite clear, attraction is incompatible with duty in the traditional, moral sense of the term.

Finally, there is what Morelly calls 'natural probity' – which, in the context of a well-constituted society, leads man to have 'only one object of his hopes, only one motive for his actions, the common good', because 'his own particular [good is] an infallible consequence of it'.[9] This seems to correspond, in Fourier, to the 'source of all passions', called 'Unityism'. He defines this as:

> the inclination of the individual to harmonise his own happiness with that of everything around him and of the whole human race, which today is so hateful. It is a boundless philanthropy, a universal well-being, which will not be able to develop until the whole human race is rich, free and just.[10]

---

8   *CN*, p. 56.
9   Ibid., p. 59.
10 Fourier, *The Theory of the Four Movements*, p. 81.

Epilogue

The growth of Unityism, like that of natural probity, follows naturally from the untrammelled satisfaction of all passions, of all subaltern needs, which they crown. There is no rupture between the individual and the collective. Rather, there is an extension and flourishing of the individual interest as part of the collective interest, so long as the social mechanism does not lead to an opposition between them.

Thus, the question again arises: was Fourier inspired by Morelly's reading, before giving his own anthropological concepts a depth that his predecessor had not even hinted at, describing in great detail the 'tree of passion', its ramifications, the human groups arising from it, the series of groups, and so on? Or, once again, do the same causes simply produce the same effects? François Villegardelle, who was the first to point out the theoretical similarity, relies on a – no doubt deliberately – ambiguous formulation:

> When we set out upon the historical study of the social ideas in which we were first initiated by Charles Fourier, we hardly expected to find the most fundamental of these ideas admirably formulated in an almost unknown writer of the last century [Morelly].[11]

Fourier's and Morelly's theories thus belong to one same family of 'social ideas', although it is impossible to define for certain the exact ancestry of these ideas. Fourier may have drawn his inspiration from the *Code de la Nature*, but he may just as easily have followed the same path as his predecessor, starting from the same kind of problem with the same kind of reformist, chimerical, and philanthropic mindset. How can we know?

But this also poses the question of what being a utopian really involves. Does it mean explicitly following in a certain tradition by adopting its themes and arguments? Or does it simply mean sharing in a theoretical attitude and a relationship with the world which – even as experienced in each particular case – naturally lead us to fall back on the same themes and the same arguments? The ambiguity at the heart of Fourier's approach – which did, after all, declare itself to be resolutely innovative and a break with the past – allows us at least to hypothesise that the theses contained in the *Code de la Nature* continued to be

---

11   François Villegardelle, 'Analyse raisonnée du système social de Morelly', in *Code de la Nature*, Paris: Masgana, 1841, p. 7.

fruitful. More than Morelly's 'Model of Legislation', which was discredited in the eyes of a Fourier who had turned away from political solutions, the *Code*'s purely philosophical dimension could perhaps serve as a wellspring of new theories on man and the social bond. If that were indeed true, then it would seem that the *Code* was important because it stood at the crossroads of the utopias of the age: opening the way simultaneously to attempts at radical reform of the state, and non-state modes of organising social relations, based on the anthropology of passion.

We have raised the problematic question of whether the utopian genre has its own specific theoretical content, actually passed down from one author to another, and on what basis we could evaluate variations. Seen by way of this nagging question, utopia appears to be both always and never the same. The break with tradition proclaimed by Fourier may not have prevented him from adopting certain essential elements from it. This would appear to corroborate the idea of the existence of a real utopian theoretical corpus ... unless this familiarity of themes simply points to similar paths taken and ways of reasoning followed. The same can be said of utopia itself, which is both a positive content and a way of relating to the world, which must always be analysed in terms of both the invariant and the unique, or, rather, in terms of what is invariant precisely by way of its uniqueness.

Utopia is a tradition more than a school of thought. In essence, it constantly reposes age-old questions: what does it mean, in the full sense of the term, to live in society? What should we imagine will bind men together, without alienating them? How can we reconcile individual flourishing with the common good? From this point of view, what remains the same in the answers to these questions is at least as revealing as what changes.

Index

Abensour, Miguel 2, 9, 308, 310, 332
Advielle, Victor 5, 349
Arendt, Hannah 119
Aristotle 108, 109, 112, 181

Bacon, Francis 7, 26, 27, 52, 61–3, 67, 89
Baczko, Bronislaw 3, 4, 40, 46, 88, 307, 333
Baker, Keith 120, 121, 235
Bernardi, Bruno 102, 117
Binoche, Bertrand 26, 27, 45, 52, 79, 90, 184, 187, 188, 225–7, 240, 242, 243, 279, 314, 315
Bloch, Ernst 2, 101
Bossuet, Jacques 45, 85–7
Brissot De Warville, Jacques-Pierre 341
Buonarroti, Philippe 344–9

Cabet, Etienne 363
Campanella, Tommaso 57, 60, 61, 180, 219
Ciceron 104, 105, 177
Collignon, Nicolas 267, 301, 305, 331
Condorcet, Nicolas De Caritat Viii, 26, 27, 52, 90–2, 232, 235–44, 276

D'alembert, Jean Le Rond 217, 259
Daline, Victor Viii, 216, 295, 297, 321
Derathe, Robert 116
Dezamy, Théodore 363
d'holbach, Paul-Henri Thiry 10, 183, 190
Diderot, Denis 4, 5, 23, 24, 45, 102, 217, 324, 363
Dommanget, Maurice viii, 221, 263, 298, 301, 329

Koselleck, Reinhart 38, 39, 120, 287

Labica, Georges 8
Lefort, Claude 188, 189, 283
Le Mercier De La Riviere, Pierre-Paul 7, 139, 140, 146–8, 155, 157
Linguet, Simon-Nicolas-Henri 276
Locke, John 101, 103, 106, 108, 110, 111, 116, 127–30, 161, 184, 248–50, 252

Macherey, Pierre 2, 31, 40, 89, 364
Machiavelli, Niccoló 7, 108, 124, 177, 191, 194, 292
Macpherson, Crawford Brough 111
Mannheim, Karl 2, 219
Marechal, Sylvain 190, 311
Marx, Karl 4, 19, 354

Mathiez, Albert 323
Mazauric, Claude 216, 298, 299, 301, 311, 313, 329, 338
Mercier, Louis-Sébastien 83, 266, 288
Montesquieu, Charles-Louis De Secondat vii, 45, 55, 124, 125, 133, 178, 180, 182, 189
More, Thomas 3, 6, 7, 15, 18–20, 22, 25, 27–31, 40, 46, 52, 57–61, 64, 68, 98, 100, 132, 133, 143, 180, 181, 188-192, 194, 195, 218, 219, 292, 346, 350, 357, 360
Moreau, Pierre-François 2, 13, 19, 31, 71, 72, 100, 325

Ozouf, Mona 3

Proudhon, Pierre-Joseph 363

Quesnay, François 146, 147, 151, 303

Restif De La Bretonne, Nicolas-Edme 4, 216–18, 267, 268, 331
Robespierre, Maximilien 8, 195, 307, 311, 323, 333, 335, 336, 348

Rousseau, Jean-Jacques vii, viii, 5, 7, 19, 46–8, 60, 61, 77, 82, 102–4, 106, 116, 117, 134, 151, 156, 159–61, 172–9, 182, 190–2, 194, 196, 207, 212–14, 223–38, 246–8, 250–4, 256, 268, 270, 272–7, 279–82, 284, 293, 304, 306, 313–17, 324, 326, 330, 342, 343, 354, 355, 358

Sade, Donatien Alphonse François 21, 22, 78–81, 187, 188–90, 335–7
Saint-Just, Antoine-Louis 306, 308–10, 332, 333, 349
Saint-Pierre, Charles-Irénée Castel 133, 135
Soboul, Albert viii, 13, 64, 296, 307–9, 327
Skinner, Quentin 8, 194

Tocqueville, Alexis De 239

Villegardelle, François 358, 363, 367
Vovelle, Michel 283, 323

Wollstonecraft, Mary 231, 232